D1457696

T.H. Shepherd Delt.   J.Brown Sc.

THE DUKE OF YORKS COLUMN

from St James's Park

LONDON

DRAWN AND ENGRAVED FOR

DUGDALES ENGLAND AND WALES

Delineated

PUBLIC LIBRARY

CURIOSITIES OF GREAT BRITAIN.

ENGLAND & WALES

DELINEATED

Historical, Entertaining & Commercial

ALPHABETICALLY ARRANGED

BY THOMAS DUGDALE, ANTIQUARIAN

Assisted by William Burnett.

VOL. VII.

THE BIRTH PLACE OF THE PRESENT
SIR. R. PEEL,
Blackburn,
LANCASHIRE.

London. Published by L. TALLIS, 3, Jewin Street, City.

RAWMARSH
PUBLIC LIBRARY

ACCESSION No.

8548

CLASS No.

R9m2   10/55

THE BIRTH PLACE OF

WILLIAM COBBETT

Farnham,

SURREY.

Drawn & Engraved for DUGDALE'S ENGLAND & WALES Delineated.

POPE'S HOUSE

Binfield,

(Adjoining Windsor Forest)

BERKSHIRE.

Drawn & Engraved for DUGDALE'S ENGLAND & WALES. Delineated.

MORLEY'S HOTEL,
AND THE
NELSON COLUMN, TRAFALGAR SQUARE, LONDON.

SHOREDITCH, LONDON.

MAIDSTONE,

KENT.

Drawn & Engraved for DUGDALES ENGLAND & WALES Delineated.

POWDERHAM CASTLE.

DEVONSHIRE.

Drawn & Engraved for DUGDALE'S ENGLAND & WALES Delineated.

BLENHEIM HOUSE, OXFORDSHIRE, THE SEAT OF HIS GRACE THE DUKE OF MARLBORO.

LONDON: L. TALLIS.

BIRTH-PLACE OF ROBT. BLOOMFIELD, HONINGTON,

SUFFOLK.

LONDON: L. TALLIS.

ST. ALBAN'S,
HERTFORDSHIRE.

HIGHBURY COLLEGE, ISLINGTON.
MIDDLESEX.

BIRTH PLACE OF THE

REV.^D JA: HERVEY

Hardingstone,

NORTHAMPTONSHIRE.

Drawn & Engraved for DUGDALE'S ENGLAND & WALES Delineated.

BIRTH PLACE OF
DRYDEN
Aldwinkle,
NORTHAMPTONSHIRE.

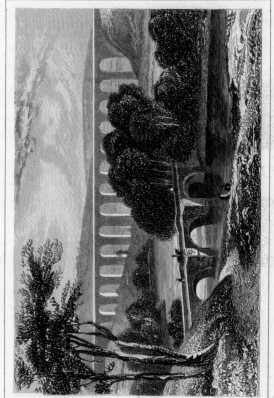

PONT-Y-CASULLTE AQUEDUCT.

IN THE VALE OF LLANGOLLEN, DENBIGHSHIRE.

This Aqueduct 1007 feet in length, carries the waters of the Ellesmere Canal over the River Dee.

BIRTH PLACE OF JOHN LOCKE, WRINGTON.

SOMERSETSHIRE.

Drawn & Engraved for DUGDALES ENGLAND & WALES Delineated.

GREENWICH HOSPITAL.

Drawn & Engraved for DUGDALES ENGLAND & WALES Delineated.

WESTMINSTER ABBEY.

Drawn & Engraved for DUGDALES ENGLAND & WALES Delineated.

HAYE'S FARM, EAST BUDLEIGH,
DEVONSHIRE.

The Birthplace of Sir Walter Raleigh.

NEAR WOKING, SURREY.

WARWICK CASTLE,
WARWICKSHIRE.

Drawn & Engraved for DUGDALE'S ENGLAND & WALES Delineated.

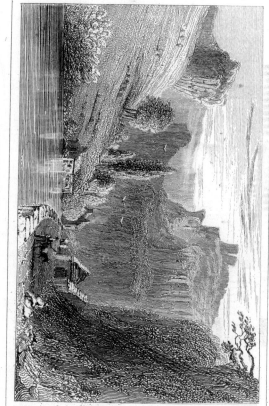

CHEDDER CLIFFS.

SOMERSETSHIRE.

Drawn & Engraved for DUGDALES ENGLAND & WALES Delineated.

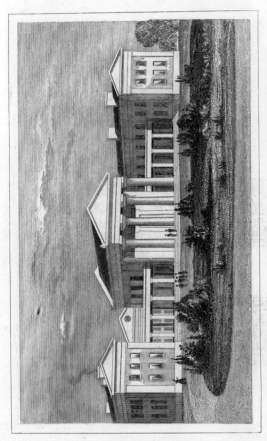

LONDON ORPHAN ASYLUM, HACKNEY ROAD.

MIDDLESEX.

Drawn & Engraved for DUGDALE'S ENGLAND & WALES Delineated.

CITY OF CARLISLE.

CUMBERLAND.

Drawn & Engraved for DUGDALES ENGLAND & WALES Delineated.

Samuel del.   Castel sc.

LLANDDEWI.   CARDIGANSHIRE.

Linwood del.   Kirk sc.

SEVEN OAKS, KENT.

BROUGH CASTLE.

WESTMORLAND.

Drawn & Engraved for DUGDALES ENGLAND & WALES Delineated.

ST JAMES'S PALACE.

PALL MALL, LONDON.

Drawn & Engraved for DUGDALE'S ENGLAND & WALES Delineated.

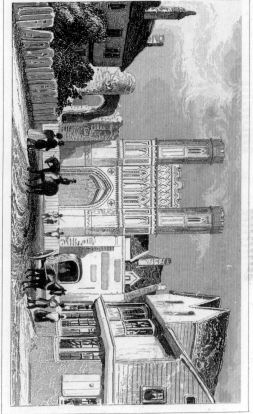

ST AUGUSTINE'S GATE, CANTERBURY.

KENT.

Drawn & Engraved for DUGDALES ENGLAND & WALES Delineated.

Map.	Names of Places.	County.	Number of Miles from			Dist. Lond.	Popu-lation.
23	Hinckley Bond......to	Leicester ...	Hinckley....1	Leicester ..12	Stapleton ..3	98	4216
36	Hinderclay ....pa	Suffolk	Bury St. Ed.14	Debenham...6	Stow Market.8	91	403
43	Hinderwell ....pa	N. R. York.	Whitby 9	Gisborough ..8	Easington ..2	255	1881
22	Hindley ......to & cha	Lancaster ..	Wigan 2	Bolton 8	Newton 7	198	....
45	Hindley, Cold......to	W. R. York.	Wakefield ..5	Barnsley....5	Huddersfield13	175	....
45	Hindley, North .....to	W. R. York.	Barnesley...6	Pontefract...5	Mirfield 11	178	....
45	Hindley, South......to	W. R. York.	6	Wakefield...4	Leeds 11	179	166
42	Hindlip ....pa	Worcester.	Worcester...3	Droitwich...3	Alcester 14	114	129
27	Hindolveston ......pa	Norfolk	Reepham ...6	N. Walsing. 10	Holt 4	115	797
41	Hindon*......bo & m t	Wilts	Wilton....12	Shaftsbury..7	Warminster .8	97	921
27	Hindringham ....pa	Norfolk ...	Walsingham.4	Holt 6	Wells......7	118	784
27	Hingham.....m t & pa	Norfolk ...	Norwich ..16	N. Walsham 10	Yarmouth ..16	125	1539
4	Hinskey, North, or Lawrence......pa	Berks	Oxford 1	Farringdon ..8	Abingdon...7	55	....
4	Hinskey, South ...pa	Berks	2	14		56	....
33	Hinstock..........pa	Salop.	Newport ...6	Drayton ...6	Hodnet......6	145	805
36	Hintlesham ....pa	Suffolk....	Hadleigh ...4	Ipswich 6	Bildeston...9	69	578
15	Hinton.............ti	Gloucester.	Chip.Sodbry.4	Marshfield ..3	Bristol 10	111	346
15	Hinton ....ti	Gloucester.	Berkeley....1	Dursley 4	Gloucester..14	113	....
28	Hinton ....ham	Northamp.	Daventry ...9	Banbury....8	Towcester..12	75	....
33	Hinton ....to	Salop.	Whitchurch. 1	Audlem.....8	Wem 10	161	....
34	Hinton ....to	Somerset ..	Wells 3	Glastonbury .3	Shep. Mallet.8	123	....
16	Hinton............ti	Hants	Christchurch 4	Lymington..8	Ringwood ..7	92	....
36	Hinton............ham	Suffolk	Southwold...4	Halesworth..3	Loxworth ..5	96	....
16	Hinton Ampner.....pa	Hants	Alresford ...4	Winchester 6	B. Waltham .7	62	325
34	Hinton Blewet ....pa	Somerset ..	Wells......8	Bristol 10	Bath 11	118	264
16	Hinton, Daubney..ham	Hants	Petersfield..8	Hambledon . 2	B. Waltham .6	62	....
41	Hinton, Great ....pa	Wilts	Trowbridge..3	Melksham ..3	Bradford 6	96	202
15	Hinton on the Green..pa	Gloucester.	Evesham ...3	Tewksbury .10	Winchcombe 8	102	195
28	Hinton in the Hedges..pa	Northamp.	Brackley ...3	Banbury....9	Aynhoe......4	66	188
41	Hinton, Little ....pa	Wilts	Swindon....5	Highworth ..4	Albourne ..7	79	284
12	Hinton Martel ...pa	Dorset.....	Wim.Minster 4	Cranborne ..6	Spittisbury .8	97	257
12	Hinton Parva.......pa	Dorset.....	2	8	7	99	25
34	Hinton St. George†..pa	Somerset ..	Crewkerne ..3	Ilminster ...4	Chard......7	134	850
12	Hinton, St. Mary ..pa	Dorset.....	Shaftesbury .7	Stalbridge.. 2	Stur. Newton 4	110	297
12	Hinton Tarrant ...pa	Dorset.....	Blan. Forum,5	Shaftesbury.10	Cranborne ..8	99	278
4	Hinton, St. Walery pa	Berks	G.Farringdon 6	Bampton ...4	Abingdon....9	65	315
35	Hints.............pa	Stafford ...	Tamworth ..3	Litchfield....5	S. Coldfield..5	119	250
3	Hinwick ....ham	Bedford	H. Ferrers ..5	Harold 4	Bedford 11	63	....
21	Hinxhill ....pa	Kent	Ashford....2	Hythe.....10	Folkestone . 13	57	146
6	Hinxton ....pa	Cambridge.	Linton 4	Cambridge...7	Royston ...9	53	312
3	Hinxworth ....pa	Bedford	Baldock ...5	Biggleswade .5	Shefford ...7	43	....
41	Hippenscombe...ex pa	Wilts	Ham......4	Marlboro'...7	Ludgershall .8	71	....
45	Hipperholme... ...to	W. R. York.	Halifax....2	Leeds......10	Otley......11	194	4977
44	Hipswell ....to	N. R. York.	Richmond ..2	Bedale 7	Middleham ..7	233	273
56	Hirnant ....pa	Montgomery	Llanfyllyn ..6	Llangadfan ,10	Llanganog ..3	194	280
22	Hisken............to	Lancaster..	Chorley 4	Ormskirk ..8	Preston 9	207	274
6	Histon.............vil	Cambridge.	Cambridge...4	Huntingdon 12	St. Ives....9	55	784
6	Hitcham ....pa	Bucks	Maidenhead .2	Beaconsfield .6	Slough 5	26	1022
36	Hitcham ....pa	Suffolk	Bildeston...2	Lavenham ..8	Stow Mt....7	66	965
5	Hitchenden ....pa	Bucks	Buckingham .2	Sto.Stratford 6	Brackley ...8	57	1457
18	Hitchin and Perton hun	Herts				....	10711
18	Hitchin‡ ....m t & pa	Herts	Baldock ...5	Stevenage ...5	Luton......8	34	5211
11	Hittesleigh ....pa	Devon	Crediton ...7	Oakhampton 10	Bow 4	187	163
35	Hoarcross ....to	Stafford	Litchfield...8	Abb.Bromley 2	Rugeley.....5	127	611

* HINDON. *Market*, Thursday.—*Fairs*, May 27, and October 29, for cattle, sheep, horses, swine, and cheese.

† HINTON ST. GEORGE. The views from this parish are very extensive and beautiful, and from one part both the North and South Seas are distinctly visible. Here is a large and magnificent seat, called Hinton St. George, surrounded by elegant parks and noble plantations.

‡ HITCHIN is situated in a fertile valley, surrounded by considerable eminences. It was given by Edward the Confessor to Earl Harold, by the appellation of Hitche. In the Domesday Book it is called Hiz, from the little river of that name, which flows through it. The jurisdiction of the manor-court extends into several neighbouring parishes. The church is a handsome structure, in the pointed style, occupying the site of a more ancient fabric near the middle of the town. The interior is spacious, and consists of a nave, chancels, and side aisles; its length is upwards of 150 feet; and its breadth, sixty-seven. At the west-end is a massive tower twenty-one feet in diameter, terminating by a small octa-

Handsome church.

6 G

Map.	Names of Places.	County.	Number of Miles from			Dist. Lond.	Popu-lation.
21	Hoathe ....pa	Kent	Canterbury . 6	Ramsgate...10	Wingham ...5	61	348
38	Hoathley, East .....pa	Sussex	Uckfield 5	E. Grinstead .4	Maresfield .. 9	34	510
38	Hoathley, West ....pa	Sussex	E.Grinstead .4	Uckfield 5	Crawley ...8	34	980
33	Hobendren........to	Salop	Bishop Castle 5	Bettus 5	Knighton .. 8	173	255
12	Hob Lench ......ham	Worcester.	Pershore....6	Alcester ...6	Evesham ...7	107	102
23	Hoby ....pa	Leicester ...	M. Mowbray.6	Mt. Sorrel ..6	Leicester ...11	110	352
7	Hockenhall.......to	Chester.....	Chester 6	Frodsham ...6	Tarvin 2	177	38
27	Hockering.........pa	Norfolk....	Dereham ...6	Norwich ...10	Reepham....7	107	392
30	Hockerton.......pa	Nottingham.	Southwell ...2	Mansfield...12	Ollerton.....8	134	115
27	Hockham*.........pa	Norfolk ,...	E. Harling...5	Watton 6	Attleboro' ..5	94	565
14	Hockley Super Mon-tem ....pa	Essex	Rayleigh 3	Chelmsford .12	Billericay...11	43	777
3	Hockliffee.........pa	Bedford	Dunstable ...5	Woburn.....4	L. Buzzard ..2	43	393
27	Hockwold.........pa	Norfolk....	Brand. Ferry.4	Methwold ...5	Stoke Ferry..9	82	878
11	Hockworth ....pa	Devon.....	Bampton ...6	Tiverton....8	Collumpton .9	157	354
18	Hoddesdon†. m t & cha	Herts.....	Ware 3	Hertford.....4	Wormley...3	17	1615

HITCHIN. gonal spire. The whole fabric is embattled; and the principal chancel is additionally ornamented by pinnacles. The north and south porches are well wrought; the latter has a groined roof, with canopied niches, and ornamentents in front. Amongst the monuments, which are very numerous, some ancient ones of the Kendale family possess considerable interest. Some very fine brasses of the fifteenth and sixteenth centuries also occur in different parts of the church. Here are likewise several monuments for the Radcliffes, of Hitchin-priory. The font has been ornamented with figures of the twelve Apostles, under niches; but they can scarcely now be traced. Near the church, formerly stood the priory of Biggin, founded for nuns of the Gilbertine order. At the Dissolution, its annual revenues were, according to the "Monasticon," estimated at £13 16s. Hitchin-priory was founded for White Carmelites, in the time of Edward II. Its annual revenues were valued at only £4 9s. 4d. when it was surrendered to Henry VIII. Very few traces of the priory remain; the immediate site is occupied by a mansion of the Radcliffe family. In the year 1668, John Skynner, Gent. gave £300 to build

Liberal bequest. alms-houses; £300 to purchase lands to endow the same; £100 to apprentice poor children; £100 towards the further endowments of the free-school, in Hitchin; and the produce of his orchard, next the church-yard, to keep the alms-houses in repair. The respective estates, now vested in trustees, produce about £21 for the alms-people; £5 for repairs, and £5 for the school, annually. In 1697, Ralph Skynner, Gent. (probably son of the above,) bequeathed £200 to buy lands, to augment the revenue of the vicarage; £800 for building and endowing eight alms-houses; and £60 for apprenticing ten poor children. Hitchin market has existed from an early period; and very large quantities of corn and grain are annually sold in it; probably in some degree from being free of toll, by prescriptive right. Formerly the wool trade was very flourishing here. The town is divided into three wards, and is governed by two constables, two headboroughs for each ward, two leather sellers, two ale-tasters, a bellman, &c. The town consists of several streets and lanes.

Market, Tuesday.—Fairs, Easter Tuesday, and Whit Tuesday, for sheep and pedlery.

* HOCKHAM. Fairs, Easter Monday, for small toys.

† HODDESDON is a handsome little market town and chapelry in the parishes of Amwell and Broxbourn. The manor, now belonging to the Marquis of Salisbury, was anciently a part of the estate of the Bassingbourns. The town consists chiefly of one street on the high road. The chapel, a neat brick structure, was erected about fifty years ago, on the site of a more ancient building. The market-house, an old and Ancient market-house. curious edifice of wood, supported on arches and pillars, is yet standing, though greatly out of repair; a number of rude and grotesque figures are carved on different parts. Near the market house is a conduit of good

Map	Names of Places.	County.	Number of Miles from			Dist. Lond.	Popu-lation.
16	Hoddington ....ti	Hants ...	Odiham . . .3	Farnham 7	Alton 5	46	....
57	Hodgeston ....pa	Pembroke ..	Pembroke ...5	Narbeth 9	Tenby 7	268	75
39	Hodnet..........ex pa	Warwick...	Southam.....3	Warwick....9	Kineton 7	81	9
33	Hodnet ....pa	Salop	Drayton 6	Wem 7	Whitchurch 10	150	1769
30	Hodsock ....lord	Nottingham	Worksop....5	Blyth 2	E. Retford...6	150	228
40	Hoffe ....ham	Westmorlnd	Appleby 2	Brough......8	Duston 6	269	93
22	Hoghton ....to	Lancaster...	Blackburn .. 6	Preston......4	Chorley 6	212	2198
10	Hognaston ....pa	Derby	Wirksworth .5	Alsop 5	Ashborn 5	144	292
5	Hogshaw ....pa	Bucks......	Winslow 4	Bicester 9	Buckingham .6	50	....
24	Hogsthorpe ....pa	Lincoln ...	Alford 5	Saltfleet . .14	Burgh 7	140	698
5	Hogston ....pa	Bucks	Winslow 4	L. Buzzard ..8	Aylesbury ...7	46	188
24	Holbeach* ...m t & pa	Lincoln.....	Spalding....8	Croyland ...12	Boston 16	109	3890

water, which is supplied by pipes from a spring at some distance. It was HODDESDON
erected by the Raudons, a respectable family of this town, and is kept in
order by a bequest of a certain sum annually, made by Marmaduke
Raudon, Esq., in the year 1679.

† HOLBEACH, a market-town and parish in the wapentake of Elloe,
parts of Holland, indifferently built, but of great antiquity. The living
is a vicarage in the archdeaconry and diocese of Lincoln. The church,
which is dedicated to All Saints, is the principal building, and is a spacious, handsome edifice, consisting of a nave, chancel, aisles, porch, and
a square tower, surmounted with an octangular spire, and contains some
very fine monuments. Here is an hospital, which was endowed by Sir
John de Kirton, Knight, about the year 1351, and was intended to support
a warden, chaplain, and fourteen poor pensioners. A free grammar-school   Charitable
was also founded here, by licence from Edward III., who granted certain   endow-
lands for its support; and another free-school was established here about   ments.
the year 1669, by George Farmer, Esq.; the revenues for the support of
which have been much increased by donations and bequests. In the
market-place was an ancient stone cross, supposed to have been raised
about the year 1253; near which period, Thomas de Malton, Lord Egre-
mont, obtained the grant of a weekly market, and an annual fair. Holbeach church is a large handsome structure, consisting of a nave, chancel,   The church.
aisles, porch, and a square tower, surmounted with an octangular ornamental spire; each angle of which is charged with crockets, and each face
has two windows, with canopies, &c. The north porch has two circular
towers, with embattled parapets at its extreme angles. The church contains some fine monuments of the Irby and Littlebury families, which
formerly resided in this neighbourhood. This town has derived some
eminence from two of its natives; Henry de Rands, called Holbech, who,
after passing through different ecclesiastical offices, was advanced to the
bishopric of Lincoln; and William Stukeley, M.D., C.M.L., F.A.S., and   Birthplace
F.R.S., whose name we have frequently had occasion to mention. He   of W.
was descended from an ancient family, and was born November 7, 1687.   Stukeley.
After receiving the first rudiments of education under Mr. Edward Kelson,
in the free-school of this town, he was admitted of Bennet-college,
Cambridge, where he made medicine and botany his peculiar study.
Taking a degree in physic, he removed to London, in 1717, where he was
elected a fellow of the Royal Society, and was one among the distinguished
number who revived the Society of Antiquaries, to which he acted many
years as secretary. He was also made a member of the College of Physicians, and became one of the censors. After residing in London a few
years, he retired to Grantham, where he married. Afflicted with the
gout during the winter, it was his custom to travel for his health in the
spring or summer; and in these journeys he acquired a particular and
zealous love of antiquities. Finding his health inadequate to the fatigue
of his profession, he turned his view to the church, and was ordained at
Croydon, July 20, 1730. He was presented to the living of All Saints,

Map.	Names of Places.	County.	Number of Miles from			Dist. Lond.	Popu- lation.
45	Holbeck......cha & to	York	Leeds 2	Huddersfield.9	Barnsley....7	179	11210
30	Holbeck...........to	Nottingham.	Worksop 4	Ollerton 8	Me...field....8	146	239
30	Holbeck Woodhouse } ....ex pa }	Nottingham.	4	7	7	145	5
11	Holberton.........pa	Devon	Modbury ...3	Plym. Earls..6	Kingsbridge .9	211	1107
10	Holbrook..........to	Derby	Derby 6	Kegworth ...8	Nottingham..11	123	703
36	Holbrook..........pa	Suffolk	Ipswich 5	Harwich.. ..8	Strat. Bridge.9	69	762
22	Holcombe .... to	Lancaster...	Bury 4	Haslingden..5	Rochdale ...8	205	....
31	Holcombe.......ham	Oxford	Wallingford .5	Oxford ...10	Watlington . 5	51	110
34	Holcombe.........pa	Somerset ..	Shep.Mallett 6	Wells 9	Frome 8	111	538
11	Holcombe Burnell ..pa	Devon	Exeter.....5	Crediton ...6	Chudleigh ...7	178	237
11	Holcombe Rogus....pa	Devon	Bampton...7	Tiverton.....7	Collumpton..8	158	915
3	Holcott..........pa	Bedford ...	Woburn.....4	Ampthill ...6	Toddington . 8	49	62
29	Holcott..........pa	Northamp ..	Wellingboro' 6	Kettering...3	Rothwell....5	73	433
15	Holden...........ham	W. R. York	Clitheroe ...6	Broughton .. 6	Newton.....6	223	....
29	Holdenby*........pa	Northamp ..	Northampt ..6	Welford.....9	Daventry .. .9	72	140
16	Holdenhurst ....pa	Hants	Christchurch 3	Ringwood ...7	Lymington..14	101	733
16	Holderness .....wap	E. R. York .	....	....	....	...	23385
12	Holdfast ....ham	Worcester..	U.-on-Severn 1	Worcester..11	Tewksbury ..6	112	89
13	Holdgate..........pa	Salop.....	Ludlow....12	M. Wenlock .6	C. Stretton ..9	149	77
24	Holdingham ....ham	Lincoln.....	Sleaford....1	Grantham ..13	Lincoln.....16	116	126
16	Holdshott ....hun	Hants	....	....	....	...	3668
16	Holdshott ....ti	Hants	Hart. Bridge .4	Basingstoke.10	Odiham 9	38	....
7	Holdford ....ham	Chester....	Northwich ..3	Knutsford ...4	Warrington.12	173	....
34	Holford ....pa	Somerset ...	Bridgewater 11	Watchet 5	Neth.Stowey 5	152	240
16	Holgate ....to	York	York 2	Selby 11	Askam......2	199	83
22	Holker, Lower .....to	Lancaster...	Ulverston...5	Cartmell ...2	Dalton 9	267	1021
22	Holker, Upper .....to	Lancaster..	5	2	Hawkshead..9	268	1095
27	Holkham†.........pa	Norfolk	Wells 2	Cley 10	Burn.Market.4	125	792

HOLBEACH. Stamford, and was afterwards rector of St. Peter's, and master of Brown's hospital, in the same place. He appears to have had the offer of several better livings, which he declined. He was presented, by the Duke of Ancaster, with the living of Somerby, who also appointed him one of his chaplains. About the time of these promotions, he published an account of Stonehenge ; a work which displays much speculation and theory ; but, exclusive of the descriptive facts which serve to perpetuate certain parts of that extraordinary monument, it is likely to deceive and bewilder the reader. At the instance of the Duke of Montague, he resigned his preferments in the country ; and, in lieu of them, accepted the rectory of

His death. St. George's, Queen-square, London. He was seized with a paralytic stroke, which terminated fatally, the 3d of March, 1765, when he had attained his seventy-eighth year. His principal works are, " Itinerarium Curiosum, or an Account of the Curiosities and Antiquities of Great Britain," folio, " An Account of Stonehenge and Avebury," 2 vols. folio. " Palæographia Sacra, or Discourses of the Monuments of Antiquity, that relate to Sacred History," quarto. " Palæographia Britannica," quarto. " History of Carausius," 2 vols. quarto. " Dissertation on the Spleen," folio.

Market, Thursday.—*Fairs*, May 17 ; September 11 ; and October 11, for horses.

Remains of a magnificent structure. * HOLDENBY, a parish in the hundred of Nobottle Grove ; living, a rectory in the archdeaconry of Northampton, and diocese of Peterborough. Here was Holdenby, or Holmby-house, which appears from remaining vestiges to have been a most magnificent structure. It was erected in the reign of Elizabeth, by Sir Christopher Hatton, a native of this place, who was bred to the law, and raised to the highest honours and preferments by that queen, who admired his comely person and graceful dancing ; and it will be ever memorable for the circumstances attending it previous to its dilapidation, as it formed first a palace, and afterwards a prison for the unfortunate monarch, Charles I.

† HOLKHAM. In this parish stands Holkham-house, the magnificent seat of Thomas William Coke, Esq., M. P. This spacious mansion was begun in the year 1734, by the Earl of Leicester, and completed by his

dowager countess, in 1760. The central part is composed of white brick, and has four wings connected with it by rectilinear corridors, or galleries; each of the two fronts, therefore, displays a centre and two wings. The south front has an air of lightness and elegance, arising from the justness of its proportions. In the centre is a bold por' co, with i.s entablature supported by six Corinthian columns. The grand entrance is at the north front. The wings have been thought to take from the general magnificence of the building, by their want of uniformity with the south front. The centre, which extends 345 feet in length by 180 in depth, comprises the principal apartments. Each wing has its respective destination. In one are the kitchens, servants'-hall, and some sleeping rooms. The chapel-wing contains the dairy, and laundry, with sleeping rooms. Another contains the suite of family apartments, and the fourth is appropriated to visitors. In appropriate arrangement and convenience, this grand residence yields to none in the kingdom. The entrance hall, which forms a cube, is encircled by a gallery, supported by twenty-four Ionic columns. Next is the saloon, on each side of which is a drawing-room; and connected with this is the state dressing-room and bed-chamber. Another drawing-room communicates with the statue gallery, which connects a number of apartments in the most admirable manner; on one side of the hall is the dining-room, and on the other is Mrs. Coke's bed-room, dressing-rooms, and closets. From the recesses in the dining-room opens a door on the staircase, which immediately communicates with the offices; and in the centre of the wings, by the saloon door, are invisible staircases, which lead to all the rooms and respective offices. Thus here are four general suits of apartments, all perfectly distinct from each other, with no reciprocal thoroughfares; the state, Mrs. Coke's, the late earl's, and the strangers'. The interior is fitted up in the most splendid style, and with the most elegant taste. The ceilings of many of the rooms are of curious gilt fret and mosaic work; the Venetian windows are ornamented with handsome pillars, and are also profusely gilded. The marble chimney pieces are all handsome; but there are three whose exquisite sculpture entitle them to particular attention. Two of these are in the dining-room, one ornamented with a sow and pigs, and a wolf; the other has a bear and bee-hives, finely sculptured in white marble. A third, in the state bed-room, representing two pelicans, is exceedingly chaste and beautiful. The marble side-boards, agate-tables, rich tapestry, silk furniture, beds, &c. are all in the same style of elegance. The statue gallery consists of a central part and two octagonal ends. The first is seventy feet long, by twenty-two feet wide, and each octagon, of twenty-two feet in diameter, opens to the centre by a handsome arch. One end is furnished with books, and is extremely fine. A Venus, clothed with neat drapery, is exquisite. The saloon is forty feet long, twenty-eight wide, and thirty-two in height. The room, appropriated for paintings, contains many by the most eminent masters; but they are not exclusively preserved in this, a vast collection being distributed over most of the apartments of the house. The pleasure grounds are highly ornamental. The first entrance is by a triumphal arch, finely imagined, and its effect is heightened by several clumps of trees, which surround it. Crossing the turnpike road, a narrow vista, through a plantation for a mile and a half, exhibits at the extremity an obelisk standing on an eminence. At the bottom of the hill are two lodges, which are small, but neat structures. Ascending the hall, through a fine plantation near the obelisk several charming vistas present to the eye the south front of the house, Holkham-quay, the town of Wells, Stiffkey-hills, Thorpe-lodge, Overy-quay, the triumphal arch, and the village church. On the north side of the park, a lake, covering about twenty acres, extends in nearly a rectilinear direction for 1056 yards; it includes a small island, and the shore is bold and clothed with wood, waving in rich and picturesque beauty.

HOLKHAM.

Splendid mansion.

Curious gilt ceilings.

Beautiful prospect.

Mars	Names of Places.	County.	Number of Miles from			Dist. Lond.	Population.
11	Hollacombe........pa	Devon......	Holdsworthy 2	Oakhampton16	Hatherleigh.11	212	96
14	Holland, Great .....pa	Essex	Manningtree 11	Colchester. 15	Harwich ...12	65	413
14	Holland, Little .....pa	Essex	Colchester..14	Harwich ...15	Gt. Holland .3	65	73
22	Holland,Upper*mt &to	Lancaster...	Wigan.....4	Ormskirk....7	Newton.....8	204	3942
28	Hollawell ....ham	Northamp..	Northampton 9	Mt.Harboro' 8	Kettering....8	75	279
36	Hollasley........pa	Suffolk	Woodbridge .6	Ipswich 14	Orford.......7	83	575
22	Holleth............to	Lancaster...	Garstang ...5	Lancaster....4	Hornby.....12	236	604
21	Hollingbourn ......pa	Kent.......	Maidstone ...6	Canterbury 18	Charing....8	41	943
22	Hollingfare ....cha	Lancaster ..	Warrington..6	Manchester .12	Newton .. 8	193	....
10	Hollington.........to	Derby......	Ashborne....5	Turnditch ...4	Derby 7	133	314
38	Hollington.........pa	Sussex	Hastings....3	Battle 3	Winchelsea..8	61	212
7	Hollingworth ......to	Chester	Chester 7	Northwich ..9	Tarporley ..6	184	1766
35	Hollings-clough ...to	Stafford	Leek 8	Longnor 5	Ashborn ...9	148	564
25	Holloway†.......ham	Middlesex ..	Hampstead ..4	Highgate 2	Islington....2	3	....
46	Hollym............pa	E. R. York	Hull 17	Patrington ..2	Hedon......10	194	260
3	Holme............ham	Bedford....	Biggleswade .1	Potton 5	Shefford 4	44	....
10	Holme.............to	Derby......	Bakewell ...1	Chesterfield 11	Brampton ..7	152	....
19	Holme.............pa	Huntingdon.	Stilton 2	Ramsey 7	Peterboro' . 8	74	311
24	Holme.............to	Lincoln.....	Gland.Bridge 7	Burton.....8	Kirton.....8	162	....
27	Holme.............pa	Norfolk.....	Mt.Downham4	Lynn.......7	Swaffham ..14	88	198
30	Holme .....to & cha	Nottingham.	Newark 4	Tuxford ...9	Southwell ..7	128	114
35	Holme.............to	Stafford	Cheadle 4	Ipstone.... 4	Leek.......5	149	527
40	Holme.............to	Westmorlnd	Kir.Lonsdale 7	Milthorpe...3	Kendal..... 9	252	649
44	Holme.............to	N. R. York .	Thirsk......5	Masham 6	Ripon......7	216	102
45	Holme.............to	W. R. York	Huddersfield.9	Hay 8	Wakefield ..17	179	630
9	Holme, Baldwin ...to	Cumberland	Carlisle 5	Wigton 7	Longtown ..9	305	234
9	Holme, Cultram‡ ..pa	Cumberland	Wigton 6	Bonus.......8	Ireby 9	314	3056
12	Holme, East ....ex pa	Dorset......	Wareham ...2	Poole......10	Bere Regis..7	114	42
27	Holme, Hale ......pa	Norfolk.....	Swaffham...5	Castle Acre. 9	E. Dereham. 8	93	422
27	Holme near the Sea.pa	Norfolk.....	Bu.Westgate 8	Lynn 16	Docking 6	126	219
43	Holme, North.......to	N. R. York .	New Malton 10	K. Moorside .2	Middleton ..6	234	24
30	Holme, Pierpoint§ ..pa	Nottingham.	Nottingham..4	Bingham 5	Ratcliffe 2	126	205

Church dedicated to St. Thomas à Becket.

* HOLLAND, UPPER, a market-town, township, and chapelry, in the parish of Wigan, and hundred of West Derby; church dedicated to St. Thomas à Becket; patron, the Rector of Wigan. Here was formerly a chantry, or college, afterwards converted into a priory of Benedictine monks, about the year 1319. It was founded by Sir Robert de Holland, whose posterity are celebrated in history both for their grandeur and their misfortunes.

Market, Wednesday.—*Fair*, July 15, for horses, horned cattle, and toys.

† HOLLOWAY, a hamlet in the parish of Islington, Finsbury division of the hundred of Ossulstone, divided into two parts, Upper and Lower Holloway, now nearly united. The whole village consists of ranges of handsome detached houses with gardens in front, and other buildings, extending along the great north road from Islington to Highgate. At Upper Holloway is an old public house called the Mother Red Cap, noticed in "Drunken Barnaby's Itinerary;" and another called the Half Moon, famous a century ago for excellent cheesecakes. A large edifice was erected at Lower Holloway some years since as a chapel of ease to Islington; and a church in the Gothic style has recently been built in Upper Holloway.

Handsome Gothic structure.

‡ HOLME CULTRAM, or Abbey Holme, a parish in Allerdale ward, below Darwent, situated on the west side, and near the mouth of that river and Solway Frith; it was formerly a market-town; living, a dis. vicarage, with that of Newton-Arlosh, in the archdeaconry and diocese of Carlisle. The church, dedicated to St. Mary, is a handsome Gothic structure. Here was formerly an abbey, founded and richly endowed in the year 1150, by Prince Henry, son of David, King of Scotland, for monks of the Cistercian order; the abbots of this establishment were, in the reigns of Edward I. and II., summoned to several parliaments.

Fair, October 29, for horses and horned cattle.

§ HOLME. In the pleasant little village of Holme Pierpoint, is Holme Pierpoint-house, a large and ancient building, though much of it

Map.	Names of Places.	County.	Number of Miles from			Dist. Lond.	Popu-lation.
10	Holme, Scales .....to	Westmorlnd	Kendal......6	Sedberg 4	K. Lonsdale 10	262	....
43	Holme, South .....to	N. R. York .	New Malton .7	K. Moorside .5	Helmsley ...8	228	66
46	Holme upon Spalding } Moor*.........pa	E. R. York .	Mt. Weighton 4	Selby......12	Pocklington .6	191	1438
46	Holme on the Wolds pa	E. R. York .	Beverley ...6	Pocklington .9	Mt. Weighton6	200	138
45	Holmefirth† .. cha & to	W. R. York	Huddersfield 6	Barnsley ...11	Wortley ...10	183	....
17	Holmer ....pa	Hereford ...	Hereford 2	Leominster .11	Weobly 10	137	524
10	Holmesfield .. cha & to	Derby	Chesterfield..6	Dronfield ...2	Brampton ...5	157	499
46	Holmpton ....pa	E. R. York .	Patrington...4	Hedon.....11	Roose.......4	196	256
13	Holmside ....to	Durham .	Durham 6	Newcastle..10	Wolsingham 15	265	228
22	Holmswood .....ham	Lancaster...	Ormskirk ..6	Chorley 6	Wigan......7	207	....
11	Holmsworthy‡ m t & pa	Devon......	Stratton 8	Oakhampton17	Torrington..14	214	1628
11	Holne.............pa	Devon......	Ashburton...4	PlymptonE. 15	Chudleigh ..12	189	410

at times has been pulled down. It stands close to the church. Cased, in imitation of stone, it forms a handsome specimen of the Gothic of the later ages. The church is rich in mural monuments, in altar tombs, and in ancient armorial brasses. Its form is Gothic, but in the style of the time of Henry VII. The family vault of the late dukes of Kingston, and of the present Pierpoint family, is in the north side of the choir, with a lofty monument over it, supported by Corinthian pillars, and gloomily ornamented with death's heads in wreaths, intermixed with fruit and foliage. Its inscription is unusual. " Here lyeth the Illustrious Princess Gertrude, Countess of Kingston, daughter to Henry Talbot, Esq., son to George late Earl of Shrewsbury. She was married to the most Noble and Excellent Lord Robert, Earl of Kingston, &c." A fine altar tomb to the memory of Sir Henry Pierpoint, knight, in 1615, is on the south side ; he is in armour, and in the usual attitude of prayer. On the sides of the tomb are a son, four daughters, and an infant in swaddling clothes ; and over it a highly ornamented tablet containing the inscription. Near it is another, who, by his habit of a pilgrim, seems to have been to the Holy Land ; he has angels playing round his head. Here too was buried young Oldham, a poet of considerable merit, and patronized by William, Earl of Kingston, who wrote the very elegant inscription on his tomb. The village of Holme, belonged, in the seventeenth century, to Sir Thomas Barton, knight, whose fortune having been acquired by the woollen manu-facture, he placed the following couplet in the windows of his mansion :

> " I thank God, and ever shall ;
> It was the sheep that paid for all."

Holme chapel has some monuments of the family in the chancel. On the north side stands a very large and curious altar tomb, with two recumbent figures of a man and woman, and below a very striking figure of an emaciated youth. Over the south porch is a chamber, called " Nan Scott's." It is said, that the last great plague was particularly fatal to this village ; at which time this Ann Scott retired to the room here men-tioned, with a sufficient quantity of food to last her several weeks. Having remained unnoticed until her provisions were expended, she ven-tured to the village, which she found entirely deserted, only one person, besides herself, of its former inhabitants, being alive. Shocked by the horrors of the scene, she is said to have returned to this chamber, where she took up her residence again for the remainder of a life of many years duration.

* HOLME-UPON-SPALDING-MOOR. Here is a small hill, which commands a very extensive prospect over the surrounding flat country ; and also a beacon, formerly used to alarm the surrounding villages, in case of invasions or internal commotions.

† HOLMEFIRTH, Fair, October 30, for horned cattle.

‡ HOLMSWORTHY. A market-town and parish in the hundred of Black Torrington, pleasantly situated between two branches of the river

(marginal notes:)
HOLME.

Curious inscription

Village depopulat by the plague.

Map.	Names of Places.	County.	Number of Miles from			Dist. Lond.	Popu-lation.
'2	Holnest............pa	Dorset......	Sherborne ...5	Stalbridge ...6	Stur.Newton 7	115	162
52	Holt* ....to	Denbigh	Wrexham .. 5	Chester.....16	New Chapel .3	188	1015
12	Holt................ti	Dorset......	Wim.Minster 3	Spittisbury .11	Blan.Forum 14	101	1265
23	Holt...............to	Leicester ...	Rockingham 3	Tugby.......6	Leicester ...18	84	53
27	Holt.............hun	Norfolk.....	....	....	....	....	10416
27	Holt† ....m t & pa	Norfolk.....	Cromer.....8	Clay. 4	Wells......13	119	1622
41	Holt..........cha	Wilts........	Bradford ...2	Melksham ..3	Trowbridge..3	100	839
42	Holt............pa	Worcester .	Worcester...6	Bewdly 8	Droitwich ...6	117	635
43	Holtley ....pa	N. R. York .	York 4	New Malton 13	Gatton......3	204	170
24	Holton............pa	Lincoln.....	Wragby 2	Spittal 12	Mt. Raisin...6	145	142
31	Holton............pa	Oxford	Oxford......6	Thame 8	Tetsworth ..6	52	260
34	Holton............pa	Somerset ...	Wincanton .3	Ilchester ...10	Castle Carey.4	111	235
36	Holton............pa	Suffolk	Halesworth ..1	Bungay....10	Beccles 10	101	399
6	Holton............pa	Suffolk	Hadleigh 4	Ipswich 8	Neyland......6	63	213
24	Holton le Clay....pa	Lincoln.....	Gt.Grimsby..6	Louth......14	Saltfleet....16	166	220
24	Holton le Moor ....pa	Lincoln.....	Mt.Raisin ...5	Castor.....4	Glan.Bridge 10	152	135
27	Holverston ....pa	Norfolk.....	Norwich ...7	Bungay......7	Loddon......6	113	26
3	Holwell ....pa	Bedford	Hitchin ...3	Baldock 5	Shefford 4	37	179
23	Holwell...........to	Leicester ...	M. Mowbray.4	Waltham....3	N.Broughton 5	109	132
31	Holwell..........ham	Oxford	Burford ...3	Bampton ...7	Witney 9	70	86
34	Holwell............pa	Somerset ...	Sherborne ..6	Mil. Port ...5	Yeovil......10	119	405
34	Holwell..........ham	Somerset ...	Frome......4	Shep. Mallett 7	Bruton......8	107	342
44	Holwick............to	N. R. York .	Greta Bridge18	Brough ...9	Bowes. ...14	262	201
16	Holybourn ....pa	Hants	Alton........1	Odiham 7	Farnham ...7	48	482
42	Holycross..........to	Worcester..	Worcester...1	Pershore ...10	Droitwich ...6	112	2145
14	Holyfield.........ham	Essex	WalthamAb. 2	B. Stortford.12	Epping......5	15	293
17	Holyhead‡........m t	Anglesea ...	Llanerchym.15	Roscolyn....5	Bangor.....25	278	428

HOLMS WORTHY. Tamar, and through which passes a canal to the Harbour of Bude. The inhabitants chiefly derive their employment from the operations of agriculture. The petty sessions are holden here.

Market, Saturday.—*Fairs*, April 27 ; July 10 ; and Oct. 2 ; for cattle.

* HOLT. A town, having a distinct jurisdiction, in the parish of Holt and hundred of Bromfield, situated upon the river Dee, here crossed by a bridge. It is governed by a mayor, two bailiffs, and a coroner, in conformity with the charter obtained by Thomas, Earl of Arundel, in the year 1410. The living is a chapelry, not in charge, to the vicarage of Gresford, in the archdeaconry and diocese of St. Asaph ; patrons, the Dean and Chapter of Winchester. **Castle besieged by the Parliamentarians.** The castle of Holt was a place of considerable strength, and garrisoned for Charles I., in 1643, but besieged, taken, and utterly demolished, by the Parliamentarians, in 1645. The lordship belongs to the crown, and its duties are discharged by a steward. Roman antiquities are frequently found in this parish, whence it is conjectured to have been a Roman station.

Fairs, June 22, and October 29.

† HOLT. A market-town and parish, pleasantly situated on a rising ground : it formerly suffered great inconvenience from want of water, which was fetched from a considerable distance. **Great destruction by fire.** Great part of the town was destroyed by fire in the year 1708, since which time many good houses have been erected. The sessions-house is a good building, and is occasionally used as an assembly-room. Here is a considerable free-school, which was founded in the year 1556, by Sir Thomas Gresham, who was a native of the town, and the well-known founder of the Royal Exchange. The surrounding scenery is particularly fine, and the air very salubrious.

Market, Saturday.—*Fairs*, April 25, and November 25, for horses, &c.

‡ HOLYHEAD. A market-town, situated upon the Irish Sea. The town consists of two good avenues and a few cross streets, and possesses an open market-place around the old cross, with two inns, and several genteel residences. It has lately undergone great improvements, and being the adopted station for the transmission and receipt of the mails between London and Dublin, an asylum harbour has been constructed at

Map.	Names of Places.	County.	Number of Miles from			Dist. Lond.	Popu. lation.
13	Holy Island* .... island	Durham	Belford 7	Berwick 12	Ancroft 9	329	836
23	Holy Oaks .... lord	Leicester ...	Rockingham .3	Mt. Harboro' 9	Tugby....... 7	85	7

the expense of government. It is formed by a pier, 900 feet in length, running in a direction west to east, faced with hewn limestone, and having a depth of fourteen feet at the pier-head, at low water. The land extremity of the pier, by the old lighthouse, is connected to the mainland by a cast-iron bridge across Salt Island Sound, and the new road continued thence to the Menai Bridge. There is a light on the pier-head; three leagues, north north-west, is the Skerries light; and a revolving light is placed upon the South Stack, at an elevation of 200 feet above sea level, bearing upon the Skerries light, south-west half west, nearly eight miles. Recently, also, two anchors, of one arm each, connected by a chain cable of 140 fathoms, have been laid down across the entrance of the harbour, to prevent vessels from being driven upon the rocks to leeward, while attempting to gain the harbour in stormy weather. The ground at the mouth of the harbour having become so broken as to afford no secure anchorage. The South Stack is approached by a suspension-bridge, thrown from the front of a magnificent rock of serpentine to the island. Besides the valuable improvements already mentioned to ensure a safe asylum for shipping here, there is a dry dock, large enough to admit a sixty-four gun ship. The church is an ancient building, disfigured by an extravagant quantity of whitewashing; it is dedicated to St. Bybi, and on the north side was inscribed *Sancte Kybi ora pro nobis*. A low wall, enclosing the church-yard, is all that remains of the piece of Roman architecture so much spoken of. The harbour improvements have brought nautical traffic into this place. Ship-building is conducted here skilfully; and repairing of vessels is a source of contstant occupation to the inhabitants. The mountain of Holyhead, which rises to an elevation of 709 feet above the sea, is almost wholly composed of beautiful serpentine. The influx of passengers ought to be a greater source of profit also than it has proved to be, but their stay is so short, that the inn-keepers alone appear to be enriched by them. In 1821, King George IV. embarked here for Ireland, and a triumphal arch upon the pier commemorates the event. There is an endowed free-school in the town. St. Gybi founded a monastery here, in the year 380. The Romans are thought to have had an intrenchment here, from the coins of that great nation found in the vicinity; and Druidical remains are yet tracticable. The South Stack lighthouse, and the bold cliffs of the Holyhead mountain, are interesting and picturesque objects. In clear weather, the Wicklow mountains, the Isle of Man, and Cumberland hills, can be seen by the aid of the telescope.

Market, Saturday.—Mail from London arrives at 11 and departs at half past 4, A. M.

* HOLY ISLAND, an island, or rather peninsula, united with Northumberland by a narrow isthmus which is covered by the flow of the tide. It belongs to Islandshire ward, county of Durham, though situated about eight miles south-east of Berwick-upon-Tweed, nearly opposite the mouth of the river Landi. It is about nine miles in circuit; and at its south-western angle is a village, principally inhabited by fishermen, near which is a commodious haven, which serves as a shelter for merchant vessels in stormy weather. On a precipitous rock, in its vicinity, stands a castle or block-house, occupied by a detachment of invalids from Berwick. During the rebellion in 1715, it was surprised by the partisans of the house of Stuart, but was speedily recaptured. Exclusive of the castle rock, the island is a continued plain, inclining to the south-west, and consisting of about 1000 acres, more than half of which is covered with sand; but the soil of the cultivated portion is rich. Fish and wild fowl are plentiful

Margin notes: HOLYHEAD. Secure harbour. Suspension bridge. Druidical remains.

6 H

Map.	Names of Places.	County.	Number of Miles from			Dist. Lond.	Popu. lation.
53	Holywell*....to & pa	Flint.... :	Hawarden..10	Flint........5	Caerwys 5	212	896?
19	Holywell. ....pa	Huntingdon.	St. Ives 2	Erith........4	Fen. Stanton 4	58	95?
24	Holywell .... ..ham	Lincoln.....	Stamford...7	Corby......7	Bourn 10	96	11?
29	Holywell..........to	Northumb ..	Shields....5	Blyth 6	Morpeth....11	284	10?

HOLY ISLAND.

here, and there are a great many rabbits. On the conversion of the Anglo-Saxons to Christianity by St. Aidan, a native of Scotland, this island was given to him by Oswald, King of Northumbria, in 635, when he founded the bishopric of Lindisfarne, and erected a cathedral church, dedicated to St. Peter. This structure was demolished by the Danes in 795, and again in 867, in consequence of which the island was deserted by Eardulph, the last bishop; and the see was subsequently united with Durham.

Cathedral destroyed by the Danes.

* HOLYWELL is a thriving manufacturing town, situated upon an eminence on the south of the estuary of the river Dee. The plan of the town is devoid of all regularity or design, and consists of one broad and good avenue, approached at each end by narrow, crooked lanes. Several small streets branch off from the main one, the best of which is the approach to the church, which possesses some beauty; it stands at the foot of the hill on which the town is erected, and was rebuilt in the year 1769, upon the site of a Norman structure, some parts of which are preserved in the interior. A square tower at the west end was added for the suspension of bells, but unluckily it lies so much below the level of the town, and is so immediately overhung by steep hills, that the toll of the bell is not heard in the town. The inhabitants are now summoned to prayers by a person having a good-sized bell suspended by a strap from his neck, and resting upon a cushion, which protects his knee; in this way regular tolls are produced as he walks along, by the advance of the cushioned knee. This town is the most important, as a place of trade, in the county, and its natural advantages are considerable. The celebrated spring, from which the place takes its name, in the short course of one mile, is employed in working eleven mills of various descriptions. Here are four cotton-mills, established by the Holywell Cotton and Twist Company; an extensive silk and ribbon manufactory; a copper smelting-house and smithy; a brass-house and foundery; a wire-mill; smelting-houses for lead; a calamine calcinary, besides water corn-mills; all of which are dependent upon the issue of the well for their supply of water-power.

Extensive mine.

The great mine, called the Holywell Level, opened in 1773, is carried into the hill for a length of one mile, the level acting as a canal for the transportation of the ore to the mouth of the Adit. Here are found petro-silex, used in the potteries; lead-ore of the cubic and steel-grained kinds; calamine, and ore of zinc. The exports consist of copper-sheets and nails for sheathing ships, and copper bolts, used in ship-building. The copper works belong to the Anglesey Company; besides the various productions of the different factories. Vessels, taking in lading, lie at the Mark, which is dry at low water, and inconvenient at all times. Steam-packets sail regularly between Bagilt and Chester, which afford an easy and cheap communication to the inhabitants of this town, in addition to the mail and stage-coaches, which pass here daily between Chester and Holyhead.

St. Winifrede's well.

The Well of St. Winifrede, the fountain of prosperity of this place, gushes up within an area of two yards in diameter. It throws up eighty-four hogsheads every minute, has not been known to freeze, yields a supply which forms instantly a tolerable river, nor is it subject to any material increase or diminution from the drought or moisture of the seasons. Over the well, which is enclosed by octagonal sides, stands a temple in an exquisitely enriched Gothic style: the ceiling is of carved stone, ornamented with sculptured pendants, and supported with light coupled pillars, which

Map.	Names of Places.	County.	Number of Miles from			Dist. Lond.	Population.
17	Hom.............pa	Hereford ...	Hereford 6	Ledbury....12	Ross........8	132	389
36	Homersfield.......pa	Suffolk	Bungay.....14	Botesdale....9	Debenham . 10	93	201
25	Homerton.......ham	Middlesex ..	Hackney 1	Tottenham .. 5	S. Newington 3	4	....
41	Homington........pa	Wilts	Salisbury....4	Wilton......4	Downton ...5	85	177
11	Honey Church .....pa	Devon.....	Hatherleigh . 6	Bow 5	Oakhampton .7	193	66
39	Honiley..........pa	Warwick...	Warwick....6	Coventry.. .7	Solihull....8	93	63
27	Honing..........pa	Norfolk....	Walsham....4	Cromer 11	Worsted . . .3	124	268
27	Honingham.......pa	Norfolk....	Norwich 7	E. Dereham .8	Hingham ...8	116	321
24	Honington........pa	Lincoln....	Grantham ..10	Sleaford....5	Lincoln.....15	118	156
36	Honington*.......pa	Suffolk	Bury St. Edm.8	Thetford ...7	Ixworth 4	81	250
39	Honington........pa	Warwick...	Shipston on S.2	Stratford ...9	Kineton ...8	85	337
11	Honiton† .... m t & bo	Devon.....	Chard......12	Axminster...9	Ott. St. Mary 7	156	3509

form a Gothic open arcade around the fountain. The water, after gushing up within the octagonal inclosure, flows rapidly away beneath a low archway into a rectangular bath, twelve feet by seven, in which the superstitious continue to immerge, in the fond hope of miraculous consequences. Two festivals are observed here in honour of the saint: the 22d of June, to commemorate her martyrdom, and the 3d of November, her translation to Heaven. St. James's-day is also observed here as a festival, and called Dydd-Sul-y-Saint, *i. e.* the Sunday of the Saints. The legend informs us that St. Winifrede was the daughter of Thewith, and niece of St. Beuno, who flourished in the seventh century. She had resolved upon founding a religious house, and devoting her life to prayer and penitence, when Cradocus, the son of King Alen, became enamoured of her charms, and resolved to use violence rather than be disappointed in his lustful passion. Having expressed to her his determination; she fled from his presence towards the church, where her parents were at prayers; but Cradocus overtaking her at the descent of the hill, drew his sword, and cut off her head. The head rolled down the hill, nor stopped until it reached the altar in the church, around which the congregation were kneeling, when instantly a fountain of clear water gushed up, and has continued to flow with an undiminished ebullition to the present day. St. Beuno caught up the head, and, *mirabile dictu*, united it to the body, and restored the beautiful virgin in all her bloom, while Cradocus fell down dead upon the spot, where he committed the impious act. At the bottom of the well, grows the *byssus jolithus*, a vegetable production of a reddish hue, which superstition points to as drops of blood. The bones of St. Winifrede were removed from Gwytherin, in Denbighshire, where she died abbess, fifteen years after her decapitation, to the abbey church of Shrewsbury.

HOLYWELL.

Legend of St. Winifrede.

Market, Friday.

* HONINGTON, an obscure village, is celebrated as the birth-place of the pastoral poet, Robert Bloomfield. His mother kept a school in a cottage, near the church, where she died in 1804. At the age of thirteen or fourteen, he was received by his brothers, to be instruced in their trade of shoe-making. At that time his knowledge of books was so small, that he was at a loss to comprehend the meaning of words that commonly occur in the newspaper; but, by a process of study unexampled in the annals of literature, and astonishing to those who witness its traces in his writings, his diction, like his understanding and poetical genius, became strong, flowing, and perspicuous. His principal production is the " Farmer's Boy," a poem displaying most of the beauties belonging to that species of composition, strength, sweetness, harmony of numbers, and simplicity. He also published a volume of " Rural Tales, Ballads and Songs," and several other productions, which are all possessed of a merit peculiar to his writings.

Birth-place of Robert Bloomfield.

His principal productions

† HONITON is situated in a delightful vale on the south side of the river Otter, and consists principally of one broad, handsome street, running

Map.	Names of Places.	County.	Number of Miles from			Dist. Lond.	Popu- lation
45	Honley.......cha & to	W. R. York	Huddersfield .3	Hay 9	Barnsley....14	148	4523
21	Hoo............hun	Kent		Chatham 4	Queensboro' .8	....	910
21	Hoo.............pa	Kent	Rochester ...4	Chatham 4	Queensboro' .8	33	960
27	Hoo.............pa	Norfolk	E. Dereham .2	Foulsham ...7	Fakenham . .9	103	228
36	Hoo.............pa	Suffolk	Mt. Wickham 4	Framlingham 4	Debenham ...6	83	174
44	Hood Grange....ham	N. R. York .	Thirsk 5	Aldborough.12	N. Allerton .13	228	30
38	Hooe............pa	Sussex	Battle 7	Hastings....9	Hailsham....7	63	525
37	Hook ....ham	Surrey......	Kingston ...3	Hounslow ..6	Chertsey ...7	15	222
12	Hooke ....pa	Dorset......	Beaminster .5	Bridport...10	Calistock....5	127	234
46	Hooke............to	W. R. York	Howden ...2	Selby......9	Thorne.....8	180	650
7	Hoole............to	Chester.....	Chester......2	Frodsham ...8	Thornton....4	182	237
22	Hoole, Little......to	Lancaster...	Preston......6	Kirkham ...3	Garstang ...11	222	934
22	Hoole, Much ....pa	Lancaster...		Ormskirk ...10	Chorley 9	220	745
10	Hoone............to	Derby	Derby......8	Uttoxeter ...10	Ashborn....11	134	40
7	Hoose............to	Chester.....	Gt. Neston ..4	Liverpool....5	Wallasea....4	199	114
7	Hooton............to	Chester.....	Chester......9	Maltby......2	Eastham ...5	192	112
46	Hooton Levet......to	W. R. York	Bawtry......9	Maltby......2	Worksop ...8	154	95
46	Hooton Pagnell ....pa	W. R. York	Doncaster ..7	Wakefield . 10	Pontefract ..6	171	425
45	Hooton Roberts....pa	W. R. York	Rotheram ..4	Barnsley....10	Sheffield.....9	163	190
31	Hopcrofts, Holt ...ham	Oxford	Deddington . 4	Bicester 8	Woodstock ..6	72	....
10	Hope.............pa	Derby	Tideswell ...6	Sheffield ...13	C. in le Frith 8	166	3927
53	Hope*........pa & vil	Flint........	Wrexham ..5	Hawarden ..5	Mold.......6	196	2747
56	Hope.............to	Montgomery	Welsh Pool..3	Llandrinio ..5	Buttington ..1	173	169
44	Hope.............to	W. R. York	Greta Bridge.5	Brough.....10	Askrigg 10	246	44
21	Hope, All Saints ...pa	Kent	Romney 1	Rye........9	Lydd........4	70	48

HONITON. from east to west, and another crossing it at right angles : through the former runs a stream of excellent water, from which the inhabitants are supplied by a dipping-place opposite almost every door. The buildings are mostly modern, and covered with slate, an improvement that originated from several fires which nearly destroyed the town at four different periods. The streets are well paved and lighted. It is said that the first manufacture of serge in Devon was established here ; but the principal manufacture at present, is that of broad lace and edgings ; it also supplies the London markets with great quantities of butter. **Church dedicated to St. Michael.** The church, which is dedicated to St. Michael, is situated on a bold eminence, a short distance from the town ; it was originally a small chapel for mendicant friars, but was enlarged about the year 1482, chiefly at the expense of Courtenay, Bishop of Exeter, who also gave the curious screen which separates the chancel from the nave ; it contains several ancient monuments. The chapel-of-ease, which is dedicated to All Saints, was erected by subscription, and is built of flint, with a tower and cupola, with six bells, a clock, and chimes.

Market, Saturday.—*Fair*, July 20, for cattle.

* HOPE, or Queen's Hope, or East Hope, a parish and village in the hundred of Mold, near to the banks of the Alen river, and at a short distance from Caergwrle. The noble castle of Hope was erected upon the summit of a lofty and precipitous rock ; its founder is not known, but in the reign of Owen Gwynedd, it appears to have been in the possession of Gryffydd Maelor. Edward I. granted the castle to Prince David, but subsequently conferred it upon his faithful Queen Eleanor, **Residence of Queen Eleanor.** who settled here upon her journey to Carnarvon, at which latter place she shortly after gave birth to Edward, surnamed Carnarvon. The name, Queen's Hope, is probably derived from the circumstance of the royal visit. In 1307, the castle and manor were granted to John de Cromwell. The ruins are now inconsiderable. In the parish church is an ancient mural monument, to the memory of Sir John Trevor, comptroller of the navy during the remarkable period of the meditated descent of the Spanish **Mineral springs.** Armada. There are two mineral springs in this parish, impregnated with muriate of soda, and believed to be efficacious in scorbutic cases. Some beautiful specimens of entrochi and astroites are found in the limestone of this district ; and the uncommon species, usually denominated the arborescent sea star, has also been discovered here.

Map.	Names of Places.	County.	Number of Miles from			Dist. Lond.	Popu-lation
33	Hope Bagot.......pa	Salop.......	Ludlow 6	C. Mortimer.7	Bridgenorth.15	144	71
33	Hope Bowdler......pa	Salop	16	Shrewsbury.11	Bishop'sCas. 10	160	179
17	Hope under Dinmore pa	Hereford ..	Leominster..5	Bromyard...10	Hereford....9	144	555
17	Hope Mansell......pa	Hereford ..	Ross.......5	Monmouth..10	Gloucester...11	118	146
33	Hope Say.........pa	Salop.....	Bishop'sCast. 6	Ludlow 10	ChurchStret. 8	152	571
17	Hope Sollers......pa	Hereford ..	Ross.......7	Monmouth..10	Gloucester ..22	126	187
17	Hopley...........to	Hereford ...	Weobly 5	Kington 5	Hay.......11	151	....
29	Hoppen..........to	Northumb..	Belford......4	Wooler......9	NewBewick 14	320	29
44	Hopperton........to	W. R. York	Knaresboro' .5	Aldborough..7	Ripon 13	201	....
39	Hopsford ....ham	Warwick...	Coventry 7	Hinckley 6	Nuneaton ...7	96	....
10	Hopton...........to	Derby	Wirksworth .2	Ashborn ...7	Winster 6	142	116
35	Hopton *.........lib	Stafford ...	Stafford ... 2	Stone 6	Eccleshall...7	142	642
36	Hopton...........pa	Suffolk	Harling......6	Thetford....5	Ixworth....6	74	581
36	Hopton...........pa	Suffolk ...	Lowestoff ..5	Yarmouth ...6	Beccles....6	119	524
33	Hopton Castle.....pa	Salop.....	Knighton....6	Bridgnorth . 10	Bewdly....9	140	150
33	Hopton in the Hole .pa	Salop.....	Ludlow 5	M.Wenlock 10	ChurchStre. 11	146	24
33	Hopton Monks......pa	Salop.....	M. Wenlock.4	Shrewsbury 15	11	153	168
33	Hopton Wafers ....pa	Salop	Tenbury....5	C.Mortimer..4	Ludlow....10	141	473
35	Hopwas.........ex p	Stafford ...	Stafford ... 2	Stone......5	Eccleshall ..5	142	3
10	Hopwell...........lib	Derby	Derby......7	Nottingham .8	Eastwood...6	130	34
22	Hopwood..........to	Lancaster..	Lancaster .. 4	Garstang 6	Hornby....14	236	1384
42	Hopwood..........ham	Worcester..	Bromsgrove..6	Birmingham .8	Alcester....10	122	1413
24	Horbling ....pa	Lincoln ...	Folkingham..3	Donnington ..5	Sleaford ...10	109	559
45	Horbury..........pa	W. R. York	Wakefield ..2	Mirfield 5	Huddersfield.8	184	2400
33	Horderley....ex pa lib	Salop.....	Bishop'sCast. 1	Montgomery .8	Church Stre..9	160	....
16	Hordle ....pa	Hants	Lymington ..4	Christchurch 7	Yarmouth ...7	88	699
33	Hordley..........pa	Salop.....	Ellesmere ..5	Oswestry....5	Shrewsbury.12	174	308
34	Horethorne........hun	Somerset ..				....	7663
15	Horfield...........pa	Gloucester..	Bristol......2	Thornbury . 10	Sodbury 10	113	198
36	Horham...........pa	Suffolk ...	Eye.........4	Debenham ..7	Harlestone...7	90	423
14	Horkesley, Great ..pa	Essex	Neyland 2	Colchester...5	Coggleshall .12	53	697
14	Horkesley, Little ...pa	Essex	3	Manningtree10	11	54	238
24	Horkstow.........pa	Lincoln ...	Barton on H. 4	Burton.......7	Glan.Bridge 12	168	200
31	Horley...........pa	Oxford ...	Banbury....3	Shennington .3	Bloxham....7	74	881
37	Horley...........pa	Surrey ...	Riegate 6	E. Grinstead.8	Capel......8	27	1063
18	Hormead, Great ...pa	Herts	Buntingford..4	Standon....5	Royston....9	31	1164
18	Hormead, Little ....pa	Herts	4	4	Hodham....5	30	576
4	Hormer.... ....hun	Berks				....	3323
32	Horn.............pa	Rutland ...	Stamford 6	Cottesmere ..4	Empingham .3	95	396
34	Hornblotton........pa	Somerset ..	Castle Carey.4	Glastonbury .7	Shep. Mallet.6	116	425
22	Hornby †...m t & cha	Lancaster..	Lancaster...8	K. Lonsdale .7	Burton.....7	248	417
44	Hornby...........to	N. R. York	N. Allerton..8	Darlington ..6	Yarm......6	233	238
44	Hornby...........pa	N. R. York	Catterick....4	N. Allerton..7	Thirsk.....6	230	102
24	Horncastle........soke	Lincoln				....	8656

* HOPTON. A severe action was fought here between the king's forces under the Earl of Northampton, and the parliamentary army, commanded by Sir John Gell and Sir William Brereton. The latter having encamped at this place, the former immediately led his forces against them; and notwithstanding their great superiority in numbers, attacked them with incredible impetuosity; and after an obstinate contest, the earl's horse having been shot under him, he was surrounded and slain; but the royalists continued the battle, and, according to their account, gained a decided victory; the parliamentary army, on the other hand, asserted that, though defeated at first, they were in the end successful.

Action between the Royalists and the Parliamentarians.

† HORNBY is a small ancient market-town and chapelry, in the parish of Melling, in the hundred of Lonsdale. The principal object of attraction here is Hornby-castle, erected by Nicholas de Mont Begons, soon after the conquest; in later years it became possessed by William, Lord Monteagles, to whom the mysterious letter was sent which led to the discovery of the gunpowder treason. The ruins of a Saxon fortification stand in this honour, and also the remains of a premonstratension priory. Hornby had once a weekly market on Friday, which has merged in the fortnight fair for cattle, held on Tuesday; there is also an annual cattle fair on the 30th of July. From Hornby-castle the scenery is very beautiful, embracing the picturesque and fertile vales of the Lune and the Wenning, and in the distance is seen the hills of Ingleborough, Whernside and Pennigent.

Ancient castle.

Map.	Names of Places.	County.	Number of Miles from			Dist. Lond.	Popu. lation
24	Horncastle* ..m t & pa	Lincoln.....	Spilsby 10	Tattershall ..9	Alford......14	136	3988
14	Hornchurch ....pa	Essex	Romford.....4	Brentwood .. 6	Grays Thurr. 8	14	2186
13	Horncliff ....to	Durham	Berwick on T.5	Coldstream ..9	Wooler 12	335	351
14	Horndon, Great.....pa	Essex	Brentwood ..4	G. Thrrock ..8	Billericay ...4	19	459

* HORNCASTLE is a neat market-town and parish, pleasantly situated at the foot of that bold and even range of hills, which, from their openness, have been termed the wolds. The principal part of the town is built in an angle, formed by the confluence of two rivers, the Bane and the Waring, where an ancient fortification formerly stood, the site of which is still visible, denoting it to have been a station of importance in early times. Within the last century, the appearance of the town is completely changed. The rebuilding of many houses in the principal streets, in a handsome manner, within the last twenty years, has given to the town an air of respectability ; but the effect which would be produced by these buildings, in its general appearance, is materially diminished by the narrowness and irregularity of the streets. Since the completion of the canal, in 1801, a considerable trade in corn and wool has been carried on here. The church, dedicated to St. Mary, though an ancient structure,

Ancient church.

from the numerous repairs which have been put upon it, has a modern look. The few portions of the original architecture which have escaped the silent ravages of time, and the hands of the innovator, bespeak the building to have been erected about the period of Henry VII. In the wall of the north aisle is a stone, containing the figure of Sir Lyonel Dymoke, in armour, kneeling. Sir Lyonel Dymoke was one of the ancestors of the present family of that name, who performed the office of champion at the coronation of the kings of England. Scrivelsby-court, the ancient baronial seat, is about two miles from Horncastle. The benefice of this church is a vicarage, in the presentation of the Bishop of Carlisle. The other places of worship are, a chapel each for the Wesleyan and primitive methodists, independents and calvinistic baptists. A building, situated on the south side of the church-yard, is appropriated for the purposes of a dispensary, which is supported by subscription. A literary society, which was established here in 1790, formed a permanent library, which is kept at the dispensary, and contains about one thousand volumes, open to the members two days in the week. In the year 1807, an act for the recovery of debts under five pounds was obtained, and the commissioners hold their courts at this place, as well as at the other towns specified

Charitable nstitutions.

in the act, every fourth Thursday. The education of the poor, which has lately excited so much attention in various parts of the kingdom, has not been neglected here. A school on the Lancasterian, or British system, and another on the plan of Dr. Bell, supported by voluntary contributions, instruct about four hundred children. The grammar-school was founded by Lord Clinton and Saye, in the year 1652. The governors of the grammar-school are also trustees of another public school, of a humbler class, for poor girls, founded by Mr. Richard Watson, in 1784. There are now three fairs for horses, cattle and sheep, held here annually. The first, which concludes on the 22nd of June, has of late years declined very much, and though chartered for eight days, seldom continues more

Great fair for horses.

than three. The second, which terminates on the 21st of August, has long been celebrated as the largest fair for horses in the kingdom, perhaps, it may be said, in the world ; it continues about ten days, being three days more than the time expressed in the charter. The third fair, which is held on the 28th and 29th days of October, was removed to this place in 1768, from Market Stainton, a decayed market-town, about eight miles distant, two hundred pounds being given to the lord of the manor of that place, to permit the removal. The market is held here every Saturday, to which it was changed from Wednesday, the day mentioned

Map.	Names of Places.	County.	Number of Miles from			Dist. Lond.	Population.
14	Horndon on the Hill* pa	Essex	Brentwood ..8	G. Thurrock 5	Billericay ...7	24	511
14	Horndon, West.....pa	Essex	4	6	6	18	45
37	Horne.............pa	Surrey	Godstone 6	Bletchinly ..6	Dorking 10	25	595
27	Horning..........pa	Norfolk	Acle.......6	Norwich ...10	Worstead ...6	119	440
23	Horninghold.......pa	Leicester ...	Rockingham .5	Tugby.......3	Leicester ...14	86	97
35	Horninglow ....pa	Stafford	Burton on T. 2	Uttoxeter ..10	Ab.Bromley 10	127	341
6	Horningsea ....pa	Cambridge .	Cambridge...5	Ely.........9	Newmarket .8	56	285
41	Horningsham.....pa	Wilts	Warminster .4	Frome.......6	Westbury ...6	101	1323
36	Horningsheath .....pa	Suffolk	Bury St.Edm.2	Newmarket 14	Clare.......12	72	586
27	Horningtoft.......pa	Norfolk	Fakenham ...4	Castle Acre..9	Foulsham....7	103	254
46	Hornsea† ...m t & ex p	E. R. York .	Beverley...13	Leaven.....6	Aldborough..6	188	780
25	Hornsey‡......pa & vil	Middlesex ..	Islington....4	Highgate 2	Hackney....5	5	4856

in the charter, probably in consequence of the markets of Boston and Louth being also on that day.

HORN-CASTLE.

Letters from London arrive (by gig from Spilsby, where it meets the London and Louth males) every afternoon at half-past three, and are despatched every morning at half-past ten. The Lincoln and North mail arrives every afternoon at three, and is dispatched every morning at four.—*Bankers*, Claypon, Garfittes and Claypons, draw on Masterman and Co.

* HORNDON-ON-THE-HILL. *Market*, Saturday.—*Fair*, June 29, for wool.

† HORNSEA. *Market*, Monday.—*Fairs*, August 13; and December 17, for horses and beasts.

‡ HORNSEY, a parish and village, in Finsbury division of the hundred of Ossulstone ; the former including the hamlets of Crouch End, Muswell-hill, Stroud-green, a considerable part of Highgate, and a part of Finchley-common. It is remarkable for its rural character. The circumjacent country is eminently attractive, by its soft ranges of hills ; and the New River, which meanders through the parish, forms, at many points, a beautiful object. The manor of Hornsey has appertained to the see of London from a period beyond the reach of any known record. The bishops formerly had a palace here. The more ancient building, occa-sionally inhabited by the prelates, is supposed to have stood on Lodge-hill, at the eastern extremity of Lord Mansfield's wood ; and the remains of a moat are still to be seen. The " great park," formerly belonging to the bishops of London, has been long under cultivation. Some passages of history, however, are connected with the district. In the reign of Richard II. the Duke of Gloucester, with the Earls of Arundel and War-wick, of Derby and Nottingham, and several other nobles, repaired to arms, for the avowed purpose of opposing Robert de Vere, Earl of Ox-ford, whom the king, in an excess of partiality, had created Duke of Ireland. The place in which they assembled was this park. Among the persons seized, in consequence of that supposed conspiracy against Henry VI., in which the Duchess of Gloucester bore a part, were Roger Bolingbroke, an astrologer, and Thomas Southwell, a canon of St. Stephen's. The former was said to have devised necromantic means for wasting and destroying the king's person ; and Southwell " said masses in the lodge at Hornsey-park, over the instruments which were to be used for that purpose." The Lord Mayor of London, and a train of citizens, met the youthful and ill-fated Edward V. in this park, when he approached the capital shortly after the decease of his father, and conducted him into the city. The citizens, in official array, also met Henry VII. at the same place, on his return from a successful Scottish war. Brownswood manor forms the chief part of a prebend in St. Paul's cathedral, once held by Bishop Fox, the founder of Corpus Christi-college, Oxford. Lands descend according to the custom of Gravel kind, in the manor of Hornsey. From Muswell-hill, at the north-western extremity of the parish, are some beautiful and varied prospects, with numerous detached villas. On this hill is a spring (formerly termed Mousewell) traditionally famous for a " great cure performed upon a king of Scots, who was, by some divine

Romantic scenery.

Celebrated in history.

Custom of Gravel kind observed here.

Map.	Names of Places.	County.	Number of Miles from			Dist. Lond.	Popu- lation.
31	Hornton..........cha	Oxford	Banbury.....6	Chip.Norton12	Deddington.12	77	551
6	Horseheath.........pa	Cambridge..	Linton 4	Haverhill....5	Cambridge .10	64	413
44	Horse House..to & cha	N. R. York.	Middleham ..7	Askrigg 8	Paitley Br. .11	231	....
27	Horseford ....pa	Norfolk	Norwich 5	Reepham....8	Aylsham ...9	114	543
15	Horsley...........pa	Gloucester .	M. Hampton.2	Dursley 6	Berkley 9	96	3565
35	Horsley...........to	Stafford	Stafford 7	Drayton....10	Eccleshall...2	150	487
37	Horseley, East .....pa	Surrey......	Leatherhead .6	Dorking 6	Guildford....7	23	192
37	Horseley, West*....pa	Surrey......	7	7	 6	24	611
37	Horsell...........pa	Surrey......	Ripley.....4	Bagshot 7	Chertsey...6	25	673
21	Horsemonden .....pa	Kent......	Lamberhurst.2	Marden 5	Cranbrook .. 5	39	1197
5	Horsendon ....pa	Bucks......	G. Missenden.7	Wendover ..6	Thame......7	38	50
23	Horsepool ....to	Leicester ...	Leicester ...8	Ashby de la Z.8	Mt.Bosworth 7	104	....
27	Horsey...........pa	Norfolk....	Caistor......9	Worstead ..10	N.Walsham 12	125	95
45	Horseforth...to & cha	W. R. York	Leeds......5	Otley......5	Bradford...5	200	3425
38	Horsham†..bo n t & pa	Sussex	Cuckfield...10	Steyning...15	Alfold.....10	36	5105
27	Horsham, St. Faiths.pa	Norfolk	Norwich 5	Reepham....9	Aylsham 8	114	1279
24	Horsington ....pa	Lincoln.....	Horncastle .3	Wragby 9	Louth 10	139	322

HORNSEY.   intelligence, advised to take the water of a well in England, called Mus-well." A chapel was consequently erected on the spot, bearing the name of our Lady of Muswell. This chapel (an appendage to the priory of Clerkenwell) had sunk, before the reign of Elizabeth; and, "Alderman Roe had a proper house occupying the site." The well yet remains, but is not known to possess any medicinal virtues. At Crouch End, on the road from Islington to Hornsey, are several substantial and desirable dwellings, and a small place of worship for dissenters. Hornsey-church, recently repaired, is a plain structure of stone, erected about the year 1500. At the west end is a weighty square tower, with graduated buttresses, and an octagonal embattled turret at one angle. The interior comprises a chancel, nave, and south aisle. The aisle is divided from the nave by a range of pillars, supporting broad, but pointed, arches. Here are numerous monuments, but none of a very striking character.

   * HORSELEY, WEST. The church, which is dedicated to St. Mary, is a small ancient structure, containing several old stalls and monuments. In the chapel, which is the burial-place belonging to the manor-house, is

Discovery of the head of Sir W. Raliegh.   interred Carew Raleigh, Esq., son of Sir Walter; near his coffin, a human skull, without any other bones or covering, was found in a niche in the rock of chalk, which is supposed to have been that of Sir Walter Raliegh, brought here by his son with the intention of having it buried with himself. Within a short distance is the venerable old mansion, which formerly belonged to the Raleigh family.

   † HORSHAM is pleasantly situated on a branch of the river Adur, and in the centre of a fertile district, surrounded by varied and interesting scenery, with excellent turnpike roads branching in every direction. The houses are in general well built, and the town is well paved. It consists principally of one long street, running east and west, and small ones branching from it; the one through which the church is approached is agreeably planted with rows of fine majestic trees. Many good seats and mansions are in the vicinity of the town, and its inhabitants generally very respectable. Its great thoroughfare situation ensures it a certain portion of business and consequence, and gives it an air of liveliness superior to most other towns in the neighbourhood. A great quantity of poultry is reared in this vicinity, for the London market; and it contains

Quarries of excellent stone.   quarries of excellent stone, which is used for flooring, paving, &c. The quarter sessions are held here in July, but the spring assizes have been removed to Lewes. Horsham is a borough by prescription, and has returned two members to parliament since the 23rd of Edward I., but now sends but one. The church, dedicated to St. Mary, is a spacious and venerable structure, in the early style of English architecture, with a lofty tower, surmounted by a spire. The east window of the chancel i

Map	Names of Places.	County.	Number of Miles from			Dist. Lond.	Population.
34	Horsington..........pa	Somerset ...	Wincanton ..4	Castle Carey.4	Somerton ..11	109	968
10	Horsley............pa	Derby	Derby 6	Ashborn....15	Alfreton ...8	132	649
27	Horsley.........to	Northumb	New.-on-T. 10	Corbridge ...9	Morpeth...13	134	257
29	Horsley, Long .....pa	Northumb .	Morpeth....7	Rothbury ..9	Elsdon 12	295	1006
10	Horsley Woodhouse.pa	Derby.....	Derby 7	Nottingham .8	Eastwood ...5	132	1948
31	Horspath........pa	Oxford	Oxford....4	Thame.....9	Abingdon...8	54	264
27	Horstead .... pa	Norfolk.....	Cottihall 1	Aylsham ...6	Reepham...9	116	593
36	Horstead, Keynes*..pa	Suffolk	Cuckfield...6	Stow Market 4	Ixworth 9	85	782
38	Horstead, Little ...pa	Sussex	Uckfield....3	Hailsham....8	Lewes.......7	50	286
5	Horton ....ham	Bucks	Ivinghoe 3	Lei. Buzzard.3	Aylesbury ..9	39	804
5	Horton ....pa	Bucks	Colnbrook ...2	Windsor ...3	Slough.....5	19	796
7	Horton ....to	Chester.....	Chester.....6	Frodsham ..6	Northwich .11	180	136
7	Horton ....to	Chester.....	6	7	10	179	40
12	Horton............pa	Dorset.....	Cranborne ...5	Wim.Minster7	Blan.Forum 10	98	420
15	Horton............pa	Gloucester..	Chip.Sodbury4	Wotton 6	Tetbury ...10	108	385
21	Horton ....cha	Kent	Canterbury ..4	Faversham .5	Ashford 9	51	....
29	Horton............pa	Northamp ...	Northampton 6	Wellingboro10	Towcester..10	60	87
29	Horton............pa	Northumb..	Morpeth.....6	Blyth 4	Newcastle..11	285	2631
29	Horton............to	Northumb..	Wooler.....3	Coldstream 12	Belford 7	323	....
31	Horton ....ham	Oxford	Oxford....7	Bicester 5	Woodstock .10	61	....
33	Horton ....to	Salop.....	Wellington ..2	Newport 5	Shiffnal 6	152	....
33	Horton ....to	Salop......	Wem.....3	Whitchurch 8	Ellesmere ..10	173	99
35	Horton..........pa	Stafford	Leek......3	Longnor 6	Flash 3	157	970
45	Horton in Craven ..to	W. R. York	Skipton....10	Clitheroe ...5	Broughton .. 6	222	187
29	Horton Grange.....to	Northumb..	Newc.-on T. 8	Blyth......9	Morpeth.....8	282	66
45	Horton,Great. cha & to	W. R. York	Bradford....2	Keighly 6	Halifax......4	198	10782
35	Horton, Hay......to	Stafford	Leek......5	Newcastle ..9	Longnor....13	157	....
21	Horton, Kirby....pa	Kent	Dartford....4	Farningham .2	Gravesend .. 7	17	666
45	Horton, Little....ham	W. R. York	Bradford....1	Halifax......4	Huddersfield 8	197	7192
21	Horton, Monks ....pa	Kent	Hythe.....5	Dover 12	Canterbury .11	63	186
44	Horton in Ribbles-} dale†..........pa {	W. R. York	Settle......6	Ingleton 4	Hawes......11	241	567
22	Horwich ....to	Lancaster...	Bolton.....5	Chorley 5	Wigan......5	202	3562
11	Horwood..........pa	Devon	Bideford....4	Barnstaple..5	Torrington ..6	201	144
5	Horwood, Great ...pa	Bucks	Winslow....3	Buckingham .5	Sto.Stratford 7	53	720
5	Horwood, Little ...pa	Bucks	3	7	Fen Stratford 7	54	429

of beautiful design ; and the interior, which preserves its original character throughout, contains several interesting and ancient monuments. The principal charities are, a free-school, founded in 1532, and now under the masters and wardens of the Mercers' Company ; and a school on the Lancasterian system, in which are instructed about 300 boys and girls. The principal weekly market (a large one for corn) is held on Saturday ; and during the spring and summer months a very considerable one for poultry takes place every Monday. The annual fairs are six in number, viz., the 3rd of April, for sheep ; the Monday before Whit-Sunday, and the 18th of July, for cattle, horses and sheep ; the 25th of the same month a pleasure fair ; November 17, or St. Leonard's fair, for Welsh cattle ; and the 27th, for cattle, generally and sundry wares. The principal is the Lamb.

HORSHAM.

Charitable institutions.

Letters from London and Brighton arrive every morning at three, and are despatched every night at ten.

* HORSTED KEYNES. *Fairs*, May 27, and September 12, for cattle and pedlery.

† HORTON-IN-RIBBLESDALE, a parish in the west division of the wapentake of Staincliffe and Ewcross. In this parish are the sources of the Ribble and the Wharfe. To the east is Pennigent-hill, a towering mountain, at whose base are two frightful chasms, called Hulpit and Huntpit-holes ; through each of them runs a subterraneous brook, which emerges at a considerable distance. On the west side of the mountain are the remains of some ancient places of interment, called the Giant's Graves, though the skeletons discovered here do not exceed the ordinary size. To the western boundary of the parish are the skirts of Ingleborough-hill ; this mountain is 2361 feet in height, the top is flat, and nearly a mile in circumference ; the summit is of a gritty sand-stone, and commands a noble view. Here was formerly a beacon, to communicate any sudden alarm. Ingleborough is the first land descried by sailors in their voyage from Dublin to Lancaster.

Subterraneous brook.

6 I

Map.	Names of Places.	County.	Number of Miles from			Dist. Lond.	Population.
23	Hose..............pa	Leicester ...	Mel.Mowbray7	Bottesford ...8	N.Broughton 4	112	320
4	Hospital.............ti	Berks	Abingdon .. 14	Farringdon ..2	Bampton.. ..4	70	....
46	Hotham............pa	E. R. York .	N. Cave.....1	Mt.Weighton4	Howden.. ..9	178	293
22	Hothersall............to	Lancaster...	Preston 7	Whalley.. ..6	Blackburn ..4	218	948
21	Hothfield...........pa	Kent..	Ashford 3	Tenterden ..10	Charing 3	53	438
28	Hothorpe.........ham	Northamp ..	Mt. Harboro'.4	Daventry ...16	Rothwell ..10	86	62
23	Hoton.. ....to	Leicester ...	Loughboro' ..3	Kegworth ...7	N.Broughton 8	112	401
7	Hough, The ....to	Chester	Nantwich .. 3	Audlem 6	Betley......5	166	202
24	Hough on the Hill...pa	Lincoln	Grantham ...8	Newark 9	Lincoln.. ..13	118	565
21	Hougham...........pa	Kent	Dover.......3	Canterbury .15	Folkestone ..4	70	834
9	Houghton...........to	Cumberland	Carlisle.. ...2	Longtown ...6	Brampton ...9	304	288
19	Houghton...... ....pa	Huntingdon.	St. Ives......2	Huntingdon. .3	Oldhurst 4	64	427
22	Houghton...........to	Lancaster...	Stockport ...4	Manchester ..7	Denham 1	182	2914
22	Houghton...........to	Lancaster...	N.in Makerfi. 4	Bolton 8	Wigan.. 7	196	280
29	Houghton...........to	Northumb ..	Newc -on-T. 8	Corbridge ...8	Morpeth....14	282	362
38	Houghton...... ....pa	Sussex	Arundel 4	Steyning....10	Petworth....7	56	162
46	Houghton ....to	E. R. York .	M.Weighton 2	Beverley 7	Pocklington .8	191	334
3	Houghton Conquest .pa	Bedford	Ampthill 2	Bedford 6	Shefford 7	47	796
3	Houghton Gildable..pa	Bedford	3	 5	6	48	
45	Houghton, Glass ....to	W. R. York	Pontefract...3	Tadcaster ..10	Abberford .. 6	180	412
28	Houghton, Great ....to	Northamp. .	Northampton3	Bozeat 7	Towcester..10	63	249
45	Houghton, Great ....to	W. R. York	Barnsley . ..6	Pontefract...8	Wakefield..10	178	287
28	Houghton,Hanging ham	Northamp ..	Northampton8	Daventry 7	Welford 9	74	111
23	Houghton on the Hill pa	Leicester ...	Leicester 6	Tugby 6	Mt.Harboro'12	90	374
27	Houghton on the Hill pa	Norfolk.....	Walton.. ...4	Watton 4	Swaffham .. 4	94	34
27	Houghton in the Hole pa	Norfolk.....	N. Walsingh. 1	Holt 10	Wells.. 4	119	206
28	Houghton, Little....pa	Northamp ..	Northampton4	Bozeat.. 7	Towcester..11	63	539
29	Houghton, Little ....to	Northumb ..	Alnwick 4	Belford 15	NewBewick14	311	77
45	Houghton, Little ....to	W. R. York	Barnesley....5	Rotheram ...8	Wakefield..10	167	112
29	Houghton, Long ....pa	Northumb ..	Alnwick 4	Belford 16	NewBewick14	310	650
27	Houghton, New ....pa	Norfolk	Fakenham ..9	Burn.Market10	Castle Rising 7	107	200
16	Houghton, North ...pa	Hants	Stockbridge .2	Salisbury. ..13	Andover 8	68	365
3	Houghton Regis.....pa	Bedford.. ..	Dunstable ...2	Leig.Buzzard 7	Toddington ..4	36	1424
13	Houghton Lee Side ..to	Durham	Darlington ..6	Sedgefield ...7	Durham 11	247	122
13	Houghton le Spring* ....m t & pa	Durham	Durham 7	Sunderland ..7	S. Shields ..20	266	20524
22	Houghton, West ....to	Lancaster...	Wigan.. 4	Bolton 5	Manchester 13	195	4211
12	Houghton Winter-borne.. ....pa	Dorset......	Bland Forum 5	Spittisbury ..6	Stur.Newton 8	108	203
16	Hound..............pa	Hants	Southampton 4	Titchfield ...6	Botley......5	74	387
34	Hound Street.........ti	Somerset ...	Pensford 2	Frome.......7	Bristol.. 8	110	73
34	Houndsborough, Ber-wick & Croker hun	Somerset ...	....	....	....	....	7914

Church dedicated to St. Michael.

* HOUGHTON-LE-SPRING. This village is situated at the head of a fine vale, opening to the west, and sheltered from the bleak winds of the north by a chain of hills. The church, dedicated to St. Michael, stands on a rising ground, in the centre of a square area, formed by the buildings in the lower part of the village. It is a valuable rectory, in the gift of the bishop; chapels-of-ease to this parish are in several of the dependent townships, and in the village are, meeting-houses for dissenters, methodists, baptists, &c. The bishop is the lord of the manor, and holds copyhold courts by his halmote clerk, twice in the year, at which petty causes of assault, and debts under 40*s.*, are tried, and nuisances within the manor presented. Near to the church is the Keepier grammar-school, founded in 1574, a girl's charity-school, and alms-houses for six poor widows. A mechanics' institute is established here, under the powerful patronage of the Marquis of Londonderry and J. G. Lambton, Esq., M.P. This parish is celebrated for having had as its rector the Rev. Bernard Gilpin, who, in the reigns of Queen Elizabeth and the ruthless Mary, was styled the apostle of the north; he was buried in the parish church in 1683. The trade of this place, and indeed an immense surrounding tract, is dependent upon the mining operations; and according to the success or declination of these subterranean works, so is the prosperity of this and the neighbouring villages controlled. A small fair for two days is held here in the beginning of October, said to have originated in a religious festival held in commemoration of the sanctification of the parish church. The parish of Houghton-le-Spring contains no less than fifteen dependent townships and the chapelry of Painshaw.

Rectory of the celebrated Bernard Gilpin.

Market, Friday.

Map.	Names of Places.	County.	Number of Miles from			Dist. Lond.	Popu- lation.
25	Hounslow*..........pa	Middlesex	Staines......7	Brentford....3	Uxbridge....9	10	....
38	Hove............ ......pa	Sussex	Brighton 2	Lewes......10	Steyning.....8	58	1360
30	Hoveringham ....pa	Nottingham	Southwell ...5	Newark ...6	Bingham ...5	129	335
27	Hoveton vil	Norfolk.....	Coltishall ...3	Worstead ...5	Aylsham 9	116	337
43	Hovingham..........pa	N. R. York	New Malton.8	Helmsley....6	Pickering....9	225	1162
9	How Bound.......to	Cumberland	Penrith......9	H.Newmarkt.4	Penrith.....11	295	....
29	Howburn............to	Northumb..	Belford.....5	Coldstream .13	Berwick....13	327	....
46	Howden†....m t & pa	E. R. York.	S. Cave.....12	Selby.......8	Snaith 9	182	4531
46	Howdenshire .....wap	E. R. York .				....	8246
29	Howden Pans.......to	Northumb..	N. Shields ..2	Newcastle...6	S. Shields....3	280	....

* HOUNSLOW, a market-town and chapelry, partly in the parish of Heston and partly in that of Isleworth, and in the hundred of Isleworth. It is situated on the principal road from London to the west of England, and has long been noted as a great thoroughfare. It is stated in the parliamentary survey, made in 1650, that the town of Hounslow then contained 120 houses, most of which were inns and alehouses, depending upon travellers; but such has since been the increase of population, that in 1795 a greater number of houses was comprised within that part of the town alone belonging to the parish of Heston. Its early importance may be inferred, from its having been the scene of a tournament, held during the insurrection of the associated barons, who procured the grant of the great charter from King John; and in the first year of Henry III., a conference took place at Hounslow between the partisans of that prince and those of the French dauphin, who had invaded England. On Hounslow Heath, both the royal and parliamentary armies were encamped, at different periods, during the civil war. Here also James II. had collected a large body of troops, in June, 1688; and when on a visit to the camp to review the soldiers, he was alarmed by the loud exclamations of joy, on the arrival of the news of the acquital of the seven prelates who had been tried for sedition, in consequence of their presenting to the king a remonstrance against his assumed power of dispensing with the established laws of the kingdom. While this encampment continued, the king granted the privilege of holding a daily market on the heath, for the convenience of the troops, and also a weekly market on Thursdays, the latter of which is still continued. There was anciently a priory at Hounslow, dedicated to the Holy Trinity, which gave rise to the foundation of the present church, as a chapel of ease to the parish of Heston. A district church has also recently been erected under the authority of the parliamentary commission. The only manufacture of importance at present, is that of gunpowder; for making which there are two establishments in the vicinity of Hounslow. Barracks were erected on the heath, by government, in 1793, calculated to afford accommodation for more than 600 men. This heath was formerly one of the most noted scenes of highway robberies in the neighbourhood of London; but almost every part of it which is capable of culture has been enclosed by act of Parliament, and numerous handsome houses have been erected, and plantations made within a few years past, which have materially changed the appearance of this formerly desolate tract of country.

Encampment of the royal and parliamentary armies.

Manufactory for gunpowder.

† HOWDEN, a market-town, parish, and township in the wapentake of Howdenshire, situated at a short distance from the river Ouse. The town is neat and well built, and has latterly been much improved; in the market-place is a large old building called the Moot-hall, where the Bishop of Durham, as lord of the manor, holds four copyhold courts in the year, two freehold courts, and a court-baron every three weeks, for causes under 40s. Henry III. granted to the Bishops of Durham, among many other privileges, those of having the property of all persons who died *felo de se* within the manor, all wrecks cast upon the shores of the river Ouse, and the power of issuing writs. The living is a vicarage in

Curious grant.

Map.	Names of Places.	County.	Number of Miles from				Dist. Lond.	Popu-lation.
27	Howe..............pa	Norfolk	Norwich ...6	Yarmouth ..13	Loddon......6		110	99
44	Howe..............to	N. R. York.	Thirsk.......6	Bedale 4	Masham....7		219	32
17	Howe Caple........pa	Hereford ...	Ross.........6	Hereford ...10	Ledbury ...9		128	117
24	Howell............pa	Lincoln....	Sleaford....5	Swinehead...7	Donington ...9		114	693
7	Howfield..........to	Chester....	Tarporley...3	Chester.....7	Malpas.....10		181	....
44	Howgill..........ham	York	Kendal 9	Sedberg 3	Hawes 15		269	....
44	Howgrave ....to	N. R. York.	Ripon 5	Masham 5	Bedale......6		217	....
22	Howick ....to	Lancaster..	Preston.....3	Kirkham 5	Garstang ...10		219	136
25	Howick ....ex pa	Monmouth..	Chepstow ..3	Usk.........9	Caerleon...10		135	34
29	Howick*..........pa	Northumb..	Alnwick 6	Belford ...13	NewBewick13		314	235
9	Howrigg..........to	Cumberland	Wigton 5	Carlisle 8	H.Newmarkt 7		303	....
24	Howsham ....to	Lincoln....	Gland.Bridge 5	Castor......5	Spittal 11		159	....
46	Howsham ....to	E. R. York.	New Malton .7	York 9	Ga.Helmsley14		209	225
42	Howshills....... ham	Worcester ..	Worcester ..8	Tenbury ...16	Upton......13		116	....
43	Howthorpe ....ham	N. R. York.	New Malton.7	Ga. Helmsley 8	York......12		212	33
29	Howtell....... ....to	Northumb..	Wooler......7	Berwick ...15	Coldstream ..5		327	192
36	Hoxne†...........pa	Suffolk	Eye...... ..3	Harlestone ..5	Botesdale...10		95	1243
36	Hoxne............hun	Suffolk	....	....	....		....	16399
25	Hoxton‡.....pa dis	Middlesex ..	Hackney... 2	Islington ...2	Edmonton ...7		2	....

HOWDEN, the archdeaconry of the East Riding, and diocese of York, not in charge; annual value P. R. £130; patron, the Lord Chancellor. The church, dedicated to St. Peter, is a handsome building, of a cruciform construction, with a fine tower rising from the centre, which contains a peal of eight bells; this tower was erected in 1390, by Bishop Skirlaw, as a place of refuge, in case of the inundations of the Ouse, which were formerly very frequent occurrences. The annual horse-fair, held at Howden, *Great fair for horses.* is, perhaps, the largest in the kingdom. John de Hoveden, an ancient monkish historian, and chaplain to Henry II., was a native of this place, as his name proves, corresponding with the ancient appellation of the town.

Market, Saturday.—*Fairs*, second Tuesday after January 11; April 5; Saturday before Holy Thursday; second Tuesday July 11; and October 2, for horses, cattle, and linen.

* HOWICK, a parish in the south division of Bambrough ward, pleasantly situated about one mile from the sea; living, a rectory in the archdeaconry of Northumberland and diocese of Durham. Howick-hall, a noble and beautiful mansion, situated in a spacious park, is the seat of Earl Grey, who takes his title of Viscount from this place. Near the *Roman encampment.* east side of the park are the remains of a Roman encampment, and several Roman coins and antiquities have been found here.

† HOXNE. It was to this place, anciently denominated Eglesdune, that King Edmund fled after his last unsuccessful encounter with the Danes, in 870. In hopes of escaping his pursuers, it is said he concealed himself under a bridge, now called Gold-bridge, from the gilt spurs which he happened to wear, and by which he was discovered. Here also the remains of that unfortunate Monarch were first interred, but afterwards removed to Bury.

‡ HOXTON, a parochial district, formerly a hamlet or liberty in the parish of St. Leonard, Shoreditch, lower division of the hundred of Ossultstone, and now forming a part of the north-east suburb of the metropolis. In the beginning of the seventeenth century, when Hoxton was a detached village, it seems to have been a favourite place of resortment for the citizens, and, like Islington, it was famous for cakes and ale, and also for custards, as appears from allusions of the dramatists and other popular writers of that period. The manor belongs to the Dean and Chapter of St. Paul's, who held it before the Norman Conquest. It gives denomination to a Prebend in St. Paul's Cathedral. Among the charitable institu- *Charitable institutions.* tions connected with London, one of the most important is Haberdashers'- hospital, in this liberty, founded in 1692, in pursuance of the will of Robert Aske, Esq., for the support of twenty poor members of the Haberdashers' Company, and the education of twenty boys. The original

Map	Names of Places.	County.	Number of Miles from			Dist. Lond.	Popu-lation.
45	Hoyland, Nether..to & cha	W. R. York	Barnsley....5	Rotheram ...4	Sheffield.....6	168	1670
45	Hoyland, Swain.....to	W. R. York.	6	Huddersfield 9	12	174	738
44	Hubberholme ...ham & cha	W. R. York	Settle......4	Hawes 12	Middleham 18	236	790
57	Hubbertson.........vil	Pembroke ..	Milford......1	Haver.West .4	Marlos......7	277	1013
44	Huby..............to	N. R. York	Easingwold..4	York 7	N. Malton.. 14	207	526
21	Hucking ....pa	Kent	Maidstone ..6	Faversham..10	Charing.....8	40	158
15	Hucklecot........ham	Gloucester..	Gloucester...3	Cheltenham..6	Painswick ...5	102	465
10	Hucklow, Great ....to	Derby	Tideswell ...3	Hathersage ..3	Dronfield ...11	164	274
10	Hucklow, Little ..lib	Derby	2	Cha. le Frith 8	Sheffield....14	160	218
30	Hucknall Forkard ..pa	Nottingham.	Nottingham..6	Mansfield....8	Worksop ..12	130	2200
30	Hucknell under Huthwaite ...ham	Nottingham.	Mansfield...5	Nottingham 14	17	138	929
45	Huddersfield* m t & pa	W. R. York.	Barnsley....13	Leeds 12	Halifax......6	189	19035
45	Huddleston .... to	W. R. York.	Ferrybridge . 7	Tadcaster ...4	Wetherby ...9	186	184
42	Huddington.....pa	Worcester..	Droitwich ...4	Bromsgrove .10	Worcester...6	120	125
44	Hudswell ...to & cha	N. R. York.	Richmond ...2	Askrigg 12	Middleham ..7	236	305
15	Huelsfield........pa	Gloucester .	Chepstow ...5	Coleford 7	Berkley 10	118	434
46	Hug-gate..........pa	E. R. York.	Pocklington .5	Sledmere ...7	N. Malton..12	198	413
23	Hug-gles-cote ....to	Leicester ...	M. Bosworth.7	Ashby de laZ. 5	Leicester ...13	110	....
33	Hughley. ....pa	Salop......	M. Wenlock.5	Shrewsbury 10	Wellington .12	143	786
40	Hugill..............to	Westmorlnd	Kendal......6	Ambleside...8	Orton 13	268	101
11	Huish..............pa	Devon	Hatherleigh . 5	Chumleigh..10	Torrington...6	204	300
34	Huish ....ti	Somerset ...	Crewkerne ..2	Chard 6	Ilminster ...6	133	118
34	Huish ....ham	Somerset ...	Axbridge....7	Bristol 17	Wells 16	138	....
34	Huish Champ-flower.pa	Somerset ...	Wiveliscobe .3	Minehead .. 10	Watchet 9	156	....
34	Huish Episcopi.....pa	Somerset ...	Langport 1	Ilchester 3	Somerton ...4	128	317
11	Huish, North........pa	Devon......	Totness 6	Plym. Earls 11	Modbury 6	202	574
11	Huish, South ......pa	Devon......	Kingsbridge .4	Dartmouth .13	9	212	484
13	Hulam ....to	Durham	Stok.-on-Tes13	Sunderland ..9	Durham....10	263	383
5	Hulcott ....pa	Bucks.....	Aylesbury...3	Ivinhoe 6	Tring 7	42	16

HOXTON.

building, from the design of the celebrated Dr. Robert Hooke, was taken down a few years since, and a new one erected, forming three sides of a quadrangle, with a chapel in the centre ; and in the area is a statue of the founder, standing on a pedestal. The annual income of this hospital, derived from Mr. Aske's and other benefactions, was, in 1798, about £800. Here are also Mr. Badger's alms-houses, founded in 1698, for six aged women ; Mr. Fuller's alms-houses, built in 1794, for twelve aged women ; besides some others.

Badger's alms-houses.

* HUDDERSFIELD, a populous and flourishing manufacturing and market-town, is situated in the hundred of Asbrigg, in the liberty of the honour of Pontefract, and in the central part of the West Riding. The town, which derives its name from Oder or Hudder, the first Saxon colonist in the place, stands on the river Colne ; the valley formed by this stream, with a small quantity of level ground upon its banks, comprehends the parish of Huddersfield. The houses are principally built of light-coloured stone, in a neat style; and the general appearance of the town is of a character calculated to inspire the traveller with the impression that its inhabitants are wealthy and respectable. The manufactures of Huddersfield and neighbourhood are principally woollens, and consist of broad and narrow cloths, serges, kerseymeres, cords, &c. ; fancy goods, to a considerable extent, are also made here, embracing shawls and waistcoatings in great variety, besides articles from silk. The cotton trade, of late years, has much increased in importance ; and at this period a great number of hands are employed in the spinning establishments. Amongst the principal buildings is the cloth-hall, erected by Sir John Ramsden, in the year 1765 ; the edifice is very large, and consists of two stories, formed into streets ; it is of a circular form ; a middle row, of one story in height, and supported by pillars, opens into the other parts, and divides the area into two courts ; above the entrance is placed a cupola, in which is a clock and bell, used for the purpose of regulating the time allowed for doing business. The amount of property that passes from the possession of one to another, in a few hours, is truly astonishing. The doors are opened early in the morning of the market-day, and closed at

Extensive manufactures.

HUDDERS-
FIELD.

half-past twelve o'clock at noon, they are again opened at three in the afternoon, for the removal of cloth, &c. The inland navigation of Huddersfield affords to its trade the most ample advantages, both to the east and to the west; the Ramsden and Huddersfield canals communicating with others and their branches, and intercourse is kept up with all the

Great com-
mercial
intercourse.

great commercial and manufacturing towns. There are many streams in the neighbourhood, and the rivers Holme and Colne here unite and fall into the Calder, three miles below the town, upon which streams vast numbers of mills are erected, principally employed in the manufacture of woollens, and fulling and washing the cloth, &c. It is now well lighted with gas, by a company established a few years since. Sir John Ramsden, Bart., is lord of the manor; and the chief, and almost sole proprietor of the property here, the revenue derived from which, at the present day, may be said to be more than princely. This gentleman holds a court leet once a year, at Almonbury; a court of requests for the recovery of debts under forty shillings is held in a neat building in Queen-street; and a court is held twice in the year, at the George-inn, for the liberty of the honour of Pontefract, for plea of debt or damages under £5. The edifices constructed for divine worship in the parish, although numerous, are not sufficiently so to accommodate its great population; others are, therefore, in progress of erection, and several sites for a still greater augmentation are fixed on. St. Peter's, or the parish church, is a plain build-

Gothic
church.

ing, but noble and stately in its appearance. Trinity, or the new church, is a beautiful Gothic structure, erected at the expense of £12,000, by B. H. Allen, Esq., of Greenhead, in 1819. Christ-church is a still more recent erection, being completed in 1824. It is situated about a mile and a half from the town, in the hamlet of Fartown, and central to a population of 4000 persons; it is a beautiful and chaste edifice, built by John Whitacre, Esq. The other places of worship, in and near the town, are two very large chapels, belonging to the methodists, and others for the use of the baptists, independents, new connexion, quakers, &c. The charitable institutions are a dispensary, established in 1814; a bible society, in 1810; a religious tract society, in May, 1816; a church missionary society, in 1813; a benevolent, or strangers' friend society; an auxiliary society for the conversion of the Jews; a school of industry for girls, established and supported by ladies residing in the town and neighbourhood; besides numerous Sunday-schools, and other benevolent institutions. A mechanics' institute was established in 1825, under highly favoured auspices; the library attached to the institution has become valuable. Naturally, this part of the country is barren and unproductive, but its local advantages for manufacture, from its waterfalls, and having coal-mines contiguous, has caused the assemblage of a great population, and the soil has gradually yielded to the labours of the agriculturist and husbandman, until at length it has become valuable, and available to the wants of those who have established themselves upon it. The hilly portion of the land is not unfertile, and the valleys are rich in pasturage, while, from many parts in this district, the views may be taken as most pleasing. There are many handsome residences and elegant seats in the vicinity of Huddersfield, and about three quarters of a mile from it are Lockwood-baths; the building is elegant and commodious, and combines

The baths.

every comfort and convenience. The baths, which are abundantly supplied with spa water, highly esteemed for its medicinal qualities, were opened to the public on the 1st of May, 1827. The establishment is the most complete in its kind, of any in the West Riding; Mr. Oates, of Halifax, was the architect. On the Castle-hill, about two miles hence, are the evident remains of an ancient Roman city; in the neighbourhood are several medicinal springs.

Market, Tuesday.—*Fairs*, March 31; May 14; and October 4; for lean, horned cattle, and horses.—Letters for London and Manchester are despatched by the Mail at five every morning, and arrive every evening at half-past eight.

Map.	Names of Places.	County.	Number of Miles from				Dist. Lond.	Population.
28	Hulcott..........ham	Northamp ..	Towcester...3	Northampton 7	Ston. Stratfo.8		63	139
7	Hull................to	Chester.....	Northwhich .3	Knutsford ...4	Warrington.10		177	137
46	Hull, see Kingston-⎰ upon-Hull*......⎱	E. R. York .	Beverley.....9	Hedon.......6	Gt. Driffield 22		147.	32958
10	Hulland ....to	Derby	Ashborne .. 4	Derby. 9	Wirksworth .9		135	221
10	Hulland Ward ..ham	Derby	5	Alfreton....11	Derby 11		137	289
10	Hulland Ward In-⎰ tacks ....⎱	Derby	6	Tideswell ...7	Wirksworth .7		132	39
41	Hullavington.......pa	Wilts	Malmsbury ..5	Chippenham. 6	Wot. Basset 12		101	563
22	Hulme ....to	Lancaster...	Warrington..2	Newton 4	Prescot......9		187	9264

* HULL, or Kingston-upon-Hull, a borough town, and county of tself, and one of the principal sea-ports in his Majesty's dominions, is in the East Riding of Yorkshire. This town is of great antiquity, and its foundation was long anterior to the date commonly ascribed to it, that of the period when Edward I. gave it the royal appellation of King's-Town-upon-Hull. Its more ancient one was Wyke, or Wyke-upon-Hull ; wick, or wyke, signifying a refuge, or place of retreat. Edward I. attempted much towards the advancement of the place, considering it an excellent situation for a commercial and fortified station ; he therefore effected an exchange of lands with the lord of the manor (the abbot of Meaux) and erecting for himself a manor-hall, issued a proclamation, offering considerable privileges and immunities to those who would build and settle in the new town, which he called King's Town. In the twenty-seventh year of his reign the harbour was finished, the town made free, all the inhabitants being free burgesses. All those benefits, however, failed, according to Leland, to give the town any great importance, for, he says, "The town of Kingston-upon-Hull was, in the time of Edward III., but a mere fishar town, and longed as a member to Hasill village, a two or three miles off, up the Humber. In Richard II. time, the town waxed very rich." An act of parliament, obtained in the 6th of Henry VI., confirmed its former charter, and afterwards this monarch made it a corporate town, constituting it and its precincts a county of itself, and authorising the mayors to have the sword carried erect before them, and granting other civic privileges. In the fifteenth, sixteenth, and seventeenth centuries, Hull suffered by the devastating effects of both flood and pestilence ; the plague that visited it in 1635 lasted three years, during which time famine was added to the other horrors sustained by the inhabitants, as the country people were afraid to bring in the usual supply of provisions. At the breaking out of the civil war between Charles and the parliament, Hull was a great depôt of arms ; the arms were, at the beginning of the contest, by order of the parliament, removed to London. The king besieged the town, but was repulsed, after repeated sanguinary contests ; equally ineffectual was the attempt of the Marquis of Newcastle ; during this struggle Sir John Hotham, governor of Hull, was detected privately negociating with the king, for which he and his son were beheaded. Its situation is on the northern side of the Humber, about twenty miles from the mouth of that river, the town extending almost in a direct line along the river Hull, and lying on a level tract of ground, washed on two of its sides by the rivers Hull and Humber. It is now well secured from inundations by embankments, and the principal streets are broad, well paved, and lighted with gas. The oil gas works is an establishment in which the inhabitants of Hull must necessarily feel considerable interest, oil being one of the staple articles of its commerce ; and we are happy to report that the institution is fast rising to a state in which it will be profitable to its proprietors. The residuum, by a process recently discovered, forms a beautiful varnish, applicable to various purposes, and which promises to constitute a considerable source of emolument to the concern. The brilliant lantern at the bottom of Queen-street, which is thirty feet high, is illuminated from

Very ancient town.

Made a corporate town by Henry VI.

Besieged by Charles I.

HULL.

these works, and is very useful to the shipping; the method of lighting it is ingenious—a tube, perforated at intervals from the bottom of the burner, admits a stream of gas by means of a stop-cock, which, issuing through the apertures, by lighting the bottom jet, the ignition passes rapidly from one to the other, till it reaches the burner in the lantern.

Excellent supply of water.

The town is well supplied with water, brought by pipes from a reservoir, which has the appearance of a canal, about five miles in length. In commercial importance, Hull ranks as the fourth in the kingdom. It is the principal port for the whale fishery, and its intercourse with the Baltic is very great. It is also one of the privileged ports for trading to the East Indies; indeed, its conveniences, as a port, and its numerous local advantages, combine to place it in the first class of commercial sea-ports. Hull does not found its claims to notice, as a manufacturing town, its chief productions, under this head, being sacking, sail-cloth, chain and chain-cables. The courts of law held here comprise sessions four times a year, before a bench of magistrates, at which the recorder presides as judge; a court of requests for the recovery of small debts, held every alternate Wednesday, at the commissioners' room; and a sheriff's court leet twice in the year. The places for divine worship in this town, under the establishment, and for the various sects of dissenters, are numerous. The church of the Holy Trinity, in the Market-place, is a conspicuous ornament to the town, and is a magnificent pile, in the cathedral style of Gothic architecture, erected about the beginning of the fourteenth century; the benefice is a vicarage, in the gift of the corporation; St. Mary's, or the Low-church, in Lowgate, is of nearly equal antiquity; St. John's, on the dock side, was erected by the Rev. Thomas Dikes, and first opened in 1792. The parish of Sculcoates contains three churches, viz., Christ-church, in Worship-street; St. Mary's, on the banks of the Hull, to the north of Wincolmlee; and St. Peter's, in Drypool. The chapels belonging to the various sects, dissenters from the church, are ten in number, including a Quaker's meeting-house; and the Jews have a synagogue.

Spacious docks and wharfs.

The docks of Hull are upon a scale of magnitude commensurate with the extent of exports and imports of this populous and great trading town. The old dock, begun in 1774, was completed in three years, it is very spacious, being seven hundred yards in length, eighty-five in width, and twenty-two feet deep; the wharfs and quays are commodious, and cover a space of more than thirteen acres; the entrance is immediately from the river Hull. The Humber dock is at the west end of the town; the first stone was laid on the 13th of April, 1807; with the wharf, it covers a space of upwards of ten acres. The custom-house, in Whitefriar-gate, is a large and elegant brick building, ornamented with stone; and the citadel, originally intended for the defence of the town and harbour, is on the eastern bank of the river, with a battery of twenty-one guns, facing the Humber.

Botanical gardens.

The botanic gardens are pleasantly situated, about a mile from Hull; they contain many scarce and valuable vegetables, and a military band plays in them occasionally; in short, the spirit of improvement and tasteful embellishment keeps pace with the commercial prosperity of the town. The country around Hull is altogether agricultural, very flat, and the land, in general, between Hull and the sea, of excellent quality, feeding very fine cattle, and producing the finest corn in great plenty. The market-days are Tuesdays, Fridays and Saturdays; the Tuesday's market is a great one for corn; and the others are large meat markets, with garden produce, &c. The annual fair is October 11, for horses, foals, and horned cattle, and the following day for toys, pedlary, &c.

Letters for London and the South, Lincolnshire, Norfolk, &c., are despatched every morning at ten minutes before ten, and arrive between four and five in the afternoon.—Letters to York, the Northern Counties, Scotland, Falmouth and the West of England, are despatched every day at half-past twelve and afternoon at four (taking also the Norfolk bags), and arrive every day at noon and twelve at night.

Map	Names of Places.	County.	Number of Miles from			Dist. Lond.	Popu- lation.
7	Hulme Curtis......to	Chester.....	Middlewich .2	Sandbach ...3	Congleton ...9	164	469
22	Hulme Kirkham ....to	Lancaster...	Manchester..2	Stockport ...4	Ash.-on-Line 5	183	....
22	HulmeLevens*to & cha	Lancaster...	4	3	5	182	4224
7	Hulme, Walfield...to	Chester.....	Congleton ..2	Knutsford ..11	Macclesfield .7	163	108
7	Hulse ....to	Chester.....	Northwich .4	5	Middlewich .5	173	54
35	Hulton Abbey ......to	Stafford	Newcastle .. 4	Leek 7	Cheadle 7	152	477
22	Hulton, Little.......to	Lancaster .	Bolton 4	Chorley.....10	Manchester. 11	193	2465
22	Hulton, Middle ....to	Lancaster...	3	11	10	192	938
22	Hulton, Over ......to	Lancaster...	3	10	11	193	591
36	Hulverstreet ....ham	Suffolk.....	Beccles 5	Lowestoff...5	Yarmouth ..15	111	241
17	Humber............pa	Hereford....	Leominster ..4	Bromyard ...3	Weobly 11	134	219
46	Humber ....ward	E. R. York .	....	....	....	....	3856
3	Humbershoe ......ham	Bedford	Luton 2	Leigh Buzzad.7	Dunstable ...3	33	363
46	Humberside ......ham	E. R. York .	Hull 19	Patrington...6	Hornsea ...19	193	....
23	Humberston ......pa	Leicester ..	Leicester ...3	Mount Sorrel 7	Mel. Mowb. 14	98	415
24	Humberston ......pa	Lincoln.....	Gt. Grimsby .5	Satfleet....16	Castor......15	161	217
44	Humberton ....to	N. R. York.	Aldborough..2	Ripon 6	Thirsk 7	210	148
29	Humbleton. ....to	Northumb ..	Wooler 1	Coldstream'.12	New Bewick.8	321	184
46	Humbleton.........pa	E. R. York.	Hull 9	Hornsea 8	Patrington...8	183	579
27	Humbleyard ....hun	Norfolk.....					5409
24	Humby, Great ....ham	Lincoln.....	Grantham ..4	Folkingham..8	Sleaford 9	114	....
24	Humby, Little ....ham	Lincoln.....	Folkingham..6	Grantham ...7	7	106	65
29	Humshaugh...to & cha	Northumb ..	Hexham ...5	Newcastle..22	Bellingham .11	290	334
22	Huncoat...........to	Lancaster...	Burnley ...5	Blackburn ..6	Preston......14	209	502
23	Huncote...........to	Leicester ..	Leicester ...7	Hinckley ...7	Mt. Bosworth7	99	289
22	Hundersfield. to & cha	Lancaster ..	Rochdale....4	Burnley 12	Haslingden..11	202	....
44	Hunderthwaite ....to	N. R. York.	Barn. Castle .5	Brough......12	Bowes......5	252	313
24	Hundleby ....pa	Lincoln.....	Caistor 1	Gland. Bdg .9	Barton 15	157	348
24	Hundon ....ham	Lincoln.....	Spilsby......1	Horncastle .10	Alford 8	134	....
36	Hundon ....pa	Suffolk.....	Clare 3	Haverhill ...7	Newmarket 14	58	1121
12	Hundesbarrow ....hun	Dorset......					539
5	Hundridge........ham	Bucks	Chesham 3	Prin. Risboro.8	Amersham ..5	30	....
4	Hungerford†. . m t & to	Berks	Newbury ...8	Lambourne .7	Wantage ...14	64	2983
23	Hungerton ....pa	Leicester ..	Leicester ...7	Mel. Mowb.10	Tugby......7	103	292
24	Hungerton ....pa	Lincoln.....	Colsterworth.4	Grantham ...5	Corby 10	106	124
39	Huningham ....pa	Warwick....	Southam....5	Coventry ...8	Warwick .. .7	84	193
43	Hunmanby‡.......pa	E. R. York .	Scarborough .8	Bridlington .10	Whitby 18	208	1079

* HULME LEVENS, a township and chapelry in the parish of Manchester, and hundred of Salford, divided from Manchester by the river Medlock, is pleasantly situated and contains many excellent houses. The living is a curacy in the archdeaconry and diocese of Chester, not in charge; patron, Manchester Collegiate-church. The church, which is dedicated to St. George, is a very beautiful modern edifice in the florid Gothic style. Here is Hulme-hall, a very ancient structure, and formerly the seat of the Prestwich family; it is a singularly curious and picturesque mansion, but has been long in a state of dilapidation. The barracks, which are generally occupied by a squadron of horse, form a large and handsome structure.

Picturesque mansion.

† HUNGERFORD, a small market-town and parish in the hundred of Kintbury Eagle, is situated on a marshy soil on the banks of the Kennet, and watered by two separate streams of that river. It consists chiefly of one long street, in the centre of which is the market-house and shambles; over the latter is a large room, used as a town-hall. In this room a curious relic of antiquity is preserved, denominated the Hungerford-horn, which was given, as a charter to the town, by John of Gaunt. The constable is lord of the manor, and holds his right immediately of the king. The town is chiefly inhabited by tradesmen, has a considerable traffic by means of its canal navigation, but no manufacture. The church, which is dedicated to St. Laurence, is an ancient structure, and contains some fine old monuments, and near it is a free grammar-school with a good endowment. Hungerford-park was formerly the residence of the Barons of Hungerford, who took their name and title from this town; a neat mansion in the Italian style, occupies the site of the old house, which was built by Queen Elizabeth and given to the Earl of Essex.

Curious relic.

Hungerford-park.

Market, Wednesday.—*Fairs,* last Wednesday in April; August 10, for horses, cows, and sheep; and Monday before and after New Michaelmas, statute.

‡ HUNMANBY. *Fairs,* May 6, and October 29, for toys.

6 K

Map.	Names of Places.	County.	Number of Miles from			Dist. Lond.	Popu- lation.
18	Hunsdon ....pa	Herts......	Sawbridgewo 5	Ware.......5	Standon 7	22	592
45	Hunshelf ....to	W. R. York.	Barnsley.....7	Sheffield....10	Holme 9	172	531
44	Hunsingore ....pa	W. R. York.	Knaresboro' .7	Boroughbridg 7	Aldborough..8	202	594
45	Hunslet ....to	W. R. York.	Leeds 2	Pontefract .. 9	Abberford ...9	193	12074
46	Hunsley, High and } Low............to {	E. R. York.	South Cave..3	Kingston 8	Mt. Weighton7	190	....
9	Hunsonby ....to	Cumberland	Penrith 6	K. Oswald . 5	Alds. Moor .10	290	151
27	Hunstanton*......pa	Norfolk	B. Westgate10	Cas. Rising .10	Fakenham . 18	127	433
13	Hunstanworth.....pa	Durham	Stanhope 8	Newcastle . 22	St. J. Chapel.9	271	511
7	Hunsterton ....to	Chester.....	Nantwich ...6	Audlem 6	Talk-on-Hill .6	163	239
36	Hunston ....pa	Suffolk	Stow Market.7	Ixworth 4	Botesdale ...8	88	178
38	Hunston ....pa	Sussex	Chichester...3	Arundel . ..12	Midhurst ...12	65	166
45	Hunsworth ....to	W. R. York.	Bradford ...4	Leeds 8	Halifax 6	192	878
36	Huntingfield........pa	Suffolk	Halesworth..4	Harlestone ..9	Framblingha .8	103	336
19	Huntingdon† ....coun	Hunts	....	....	....	....	53149

Remarkable cliff.

* HUNSTANTON is remarkable for a cliff a hundred feet high, called St. Edmund's-point, from a supposition that Edmund the Martyr landed here when he was brought from Germany to be crowned King of East Anglia. He is said to have built a tower here, in which he committed to memory the whole book of Psalms, in compliance with a previous vow. Some remains of an old chapel on the cliff, dedicated to St. Edmund, probably gave rise to this story. Near these ruins tands a light-house, the light of which is visible for seven leagues. Here is Hunstanton-hall, an ancient family mansion, erected in the time of Henry VII., and once the seat of the distinguished family of Le Strange. The celebrated political writer, Sir Roger Le Strange, was born here, December 17, 1616.

† HUNTINGDON, a small inland county, bounded on the north and west by Northamptonshire, on the south-west by Bedfordshire, and on the south and east by Cambridgeshire; from the first of these counties it is separated on the northern border by the river Nene; from the last-mentioned, partly by the Ouse, and the dykes, and canals which unite it with the Nene; the Ouse, also, previously to its entrance into this county, for a short distance, forms the line of separation from Bedfordshire. When the Normans became masters of England, William the Conqueror, in 1068, gave the earldom of this county to Waltheof, a noble Saxon, on whom he also bestowed the hand of his niece, Judith; but

Treachery of a wife.

that lady betrayed her husband, who was executed for a treasonable conspiracy against the government. David, Prince of Scotland, having married the heiress of Waltheof, was made Earl of Huntingdon, in 1108, and the honour continued in his family till 1219. Almost the whole county is said to have been forest land till the reign of Henry II.; but it is now open and well cultivated. The face of the country displays three varieties. That part bordering on the Ouse, which flows across the county from the south-west, consists of a tract of the most fertile and beautiful meadows, of which Portholm Mead, near Huntingdon, almost enclosed by a bend of the river, is especially celebrated. The middle and western parts present an agreeable variety of surface, fertile in grain, and sprinkled with woods. In the north-east are fens, which unite with those of Ely, and are supposed to cover nearly one-fifth of the county. Considerable portions of these are drained, so as to afford rich pasturage for cattle, and produce heavy crops of corn. In the midst of them are shallow ponds, abounding with fish; the largest, called Whittlesey Mere,

Extensive pond.

almost deserves the appellation of a lake, being between five and six miles in length, and three in breadth. The climate is healthful, except in the fens, where the damp, foggy atmosphere gives rise to the diseases common in marshy countries; but the cutting of dykes and drains has greatly contributed to lessen this evil. The principal native products are corn and horned cattle, besides wild fowl and fish, which are very abundant. Peat or turf is in many places the usual kind of fuel, especially

Map.	Names of Places.	County.	Number of Miles from			Dist. Lond.	Popu-lation.
19	Huntingdon*mt b & c t	Hunts	St. Neots....9	St. Ives......7	Kimbolton..10	59	3267
15	Huntingford ....to	Gloucester..	Gloucester .19	Thornbury...5	Wickwar...3	108	....
7	Huntington ....to	Chester...	Chester.....3	Tarvin 6	Tarporley...9	180	133
17	Huntington ......hun	Hereford . ..				....	5971
17	Huntington.......pa	Hereford ...	Kington....4	Hay 9	Presteign....6	159	215
17	Huntington...to & cha	Hereford ...	Hereford.....2	Weobly.....9	Hay 19	137	82
43	Huntington...pa & to	N. R. York.	York 3	NewMalton 12	Sutton 5	203	626
15	Huntley...........pa	Gloucester..	Newent 4	Mitch. Dean.4	Gloucester ..8	112	405
21	Hunton ....pa	Kent	Maidstone ...4	Tunb. Wells.9	Cranbrook..10	38	765
16	Hunton......to & cha	Hants	Whitchurch .5	Basingstoke.13	Winchester..7	55	122
44	Hunton............to	N. R. York.	Richmond ..6	Bedale 4	Middleham ..5	227	535
11	Huntsham........pa	Devon	Bampton ...3	Tiverton 6	Dulverton ..8	162	153
11	Huntshaw.........pa	Devon	G.Torrington 3	Barnstaple ..8	Chumleigh..13	201	291
34	Huntspill and Puri-}ton ....hun{	Somerset ...				....	2012
34	Huntspill..........pa	Somerset ...	Bridgwater .7	Glastonbury 13	Axbridge...10	141	1503
45	Huntswick ....ham	W. R. York.	Pontefract...4	Wakefield ...5	Barnsley....7	172	....
13	Hunwick ....to	Durham	Bish. Auckla.2	Walsingham .8	Durham. 9	251	160
27	Hunworth ....pa	Norfolk....	Holt 2	Cley 5	N.Walsingh. 8	118	220
7	Hurdsfield ....to	Chester....	Macclesfield .2	Chap. le Frith8	Stockport ..11	170	3083
7	Hurleston ....to	Chester.	Nantwich ...3	Tarporley ..7	Middlewich .9	172	191
4	Hurley†..........pa	Berks	Maidenhead .5	Gt. Marlow..3	Henley 5	31	1150

among the common people. Agriculture occupies the chief attention of the inhabitants; the manufactures, therefore, are trifling, consisting of woolstapling, and spinning yarn, the latter principally practised by the women and children during the winter season, when they are prevented from finding more profitable employment in the fields. **HUNTING-DON.**

* HUNTINGDON, a market, borough, and county-town, forming a distinct liberty, under separate jurisdiction, but locally in the hundred of Toseland. It is situated at the junction of several other roads with the great north road from the metropolis, and on a rising ground to the north of the river Ouse. It was a place of some importance in the reign of Edward the Elder, who is said to have erected a castle here, in 917, which was enlarged and strengthened with new buildings and ramparts, by David, King of Scotland and Earl of Huntingdon, in the reign of Stephen, but was afterwards demolished by order of Henry II. At the period of the Norman Conquest, here was a mint for coinage; and Matilda, the wife of William I., founded a monastery at this place, which must have been anciently much more extensive than it is at present, as there were fifteen churches, which in Camden's time were reduced to four, and at present there are only two. The first charter to this borough was granted by King John. Here are a free grammar-school, which is well endowed; and a green-coat school, called also Walden's-charity, for clothing and educating twenty-four boys. The town is of moderate size, consisting principally of a street, extending north-westward from the banks of the Ouse, about a mile in length, with several lanes branching from it at right angles, which are well paved and lighted during the winter season. The town-hall is a neat and commodious building, standing on one side of a large square; and in the interior are two courts, for the trial of civil and criminal causes at the assizes; over these courts is a handsome assembly-room. Huntingdon was the birthplace of the celebrated Oliver Cromwell, who was born in the parish of St. John, April 25, 1599. It gives the title of Earl to the noble family of Hastings. **Charter granted by King John.** **Birthplace of Oliver Cromwell.**

Market, Saturday.—*Fair,* March 25, for pedlers' ware, disused.—*Mail,* arrives 2. 44 f. departs 10. 53. a.

† HURLEY, a parish in the hundred of Beynhurst, beautifully situated on the banks of the Thames. Hurley-house, a spacious mansion, occupies the site of a monastery, which was founded here, in 1086, for Benedictines; the remains of the monastery may still be traced in several of the apartments, and, in a vault beneath the hall, some bodies have been **Hurley-house.**

Map	Names of Places.	County.	Number of Miles from			Dist. Lond.	Popu- lation.
39	Hurley ....to	Warwick...	Coleshill 5	Atherstone ..5	Tamworth .. 7	110	....
16	Hurn ....ti	Hants	Southamptn.2i	Christchurch.3	Lymington ..15	97	....
16	Hursley* ....pa	Hants	Winchester..5	Stockbridge . 8	Romsey 6	67	1418
4	Hurst ......pa & cha	Berks	Wokingham .3	Reading .. .6	Maidenhead .9	....	1650
21	Hurst ....pa	Kent	Hythe......5	Ashford 8	NewRomney 7	63	30
16	Hurstbourne-priors .pa	Hants	Whitchurch .2	Andover 5	Stockbridge . 9	58	484
16	HurstbourneTarrant.pa	Hants	Andover....7	Whitchurch .7	Kingsclere..10	64	786
29	Hurst, Long ....to	Northumb ..	Morpeth....2	Felton 7	Rothbury...13	291	176
29	Hurst, North ......to	Northumb ..	5	9	Blyth.......7	294	42
19	Hurst, Old ....pa	Hunts	St. Ives....4	Ramsey 6	Warboys ..2	64	427
38	Hurst Pierpoint†..pa	Sussex	Chichester..32	Cuckfield...7	Steyning.....8	46	1484
46	Hurst, Temple......to	W. R. York.	Snaith 3	Howden 4	Selby........6	178	141
19	Hurstingstone ....hun	Hunts				....	17427
18	Hurstley..........to	Hereford ..	Weobly 5	Hay........9	Kington 8	147	68
13	Hurworth ...to & pa	Durham....	Darlington..4	Yarm.......7	Stockton ..11	237	1348
23	Husband Bosworth..to	Leicester ..	Mt. Harboro .6	Lutterworth .7	Leicester. ..13	84	865
44	Husthwaite ....pa	N. R. York.	Easingwold .4	Thirsk 4	Aldboro.....7	219	539
24	Huttoft ....pa	Lincoln	Alford......4	Saltfleet ...13	Burgh.......8	144	401
9	Hutton............to	Cumberland	Penrith ...10	H. Newmark.3	Ireby......9	299	214
14	Hutton ....pa	Essex	Billericay ...3	Chelmsford .10	Chip. Ongar .9	19	418
22	Hutton............to	Lancaster..	Preston.....4	Blackburn ..12	Chorley.....6	214	715
34	Hutton ....pa	Somerset ..	Axbridge .. 5	Bristol 17	Bridgewater 11	136	325
44	Hutton ....to	N. R. York.	Stokesley...4	Darlington..12	N. Allerton.10	238	1027
44	HuttonBonville t & cha	N. R. York.	N. Allerton..4	9	Stokesley. ..13	229	107
43	Hutton Bushell pa & to	N. R. York.	Scarborough .6	Pickering..10	Hunmanby ..9	211	671
44	Hutton Conyers..ex pa	N. R. York.	Ripon 2	Masham 7	Thirsk 8	214	127
43	Hutton Cranswick } pa & to {	E. R. York.	Gt. Driffield .3	York.......22	Humanby .. 15	193	1118
9	Hutton in the Forest pa	Cumberland.	Penrith 5	H. Newmark.6	Carlisle 15	291	157
44	Hutton Hang ......to	N. R. York.	Middleham ..2	Richmond...6	Bedale 6	236	25
40	Hutton in the Hay.ham	Westmorlnd.	Kendal 3	Sedberg....9	Kir.Lonsdale10	261	....
13	Hutton, Henry......to	Durham ...	Stock. on T.12	Durham 7	Sedgfield 7	258	174
43	Hutton in the Hole ..to	N. R. York.	Pickering...8	Guisborough 12	Whitby ...13	233	304
9	Hutton John ......to	Cumberland.	Penrith 6	Keswick ...10	H.Newmarkt 8	287	30
43	Hutton Locras ......to	N. R. York.	Guisborough 2	Helmsley ...20	Whitby ...23	250	56
44	Hutton Magna pa & to	N. R. York.	Greta Bridge.2	Richmond...8	Bar. Castle ..5	241	248
43	Hutton Mulgrave ....to	N. R. York.	Whitby 4	Guisborough18	Pickering .. 15	245	90
40	Hutton, New..to & cha	Westmorld.	Kendal 4	Sedberg....4	Kir.Lonsdale10	261	127
40	Hutton, Old ....to	Westmorld.	5	Burton 9	9	260	424
22	Hutton Priest.......to	Lancaster...	Lancaster...4	Kr. Lonsdale 6	Burton.....2	249	213
40	Hutton Roof..to & cha	Westmorld.	K. Lonsdale..3	Burton 3	Milthorpe...5	253	257
44	Hutton Sand..to & cha	N. R. York.	Easingwold . 8	Thirsk......4	N. Allerton..7	216	272
44	Hutton Sand .to & cha	N. R. York.	Thirsk......4	N. Alletorn..7	Bedale.....7	223	202
44	Hutton Sessay ......to	N. R. York.	Easingwold..6	Thirsk......3	Ripon......9	215	129
43	Hutton Sheriff .pa & to	N. R. York.	York 10	New Malton.8	Helmsley ..10	208	756
9	Hutton Soil.........to	Cumberland.	Penrith 6	H. Newmk .12	Keswick ...12	289	280
45	Hutton Wandesley..to	E. R. York.	Tadcaster ..5	Wetherby ..7	Abberford ..10	196	125
46	Huttons Ambo ....pa	N. R. York.	New Malton. 3	York........14	Helmsley ..14	214	455
11	Huxham ....pa	Devon	Exeter 4	Collumpton..8	Tiverton...10	169	172
7	Huxley............to	Chester....	Chester.....7	Tarporley...3	Tarvin......3	181	247
28	Huxloe ....hun	Northamp ..				....	12711
22	Huyton ......pa & to	Lancaster...	Lancaster ..2	Garstang ..12	Burton....12	242	13412
24	Hyckham, North ..pa	Lincoln	Lincoln.....6	Newark ...10	Sleaford ..16	129	296
24	Hyckham, South...pa	Lincoln	5	10	15	128	102
7	Hyde‡........to & cha	Chester	Stockport...4	Ashton 4	Manchester .10	182	3355

HURLEY.
Subterrane-ous vault.

found buried in Monkish habits. During the reigns of Charles II. and his successor, the principal nobility held frequent meetings in a subterraneous vault beneath this house; and it is also reported, that the principal papers which produced the revolution of 1688, were signed in the dark recess at the end of this vault.

Discovery of the Commonwealth seal.

* HURSLEY. Richard, son of Oliver Cromwell, resided at the old mansion in Hursley-park, during great part of the time that his father held the protectorate. Hursley-lodge is a substantial, spacious edifice, occupying the site of the old house, which was pulled down; and in one of the walls, the dye of a seal was discovered, which, being cleaned, proved to be the seal of the Commonwealth of England, and was supposed to be the identical seal which Oliver Cromwell took from the Parliament.

† HURST-PIERPOINT. Fairs, May 1, and August 10, for pedlers' ware.

‡ HYDE, a township and chapelry in the parish of Stockport, which obtained its name from a chapel for dissenters, which, with a solitary

Map.	Names of Places.	County.	Number of Miles from			Dist. Lond.	Popu- lation.
17	Hyde Hill ....to	Hereford ...	Leominster . .6	Weobly 3	Hereford 10	145	....
56	Hyssington ....pa	Montgomery	Bish. Castle. .4	Montgomery .4	Newtown . . .11	163	230
21	Hythe ....hun	Kent	....	....	....	....	2387
21	Hythe, West ....pa	Kent	Hythe. 2	Folkeston . . .7	N. Romney . .7	68	119
21	Hythe* . . . . . .m t & to	Kent	Folkstone . . 5	N.Romney . .9	Ashford 12	65	2287

house, were the only buildings here till within these forty years; but the place now resembles a small town, and the houses range along each side of the road for nearly a mile. Hyde-hall, an ancient brick edifice, is situated in a romantic spot, on the banks of a small river, and surrounded with bold swelling eminences, gradually sloping to the water's edge. At a short distance from the house is a neat bridge of one arch, for the accommodation of those who frequent the coal-mines that are worked on this estate, which includes both sides of the river Tame. A weir, formed to supply a water-engine, causes the river above to assume the appearance of a large lake, which, with the cascade produced by the falling of the water to a considerable depth, adds great interest to the surrounding scenery.

Margin note: HYDE.

Margin note: Coal mines.

    * HYTHE is a market town, and one of the cinque-ports, in the parish and hundred of its name, and lathe of Shepway. It is situated at the distance of about three quarters of a mile from the sea, in the midst of a valley, enclosed on each side by high hills, commanding, in clear weather, a view of the coast of France. The town consists principally of one long street, running parallel with the sea, and intersected by several smaller ones. This part of the coast is defended by a range of strong forts, and a line of martello towers, the latter erected during the late war with France, when this country was threatened with invasion by Bonaparte. The Royal Military canal from Hythe to Appledore affords a facility of conveyance for goods and merchandize; but the commerce of this place is at a very low ebb; its trade being but that of a domestic character, and its manufactures include only that of paper to a small extent. The principal public buildings are the barracks, the court-house, the borough gaol, and a small but neat theatre. Here are two book societies; another for debating, or lecturing; and a well-selected library, and agreeable reading-room. The places of worship are, the parish church, and chapels for independents and Wesleyan methodists. The church, which is dedicated to St. Leonard, is a spacious and handsome structure, partly in the Norman and partly in the early style of English architecture, with a tower at the west end in the former style, and one in the centre of the latter character. In the crypt, under the chancel, is a large pile of human bones, supposed to be the remains of Britons slain in a sanguinary battle, fought in the year 456, on the shore between this place and Folkestone, with the retreating Saxons; and to have obtained their whiteness by long exposure on the sea-shore. The principal charities are, national schools, supported by subscription; St. Bartholomew's-hospital, for five poor men and five poor women; and St. John's-hospital, for six poor persons. The vicinage of Hythe abounds with romantic scenery, and affords numerous pleasing walks and rides; and during the bathing season is much frequented; also, as a thoroughfare, by the way of the coast upon improved roads, for visitors of all classes who visit Margate, Ramsgate Deal, Dover, &c. The air may be fairly averaged as equal to most near the sea, along the coast, and it is probable that an excellent supply of gas and water may be soon at disposal, having been for some time in contemplation, if not already substituted; indeed we may safely add, that a branch may be laid from one of the intended, or proposed Railways.

Margin note: Strong fortifications.

Margin note: Handsome and spacious church.

    Fairs, July 30, and December 1.—*Principal Inn*, the Swan.

RIVERS.

Name.	Rises.	Falls.	Name.	Rises.	Falls.
Hale............	Cornwall ...	Irish Sea.	Helter..........	Northumber	Bowbent.
Hans*........	Staffordshire	Manyfold.	Hirgum........	Merionethsh.	Avon.
Harburn........	Devonshire .	Dart.	Hodder..........	Yorkshire...	Ribble.
Hartley	Northumber	South Tyne.	Holgate	Yorkshire...	Swale.
Haws...........	Montgomery	Severn.	Howley..	Chester.....	Paver.
Haws	Radnorshire	Ithon.	Hude...........	Durham	Tees.
Hebden..	Yorkshire ..	Calder.	Hull‡.........	Yorkshire...	Humber.
Heckdyke	Nottinghams	Funt.	Humber§	Yorkshire...	German Ocean.
Hel†...........	Cornwall ...	Sea.			

Forms a commodious haven.

* THE HANS and Manyfold both rise in the parish of Ilam, in Staffordshire, from some lime-stone rocks, under which they run in separate streams, for several miles.

† HEL, a river in Cornwall, rising among the hills in Wendron parish, whence it runs about three miles, to a village called Guyke, up to which the barks come with the tide. Hence it pursues its course about three miles, and then falls into the sea, forming a haven, which, within a mile of its mouth, is deep enough for ships of 200 tons to ride in safety, and is about a mile in width, where it unites with the sea.

Abounds with trout.

‡ HULL. This river gives name to Kingston-upon-Hull, and runs into the Humber. It flows near Beverley, and by means of a canal communicates with that town, and is navigable up to Fordingham-bridge. The Hull abounds with trout of peculiar excellence and large size.

Extensive navigable communication.

§ HUMBER, an estuary dividing Yorkshire from Lincolnshire, is formed by the Trent, Ouse, Derwent, and several smaller streams; by the late inland navigation, it has a navigable communication with almost every capital town and city in England; and empties itself into the German Ocean.

I.

Map.	Names of Places.	County.	Number of Miles from				Dist. Lond.	Popu-lation.
12	Ibberton..........pa	Dorset......	Blan. Forum.8	Stalbridge ..6	Stur.Newton 4		109	222
10	Ible...............to	Derby	Wirksworth .4	Winster 3	Ashborn ...9		144	135
16	Ibsley.............pa	Hants	Ringwood ...2	Fordingbridg 6	Lymington ..12		89	317
23	Ibstock...........pa	Leicester..	Mt.Bosworth 5	Ashby de laZ.5	Mt. Sorrel..12		111	1830
42	Iccombe ....pa	Worcester..	S.on theWold3	Burford 9	Northleach ..9		84	164
27	Ickborough........pa	Norfolk....	Bran.Ferry ..5	Thetford 8	Watton 8		84	154
25	Ickenham..........pa	Middlesex ..	Uxbridge ...3	Ricksmansw. 6	Stanmore ..8		16	281
5 & 31	Ickford...........pa	Bucks and Oxford	Thame 4	Bicester 10	Aylesbury ..13		49	324
21	Ickham...........pa	Kent	Wingham ...2	Canterbury . 4	Ashford 11		59	567
18	Ickleford*........pa	Herts	Hitchin 2	Baldock ...5	Luton 10		36	502
38	Icklesham..........pa	Sussex	Winchelsea..2	Rye........5	Hastings....6		64	604

* ICKLEFORD. In this church was buried Henry Boswell, king of the gipsies, who died in 1780.

Marg.	Names of Places.	County.	Number of Miles from			Dist. Lond.	Popu- lation.
6	Ickleton ....pa	Cambridge..	Linton.....4	Royston.....8	Cambridge ..8	48	682
36	Icklingham.........vil	Suffolk	Mildenhall ..4	Thetford....10	Bury St. Ed. 10	67	424
3	Ickwell ....ham	Bedford	Biggleswade .3	Bedford 7	Shefford ...5	48	....
36	Ickworth* . ...pa	Suffolk	BurySt.Edm. 3	Newmarket 14	Lavenham ..8	69	82
31	Idbury...........pa	Oxford	Burford 5	Chip. Norton 7	Deddington 17	77	193
11	Iddesleigh..........pa	Devon	Hatherleigh..4	Chumleigh ..8	Torrington ..9	203	574
11	Ideford ....pa	Devon	Chudleigh ...2	New. Bushel.5	M.Hampste. 10	183	356
11	Ide Hill ....ham	Kent	Seven Oaks..4	Westerham..4	Tunbridge ..8	25	....
38	Iden................pa	Sussex	Rye 2	Winchelsea . 5	Battle......12	63	572
11	Idle...............pa	Devon	Exeter 2	Oakhampton19	Chudleigh ..8	175	757
45	Idle.........to & cha	W. R. York	Bradford 4	Leeds 4	Otley.......6	200	5416
39	Idlicote...........pa	Warwick...	Shipston on S.3	Kineton 6	Warwick ..14	86	88
41	Idmiston......pa & ti	Wilts	Salisbury 6	Amesbury ...5	Old Sarum ..6	75	520
10	Idridge............to	Derby	Wirksworth 4	Ashborn 7	Alfreton ...9	135	160
4	Idstone........ham	Berks	Lambourn .. 6	Highworth ..7	Wantage ...10	71	154
16	Idsworth......ti & cha	Hants	Petersfield...7	Hambledon ..3	Fareham 9	61	315
21	Ifield................pa	Kent	Gravesend ..3	Rochester ...5	Farningham . 7	25	55
38	Ifield ....pa	Sussex	Horsham 7	E.Grinstead 10	Cuckfield ..10	30	918
31	Ifley†...;.....pa & vil	Oxford	Oxford......2	Abingdon....5	Wallingford 12	52	881
16	Iford ....ti	Hants	Christchurch 2	Ringwood ...8	Lymington..14	99	....
36	Iford ....pa	Sussex	Lewes 2	Seaford ...10	Brighton 6	52	157
41	Iford ....to	Wilts...	Bradford 2	Bath 6	Melksham ..7	102	....
26	Ifton ....pa	Monmouth..	Chepstow ..6	Caerleon ...8	Usk 9	141	50
22	Ighton-hill Park ....to	Lancaster...	Burnley 2	Clitheroe 7	Colne 6	212	208
33	Ightfield ....pa	Salop......	Whitchurch 4	Drayton 7	Wem 8	158	261
21	Ightham..........pa	Kent........	Wrotham ...2	Westerham 10	Seven Oaks..5	25	1017
36	Iken ....pa	Suffolk	Orford 4	Aldborough..3	Saxmundham6	91	363
35	Ilam‡..............pa	Stafford	Ashborne... 3	Leek 10	Longnor ...10	142	253
34	Ilchester§ ....m t & bo	Somerset ...	Somerton ...5	Yeovil 5	CastleCarey 11	121	1095

* ICKWORTH. In Ickworth-park, which comprises the whole of the parish, being eleven miles in circumference, and containing 1800 acres, is the handsome seat of the Hervey family, one of whom, John Hervey, was created a peer of the realm, by Queen Anne, in 1703, and was invested, by George I., in 1714, with the title of Earl of Bristol. *[Extensive park.]*

† IFLEY, a parish and village in the hundred of Bullington, anciently called Gifteley. The village, which is but inconsiderable, is situated on the bank of the river Isis, near its confluence with the Cherwell. The living is a vicarage in the archdeaconry and diocese of Oxford. The church, dedicated to St. Mary, was formerly regarded as a specimen of Saxon ecclesiastical architecture, and is mentioned as such by Dr. Ducarel, in his "Anglo-Norman Antiquities," but the style it displays is purely Norman, and it was probably erected in the twelfth century; the western portal, with its receding arch-mouldings, richly ornamented, is peculiarly characteristic of the Norman style of building. In the interior is an antique square stone font, supported on four pillars.

‡ ILAM, a parish in the north division of the hundred of Totmonslow, situated in one of the most romantic spots in the country; the rivers Hans and Manyfold rise from some limestone rocks in this parish, under which they run in separate streams for several miles. The living is a vicarage, in the archdeaconry of Stafford and diocese of Lichfield and Coventry. In the church, dedicated to Holy Cross, St. Bertram is recorded to have performed many miracles. *[Subterraneous streams.]*

§ ILCHESTER. It is supposed to be the place mentioned by Ptolemy and Richard of Cirencester, under the appellation of Ischalis, as one of the towns belonging to the Hedui, an ancient British tribe, and afterwards occupied by the Romans. Traces are still visible of the extent of the walls and fortifications of the Roman station, which, according to Dr. Stukeley, formed an oblong square, crossed from the north-east to the south-west by the old road called the Fosse-way, passing in the line of one of the principal streets. In and near the town Roman coins, and other antiquities, have repeatedly been discovered. It seems to have been a *[Roman fortifications.]*

Map.	Names of Places.	County	Number of Miles from				Dist. Lond.	Popu- lation.
29	Ilderton*......pa & to	Northumb ..	Wooler 4	New Bewick 3	Rothbury ..13		317	602
34	Ilford ....ham	Somerset ...	Ilminster 2	Ilchester ...10	Somerton ..11		134	....
14	Ilford, Great†..ward } ....& cha }	Essex	Romford 5	Barking 1	Chigwell 5		7	3512

ILCHESTER. place of some importance at the time of the Norman Conquest, and had then belonging to it 107 burgesses. In the reign of William Rufus it was besieged by Robert de Mowbray, the leader of an insurrection against that prince; and the town was successfully defended by the inhabitants. In the thirteenth century the manor belonged to Edmund, Earl of Cornwall, and afterwards to John of Eltham, son of Edward II., on whose death it reverted to the crown. It was considered as the county-town in the time of Edward III., who granted a patent, or charter, for holding the county assizes at Ilchester; but they have been since held at this place, alternately with Taunton, Wells, and Bridgewater. Among the

Public buildings. few public buildings are a county court-house, and a county gaol, the latter erected on the plan proposed by Howard, and it has been occasionally the place of confinement for persons prosecuted by Government, and convicted of sedition. Leland says the town had anciently four churches, only one of which was entire when he wrote, just before the Reformation, but there were then traces of two of the others remaining. The living is a rectory in the archdeaconry of Wells and diocese of Bath and Wells, and in the patronage of the Bishop of the diocese. The church, dedicated to St. John the Baptist, is an old edifice, with an octangular stone tower. An hospital, dedicated to the Holy Trinity, was founded here about 1220; and it is said to have been subsequently converted into a nunnery, and at length into a free chapel. Here was also a convent of the Black Friars, or Dominicans. There is an alms-house for sixteen poor women. The town has a small manufacture of lace, thread, and silk; but it has long been in a state of decline. Ilchester is com-

Birthplace of Roger Bacon. monly stated to be the birthplace of Roger Bacon, the great luminary of science, in the thirteenth century; and here, likewise, was born, in 1674, Mrs. Elizabeth Rowe, a popular writer on devotional subjects, whose family name was Singer.

Market, Wednesday.—Fairs, Monday before Palm Sunday; July 2, and August 2, for all sorts of cattle.

Druidical temple. * ILDERTON. Between this village and one of the highest of the Cheviot mountains, called Hedghope, is a Druidical temple, consisting of ten large, rude, and unequal stones, placed in an oval form, from east to west. This neighbourhood was a favourite place with the Druids, who generally fixed their temples amongst towering hills and thick woods.

† ILFORD, Great, a ward and chapelry in the parish of Barking, hundred of Becontree, situated on the high road from London to Chelmsford, Colchester, &c. Morant supposes the name of this place to have been derived from the existence of an "ill ford" here, over the river Rodon, previously to the erection of the bridge and causeway; to which point the river is now navigable, having been made so about 1738. The living is a curacy, subordinate to the vicarage of Barking, in the archdeaconry of Essex, and diocese of London, not in charge. In the village, an hospital for lepers, dedicated to the Virgin Mary, was founded in the reign of Stephen, by Adeliza, Abbess of Barking; and its revenues, at the dissolution of monasteries, amounted to £16 1s. 6½d. Queen Elizabeth granted the property to Thomas Fanshaw, Esq., remembrancer of the exchequer, on condition that the chapel should be kept in repair for the use of the village, and also apartments for six paupers, with pensions of £2 5s. per annum each. The hospital stands to the north of the turn-

Map	Names of Places.	County.	Number of Miles from				Dist. Lond.	Population.
14	Ilford, Little ..vil & pa	Essex	Romford 4	Barking.....8	Chigwell.....4		8	....
11	Ilfracombe*...m t & to	Devon	Barnstaple ..9	Bideford....17	S. Molton ..21		202	3201
10	Ilkeston.............pa	Derby	Derby 9	Alfreton 4	Wirksworth 13		135	4446
45	Ilkley†........ pa & to	W. R. York.	Otley 6	Skipton 7	Keighley 5		211	1063
27	Illington ....pa	Norfolk.....	E. Harling ..4	Watton 8	Thetford 6		86	96
45	Illingworth .ham & cha	W. R. York	Halifax.....3	Colne 12	Keighley ...7		200	....
8	Illogan.............pa	Cornwall ...	Redruth 3	Camborne ...4	St. Agnes...6		264	5170
5	Illmire............pa	Bucks	Thame 4	Wendover ..7	Aylesbury ...7		40	68
39	Ilmington ....pa	Warwick...	Shipston on S.4	Stratford 8	Kineton 10		87	836

pike-road, forming three sides of a quadrangle, the chapel being situated on the south side. The latter appears to have been built in the fifteenth century, but has undergone many subsequent alterations and repairs; some of the windows contain armorial bearings in stained glass. In 1812, on digging for brick-earth in a field near the bank of the river Rodon, and about two miles north of the Thames, various fossil remains were discovered, consisting of very large bones of oxen, horns and bones of stags, a spiral horn thirteen feet long, and the head, bones, and teeth of an elephant, differing, on examination from those of the Asiatic, or African elephants. In a neighbouring field, other remains were disinterred, including the teeth and tusks of the hippopotamus.

GREAT ILFORD.

Discovery of fossil remains.

* ILFRACOMBE, a seaport, market-town, and parish, at the northern extremity of the county, bordering on the Bristol Channel. Its maritime importance was considerable at an early period; and it contributed six ships and eighty-two mariners towards the expedition fitted out against Calais, in 1346. In the civil war under Charles I., this place was garrisoned for the Parliament, and it was taken in September, 1644, together with a quantity of arms and ammunition, by Sir Francis Doddington, a royalist officer. The church, dedicated to the Holy Trinity, is a large, plain building, containing some handsome monuments, particularly one erected by government, in memory of Captain Richard Bowen, who fell in July, 1797, in the memorable attack on Teneriffe, under Admiral Nelson. There is a place of worship for Dissenters, who have been established at Ilfracombe for more than a century. Here is a school for the gratuitous instruction of boys, and another for girls, partly supported by the benefactions of Mrs. Gertrude Pyncomb, and partly by subscriptions; and here are also a school of industry for girls, and other charitable foundations. The harbour, which is safe and commodious, is greatly resorted to, particularly in the winter season, by vessels passing up and down the Channel, from Ireland and other places. It consists of a natural basin, defended from the violence of the sea by a bold mass of rock, stretching nearly half way across the entrance, and an artificial pier, 850 feet in length, which was repaired by an act of parliament, in 1731, and partly rebuilt in 1761, by Sir Bourchier Wrey, the lord of the manor. The rock, forming the mouth of the harbour, rises almost to a point, and on its summit has been erected a lighthouse, somewhat in the style of an ecclesiastical structure. There is a daily intercourse, by means of packets, with Swansea and Milford Haven, in Wales, and also with Bristol. A considerable coasting-trade is carried on here, the grand article of export being oats; the herring-fishery is likewise considerable. The number of vessels belonging to this port, in 1820, was about seventy. Ilfracombe has, of late years, been much frequented as a watering-place; in consequence of which, a number of good houses for the accommodation of visitors have been erected along the side of the harbour; and there are bathing-machines, and warm baths for the use of invalids.

Commodious harbour.

Curious lighthouse.

Market, Saturday.—*Fairs*, April 14, and the first Saturday after August 22, for cattle.

† ILKLEY, an ancient parish and township, in the upper division of the wapentake of Skyrack, considered by antiquaries to have been the

Map.	Names of Places.	County.	Number of Miles from			Dist. Lond.	Population.
34	Ilminster*....m t & pa	Somerset ...	Crewkerne ..7	Taunton 9	Chard 5	133	2957
11	Ilsington ....pa	Devon	Chudleigh ...5	New. Bushel 5	M. Hampste. 7	187	1298
4	Ilsley, East†..m t & pa	Berks	Newbury...11	Lambourn ..12	Wallingford 10	54	738
4	Ilsley, West........pa	Berks	E. Ilsley ...2	Wantage ...7	Abingdon ..10	56	328
54	Ilston ....pa	Glamorgan..	Swansea ...7	Llangynedd..8	Lochor......5	213	279
23	Ilston on the Hill } ....to & cha }	Leicester ...	Leicester 9	Tugby 4	Mt. Harboro' 8	92	125
34	Ilton ....pa	Somerset ...	Ilminster ...2	Taunton 9	Somerton ..10	131	530
44	Ilton ....to	N. R. York .	Bedale 9	Askrigg 9	Masham ...8	228	266
41	Imber............pa	Wilts	E. Lavington.5	Warminster .6	Westbury ..7	92	414
24	Immingham ....pa	Lincoln.....	Gt. Grimsby .8	Barton.....11	Glan.Bridge 14	166	207
6	Impington‡.....pa	Cambridge..	Cambridge ..3	Ely 11	St. Ives 12	54	149

ILKLEY.

Olicana of the Romans; it is situated on the river Wharfe, to the south of which, on a lofty bank, is the outline of a Roman fortification, still in very good preservation; at Middleton-lodge is an altar inscribed to Verbeia, probably the tutelary nymph of the river. From a neighbouring hill issues a fine, clear, and cold stream, forming an excellent bath, which is much resorted to in the summer season.

* ILMINSTER, a market-town and parish, situated at the southern angle of the county, on the river Ile, from which it derives its name, signifying the minster, or church on the Ile. It stands low, but pleasant, at the intersection of two turnpike-roads which cross this part of the county. The town is said to have been privileged with a market before the Norman Conquest; and it was formerly much larger than at present, its limits having been reduced by frequent conflagrations, especially in 1491, when the place was nearly reduced to ashes. The church, dedicated to St. Mary, is a handsome structure, in the decorated Gothic style, consisting of a nave, south porch, transepts, and chancel, with a centra. square tower, ornamented with pinnacles and battlements. In the north transept is a sepulchral monument for Nicholas and Dorothy Wadham, the founders of Wadham-college, Oxford, in the beginning of the seventeenth century. A free grammar-school was founded here, in 1550, by Humphry Walrond and Henry Greenfield, who gave considerable estates for the endowment of this charity. The town comprises two streets, intersecting each other, one of them being nearly a mile in length. Many of the houses were formerly thatched; but considerable improvements have been made, and good houses erected within a few years past. The manufacture of woollen cloth was at one period largely carried on here, but the trade is now in a state of decay. At Horton, about a mile and a half from Ilminster, is a mineral spring, said to be efficacious in curing diseases of the eyes.

The town nearly destroyed by fire.

Mineral spring.

Market, Saturday.—Fair, last Wednesday in August, for horses, bullocks, pigs, sheep, cheese, &c.

† ISLEY, East, a market-town and parish in the hundred of Compton, situated on a gentle eminence, in a pleasant valley, in the centre of a range of downs, and celebrated for its sheep-market, which, next to the metropolis, is said to be the largest in England, not less than 20,000 sheep having been sometimes sold in one day; the annual average is upwards of 250,000, which are principally purchased for the farmers of Hertfordshire and Buckinghamshire, where they are afterwards fatted for the London market. The number of houses does not exceed 200. The inhabitants are chiefly employed in agriculture.

Great sheep market.

Market, Wednesday,—Fairs, Wednesday in Easter week; and every other Wednesday till July, for sheep; August 26, for sheep and lambs; first Wednesday after September 29; Wednesday after October 17; and Wednesday after November 12.

‡ IMPINGTON. During the inclement weather of 1799, a poor woman lost her way in this parish, and was overwhelmed in a snow-drift,

Map	Names of Places.	County.	Number of Miles from				Dist. Lond.	Popu-lation.
22	Ince Blundell ......to	Lancaster...	Liverpool...8	Ormskirk 8	Wigan ...18		208	505
22	Ince in Makerfield ..to	Lancaster ..	Wigan 2	Bolton 7	Newton ...8		204	1903
14	Ingatestone * ....to	Essex	Billericay....5	Chelmsford ..6	Brentwood ..6		23	789
45	Ing Birchworth .....to	W. R. York	Barnsley ...9	Huddersfield 8	Sheffield....16		179	367
23	Ingersley ....ham	Leicester ...	Leicester 6	Tugby 6	M.Mowbray 11		94	14
44	Ingerthorpe........to	W. R. York	Ripon 4	Ripley 3	Boroughbrid. 7		218	44
35	Ingestry.............pa	Stafford	Stafford 4	Uttoxeter ..10	Rugeley 5		136	125
24	Ingham ....pa	Lincoln.....	Lincoln 8	Gainsboro' ..10	Kirton.....11		141	287
27	Ingham ....pa	Norfolk.....	Walsham ...7	Norwich ...15	Worstead ...6		124	418
36	Ingham ....pa	Suffolk	BurySt.Edm. 5	Mildenhall ..7	Thetford ...12		76	185
24	Ingleby............ham	Lincoln.....	Lincoln......6	Spittal 6	Kirton 13		139	....
10	Ingleby.............to	Derby	Derby 7	Ashborn....12	Burton 6		131	141
43	Ingleby Arncliffe ..to & cha }	N. R. York .	Stokesly ...7	Guisborough .6	Whitby ...16		233	331
43	Ingleby Greenhough.pa	N. R. York ..	5	6	Helmsley ...12		234	158
41	Inglesham ....pa	Wilts	Highworth ..3	Farringdon ..4	Cricklade ...7		79	129
13	Ingleton............to	Durham	Bar. Castle ..8	Staindrop....3	Darlington..11		252	....
44	Ingleton†....to & cha	W. R. York	Settle 10	Hawes 15	Sedberg ...12		245	1228
29	Ingoe...............to	Northumb ..	Newc.-on-T. 3	Corbridge ..13	Morpeth....14		277	239
22	Ingol..............to	Lancaster...	Preston.....3	Garstang ...7	Kirkham ...6		219	658
24	Ingoldmells ....pa	Lincoln.....	Alford 8	Wainfleet ...8	Burgh 6		137	155
24	Ingoldsby ....pa	Lincoln.....	Corby 4	Grantham .. 8	Folkingham .7		109	360
27	Ingoldesthorpe......pa	Norfolk.....	Castle Rising 5	Burn.Market11	Lynn 10		116	247
29	Ingram........pa & to	Northumb ..	Wooler......9	Alnwick ...9	Belford......6		316	354

where she continued nearly eight days and nights, but was discovered alive, and survived her confinement several months.

IMPINGTON.

* INGATESTONE, a small town and parish, in the hundred of Chelmsford, situated on the main road from London to Colchester and Harwich. The town consists chiefly of one street, a part of which extends into the parish of Frierning; and being a great thoroughfare, it contains a considerable number of inns for the accommodation of travellers. The name of this place is from the Saxon *Ing atte Stone*, or the Meadow *ad Lapidem, i. e.* at the military stone; and in some old records it is called *Ging*, or *Yng ad Petram*.

† INGLETON is pleasantly situated near the junction of two rivers; its collieries nearly supply the country around with coals, but the inhabitants are chiefly employed in the manufacture of cotton yarn. Here are several of those celebrated natural curiosities, the Caves of Craven; about four miles north of the town is Gingle-pot, ten yards across, and about twenty deep; and one hundred and fifty yards further is Hurtle-pot, about forty yards in diameter, and forty feet in depth; round this abyss the branches of several trees almost meet in the centre, and shed, by their gloomy foliage, additional horror on the yawning gulf; at the bottom is a deep lake, in which are several large black trout; in great floods both these pots run over. At a short distance is Weathercoat-cave, perhaps the most surprising natural curiosity in Great Britain; it is situated in a low field, where such a phenomenon would not be expected, and is about one hundred feet deep, sixty yards long, and thirty broad, and divided into two parts by a rude and grotesque arch of limestone-rock; at the south end is an entrance down into this abyss, where the astonished visitant sees a cataract issuing from an immense aperture in the rock, and falling twenty-five yards in an unbroken sheet, and with a deafening noise, disappears amongst the rocks at the bottom, and running about a mile through a subterraneous passage, again emerges; the cave is filled with the spray of the dashing water, which sometimes produces a small rainbow of surprising brilliancy. One of the most astonishing features of the scene is a stone of enormous magnitude, suspended by its opposite angles, touching the sides of a crevice, over the orifice, whence the cataract issues. About a mile to the south is Dauk-cave, resembling Weathercoat, on a smaller scale, its stream not falling more than eight or nine yards.

Natural caves.

Remarkable cataract.

Map	Names of Places.	County.	Number of Miles from			Dist. Lond.	Popu- lation.
14	Ingrave............pa	Essex......	Brentwood..2	Billericay....4	Romford....9	19	427
40	Ings in Hugill....ham	Westmorlnd	Kendal......6	Troutbeck...5	Ambleside..11	268	....
27	Ingworth..........pa	Norfolk....	Aylsham....2	Cromer......8	Reepham....8	120	161
42	Inkerbarrow.......pa	Worcester..	Alcester....4	Droitwich...9	Worcester..12	106	1734
4	Inkpen............pa	Berks....	Hungerford..4	Newbury....7	Reading...23	63	729
22	Inskip............to	Lancaster...	Kirkham...5	Garstang....5	Preston.....5	221	798
11	Instow............pa	Devon......	Bideford....4	Barnstaple..4	Torrington..8	206	369
27	Intwood...........pa	Norfolk....	Norwich....4	Wymondham5	Hingham...11	106	44
11	Inwardleigh.......pa	Devon......	Hatherleigh..2	Holsworthy.13	Oakhampton 4	203	638
14	Inworth...........pa	Essex......	Kelvedon...2	Colchester..9	Coggleshall..4	42	437
38	Iping.............pa	Sussex.....	Midhurst....4	Petersfield..8	Haslemere..7	49	305
11	Ippleden..........pa	Devon.....	Abb.Newton..4	Ashburton..5	Totness.....4	162	1164
18	Ippolets..........pa	Herts.....	Hitchin.....2	Hertford....15	Buntingford.13	32	874
31	Ipsden............pa	Oxford...	Wallingford.4	Watlington..7	Reading....10	42	582
39	Ipsley............pa	Warwick...	Alcester....6	Solihull....12	Henley.....7	109	830
5 & 31	Ipstone...........pa	Oxford and Bucks......	Gt. Marlow..7	H.Wycombe 7	7	38	272
35	Ipstones..........pa	Stafford....	Cheadle.....4	Leek........5	Longnor....12	150	1325
36	Ipswich*.....m t & bo	Suffolk.....	Woodbridge.7	Needham....9	Hadleigh....9	69	20454

Pillaged by the Danes.

First Charter granted by King John.

Three churches destroyed by a tempest.

* IPSWICH, a market, borough, and county-town, under a separate jurisdiction, as forming a distinct liberty, which includes the town and suburbs, with the hamlets of Stoke-hall, Brooks-hall, Wykes Ufford, and Wykes Bishop. It stands on the banks of the river Orwell, just below its junction with the Gipping, from which the town derives its appellation. It was anciently fortified and encompassed by a ditch and rampart, which were partially destroyed by the Danes, who took and pillaged the place in 991, and again in 1000. A castle is said to have been erected here by William the Conqueror, which was demolished by King Stephen; but the fortifications were renewed in the fifth year of John, when a wall was built round the town, with four gates, denominated from the four cardinal points of the compass; and of this wall a portion is still remaining. The first charter of incorporation was granted to the inhabitants, in 1199, by King John; but Edward I., in the thirteenth year of his reign, deprived them of their franchises, which, however, on their subsequently furnishing ships for his service, he restored; and in 1291 granted a new charter, confirming those of John and Henry III. Other charters were granted by succeeding princes, the last being that of Charles II. Ipswich has sent members to Parliament ever since the twenty-sixth of Edward I. The corporation has the power of passing fines and recoveries, trying civil and criminal causes, and holding pleas of the crown; as likewise of holding assizes of wine, bread, beer, &c.; and also of maintaining an admiralty jurisdiction, extending to the claim of all waifs, strays, and goods, cast on shore. No freeman can be compelled to serve on juries out of the town; and all the burgesses are entitled to various advantageous privileges on sailing to different ports. The jurisdiction of the corporation extends not only throughout the liberty of Ipswich, on land, but also over the estuary of the Orwell, on the Essex coast, beyond Harwich, and on both sides of the Suffolk coast, beyond Landguard-fort. At the period of the Norman Conquest, the town contained nine parish churches, three of which are supposed to have been destroyed by a tempest, recorded by Stow to have happened January 1, 1287, notwithstanding which the number afterwards increased to twenty-one; but at present there are only twelve remaining. A free grammar-school existed here previously to 1477, and after the termination of Cardinal Wolsey's Collegiate Institution, Henry VIII. renewed the school by a royal charter, which was confirmed and enlarged by Queen Elizabeth, in 1565. It is endowed for the support of a master and usher, under the patronage of the corporation; and the number of scholars is at present restricted to thirty. There are also three charity-schools, in two of which are seventy boys, and in the third, forty girls. Besides these there is a Lancasterian-school, founded in 1811, for 200 boys. In the town are various alms-houses; and in

Maŷ	Names of Places.	County.	Number of Miles from			Dist. Lond.	Popu. lation.
7	Irby..............to	Chester.....	Gt. Neston ..5	Liverpool....8	Eastham 8	197	145
24	Irby-on-Humber....pa	Lincoln.....	Gt. Grimsby.5	Castor 6	Glan.Bridge 15	162	217
24	Irby in the Marsh...pa	Lincoln	Spilsby......6	Wainfleet .. 3	Burgh 3	134	78
28	Irchester ....pa	Northamp ..	Wellingboro' 3	High Ferrers 4	Bozeat 5	65	797
22	Ireby ....to	Lancaster...	K. Lonsdale .3	Hornby......8	Burton 9	249	115
9	Ireby, High ....to	Cumberland	Wigton 7	H.Newmark. 9	Ireby........2	304	499
9	Ireby, Low*...m t & to	Cumberland	 7	 6	Mary Port ..13	303	293

1704 was established an institution for the relief and support of the widows and orphans of poor clergymen, which is supported by subscription. The streets in general are narrow, and disposed without much attention to regularity; but they are well paved and lighted with gas. Many of the shops and private houses are handsome modern buildings; and among the number which have an antiquated appearance, many are spacious, comfortable, and convenient. The town-hall formerly constituted part of the parochial church of St. Mildred, said to have been one of the most beautiful structures in Ipswich; the custom-house, situated on the quay, is a commodious brick building; and the corn-exchange, standing on Corn-hill, is well arranged, and furnished for the business there transacted. A handsome market-cross, which had been erected in 1510, was taken down in 1812, and the square in which it stood enclosed for a market-place. At no great distance from the former is another market-place, built at the joint expense of five persons, in 1811, and consisting of inner and outer quadrangles, round both of which are covered colonnades, affording to the market-people protection from the weather; and adjoining is an enclosed cattle-market, constructed at the expense of the same proprietors. The county gaol, the plan and disposition of which have been highly praised, stands within a boundary wall, twenty-four feet in height, and enclosing about an acre and a half of ground. At a short distance from this edifice is the house of correction, in an airy situation, surrounded by a wall seventeen feet high; it includes three court-yards; and in the keeper's house is a chapel for the prisoners. The Borough goal, in St. Matthew's-street, is described as a handsome and commodious building. The spinning of woollen yarn is the only manufacture carried on here at present, to any extent, except ship-building, sail-making, &c. The principal commerce of the town arises from the exportation of corn, malt, cheese, and butter, the produce of the neighbouring country. A good harbour for light vessels is formed by the estuary of the Orwell, which is navigable, at high water, up to the bridge, except for ships of considerable burden, which pass no farther than Downham-reach, three or four miles nearer the sea. The Orwell, which is noted for the beauty of its adjacent scenery, affords the means for a pleasant excursion to Harwich in the summer season; and to that place wherries go and return regularly every tide. On the quay is a custom-house. In the reign of Edward III. it was decided that the bailiff and burgesses of Ipswich possessed the sole right to take custom-house duties for goods landed at the port of Harwich; whence it is to be inferred that the latter was then a subordinate and dependent port, with respect to Ipswich. Among the eminent natives of Ipswich, the most distinguished was Thomas Wolsey, born in March, 1471, who, after attaining the official dignities of Archbishop of York, cardinal, and prime minister of Henry VIII., died, under arrest for treason, at Leicester-abbey, Nov. 29, 1530.

Market, Wednesday, Friday, and Saturday.—*Fairs*, May 4 and 18, for lean cattle and toys; July 25, for toys; August 22, for horses and lambs; September 25, for butter and cheese.

IPSWICH.

The town-hall.

Its commerce.

Birthplace of Cardinal Wolsey.

* IREBY, Low, a market-town and township, forming, with High Ireby, a parish, in Allerdale-ward, below Darwent, situated near the source of the river Ellen. It is called Low Ireby, and also Market Ireby,

Map	Names of Places.	County.	Number of Miles from			Dist. Lond.	Popu-lation.
3	Ireland ....ham	Bedford	Biggleswade .5	Bedford 6	Ampthill 6	45	....
22	Ireleth ......to & cha	Lancaster...	Ulverston ...5	Hawkshead.17	Dalton 3	277.	513
10	Ireton Kirk.........pa	Derby	Wirksworth 3	Winster 6	Ashborn 6	143	826
10	Ireton Wood........to	Derby	Derby 4	Uttoxeter ..13	11	130	165
22	Irlam ....ham	Lancaster...	Manchester..9	Newton 7	Warrington..8	191	....
22	IrlamO"The Height ham	Lancaster...	 4	Bolton 7	Bury........8	186	....
27	Irmingland .... pa	Norfolk.....	Norfolk 5	E. Dereham .9	Reepham 8	114	16
24	Irnham............pa	Lincoln.....	Corby 2	Folkingham..6	Bourn 9	107	413
10	Iron Brock Grange.ham	Derby	Derby.....13	Winster 5	Bakewell...9	139	34
27	Irstead ....pa	Norfolk.....	Cottishall ..6	N. Walsham 8	Norwich ...13	122	152
9	Irthington ...pa & to	Cumberland	Carlisle 8	Longtown ...6	Brampton ..6	310	251
28	Irthlingborough ...pa	Northamp ..	High.Ferrers 2	Kettering...8	Thrapston ...7	70	1072
9	Irton ....pa	Cumberland	Ravenglass ..5	Egremont ..12	Whitehaven 17	295	566
43	Irton ....to	N. R. York.	Scarborough 4	N. Malton ..12	Hunmanby ..8	213	105
9	Isall ....pa	Cumberland	Cockermouth 3	Ireby.......6	Keswick ...10	300	508
9	Isall Old Park ......to	Cumberland	5	4	H.Newmark. 9	301	90
56	Is Carneg... ......to	Montgomery	Machynllath .1	Llanidloes ..18	Di.Y.Moddu13	206	338
49	Is Coed...........ham	Carmarthen.	Carmarthen..6	Kidwelly....4	Lland. Vawr 22	224	169
52	Is Coed ....pa	Denbigh	Wrexham ..5	Llangollen..12	Holt 8	185	509
38	Isfield ....pa	Sussex	Uckfield 3	Cuckfield ..12	Lewes 8	43	581
28	Isham............pa	Northamp ..	Kettering....4	Thrapston ..7	H. Ferrers ..6	71	322
26	Ishlawrcoed.......pa	Monmouth..	Newport ...16	Crickhowell .5	Abergavenny 7	158	2070
49	Ishmaels, St.........pa	Carmarthen	Kidwelly....3	Llaugherne ..5	Carmarthen..7	225	944
57	Ishmaels, St.........pa	Pembroke ..	Milford 5	Haverford,W 9	Marlos......3	275	527
34	Isle, Abbot's ....pa	Somerset ...	Ilminster 4	Taunton.....9	Somerton ...10	133	342
34	Isle, Brewers ....pa	Somerset ...	Langport 5	9	10	133	219
44	Isle, Beck ....to	N. R. York.	Thirsk.....4	Aldborough..9	Ripon 10	219	221
16	Isle of Wight ....co					....	13431
6	Iseham............pa	Cambridge..	Mildenhall...3	Ely 7	Newmarket..7	67	1942
25	Isleworth........hun	Middlesex ..				....	13568
25	Isleworth* ....vil & pa	Middlesex ..	Brentford ...2	Hounslow ..3	Staines 9	9	5590
23	Isley Walton ....pa	Leicester ...	Ashby de la Z.7	Kegworth ..4	Loughboro ..6	123	65

Low IREBY.

Ancient origin.

to distinguish it from the village of High Ireby, in its vicinity. Though now an inconsiderable place, its origin has been referred to a remote period; for Camden supposes, from the similarity of names, that it was the Arbeia of the Romans, where the military corps of the Barcarii Tigrienses was stationed; but this opinion is controverted by Horsley, who observes that no Roman antiquities have been discovered here. The living is a perpetual curacy in the archdeaconry and diocese of Carlisle; certified value £25; annual value P. R., £45; in the patronage of the Dean and Chapter of Carlisle. The grant for holding the market was obtained in 1237; and in 1688 it was frequented as a great corn-mart, but at present there is only a small market for butcher's meat. A free-school was founded here in 1726, by Matthew Caldbeck, and endowed with £5 per annum.

Market, Thursday.—*Fairs*, February 24, and September 21, for horses and horned cattle.

Insurrection against Henry III.

* ISLEWORTH is pleasantly situated on the north bank of the Thames, opposite to Richmond. In 1263, the barons, in insurrection against Henry III., encamped in Isleworth-park, which at that time belonged to Richard, Earl of Cornwall, the king's brother. The following year, the citizens of London, headed by the constable of the Tower, destroyed the manor-house and two mills, besides committing other ravages. The property subsequently became vested in the crown; and Henry V., in 1414, founded, within the manor of Isleworth, a convent of Bridgetine nuns, called the Monastery of Sion. The original site of the convent was within the parish of Twickenham; but in 1432 a new and more spacious nunnery was erected in the parish of Isleworth, to which the sisterhood removed; and there continued till the dissolution of monasteries. Edward VI. granted the conventual estate to his uncle, the Duke of Somerset, who erected a noble mansion at Sion, and formed a botanic garden. The property, on his attainder, fell to the crown; and in 1604, it was re-granted to Henry, Earl of Northumberland, who laid out £9000 on the house and gardens, which have been since variously improved by later proprietors. This noble mansion, now belonging to

Map.	Names of Places.	County.	Number of Miles from			Dist. Lond.	Popu- lation.
25	Islington*.....vil & pa	Middlesex ..	Hackney....3	Hampstead ..4	Highgate 3	1	37316
27	Islington ....pa	Norfolk.....	Lynn Regis ..4	CastleRising10	Wisbeach ..10	94	236

the Duke of Northumberland, is of magnificent dimensions, and of a quadrangular form, and is built of white stone. The living of Isleworth is a vicarage in the archdeaconry of Middlesex, and diocese of London; and in the patronage of the Dean and Canons of Windsor. The church, dedicated to All Saints, consists of a nave, aisles, and chancel, with an ancient Gothic tower at the west end. The whole structure, except the tower, was rebuilt of brick, in 1706. An alms-house for six poor women was founded here, and endowed with an estate in Yorkshire, by Sir Thomas Ingram, in 1664; another alms-house for six poor men and six women, was erected in pursuance of the munificent bequest of £5000, by Mrs. Tolson, who died in 1750; and there is a third, for six women, built in 1738, and subsequently endowed by Mrs. Mary Bell. There is likewise a charity-school for children of both sexes, originally founded by Dame Elizabeth Hill, in 1630. Anthony Collins, a noted writer on philosophical necessity, the friend and correspondent of Locke, was born at Isleworth, in 1676.

ISLEWORTH

Munificent bequest.

*ISLINGTON is an extensive village, situated between the ancient channels of the little rivers Fleet and Walbrook, which mark its western and eastern borders, in the course of their subterraneous passage to the Thames. The village, which was long one of the principal rural haunts of the metropolitan citizens, is now so closely connected with Clerkenwell, St. Luke's, Old-street, and Shoreditch, that, like those places, it may be regarded as forming an integrant portion of the vast metropolis. Besides Islington, the parish includes the villages or hamlets of Battlebridge, Upper and Lower Holloway, Highbury, Ball's-pond, part of Newington-green, Kingsland-green, and City-gardens. Battlebridge is supposed, with great probability, to have been the place where Suetonius Paulinus, the Roman governor, defeated the multitudinous army of the Britons, under the celebrated Boadicea, queen of the Iceni, A. D. 61. As early as the reign of Henry II., Islington was noted as the scene of public recreation, where wrestling, casting quoits, shooting at butts, and other athletic pastimes were practised. In 1514, the Londoners, displeased at the abridgment of their pleasures, by the enclosure of common fields about Islington, Hoxton, and Shoreditch, which they had been accustomed to frequent for the sport of archery, assembled in great numbers, and levelled the enclosures. On the commencement of war between Charles I. and the Parliament, trenches and ramparts were constructed at this place, for the defence of the city. The living of Islington is a vicarage in the arch-deaconry of Middlesex and diocese of London. Islington also gives title to a prebendary in St. Paul's-cathedral, and the value of the benefice in K. B. is £11 10s. 10d. The parish church, dedicated to St. Mary, is a modern structure of brick, with stone quoins and cornices, having at the west end an entrance-portico, and a square tower, surmounted by an octangular steeple. It was erected in 1751—1754; and when some repairs took place, in 1787, it being requisite to make some alterations in the vane, that object was effected by means of a scaffolding of wicker-work round the steeple, ingeniously constructed, on a novel plan, by Thomas Birch, a basket-maker. Besides the parish church, there are in the parish episcopal churches or chapels at Holloway, Ball's-pond, and Cloudesley-square, Liverpool-road. There are also various places of worship belonging to the Independents, Methodists, and Baptists. Part of the village of Islington, adjoining Pentonville, extends into the parish of Clerkenwell, where stands the free-school and alms-houses, founded and endowed by Dame Alice Owen, about 1610, for the benefit of both

Battle between the Romans and the Britons

Singular scaffolding

Map.	Names of Places.	County.	Number of Miles from				Dist. Lond.	Popu- lation.
28	Islip ....pa	Northamp ..	Thrapston ...1	Oundle......7	Rockingham 12		77	562
31	Islip*. ......vil & pa	Oxford	Oxford 6	Bicester 7	Woodstock ..7		60	645
57	Issells, St...........pa	Pembroke ..	Tenby 4	Narbeth 5	Pembroke ..11		260	1266
8	Issey, St..........pa	Cornwall ..	Padstow.....3	Col. Major...7	Bodmin 10		242	720
16	Itchen Abbots......pa	Hants	Alresford ... 4	Winchester..4	Basingstoke.14		59	251
16	Itchen Stoke .. ....pa	Hants	2	6	13		56	248
38	Itchinor, West......pa	Sussex	Chichester..5	Arundel ..14	Midhurst...15		67	181
38	Itchingfield ....pa	Sussex	Horsham 3	Petworth ..12	Cuckfield...12		39	349
16	Itchingswell......cha	Hants	Whitchurch .8	Kingsclere ..2	Basingstoke.11		56	399
15	Itchington ....ti	Gloucester..	Thornbury ..4	Wickwar....6	Bristol 9		105	144
39	Itchington, Bishop's.pa	Warwick....	Southam 4	Warwick ...10	Kineton 7		80	430
39	Itchington, Long....pa	Warwick....	3	Coventry ...16	Rugby 8		85	911
39	Itchington,Old to & cha	Warwick...	4	Kineton 7	Warwick ..11		81	....
9	Itonfield............to	Cumberland	Penrith 10	Carlisle.....9	H.Newmark.9		292	544
27	Iteringham ....pa	Norfolk.....	Aylesham ...4	Holt 7	Foulsham ...8		122	334
26	Itton ....pa	Monmouth..	Chepstow ...3	Usk 8	Caerleon ...11		138	123
8	Ive, St. ....pa	Cornwall ...	Callington .. 4	Liskeard 4	St. Germans .7		219	656
9	Ivegill........to & cha	Cumberland	Carlisle 9	K. Oswald ..6	H.Newmark. 7		292	129
5	Iver...............pa	Bucks	Colnbrook ...3	Uxbridge....3	Beaconsfield .7		20	1870
9	Ives, St.† ....bo & m t	Cornwall ...	Camborne ..10	Penzance....8	Merazion ...7		276	4776

ISLINGTON. parishes. A charity-school for boys and girls was established here in 1710, the house belonging to which was rebuilt, on an enlarged scale, in 1788 ; there are also parochial schools at Lower Holloway, besides which there are some others. In Queen's Head-row are alms-houses, founded in 1640, by John Heath, for ten decayed members of the Company of Clothworkers ; and another set of alms-houses, founded and endowed by Mrs. Jane Davis, in 1794 ; and in Frog-lane are six alms-houses for widows, originally founded at White-friars, by Margaret, Countess of Charitable Kent, in 1538, but subsequently removed to this place. At Islington is a institutions. handsome and spacious building, erected in 1825, for the use of the Church of England Missionary Institution ; and at Highbury is a college or academy for the education of Congregational, or Independent Dissent-ing ministers, removed hither from Hoxton. The Regent's-canal passes through the parish, being conveyed by a tunnel under the High-street and the New River, and having on its banks convenient wharfs and ware-houses. A considerable part of the course of the New River extends through this parish, but it terminates in that of Clerkenwell. In that parish also are situated Sadler's-wells Theatre. Copenhagen-house, Highbury-barn, and Canonbury-house, are places of public entertain-ment, much frequented in the summer season.

Ancient palace. * ISLIP. It is pleasantly situated on an elevated spot on the north side of the river Ray, near its confluence with the Cherwell, and over the former of these streams there is a neat stone bridge. Near the centre of the village anciently stood a palace belonging to King Ethelred II., whose youngest son, Edward, surnamed the Confessor, was born here. A build-ing, long used as a barn, but supposed to have been a chapel connected with the palace, was taken down in 1780. The manor of Islip was given by the Confessor to the abbot and monks of Westminster ; and in the manor-house Isabel of France resided for a short time, in 1326, while concerting measures for the dethronement of her husband, Edward II. In 1644 and 1645, this village, and its vicinity, were the scenes of repeated skirmishes between the troops of Charles I. and the Parliament.

Origin of the name. † IVES, ST. It is a place of great antiquity, and is said to derive its name from Iva, a woman of great sanctity, who came here from Ireland, about the year 460. It is situated at the north-east of the fine bay of St. Ives, in the Bristol-channel, and bounded by rocks of black killas. Previously to the year 1816, the harbour was greatly incommoded by immense shoals of sand driven upon the coast by the north-west winds ; the pier was then extended, and a breakwater constructed for its protection ; it will now afford, at spring tides, accommodation for 200 large vessels. The

Map.	Names of Places.	County.	Number of Miles from				Dist. Lond.	Popu- lation.
19	Ives, St.* .....m t & to	Huntingdon.	St. Neots...14	Huntingdon..6	Somersham ..6		59	3314
45	Ives, St............ham	W. R. York	Keighly 3	Bradford 5	Halifax......6		205	...
13	Ivestone .... to	Durham	Durham 10	Wolsingham .8	Stanhope ...11		268	238
5	Ivinghoe†.....m t & pa	Bucks	Tring 4	Aylesbury .. 9	Lei. Buzzard.8		34	1648

chief articles of exportation are slates and pilchards; the latter are taken here in great abundance. In the neighbourhood are some copper-mines, and in the above rocks are some streaks resembling that metal. A very singular custom prevails in this town, namely, that on the death of every individual worth £10, ten shillings shall be paid to the curate. The church is a low, but spacious building, consisting of a nave and two aisles, and situated so near the sea, that at high tides it is covered with the spray. Here, also, are meeting-houses for Dissenters, who have Sunday-schools for their poor children. The town has likewise the advantage of a free grammar-school, founded by Charles I. At a short distance from the town is a seat called Tregony-castle, and about a mile farther, on the summit of a lofty hill, a pyramid, which was erected by John Knoll, Esq., an eccentric individual, who died in 1811, and left in his will, that at the end of every five years an old woman and ten girls, under the age of fourteen, dressed in white, should parade from the market-place around this pyramid, where they should dance, and sing the 100th psalm. To defray the expenses of this singular desire, he left freeholds vested in the minister, to whom, with the port-collector, he bequeathed £10 for a dinner.

Market, Wednesday and Friday.—*Fair*, Saturday before Advent, for cattle.

ST. IVES.

Singular custom.

* IVES, ST., is situated on the river Ouse, over which there is a handsome stone bridge of six arches; it was called Slepe, by the Saxons, and is thus entered in Doomsday Book, but derives its present appellation from St. Ivo, a Persian saint, who travelled through England, about the year 600. Most of the buildings are of modern erection, nearly the whole of the town having been destroyed by a dreadful fire, in 1689. Here are several ale-breweries and malt-kilns, as the inns and public-houses are numerous, the town being a considerable thoroughfare for travellers. Here was formerly a priory, founded by Ivo, for monks of the Benedictine order; the priory-barn and dove-house are yet remaining. Slepe-hall, also called Cromwell-place, was for some time the residence of the Protector, and possesses a curious picture of two half-length figures, said to be of Sir Oliver Cromwell and another of his family, though this is far from being certain, and indeed from the figures themselves, is scarcely probable.

Destructive fire in 1689.

Market, Monday.—*Fairs*, Whit Monday, and October 10, for cattle of all sorts, and cheese:

† IVINGHOE is on the eastern side of the county, where a part of it projects between Bedfordshire and Hertfordshire. It consists of two streets, one of which extends through the whole length of the town, and the other branches off from it near the centre, so that the ground-plan takes somewhat the form of the letter T. A traditional tale and distich prevails in the neighbourhood, purporting that the manor of Ivinghoe, with others near it, anciently belonged to the family of Hampden; and that they were forfeited to the crown, as a fine or composition, for an act of personal violence towards the Prince of Wales, son of Edward III., the circumstances of which are not recorded. The antique couplet is thus worded :—

Curious tradition.

> " Tring, Wing and Ivinghoe did go,
> For striking the Black Prince a blow.''

The church, dedicated to St. Mary, is a handsome Gothic structure, which appears to have been erected in the reign of Edward IV., and

6 M

Map.	Names of Places.	County.		Number of Miles from		Dist. Lond.	Popu-lation.
17	Ivington.....to & cha	Hereford ...	Leominster ..3	Kington 10	Tenbury....12	140	602
11	Ivybridge.....to & cha	Devon......	Totness 13	Plymouth ..10	Ply. Earls. ..6	209	....
21	Ivy Church........pa	Kent	Romney 3	Ashford 10	Rye........10	68	252
41	Ivy Church ......ham	Wilts	Salisbury...3	Downton 5	Old Sarum ..5	85	....
21	Iwade ....pa	Kent	Milton 3	Queensboro'.3	Chatham ..10	41	....
12	Iwerne Courtney....pa	Dorset......	Blan. Forum 5	Shaftesbury..7	Stalbridge ...8	110	557
12	Iwerne Minster ...pa	Dorset.....	Shaftesbury..6	Cranborne..14	Blan. Forum.6	106	634
36	Ixworth*.....m t & to	Suffolk.....	BurySt.Edm. 8	Botesdale....9	StowMarket 12	77	1061
36	Ixworth Thorpe ....pa	Suffolk.....	 7	Thetford 8	Mildenhall .15	79	148

IVINGHOE.   within it are sepulchral monuments of the family of Duncombe, formerly the possessors of a seat in this parish, called Barley-end House. The market, granted in 1318, was once large, but is now almost discontinued. Berrysted-house, in this parish, now a farm-house, is said to have been the seat of Henry de Blois, Bishop of Winchester, brother of King Stephen, to whom also is attributed, but without any probability, an altar-tomb and statue in the chancel of the church.

Market, Saturday.—*Fairs*, May 6, and October 17, for cows, sheep, and hogs.

Discovery of Roman coins.   * IXWORTH, a small market-town, pleasantly situated in a valley, on the bank of a small river, which falls into the Little Ouse. Roman coins are said to have been repeatedly found here; but it may be questioned whether it was the site of any Roman settlement, and the origin of the town may with more probability be traced to the foundation of a priory of Canons Regular of St. Augustin, by Gilbert Blund, or Blount, about the year 1100. The town is a considerable thoroughfare, being situated on the road from Bury to Norwich and Yarmouth; but it has no manufacture, and its market is now inconsiderable.

Market, Monday.—*Fair*, Whit Monday, for toys.

RIVERS.

Name.	Rises.	Falls.	Name.	Rises.	Falls.
Idle..........	Nottingham	Trent.	Irvon	Brecknocksh	Wye.
Illen........	Pembrokesh	Irish Sea.	Irwell*.......	Lancashire..	Mersey.
Irk....... ...	Lancashire.	Irwell.	Isist..........	Wiltshire...	Thame.
Irt, or Irthing..	Cumberland	Irish Sea.	Isker, or Isis	Brecknocksh	Uske.

Romantic scenery.   * THE IRWELL rises in the moors, about the parallel of Haslingden, near the Yorkshire and Lancashire boundaries; whence it flows, swelled by other little streams, through the manor of Tottington to Bury; below which it forms a junction with the Roch, and afterwards makes a considerable curve to the west. Meeting with a rivulet from Bolton, the Irwell then suddenly winds towards the south-east; and proceeds, in that direction, to Manchester, where it unites with the Medlock and the Irk. Shifting its course to the west, and passing through Barton, where the Duke of Bridgewater's canal is carried over its surface, it falls into the Mersey, below Flixton. The country, from Bury to Manchester, through which the river pursues its course, is very romantic, and extremely populous. The scenery, from Lever to Clifton, is peculiarly attractive.

† ISIS, a river, rises in Wiltshire, on the borders of Gloucestershire, and flowing through only a small part of Wiltshire, begins to be navigable for boats at Cricklade; but after running in a serpentine manner

Name.	Rises.	Falls.	Name.	Rises.	Falls.
Istwith.........	Cardigansh .	Irish Sea.	Ivil, or Ivel.....	Bedfordshire	Ouse.
Istrad..........	Denbighshire	Cluyd.	Ivil........	Somersetshire	Parret.
Itching, or Alr *	Hampshire	Southampt. Water			

about four miles, to Castle Eaton, it passes the town of Lechlade, dividing the counties of Oxfordshire and Berkshire in its whole remaining course; and running through Oxford, where it is joined by the Cherwell, passes Abingdon, and above a mile below Dorchester unites with the Thame, and forms the noble river Thames. **RIVER ISIS.**

* ITCHING, or Alre, a river in Hampshire, rising at Chilton Candover, near Alresford, thence running S. W. to the city of Winchester, where it begins to be navigable till its fall into Southampton Water.

J.

Map.	Names of Places.	County.	Number of Miles from				Dist. Lond.	Popu-lation.
11	Jacobstowe.........pa	Devon..	Hatherleigh , 4	Oakhampton.6	Chumleigh .. 8		200	638
8	Jacobstowe .... pa	Cornwall ...	Stratton ... 8	Launceston 12	Bossiney....11		225	571
13	Jarrow* ....pa & to	Durham	S. Shields ...3	Newcastle...6	Sunderland ..7		276	27995
57	Jeffreston... ..... pa	Pembroke ..	Narbeth 4	Tenby.......5	Pembroke ...9		262	610
	Jersey, Island of†......	Hants......	Portland....84	Southampt 124	Portsmouth134		220	29855

* JARROW is pleasantly situated on the south side of the Tyne, at the point where that river expands and forms the fenny pool called Jarrows-lake, which covers 460 acres of ground. It was formerly called Gyrvy, which is the Saxon name for a marsh. The church, which is dedicated to St. Paul, was rebuilt in 1783, except the chancel and tower, which are very ancient. In the vestry is a rudely-formed and very ancient oaken chair, which is said to have belonged to the venerable Bede, who was born at Monkton, in this parish. Here are the remains of an ancient monastery, said to be founded by King Egfrid. *Birthplace of the Venerable Bede.*

† JERSEY, ISLAND OF, Hampshire, in the diocese of Winchester, is situated about twenty-five leagues south from the continent of Britain, five leagues west from Cape Carteret, in Normandy, three leagues south from Sarke, seven leagues south-east from Guernsey, and nine leagues south from Alderney. It is of an oblong figure, measuring twelve miles from west to east, and six from north to south, in circumference, between thirty-five and thirty-six; and in point of extent, nearly equal to, but somewhat larger than, Guernsey; elevated like that, but on the opposite side declining from south to north. The cliffs on the side fronting Guernsey being forty or fifty fathoms in height, but on the south it is almost level with the sea. The country is beautifully diversified with little hills, warm valleys, and, towards the sea, with pleasant plains. The soil also varies much, in some places gravelly, in others sandy; but the greatest part is a deep, rich, fertile mould, with scarcely any spot in the island which can be called barren. This island is better watered than Guernsey, abounding every where with rills, rivulets, and springs. The produce of this island is much the same with that of Guernsey; the pasture so sweet, that no country in Europe can boast of richer milk, or finer butter; grain of all kinds, and particularly a sort of wheat called *froment tremais*, from its being sown in the latter end of May, and *Description of the soil.*

ISLAND OF
JERSEY.

reaped in the beginning of August. But what chiefly distinguishes this island at present, are its orchards, which are very well fenced, regularly planted, and commonly yield immense quantities of fruit. On the south of the island the sea seems to have encroached upon the land, and to have swallowed upwards of six square miles, making a very beautiful bay, between two and three miles broad, and nearly the same in depth. In the east corner of this bay stands the town of St. Hellier, very pleasantly situated, having a prospect open to the sea, covered with hills to the north, with meadows between them and the town, through which runs a copious and delightful stream. The streets are open and well built, with a handsome square in the centre, and well accommodated in point of markets, and every other thing contributing to the convenience of the inhabitants. Here a pier has been raised, which is a great advantage to the port. But the principal haven is on the other side, in the west corner of the bay of St. Aubin's, from which it receives its name. It is about half the size of St. Hellier, chiefly occupied by merchants and masters of ships; and most of the buildings being new, make a very neat and elegant figure. A little to the east of the town a rock rises up in the sea, upon which the fort of St. Aubin is erected; to which the inhabitants having joined a well-built pier, their haven is now equally secured against the fury of the winds, and the insults of an enemy. Within the pier, a sixth-rate just floats at a dead neap, and a vessel of 200 tons at all times; but ships of superior size must lie without, in the road, where there is good anchorage; and the whole bay being a fine, clean, hard sand, renders the intercourse between the two towns, which are about three miles distant, perfectly easy. There are besides these, several other havens of less note; as St. Brelade's-bay, at the back of St. Aubin's; the great bay of St. Owen, taking in the greatest part of the west side of the island, where the largest ships may ride in twelve and fifteen fathoms, safe from all but east winds. La Crevasse is a port only for boats; Greve de Lecq, and port St. John, are also small havens on the north side; where is likewise Bonnenuit. On the east is the bay of St. Katherines, and the harbour of Rosel; to the south of which lies the famous Mount Orgueil-castle; to the south-west lies the haven De la Chaussée; to the east of St. Aubin's-bay is the port de Bas. All these are covered with breast-work, well defended by cannon. Formerly the chief employment and dependence of the inhabitants were placed in agriculture, but now every house has its orchard, and there is such abundance of fruit, that in a good year, between 20,000 and 30,000 hogsheads of cyder are made here. Their great manufacture is the same with that of Guernsey, the working up of their wool, and 4000 tods, which by act of parliament they are empowered to import annually from England. The articles chiefly manufactured are stockings. In ancient times they depended greatly upon their fishery, in which they are much inferior to Guernsey. In war time, several privateers are fitted out by the inhabitants of the island, by which immense riches are frequently gained. For the defence of the island, they have two troops of horse, five regiments of infantry, and a fine train of artillery, exclusive of what is in their several castles, and on the redoubts and breast-works upon their coasts, amounting, in the whole, to 115 eighteen-pounders, given by King William to the island, in 1692. There are always regular troops in Elizabeth-castle, and in Fort St. Aubin; and in time of war, they have commonly a body of forces from England. The whole number of inhabitants is computed at about 25,000, all of whom (with a very few exceptions) are natives of the place. Originally, all these islands were under the jurisdiction of one great officer, styled sometimes Lord, sometimes Bailiff, and sometimes Guardian of the Isles. At present the government of Jersey is vested in the governor or his deputy, and the bailiff, who are appointed by the king. The former is at the head of the state, and of

St. Hellier,
its chief
town.

Capacious
bay.

Produces
great quantities of
cyder.

the military government; the latter is the chief magistrate, and precedes the governor in courts of justice, but no where else; and is entrusted with the custody, and, under certain restrictions, with the use of the great seal; he has likewise his lieutenant.   There are also twelve justices of the peace, elected by the people; an attorney-general; solicitor-general; sheriff; recorder; two under sheriffs, and a keeper of the rolls.   Every parish has its constable, which is a triennial office of great honour and trust; each constable having under him two lieutenants, and twelve sworn assistants.   There is also in every vinton, a vintonier; these officers execute justice, suppress disorders, levy all taxes, and with very little expense to the public.   In the states of the island, the governor, or his deputy, presides, having first called them together; and he has also a negative voice.   They pass laws, raise money, naturalize strangers, and appoint deputies to carry addresses or representations on their behalf to the crown. This island is governed by its own laws, but an appeal lies to the king in council.   The lands and estates descend in gavel-kind.   The steady and intrepid courage which the inhabitants have often displayed when attacked, have induced several monarchs to confer very extraordinary marks of their favour.   Henry VII. gave them his sanction for the erection of two free-schools; Queen Elizabeth honoured them with larger and more explicit charters than any of her predecessors; James I. redressed several griev-ances; King Charles I. gave lands for the endowment of three fellow-ships in as many colleges at Oxford; King Charles II. sent a mace, with a most honourable inscription, to be carried before the magistrates of the island; King William III. gave all the artillery requisite for their breast-works and other fortifications; and they have deserved and received many benefits from the crown in succeeding reigns.

Government of the island.

Its climate. The climate is extremely mild, in consequence of the southern site and aspect of the island; and the temperature being equalized by the surrounding sea.   Snow seldom falls, and frosts are of transient occurrence; hence, myrtles and other shrubs, which in the south of England require protection, grow here luxuriantly in the open air; and melons are raised in gardens without artificial heat.   The pulse and corn grown here are smaller than the pro-duce of England; yet, formerly enough was raised to form a considerable article of exportation, but now the inhabitants are obliged to procure from other countries nearly one-half of the grain they consume.   The horses are small, but strong and hardy; the cows are of the Alderney breed; and the sheep appear to be chiefly Southdowns, the six-horned variety, for which the island was once noted, having become extinct. Game does not abound here; but the Jersey partridge, with red feet, pheasant's eyes, and variegated plumage, may be noticed as a curiosity. The weasel and the mole are almost the only noxious animals; and it is believed that the island contains no venomous reptiles, though toads of a large size are found here, whilst there are none at Guernsey, where it is said the air proves destructive to them.   Fish are plentiful, including conger eels, sometimes weighing fifty pounds; and the curious shell-fish, called the ormer, or sea-ear.

Quarries of sienitic granite. The only remarkable mineral substance is the sienitic granite, of which the cliffs are composed.   It is raised from quarries at Mount Mado in large quantities, and sent to Guernsey and to England, to be used for paving.   Its colour is a reddish white, and it may be polished so as to resemble marble, when it is adapted to the pur-poses of ornamental architecture.   Ochre and tripoli are found here; and there are several chalybeate springs in the island.   The contest with Bona-parte became productive of great advantage to Jersey, in consequence of its being made a grand military depot.   Its shores were then crowded by French emigrants and other strangers; workmen arrived here from England, to labour at the forts and other public works; the harbours were filled with shipping; and every thing contributed to give an extra-ordinary impulse to commerce, so that the whole island displayed a scene

Map.	Names of Places.	County.	Number of Miles from			Dist. Lond.	Popu-lation.
29	Jesmond*..........to	Northumb .	Newc.-on-T. 1	N. Shields ..7	S. Shields....8	275	....
38	Jevington.........pa	Sussex	Eastbourne..3	Seaford......5	Lewes......12	62	300
8	John, St..........pa	Cornwall ...	Saltash.....4	Plymouth ...6	St.Germans..5	221	178
25	John, St..........pa	Middlesex .	Westminster..	Hammersmith5	Brentford....8	1	22648
9	John, St..........pa	Cumberland	Egremont....4	Keswick ...14	Ravenglass ..8	292	567
16	John, St..........pa	Hants	Winchester..1	Stockbridge..9	Romsey ...11	62	785
42	John, St., the Baptist pa & to	Worcester..	Worcester...1	Droitwich ...6	Upton......10	111	2661
9	John, St., Castlerigg to & cha	Cumberland	Keswick.. ..3	H.Newmark12	Penrith.....14	289	567
36	John, St., Ilketshall .pa	Suffolk....	Bungay......3	Beccles......6	Halesworth..7	106	66
54	John's, St ....pa	Glamorgan.	Swansea ...1	Lochor......6	Neath 9	207	690
9	Johnby ....to	Cumberland	Penrith.....5	H.Newmark. 9	Keswick ...14	293	99
57	Johnston ....pa	Pembroke ..	Haverford,W 4	Pembroke ...6	Milford......3	270	186
57	Jordanstown ......pa	Pembroke ..	Fishguard ...4	St. Davids ..13	Newport ...11	261	150
8	Juliet, St ....pa	Cornwall ...	Camelford ...5	Bossiney 6	Launceston .14	227	263
8	Just, St. ....pa	Cornwall ...	St. Mawes...1	Truro......6	Penryn 6	260	4667
8	Just, St. ....pa	Cornwall ..	Penzance 7	St. Ives 12	Merazion ...11	287	1558

ISLAND OF JERSEY.

of active industry and increasing wealth. Steam-packets, carrying the mail, pass regularly between St. Hellier and Weymouth; and there are likewise steam-packets to Southampton, which touch at Guernsey.

Exports and imports.

The exports to England, besides cider, are fruit, potatoes, and cattle; and the chief imports, corn, flour, seeds, live and dead stock, coal, cloth, earthenware, and glass. Salt-fish is brought hither from Newfoundland, and much of it is shipped again for the Mediterranean; commerce is also carried on with America, and with several parts of Europe. The grand staple article of manufacture, at Jersey, consists of worsted stockings, which are made of the finest quality, and the trade in which has been protected by various regulations of the English parliament. The language of Jersey, as well as the neighbouring islands, is the Norman-French, much corrupted, and said to be on the decline, but still used in the pulpits and the courts of law. Among the eminent natives of Jersey may be mentioned Philip Falle, historian of the island; Daniel Brevint, dean of Lincoln; Dr. David Durell, a biblical critic; and Dr. John Lempriere, author of a " Classical Dictionary," and other useful publications. Jersey gives the title of earl to the family of Villiers.

* JESMOND, or Jesmont. At Jesmond-grove are the ruins of the chapel and hospital, dedicated to the Virgin Mary, to which so many pilgrims anciently resorted. Near these ruins is St. Mary's well, which was anciently in great estimation among the religious. To the south of Jesmond, at a sudden turn of the road, the Sandyford Dean is crossed by a small bridge, at the point where the rivulet falls over a rocky precipice, forty-five feet in perpendicular height, and is commonly called Lambert's-leap, on account of the singular escape of Mr. Cuthbert Lambert, whose

Extraordinary escape.

mare took fright, and bounding over the low battlements of the bridge, fell with her rider into the dreadful abyss below; the horse was killed on the spot, though Mr. L. having kept his seat, most miraculously escaped with his life, and soon recovered from the violent shock which he sustained. In 1827 another accident of the kind took place, but the unfortunate rider met with instant death.

† JOHN, ST., CASTLERIGG, a township and chapelry in the parish of Crosthwaite, Allerdale ward below Darwent, comprising the two romantic vales of St. John of Wanthwaite. A branch of the river Greta flows from Thirlmere, through the deep and narrow dell of Wanthwaite,

Devastation produced by a water-spout.

where a water-spout fell in 1749, and in two hours covered the whole vale many feet deep in water, forced down all the walls, houses, and bridges, and so completely carried away the corn-mill, that not a single stone was to be seen; the side of a mountain was excavated into a large and deep gully, and in some places stones of twenty tons weight were piled up in heaps twelve yards high. In the widest part of the dale is a rugged rock, called Green Crag, which, at a distance, has the appearance of a ruined castle, and greatly heightens the grandeur of this wild and discordant scene. St. John's vale is of a more verdant and chaste character than the former, but like it, is a deep and narrow glen, affording many picturesque beauties.

ST. JOHN, CASTLE-RIGG.

K.

Map	Names of Places.	County.	Number of Miles from			Dist. Lond.	Population.
40	Kaber*.............to	Westmorlnd	Brough 2	Kir. Stephen 3	Appleby ...11	263	164
46	Kayingham	E. R. York .	Hull 14	Hedon 4	Patrington..5	288	639
8	Kea, St. ....pa	Cornwall ...	Truro 4	Tregony 5	Penryn.....6	262	3896
24	Keadby............to	Lincoln.....	Glan.Bridge 12	Burton.....5	Kirton 13	164	279
24	Keal, East.........pa	Lincoln....	Spilsby......2	Horncastle...9	Burgh......8	132	313
24	Keal, West ....pa	Lincoln.....	 3	9	8	131	502
22	Kearsley .... .to	Lancaster...	Bolton ...:..4	Manchester ..7	Newton ...12	189	2705
29	Kearsley...........to	Northumb ..	Newc.-on-T 12	Hexham....10	Corbridge ...7	286	11
14	Keddington ......pa	Essex and Suffolk ...	C.Hedingham 9	Clare........5	Haverhill ..3	61	625
24	Keddington ....pa	Lincoln.....	Louth 2	Saltfleet 8	Alford......9	150	607
10	Kedleston† ....pa	Derby.....	Derby 4	Ashborn...11	Alfreton...14	130	109
24	Keelby ....pa	Lincoln.....	Gt. Grimsby .6	Barton 13	Glan.Bridge 13	165	638
35	Keele.........pa & vil	Stafford	Newcastle...3	Gt. Madeley .4	Drayton....12	152	1130
41	Keevil ....pa	Wilts.......	Trowbridge..4	Melksham ...4	Bradford ...6	95	692
23	Kegworth‡ ....pa	Leicester ...	Loughboro' ..6	Ashby de laZ11	Mt. Sorrel ..10	115	1821

* KABER, or Kabergh, a township, partly in the parish of Brough, and partly in that of Kirby Stephen, East ward. Here is a small endowed school. In 1663, after the restoration of Charles II., an insurrection of the republican party was intended, and meetings were held for that purpose at Kaber Rigg, where several were taken prisoners by the militia, and executed at Appleby, for joining in this conspiracy, which was called the Kaber Rigg plot.

Insurrection of the republican party.

† KEDLESTON. Lord Scarsdale has a most magnificent seat here; it is situated on a gentle ascent, is 360 feet in extent, consisting of a centre and two pavilions connected with the main buildings by corridors of the Doric order; in the centre of the north front is a double flight of steps leading to a grand portico, whose pediment is supported by six columns of the Corinthian order. The hall is a most beautiful apartment planned after the ancient Greek mode, and the ceiling is supported by twenty columns of alabaster. The saloon is an extremely elegant apartment, and is deservedly admired for the classic taste displayed in its various decorations. Almost every room in this splendid mansion is decorated with paintings, comprising many valuable works by the most eminent masters. The park-lodge was designed from the arch of Octavia, and gives admission to the grounds, which are about five miles in circumference, and display some flourishing plantations, and also a grove of venerable oaks, some of them of enormous magnitude. In the park is a neat building, erected over a spring, which is greatly valued for its antiscorbutic qualities; it has also been found efficacious, from external application, in various cutaneous diseases, but more especially in ulcerous complaints. The temperature of the spring is about forty-seven degrees.

Magnificent mansion.

Medicinal spring.

‡ KEGWORTH is situated on an eminence near the Trent, over which there is a handsome stone bridge, built at the expense of the Duke of

Map.	Names of Places.	County	Number of Miles from			Dist. Lond.	Population.
45	Keighley*.....to & pa	W. R. York	Skipton......7	Otley........8	Halifax.....10	208	11176
24	Keisby............ham	Lincoln....	Corby.....5	Folkingham..4	Grantham ..12	110	80
24	Kelby...........cha	Lincoln.....	Sleaford.....5	Grantham.....7	Folkingham..9	115	124
24	Kelfield..........ham	Lincoln.....	Gainsboro'..7	Spittal.....17	Glan.Bridge 12	158	....
46	Kelfield............to	E. R. York.	Selby.....5	York.....9	Snaith.....12	193	286
30	Kelham...........pa	Nottingham.	Newark...2	Southwell..5	Ollerton....11	127	199
43	Kelk, Great.......to	E. R. York.	Gt. Driffield .5	Bridlington ..7	Rudstone....7	201	158
43	Kelk, Little .....ext p	E. R. York.	6	6	5	202	51
22	Kellamergh ......to	Lancaster...	Kirkham...3	Preston....10	Poulton.....8	226	145
51	Kellan.............pa	Cardigan..	Lampeter...4	Tregaron...7	Llanhir......6	208	460
41	Kellaways ....pa	Wilts	Chippenham .3	Calne.....4	Wott. Basset.9	90	15
40	Kelleth...........ham	Westmorlnd	Orton.....4	Kir.Stephen 11	Kendal ...12	274	....
22	Kellet Nether ......to	Lancaster...	Lancaster...6	Kir.Lonsdale.9	Burton.....8	246	358
22	Kellet Overt..to & cha	Lancaster...	8	8	9	248	531
11	Kelley..........pa	Devon......	Launceston ..5	Oakhampton14	Tavistock ...7	209	218
43	Kelleythorpe ......to	E. R. York.	Gt. Driffield .2	Sledmere....6	Bridlington .15	196	....
27	Kelling ....pa	Norfolk....	Holt......3	Cley.....3	Cromer......8	121	163
46	Kellington.......pa	W. R. York	Pontefract..6	Selby.......6	Snaith 6	174	1388
13	Kelloe.......pa & to	Durham	Durham 6	Sheraton ...6	Sedgefield ...5	256	663
28	Kelmarsh.........pa	Northamp..	Mt. Harboro'.5	Rothwell...6	Northampt. 13	79	172
31	Kelmscott...........pa	Oxford....	Lechdale 2	Bampton....5	Burford 8	73	188
36	Kelsale...........pa	Suffolk	Saxmundham1	Framlingham 7	Halesworth..9	90	1103
7	Kelsall...........to	Chester....	Chester 9	Northwich ..8	Overton 7	177	648
24	Kelsey, North.....pa	Lincoln....	Glan. Bridge..6	Mt. Raisin..10	Castor 6	151	648
24	Kelsey, South.....vil	Lincoln.....	Castor......6	Glan. Bridge.7	Kirton 8	150	632
18	Kelshall.........pa	Herts	Royston ...3	Baldock 7	Hitchin ...12	36	208
24	Kelsterne ....pa	Lincoln....	Louth......4	Mt. Raisin..13	Wragby...13	145	179
34	Kelston‡..........pa	Somerset ..	Bath........4	Bristol 9	Pensford...6	112	248

KEGWORTH. Devonshire; it formerly had a market, which is now discontinued. The church, which is dedicated to St. Andrew, is a handsome light building, with a nave, aisles, transepts, chancel, and tower with a spire. Most of the windows are large, and some of them have pieces and complete figures of painted glass. Queen Elizabeth founded a free-school here, in 1575. The petty sessions for the hundred of West Goscote are holden here occasionally.

Fairs, February 18; Easter-Monday; April 30; and October 10, holyday-fair, toys, &c.

Extensive manufactories.

* KEIGHLEY, or KIGHLEY, a market-town and parish, situated in a deep valley, near the south-west bank of the river Aire, over which is a stone bridge; its principal manufactures are woollen cloth, cottons, linseys, worsted and Manchester goods, the prosperity of which is much increased by the Leeds and Liverpool canal, which passes within two miles. The town is well built of stone, and is amply supplied with water, which is brought from a spring on the west side of it.

Market, Thursday.—*Fairs*, May 8, for horned cattle, brass, and pewter; and November 8, for horned cattle, brass, pewter, and pedlery.

Subterraneous stream.

† KELLET OVER, a township and chapelry, in the parish of Bolton by the Sands, and hundred of Lonsdale, south of the Sands. At a short distance is a natural curiosity, called Dunald's Mill-hole, a cave at the foot of a mountain, into which the water of a large brook, after having given motion to a mill, falls and disappears. After a subterraneous course of two miles, it again emerges at Cranforth, and falls into the river Keer. The cave consists of many apartments, the roofs of which are adorned with incrustations, reflecting the light of tapers in a variety of colours.

‡ KELSTON, a parish in the hundred of Bath Forum, anciently written Kelveston, is beautifully situated, and commands an extremely pleasing and rich prospect. Here is a fine eminence, called Kelston Round-hill, which rises to an immense height above the bed of the river; its summit is crowned with a range of firs, surrounded with a circular wall; the prospect from this hill is very extensive. The old manor-house, which was erected about the year 1587, and the only remains of which is the court-yard, was the seat of Sir John Harrington, chiefly known as the

Map.	Names of Places.	County.	Number of Miles from			Dist. Lond.	Popu-lation.
32	Kelthorpe........ham	Rutland	Stamford....4	Uppingham ..9	Ketton......1	89	....
9	Kelton......to & pa	Cumberland	Whitehaven .8	Keswick ...10	Egremont....9	292	....
14	Kelvedon* ......pa	Essex	Chelmsford .12	Coggleshall ..4	Baintree....10	41	1463
14	Kelvedon Hatch ....pa	Essex	Chip. Ongar .3	Brentwood ..6	Romford ...9	21	336
33	Kemberton ......pa	Salop.......	Shiffnal 3	Wellington ..6	Madeley 4	146	260
41	Kemble..........pa	Wilts	Malmsbury ..6	Cricklade....8	Tenbury ...7	102	435
15	Kemerton ......pa	Gloucester..	Tewksbury ..4	Evesham ...10	Winchcomb 10	105	599
26	Kemys ......pa	Monmouth..	Usk........4	Abergavenny 6	Monmouth..11	145	72
26	Kemys Inferior ....pa	Monmouth ..	Caerleon ...3	Usk 5	Newport ...6	141	109
15	Kempley ....pa	Gloucester..	Newent 5	Ledbury....6	Ross 7	105	301
15	Kempsford† ......pa	Gloucester..	Fairford ...2	Lechdale ...4	Cricklade ..4	88	885
16	Kempshot..........ti	Hants	Basingstoke..4	Kingsclere...8	Whitchurch 8	49	....
3	Kempston..........pa	Bedford	Bedford 3	Harrold....7	Ampthill ...7	53	1571
27	Kempston ....pa	Norfolk.....	Swaffham ...6	E. Dereham .7	Castle Acre .6	99	56
42	Kemsey‡ ....pa	Worcester .	Worcester....4	Upton 6	Pershore ...7	115	1314
21	Kemsing..........pa	Kent	Seven Oaks ..7	Rochester ...9	Maidstone ..9	29	359
21	Kenardington ....pa	Kent	Tenterden ...7	N. Romney..8	Rye 8	56	196
17	Kenchester§......pa	Hereford ...	Hereford.. ..5	Kington ...14	Weobly....8	140	94
31	Kencott..........pa	Oxford	Burford 5	Bampton ...5	Witney 9	75	174
40	Kendal..........ward	Westmorlnd				....	17237
40	Kendal‖ ......m t & to	Westmorlnd	Sedberg ...10	Ambleside..14	Orton 12	262	10015
17	Kender Church....pa	Hereford...	Hereford ...11	Hay........17	Monmouth.14	139	77

first English translator of the "Orlando Furioso" of Ariosto. Sir John was born here about 1561, and had for his godmother no less a personage than Queen Elizabeth, who did his parents this honour from motives of gratitude for the services they had rendered her before she ascended the throne. The present manor-house was erected near the site of the old mansion, and is an elegant modern structure. pleasantly situated on a rising ground.

KELSTON.

Birthplace of Sir John Harrington.

* KELVEDON, or Easterford. *Fair*, Easter Monday, for toys.

† KEMPSFORD. A battle is said to have been fought here about the year 800, between Æthelmund, chief of the Wiccii, or inhabitants of Gloucestershire, and Wearitan, general of the Walsati, who inhabited Wiltshire; both generals were killed, but the Walsati were victorious.

‡ KEMSEY, or KEMESEY, is a handsome place, and is rapidly increasing, it being the thoroughfare between Bristol and Worcester, it has several good inns. Here was anciently a monastery, which flourished about 799. This place seems to have been of great consequence formerly, for Henry II. held his court here, and was attended by the principal nobility and bishops of the kingdom; and in 1265, just before the battle of Evesham, Simon de Montfort, and his unfortunate prisoner, Henry III., were for some time here, and lay at the bishop's-palace. Near the church are the ruins of an ancient camp, which appears to have been of considerable strength.

Ruin of an ancient camp.

§ KENCHESTER is extreme y ancient, having been a famous Roman town, and the Magna of the Itinerary. Great numbers of Roman antiquities have from time to time been discovered, and may yet be traced in different parts of the parish. Among the chief which have been found are a part of a Roman temple, a hypocaust, and an aqueduct of considerable extent.

Roman antiquities.

‖ KENDAL, or KIRKBY-KENDAL, a well-built market-town, the largest and most populous in this county. It is situated in a pleasant and healthful valley, with the river Kent washing its southern side. Many of the streets are narrow about the centre of the town, but those which run from thence to the extremities, in various directions, are more spacious; and the houses being generally whitened, and the roofs covered with blue slates, give the whole a very clean and striking appearance. The situation of the city of Bath, in Somersetshire, may be considered as greatly

Map.	Names of Places.	County.	Number of Miles from				Dist. Lond.	Popu- lation.
33	Kenelm, St. ..to & cha	Salop... ...	Hales Owen .1	Dudley 5	Oldbury 6	123	....
54	Kenfig ....to & pa	Glamorgan..	Bridgend ...6	Aberavon....7	Neath......11	187	222
39	Kenilworth* .m t & pa	Warwick...	Coventry 5	Warwick ...5	Solihull 10	95	3097

KENDAL.

Remains of an ancient castle.

similar to that of Kendal, hanging on the southern declivity of a range of hills, bordering a low vale, which is watered by the Avon, as this town is by the river Kent. The vale through which the Kent flows spreads itself considerably on each hand, varying its dimensions, and winding its course till it reaches the estuary at Milnthorpe. On the opposite side of the water are the noble ruins of a once strong castle, which stands on a fine green hill, and forms a picturesque and conspicuous object from most parts of the vale. Much of the enclosure wall of this castle still remains, a small part of two towers, one round and one square. The entire building appears to have been extensive, and built of rough stone, strongly cemented. It is generally believed to stand on the site of a Roman station, and to have been erected by the first barons of Kendal. At the east end of the town is an extensive house of industry, built some years since; and the house of correction stands near to this establishment. The public buildings and institutions are, a theatre, assembly-rooms, several valuable and well-stored libraries, philosophical and natural history societies, mechanics' institute, a savings' bank, Bible societies, &c. The schools consist of a well endowed free grammar-school, a school of industry, a large national, and several Sunday-schools. The quarter sessions are held here for the burgh, and the adjourned sessions from Appleby, for the Kendal and Lonsdale wards; a court of record is held in the town-hall every three weeks. The places for divine worship, in Kendal, are numerous and respectable. The church is a very ancient edifice, composed of many orders of architecture, but there is no record when it was built; the benefice is a vicarage in the gift of Trinity-college, and incumbency of the Rev. John Hudson. Besides the church there are two chapels under the establishment, in the town, and no fewer

Important manufac- tures.

than ten others belonging to the various sects of dissenters. The manufactures of Kendal are of an important character, and embrace the making of waistcoating in all its branches; kerseymeres, linsey wolsey, serges, baizes, knit woollen caps and jackets, carpetings of various textures, &c. Great numbers of hands are employed in the combing and spinning wool, and many valuable improvements have been made in machinery, applicable to the various processes of manufactures in this flourishing town. The marble works of Kendal are perfected by machinery, both in sawing and polishing, upon an entirely new construction; and this branch of

Gunpowder works.

business is in high repute for all purposes of statuary. There are gunpowder works in the neighbourhood, and upon the river Kent are corn and paper-mills, dye-works, &c. The land around the town is generally in a good state of husbandry, rising in gentle undulations; and the roads, in nearly all directions, are in excellent repair. Kendal has long been a populous town, for it is recorded that in June, 1598, 2,500 inhabitants were carried off by the plague.

Letters for London, Liverpool, Manchester, and the south, are despatched at ten minutes before twelve at night, and arrive at a quarter past one in the morning. Letters for the north are despatched at twenty minutes past one in the morning, and arrive at a quarter before twelve at night.—*Market*, Saturday.—*Fairs*, April 27, and November 8.

* **KENILWORTH,** a market-town and parish. It consists principally of an irregularly-built street, nearly a mile in length, and it is now a place of little importance, its chief claims to notice arising from the ruins of its ancient baronial castle. This structure was founded by Geoffrey de Clinton, chamberlain and treasurer to Henry I.; but the existing remains are part of a fortress subsequently erected by John of Gaunt, whose son becoming king, under the title of Henry IV., the castle, with the exten-

Map	Names of Places.	County.	Number of Miles from			Dist. Lond.	Popu- lation.
33	Kenley.............pa	Salop.....	M. Wenlock.4	Shrewsbury..8	Wellington 10	145	321
34	Kena ....pa	Somerset ...	Axbridge ..10	Bristol 11	Pensford....12	125	276
49	Kennarth ....pa	Carmarthen	Carmarthen 12	Newcastle ..2	Clydey 4	232	1935
58	Kennarton.........to	Radnor.....	New Radnor 2	Presteign....4	Kington 6	160	....
11	Kenne.............pa	Devon	Exeter 4	Topsham ...5	Chudleigh ..6	177	982
11	Kennerley.........pa	Devon......	Crediton 5	Chumleigh...9	SouthMolton17	185	93
6	Kennet ....pa	Cambridge .	Newmarket .5	Ely........11	Mildenhall...6	66	164
41	Kennet, East*......pa	Wilts	Marlborough.5	Calne 8	Devizes......9	79	91
41	Kennet, West......ti	Wilts	 6	 7	10	80	....
27	Kenninghall.......pa	Norfolk	E. Harling...3	N.Buckenha. 4	Diss 7	92	1251
4	Kennington.......to	Berks	Abingdon....3	Oxford.....3	Wallingford 10	53	171
21	Kennington ....pa	Kent	Ashford.... .2	Faversham ..8	Canterbury .11	54	447
37	Kennington†.....ham	Surrey......	Clapham ...3	Brixton 2	Pimlico 2	1	....
43	Kennythorpe ......to	E. R. York .	New Malton.4	Bridlington .18	York 18	214	83
25	Kensington‡........pa	Middlesex .	Hammersmith2	Brentford ...5	Chelsea 2	2	20902

sive demesne belonging to it, was vested in the crown. Queen Elizabeth gave Kenilworth to her favourite, Robert Dudley, Earl of Leicester, who enlarged the chase, and made various improvements in the buildings and decorations of the castle, on which he is said to have expended £60,000. In July, 1575, he celebrated here a grand festival, in honour of his royal mistress, the particulars of which have been described by the late Sir Walter Scott, in one of his most interesting historical romances. During the barons' wars, this fortress sustained a siege of six months, in which the decree, called "Dictum de Kenilworth," passed, which mitigated the severity of the "Dictum de Winchester." Here, too, the unfortunate Edward II. was imprisoned by his queen and her favourites, prior to his inhuman murder in Berkley-castle. The principal manufacture carried on here is that of horn combs; and there are also chemical works for the preparation of volatile salts and hartshorn, and a blue manufactory. A monastery of canons regular of St. Augustin, was founded here by Geoffrey de Clinton, in the twelfth century, and was so richly endowed, that at the dissolution the revenues amounted to £643 14s. 9d.

KENIL-WORTH.

Edward II. confined here.

Market, Wednesday.—Fairs, April 30, and September 30, for cattle and pedlery.

* KENNET, EAST. A parish in the hundred of Selkley. It is situated south of the river Kennet, and on the road from London to Bath, and is supposed by some antiquaries to occupy the site of the Roman station of Cunatio. This opinion is doubtful, but the place is interesting on account of its vicinity to the great tumulus, called Silbury-hill, and the barrows by which it is surrounded. Kennet is now famous for a brewery of strong ale, which forms a considerable article of commerce with London, where it is known by the appellation of Kennet ale.

Famous for the brewery of ale

† KENNINGTON, a hamlet in the parish of Lambeth, eastern division of the hundred of Brixton, which formed a distinct manor in the reign of Edward the Confessor, called in the Doomsday Book, the lordship of Chenintune. After having been held by various persons under royal grants, it was, in the 11th of Edward III., annexed to the duchy of Cornwall, to which it still belongs. Henry III. is supposed to have had a palace here, in which several of his successors occasionally resided, and which appears to have been pulled down when the manor was let on lease by Henry VIII. Kennington-common was formerly the place of execution for malefactors in the county of Surrey; and after the suppression of the rebellion in Scotland, in 1745, many of the insurgents, having been convicted of treason at Southwark, here suffered the sentence of the law.

Formerly a place of execution.

‡ KENSINGTON is situated on the grand western road, about a mile and a half from Hyde Park-corner, and by means of the intervening hamlet of Knightsbridge, it is connected, by an almost uninterrupted range

Map.	Names of Places.	County.	Number of Miles from				Dist. Lond.	Popu- lation.
42	Kenswick..........pa	Worcester ..	Worcester...4	Droitwich ...8	Upton......10		115	15
18	Kensworth ...... pa	Herts	Mark. Street 2	Luton 5	Dunstable ...3		30	732
21	Kent*...........co	Kent	....	....	....		....	479155
17	Kentchurch ....pa	Hereford ...	Hereford ...13	Ross 12	Monmouth..11		136	311

KENSING-TON.
The palace.

of buildings, with the metropolis. The parish includes the hamlets of Brompton, Earl's-court, Kensington-gore, the Gravel-pits, and a part of Little Chelsea; but the royal palace and several houses on the north side of the High-street are within the parish of St. Margaret, Westminster. Kensington-palace was a favourite residence of royalty till the death of George II., which event took place here, and it has since been entirely deserted by the reigning monarchs. It is a spacious, irregular brick edifice, built at different times, and containing a suite of twelve rooms, called the state apartments, in which are a considerable number of paintings by eminent masters, including many portraits of persons distinguished in the annals of our native country. Kensington-gardens, attached to the palace, were enlarged by Queen Anne, and much more extensively by Queen Caroline, the wife of George II., who added nearly 300 acres out of Hyde-park. The parish includes several large nurseries and gardens, one of the former of which was established at the latter end of the seventeenth century. Kensington has been the residence of many

Lord Chancellor Camden born here.

distinguished individuals, and it was the birthplace of the Lord Chancellor Camden, who died in 1794, at the age of eighty. The Irish title of Baron Kensington, belonging to the family of Edwardes, is derived from this place.

* KENT is a maritime county, situated in the south-eastermost part of Great Britian, and including the angle nearest to France, from which its nearest point is about twenty-four miles distant. Its figure is irregular, but approaches more to the trapezium than to any other. On the north, with the exception of a small tract on the Essex side, it is bounded by the river Thames; on the east and part of the south sides, it opens to the German Ocean, and British Channel; on the south it is skirted by Sussex; and on the west by Surrey. Its medium length from west to east is about sixty-six miles; its breadth about twenty-six; and its circumference is nearly 174 miles. For local purposes, this county has been long divided into the two districts of East and West Kent; the eastern division contains the lathes of Sutton, Ford, and part of Scray; the western, Shepway, Augustine, and the remaining part of Scray; within these lathes are comprehended all the smaller divisions, as bailiwicks, hundreds, liberties, &c. In each of the great districts, East and West Kent, a court of sessions is holden four times every year, viz. twice originally and twice by adjournment. The justices, though appointed for the whole county, generally confine their attention to that particular district in which they reside. The present flourishing condition of Kent has doubtless originated from the peculiar customs by which the descent of the landed property is regulated, and which are comprehended under the

Custom of gavelkind.

term gavelkind. The law of gavelkind comprehends the joint inheritance of all the sons to the estate of their father; and should the father survive, the inheritance devolves to his grandsons, if there are any, or else to his daughters. The partibility of this custom is not restrained to the right line of consanguinity; for all brothers may jointly inherit the estate of a deceased brother; and agreeably to the same rule, nephews and nieces, by the right of representation, are in their degrees entitled to the same division of property. The general aspect of Kent is very beautiful, arising from the inequality of the surface, the diversity of the scenery, and the variety of the verdure. The whole county, excepting the marshes and the weald, is a general cluster of small hills; two chains of which, higher than the rest, run through the middle of the county, from east to west, in general at about eight miles distance from each other (though in some places much less), and extend from Surrey to the sea. These are called the Upper and Lower Hills, and are mostly covered with coppice and woodlands. The north range, and indeed the whole north side of the county, is composed chiefly of chalk and flints, as well as a large tract on the east coast; the southern range is chiefly of iron-stone and rag-stone; more westerly, clay and gravel prevail on the eminences. The hop grounds, extending from Maidstone and Canterbury, and from thence to Sandwich, are very productive, and under a good system of management, though the soils are different, as well as the kind of hops cultivated. The plantations have, of late years, been greatly increased, particularly in the vicinity of Maidstone, Faversham, and Canterbury. The plantations, called the City-grounds, extend through a circuit of two miles and a half round the latter city, and are estimated to include from 2500 to 3000 acres. The hops grown here, and in the grounds running hence to Sandwich, are very rich in quality, and in much request for their great strength; if well managed, they are also of a good colour. The Weald of Kent is a considerable and remarkable tract, stretching along the south side of the county, from Romney Marsh to Surrey; on the north it is bounded by the range of hills which enter the county near Well-street, and extends in nearly a due west direction to Sutton and Egerton, and thence stretches south-east to Hythe; on the south it extends to the confines of Sussex, and includes the Isle of Oxney. The whole of this district was, in ancient times, a demesne of the Saxon kings; and there are still certain privileges annexed to the possession of the lands, which induce the proprietors to contend for their being within its limits. The Weald, when viewed from the adjoining hills which command the whole extent, exhibits a most delightful landscape, interspersed with small eminences, highly cultivated, and animated by farm-houses, seats, and villages, promiscuously scattered among towering oaks and other trees. Romney Marsh is an extensive level tract of rich land, lying on the south coast, and in itself comprehending about 23,925 acres. These marshes are almost entirely appropriated to the grazing and fattening of sheep and cattle, but chiefly to the former, which are bred and fed here in immense numbers, perhaps exceeding that of any other district in the kingdom. The breed of sheep kept here is peculiar to these marshes, and from them takes its name. The beautiful appearance of these levels in the summer season, when the entire surface is clothed with luxuriant verdure, and covered with numerous flocks of sheep, and droves of cattle, cannot fail to excite considerable interest in every observer. The manufactures carried on in Kent are various, though not particularly extensive. The clothing trade, which once gave employment to great numbers of its inhabitants, is now nearly forgotten in the county. The various dock-yards at Deptford, Woolwich, Chatham, &c., give employment to numerous artisans in all the different branches of naval affairs; ship-building is also carried on at other places on the sea-coast. The religious houses in Kent were numerous, and their net annual income, at the dissolution, amounted to £9000. The Roman Watling-street entered this county from London, and passed through Dartford, Rochester, Canterbury, and across Barham Downs to Dover. The number of castles that have been erected in this county is very considerable, and many of them yet remain either more or less perfect. Of these, the immense fortress of Dover may be regarded as the principal; and this is now garrisoned with a strong force, as are also several others on the sea coast; but most of the castles in the interior of the county are dismantled, and mouldering in ruins. The principal rivers that intersect or bound this county, are the Thames, the Medway, the Greater and Lesser Stour, the Darent, the Cray, and the Raversbourne. At Dartford began the insurrection of Wat Tyler and

COUNTY OF KENT.

The Weald.

Romney Marsh.

Rivers.

Map.	Names of Places.	County.	Number of Miles from			Dist. Lond.	Popu-lation.
36	Kentford ....pa	Suffolk	Newmarket .4	Mildenhall...4	Bury St. Ed. 12	67	109
11	Kentisbeare ....pa	Devon	Collumpton..3	Honiton 8	Ott. St. Mary 9	161	1336
11	Kentisbury ....pa	Devon	Barnstable ..9	SouthMolton14	Dulverton ..21	189	307
25	Kentish Town* ..ham	Middlesex ..	Highgate....2	Hampstead ..2	Islington 3	3	....
40	Kentmere ....to	Westmorlnd	Kendal......9	Chudleigh ...6	Troutbeck ..7	271	212
11	Kenton† .... .pa	Devon	Exeter 6	Chudleigh ...6	Topsham 4	174	2050
29	Kenton............to	Northumb ..	Newcastle ..3	N. Shields ..7	S. Shields...8	277	1204
36	Kenton............pa	Suffolk	Framlingham 6	Debenham ..2	Needham...10	93	252
34	Kenton Mandeville. pa	Somerset ...	Somerton ...4	Glastonbury .7	Castle Cary..7	120	349
8	Kenwyn ....pa	Cornwall...	Truro 1	Redruth 7	St. Michael ..6	258	8492
22	Kenyon ....to	Lancaster...	Newton 3	Manchester 13	Warrington..7	195	396
44	Kepwick...........to	N. R. York.	Thirsk 6	Stokesley....9	N. Allerton..7	225	170
27	Kerdeston.........pa	Norfolk	Reepham....2	Holt 8	Aylesham ..7	113	160
39	Keresley ....ham	Warwick ..	Coventry ...3	Nuneaton ...6	Coleshill .. .10	94	386
7	Kermineham........to	Chester ...	Congleton ..6	Knutsford ..7	Middlewich .6	167	176
8	Kerrier ....hun	Cornwall ...	....	....	....	....	51313
30	Kersall...........ham	Nottingham.	Ollerton 5	Southwell ...5	Kneesall 2	137	82
36	Kersey............pa	Suffolk.....	Hadleigh 2	Lavenham ..7	Sudbury....10	66	700
11	Kerswell, Abbots...pa	Devon	Newton 2	Ashburton ..6	Totness 6	198	437
11	Kerswell, Kings ...pa	Devon	4	8	6	192	679
36	Kesgrave..........pa	Suffolk	Ipswich ...4	Woodbridge 4	Needham .. 12	73	102
36	Kessingland‡ .. ...pa	Suffolk	Lowestoff ...6	Beccles 9	Southwold ..7	112	666
21	Keston§...........pa	Kent	Bromley 5	Westerham ..6	Farningham 10	16	252

COUNTY OF KENT. Jack Straw, who afterwards mustered a vast force on Blackheath, near Greenwich, and marched to London. Swanescombe, near Gravesend, is the place where, it is said, the Kentish men, concealed by boughs of trees, met William the Conqueror, and demanded and obtained the confirmation of all their rights and privileges, as the condition of their submission.

* KENTISH TOWN, a hamlet and chapelry in the parish of St. Pancras, Holborn division of the hundred of Ossulton. This place is described in Doomesday Book as a manor belonging to the canons of St. Paul's; and it gives title to the Prebendary of Cantelows, or Kentish Town, who is now lord of the manor, and holds a cout-leet and court-baron. Here, William Bruges, garter king at arms, in the reign of Henry V., had a country house, at which he entertained the German Emperor, Sigismund, who visited England, in 1416, to promote a negotiation for peace with France. The situation of Kentish Town is pleasant and healty; and the limits of the village have, within a few years past, been considerably extended, by the erection of new streets and ranges of handsome houses.

Visit of the German Emperor.

† KENTON, a parish in the hundred of Exminster, situated at the confluence of the rivers Ken and Ex. A custom prevails here that if the issue of any of the tenants hold their tenements for three successive descents, they may claim it as their inheritance.

Curious custom.

‡ KESSINGLAND, a parish in the hundred of Mutford and Lothingland; it formerly had a weekly market, and was a place of much greater importance than at present. The church, which is dedicated to St. Edmund, has a lofty square steeple, containing five bells; the font, which is very ancient, is of an octagonal form, having on each of the eight sides the figure of a saint in a sitting posture, and, underneath each of these, the figure of another saint, standing on a pedestal. The old church was considerably larger than the present structure, which was erected about 1694.

Ancient church.

§ KESTON, a parish in the hundred of Ruxley, lathe of Sutton-at-Home. On the west side of Holwood-hill are the remains of an immense Roman encampment; its form is elliptical, but approaching to a circle; it is surrounded by triple ditches and ramparts of vast height and depth, and measures nearly two miles in the outward circumference.

Roman encampment.

Map.	Names of Places.	County.	Number of Miles from			Dist. Lond.	Popu- lation.
9	Keswick* ...m t & cha	Cumberland	Cockermout 12	Penrith 17	Workington 20	290	2159
27	Keswick............pa	Norfolk.....	Norwich 3	Wymondham 6	Attleboro' ..11	106	104
27	Keswick ....ham	Norfolk....	N. Walsham 5	Holt.......4	Wells 8	118	....
45	Keswick, East......to	W. R. York.	Wetherby ..5	Otley 7	Leeds 6	201	296
33	Ketley.............to	Salop	Wellington ..2	Newport 7	Shiffnal......6	146	....
28	Ketering† ...m t & pa	Northamp..	Rothwell....4	Thrapston ..10	Wellingboro' 8	74	4099
27	Ketteringham ......pa	Norfolk...	Wymondham 4	Norwich 6	Attleborough 9	103	175
36	Kettlebaston ......pa	Suffolk	Bildeston... 2	Lavenham ..6	Sudbury....11	65	190
36	Kettleburgh........pa	Suffolk	Framlingham 2	Debenham ..7	Woodbridge .9	88	360

KESTON.

At a short distance from the outer ditch is the spring-head of the river Ravensborne, from which the soldiers were supplied with water, and a plain way leading down to it can still be traced.

Romantic country.

* KESWICK, an ancient market-town and chapelry in the parish of Crosthwaite, ward of Allerdale, below Darwent, situated on the eastern side of the vale of Keswick, and on the banks of the lake of Derwentwater, in a most romantic tract of country, encompassed with rocky hills, rich in mineral productions, and watered by the rapid river Greta. On the north rises the lofty mountain of Skiddaw, and near its base is the lake of Bassenthwaite, or Broadwater. The town consists of one long street, and the houses are built of stone. It was a place of some note in the beginning of the fourteenth century, as it appears that a customary market was then held here. The manor is now vested in the commissioners and governors of Greenwich-hospital, as part of the forfeited estate of the Earl of Derwentwater; and manor courts are held in the town-hall, at spring and autumn, when a constable is appointed for the government of the town. The parish church of Crosthwaite stands about three quarters of a mile north-west of the town; and within the parish there are five chapels-of-ease, besides places of worship for Dissenters. In the town are a free-school and a workhouse.

Manufac- tures.

The manufactures of Keswick consist principally of coarse woollens, but more recently cloth of a finer texture has also been made here. Blacklead pencils are made here in considerable quantities; and though the copper-works are extinct, a vein of lead ore, which is very productive, is now worked not far from the lake of Derwentwater. There are in the town two museums of mineral specimens and other curiosities, collected by individuals, for public exhibition. Keswick is highly worthy of the note it enjoys, as the fashionable resort of a great number of strangers in the summer season. Its situation is of the romantic and picturesque character, diversified by lofty mountains, lakes, woods, and water-falls. The beautiful limpid lake of Derwent is half a mile south of the town, the banks of which are ornamented by several tasteful and rural seats, the summer residences of opulent individuals. A mile and a half south of Keswick is a remarkable arrangement of rude granite stones, of various forms, about fifty in number, which form a circle, and is called the Druid's Temple; they are rough and unhewn, of different sizes, some being upwards of eight feet in height. A short distance to the south of Derwent lake are two mineral springs, which were formerly in high repute.

Market, Saturday.—*Fair*, August 2, for leather and woollen yarn.

TheChurch.

† KETTERING, a market-town and parish, situated on a gentle ascent, near a rivulet that runs into the Nen; the inhabitants are chiefly employed in sorting, working, combing, and spinning wool. The church, which is dedicated to St. Peter and St. Paul, consists of a nave, north and south aisles, and a chancel, with a handsome tower and spire, containing eight bells and a set of chimes. The tower consists of three stories, in each of which are large windows of several compartments; the angles are flanked with double buttresses; under the embattled parapet runs an ornamented fascia, and at each corner is raised a small hexan-

Map	Names of Places.	County.	Number of Miles from			Dist. Lond.	Popu lation.
23	Kettleby ....ham	Leicester ...	Mel.Mowbray2	Leicester ...13	Loughboro' .14	108	....
24	Kettlesby ....pa	Lincoln ...	Spilsby 6	Louth 9	Horncastle ..9	139	....
7	Kettles Hulme......to	Chester.....	Macclesfield .7	C. in le Frith 5	Buxton.....8	153	354
27	Kettleston ....pa	Norfolk.....	Fakenham ...4	N.Walsingha 4	Holt.......8	113	230
24	Kettlethorpe ....pa	Lincoln ...	Lincoln.....9	Gainsboro'..10	Newark....16	142	399
45	Kettlewell*.......pa	W. R. York	Skipton 14	Askrigg 12	Hawes 12	232	673
32	Ketton...........pa	Rutland ...	Stamford 4	Uppingham..9	Empingham 4	91	810
58	Kevenleece ....hun	Radnor ...				....	3135
8	Keverne ....pa	Cornwall ...	Falmouth ...9	Helstone .. 10	Penryn ...10	279	2437
37	Kewt.............pa	Surrey.....	Kingston ...6	Wandsworth 5	Hounslow ...4	6	837
8	Kew, St...........pa	Sussex	Hurst 2	Lewes 8	Steyning ...10	45	1218
8	Keyne............pa	Cornwall ...	Liskeard 3	L. Withiel..10	West Looe ..5	227	153
34	Keynsham ....hun	Somerset ...				....	9029
34	Keynsham‡...m t & pa	Somerset ...	Bristol 5	Bath.......7	Pensford 4	109	2142

KETTERING. gular embattled turret; the whole surmounted by a handsome hexagonal crocketed spire, with three windows, diminishing in their size upwards, on the alternate sides. Dr. John Gill was born here, in 1697.

Market, Saturday.—*Fairs*, Thursday before Easter; Friday before Whit Sunday; Thursday before October 11, for horses and horned cattle, sheep, hogs, and pedlery; Thursday before December 21; and a Friday fortnight market for sheep and cattle.

* KETTLEWELL. *Fairs*, July 6, and September 2, for sheep.

† KEW, a village and parish, agreeably situated on the southern bank of the Thames. This place has been chiefly distinguished as the site of a royal mansion, which was the residence of Frederick, Prince of Wales, who held the property on lease. The freehold was purchased by George III., who enlarged the gardens belonging to the mansion. The Orangery and the Pagoda, which is 163 feet high, were open to the public, until the absurdity of the visitors, in carving their names on every plain piece of wood they could find, produced an order against their admission. Celebrated for its botanic garden. Besides the garden belonging to the palace, Kew has long been celebrated for its botanic garden, which was enriched, by George III., with a vast multitude and variety of exotic trees, shrubs, and plants, from every quarter of the globe. The old palace, in which Queen Charlotte died, and all the royal family were brought up, a plain brick building, is still standing, and occasionally visited by the royal family. An unfinished palace, built by Mr. Wyatt, in conformity with the taste of George III., has, since his death, been pulled down. Kew was formerly a hamlet of the parish of Kingston; but, in 1769, it was constituted, by act of Parliament, a distinct parish. The living is a vicarage, with Petersham, in the archdeaconry of Surrey, and diocese of Winchester. The church, dedicated to St. Anne, is a brick structure, built and consecrated, in 1714, on ground given to the parish by Queen Anne. It was designed as a chapel-of-ease to Kingston; and was erected instead of another, which had been originally founded as a private chapel, in 1522. The approach to this village, from the great western road, is by a stone bridge of seven arches over the Thames, besides a land-arch on each side, which was erected in 1789, and is now the property of a private individual. Kew is lighted with gas from Brentford.

‡ KEYNSHAM, a market-town and parish, situated on the south bank of the river Avon, over which is the county bridge, built of stone, and consisting of fifteen arches, leading to Gloucester; and another over the river Chew, which here falls into the Avon, leading to Bath. It is Founded by Princess Keyna. supposed to have derived its name from Keyna, daughter of Braganus, Prince of the province of Wales, now called Brecknockshire, who is said to have been the foundress of the town, the site of which was previously a wild forest. The town is built upon a rock, and consists of one street, nearly a mile in length. Here was formerly a considerable clothing-trade, which has now almost totally declined; but the poorer inhabitants are

Map	Names of Places.	County.	Number of Miles from			Dist. Lond.	Popu-lation.
12	Keynston Tarrant...pa	Dorset......	Blanford.....4	Wimborne...8	Bere Regis..10	105	220
3	Keysoe............pa	Bedford	Kimbolton ..4	H. Ferrers ..9	St. Neots 8	58	718
19	Keyston...........pa	Huntingdon.	Huntingdon..6	Peterboro'..13	Spaldwick ...5	65	196
23	Keythorpe.........lib	Leicester ...	Mt. Harboro'.9	M.Mowbray 14	Leicester ...10	86	26
30	Keyworth.........pa	Nottingham.	Nottingham .7	Bingham ...10	Broughton .. 6	117	552
35	Kibblestone.......lib	Stafford	Stone 1	Newcastle..10	Cheadle....10	140	1089
13	Kibblesworth......to	Durham	Gateshead ..4	Sunderland .10	Durham....10	269	237
54	Kibbor.... ......hun	Glamorgan..	....	....	....	....	2609
23	Kibworth Beau- champ ....pa }	Leicester ...	Mt. Harboro'.6	Leicester 9	Billesden....7	89	1500
23	Kibworth Harcourt .pa	Leicester ...	5	10	8	88	396
21	Kidbrook ....lib	Kent	Blackheath ..1	Bromley.. ..5	Greenwich ..1	5	458
42	Kidderminster*....m t	Worcester..	Worcester..15	Stourbridge..9	Bewdley ...3	126	20865

employed in spinning for those of Bradford and Shepton. Its chief trade now consists in malting. The petty sessions for the hundred are holden here. The church is a large, handsome building, with a fine lofty tower, situated nearly in the centre of the town ; it contains many ancient and curious monuments, and was appropriated to an abbey of black canons, which formerly existed here, and was founded by William, Earl of Gloucester. Here also is a good charity-school, where the children of the poor receive the rudiments of education.

Market, Thursday.—*Fairs*, March 24, and August 15, for cattle and cheese.

KEYNSHAM

* KIDDERMINSTER, a large and populous market and corporation town, having separate jurisdiction, but locally situated in the lower division of the hundred of Halfshire. It stands on the river Stour, not far from its confluence with the Severn ; and close to the town passes the Staffordshire and Worcestershire canal. Members were returned to Parliament for this place in the reign of Edward I., but the privilege was lost by disuse, till the passing of the Reform Bill, and now sends one member. A charter of incorporation was granted by Charles I., in the twelfth year of his reign. The lord of the manor also holds a court-baron ; besides which there is a court of requests held once in three weeks for the recovery of debts under forty shillings. The church is a spacious and venerable Gothic structure, with a lofty tower. There is another episcopal place of worship called St. George's-chapel, a handsome edifice in the Gothic or pointed style of architecture, erected in 1823, at the estimated expense of £16,401, under the sanction of the commissioners for building new churches and chapels. Over the altar is suspended a beautiful specimen of carpet weaving, exhibiting a picture of the Descent from the Cross, interesting as an example of the progress of arts and manufactures in the town. Here are chapels for the Independents, Wesleyan Methodists, Unitarians, and Baptists. At the east end of the old church, adjoining the choir, is a room appropriated to the free grammar-school, and in the town are two national schools and an infant school, besides which there are Sunday schools connected with the church, and others supported by the dissenters. Among the other charitable institutions are twelve alms-houses, and a dispensary for the gratuitous supply of medicines to the sick. The town consists of ranges of buildings extending nearly a mile from north to south-east, and about half a mile in breadth ; the streets are well paved, and lighted with gas, and are kept clean by means of underground sewers, which prevent, in some degree, the inconvenience to which the inhabitants of the lower streets were formerly exposed from inundations. Kidderminster was noted, in the reign of Henry VIII., for the manufacture of broad-cloth, afterwards for that of linsey-woolsey, and more recently for the making of crapes, bombazines, and poplins. In 1735, the manufacture of Scotch carpeting was introduced, and subsequently that of cut carpets was established, which sort of goods having been invented here, has obtained the distinction of Kidderminster carpets. Brussels carpets are likewise made here in a style

A very respectable market town.

Beautiful specimen of carpet weaving, representing the Descent from the Cross.

Celebrated for carpet weaving.

6 o

Map.	Names of Places.	County.	Number of Miles from			Dist. Lond.	Popu-lation.
31	Kiddington, Nether .pa	Oxford.....	Enstone....3	Woodstock.5	Deddington.8	71	....
31	Kiddington, Upper .div	Oxford....	3	Chip.Norton.7	11	70	252
45	Kid Hall.....ham	W. R. York	Leeds......8	Wetherby..5	Tadcaster...3	203	124
29	Kidland........ex pa	Northumb..	Rothbury...12	Wooler....6	New Bewick 5	315	62
31	Kidlington.........pa	Oxford....	Woodstock..4	Oxford.....6	Bicester...8	70	1217
49	Kidwelly*....m t & pa	Carmarthen.	Carmarthen.8	Llaugharne..9	Lochor.....12	231	10001
15	Kiftsgate.........hun	Gloucester.				....	15087
11	Kighbeare.......ham	Devon......	Oakhampton.2	Hatherleigh..5	Holsworthy.17	196	116
25	Kilbourne †......ham	Middlesex..	Stanmore...9	Brentford...8	Paddington ..2	3	....
10	Kilburn ....to	Derby.....	Derby 7	Alfreton ...6	Eastwood ...6	133	590
44	Kilburn...........pa	N. R. York.	Easingwold..7	N. Allerton..9	Aldborough.11	224	529
23	Kilby............pa	Leicester...	Leicester 6	Lutterworth.9	Mt.Harboro'10	90	409
44	Kildale...........pa	N. R. York	Stokesley....6	Guisborough 4	Whitby 16	246	209
45	Kildwick..........pa	W. R. York	Skipton 4	Keighley....4	Broughton...7	214	9926
57	Kilgarran† .....hun	Pembroke...				....	5021

KIDDER-MINSTER.

of excellence highly creditable to the skill and taste of the Kidderminster manufacturers, whose productions are said to be unrivalled for elegance of design, and permanence, and brilliancy of colour. There is a considerable market for the sale of corn, held by charter, on Thursdays; and a market on Saturdays, for butcher's meat and other provisions, has been established within a few years.

Market, Thursday.—Fairs, Palm Monday, for cattle, sheep, and pedlery; Holy Thursday; June 20; September 4; and November 26, for horned cattle, horses, cheese, linen, and woollen cloths.

* KIDWELLY, a market-town and parish, situated on the banks of the river Gwendraeth, which, about a mile and a half hence, falls into another, called Gwendraeth Fawr; from this junction, and the circumstance of their afterwards falling into Carmarthen Bay, the town derives its name, as the Welsh word Cidwelli signifies to go into one place. The town is divided into old and new, by the river, and united by a bridge; the former, now in a decayed state, was anciently defended by a strong wall; and over one of its old gates is the present town-hall and prison. Its chief trade is in coals, raised about four miles hence, which

Considerable trade in coal, iron, tin, &c.

are conveyed by a canal to the vessels lying in the docks, where there is also a very commodious quay. The manufactures are in iron and tin, there being an iron-foundry of considerable extent in the town, and a tin-mill at about a mile distant; the latter exports a large quantity of tin annually, to all parts of the kingdom. The port has been latterly much improved by Lord Cawdor. The town, which is within the jurisdiction of the Duchy of Lancaster, was incorporated in the reign of Henry VI.

Market, Tuesday and Friday.—Fairs, May 24; July 22, and October 29, for cattle and pedlery.

† KILBOURNE, a hamlet in the parish of Hampstead, and Holborn division of the hundred Ossulton. This place has been rapidly increasing, in extent and population, for some years past. Coldbourne-stream, which rises near Westend, Hampstead, and from which this place takes

A stream here supplies the Serpentine river in Hyde-park.

its name, passes through Kilbourne to Bayswater; and after supplying the Serpentine reservoir, in Hyde-park, flows into the Thames, at Ranelagh.

‡ KILGARRAN, or Cil-Geran, an ancient town, situated upon the river Teifi. The town, which is without any regular plan, contains chapels for Baptists and Wesleyans, but the church stands at a little distance. Every burgess has an undisputed right of opening a quarry within the lordship, in consequence of which many quarries of excellent slate are worked here, and a valuable export-trade carried on from the port of Cardigan. There

Celebrated for its salmon fishery.

is also a manufacture of strong shoes here, which employs many hands, and the salmon-fishery of the Teifi is an incessant source of profit, and an auxiliary to subsistence, almost every poor person being an accom-

Map.	Names of Places.	County.	Number of Miles from			Dist. Lond.	Popu- lation.
57	Kilgarran......to & pa	Pembroke ..	Cardigan 4	Newport ...11	Narbeth 16	239	879
26	Kilgwrwg...........pa	Monmouth..	Usk 6	Chepstow ...6	Caerleon ...10	136	113
29	Kilham............to	Northumb..	Wooler 7	Coldstream ..6	NewBewick14	327	246
46	Kilham*..........pa	E. R. York.	Gt. Driffield .5	Rudstone....3	Hunmanby ..9	201	1022
8	Kilkhamp on†.....pa	Cornwall ...	Stratton ...4	Newport ...20	Camelford ..19	226	1126
10	Killamarsh..........pa	Derby	Chesterfield .9	Sheffield 9	Dronfield....8	159	774
13	Killerby...........to	Durham ...	Darlington ..7	B. Auckland.5	Staindrop ...5	244	107
28	Kill sby...........pa	Northamp..	Daventry ...6	Crick 6	Welford....12	78	687
51	Killian Avron ...pa	Cardigan....	Lampeter....8	Llan.Rhystyd5	Tregaron ...9	219	320
24	Killinghall.........to	W. R. York	Knaresboro' .4	Ripon 7	Harrowgate.4	216	545
24	Killingholme, North } and South ......pa }	Lincoln ..	Gt. Grimsby .9	Barton....10	Castor......12	168	438
40	Killington....ti & cha	Westmorlnd.	Kir.Lonsdale 8	Kendal......8	Sedberg 3	260	335
46	Killingwold Grove ham	E. R. York .	Beverley ...2	Mt. Weighton 7	Pocklington 13	185	....
29	Killingworth.......pa	Northumb..	Newcastle ..6	Blyth 7	Morpeth....10	280	....
31	Kilmersdon.......hun	Somerset ..	....			....	6622
34	Kilmersdon..........pa	Somerset ...	Frome 6	Bath 9	Wells......11	109	2129
16	Kilm ston.........pa	Hants	N. Alresford.5	Petersfield ..11	Hambledon ..8	62	212
11	Kilm ngton........pa	Devon......	Axminster ..2	Honiton 6	Colyton 4	149	540
34	Kilmington‡........pa	Somerset ...	Bruton 6	Frome 8	Wincanton ..7	106	580
44	Kilnsea §..........pa	W. R. York	Settle 11	Masham 12	Askrigg 10	229	137
43	Kilnwick .....pa & to	E. R. York .	Gt. Driffield .6	NewMalton 14	Sledmere ...8	192	230
34	Kiloe ....pa	Somerset ...	Bridgewater 11	Watchet ...7	N. Stowey ..5	152	263
17	Kilpeck............pa	Hereford ..	Hereford 9	Monmouth .12	Ross 12	136	265
46	Kilpin............to	E. R. York .	Howden 2	Burton......7	South Cave .9	183	318

plished fisherman, and proprietor of a species of boat called a coracle, a simple invention, of early origin, and well known, to this day, both in Wales and Ireland. The castle, once the great boast of Kilgarran, is now much ruined. The magnificent remains occupy the crown of a lofty and precipitous rocky promontory, standing boldly out into the river, and all tourists are recommended to survey its noble proportions, and to enjoy the fine landscape which it helps to compose, from the surface of the water only.

Market, Wednesday, now discontinued.—*Fairs*, August 21, and November 12.

* KILHAM, a parish, partly within the liberty of St. Peter of York, and partly in the wapentake of Dickering, nearly a mile and a quarter long, running from east to west. It is pleasantly situated amidst the Wold hills, in a fertile soil; and seems to have been formerly of much greater importance than at present, having once had a market which is now disused. Here, after a wet autumn, the Vipsey, or Gipsey, bursts out, and the violence of the spring, when it first issues from the ground, is said to be so great, that a man on horseback may ride under its arched stream.

The violence of the Gipsey spring.

Fairs, August 21, and November 12, for horses and beasts.

† KILKHAMPTON. The church is a light and handsome edifice, consisting of three aisles divided by slender pillars, supporting obtuse pointed arches, and containing many handsome monuments, amongst which is one to the memory of Sir Bevil Grenville, who was killed in the celebrated battle of Lansdown, near Bath.

Sir Bevil Grenville.

‡ KILMIGTON. About two miles from the church is a stately tower, and on a tablet over the entrance is the following inscription:— " Alfred the Great, A. D. 879, on this summit erected his standard against Danish invaders. To him we owe the origin of juries, and the creation of a naval force. Alfred, the light of that benighted age, was a philosopher and a Christian, the father of his people, and the founder of the English monarchy and liberties."

Monument to Alfred the Great.

§ KILNSEA, a parish in the south division of the wapentake of Holderness. The church is in a very dilapidated state, and will probably soon become a prey to the depredations of the ocean, which has been making progressive encroachments on this coast for many years. Here is

Map.	Names of Places.	County	Number of Miles from			Dist. Lond.	Popu-lation.
34	Kilton ....pa	Somerset....	Bridgewater 10	Watchet 7	N. Stowey ..4	152	149
13	Kilton.............to	N. R York .	Guisboro'...5	Whitby 11	Easington ...4	255	100
27	Kilverston ....pa	Norfolk.....	Thetford ...2	E. Harling...7	Attleboro ..12	82	31
30	Kilvington ....pa	Nottingham.	Newark ...7	Southwell ..11	Bingham 7	125	24
14	Kilvington, North...to	N. R. York .	Thirsk ...2	N Allerton..6	Stokesley...14	225	68
44	Kilvington, South pa & to	N. R. York.	1	7	15	224	260
23	Kilworth, North....pa	Leicester ...	Lutterworth .5	H. Bosworth.2	Hinckley ...15	82	391
23	Kilworth, South ...pa	Leicester ...	5	3	14	82	450
27	Kimberley ....pa	Norfolk.....	Wymondham 3	E. Dereham..9	Norwich ...12	103	145
14	Kimberworth.......to	W. R. York	Rotheram....2	Sheffield 8	Barnsley 7	161	3797
5	Kimble, Great* .....pa	Bucks......	Wendover ..3	P. Risboro' ..4	Amersham ..9	36	360
5	Kimble, Little ......pa	Bucks	3	5	8	35	165
13	Kimblesworth ..ex pa	Durham ...	Durham 3	Newcastle..12	Wolsingham 12	262	32
17	Kimbolton† ....pa	Hereford ...	Leominster ..3	Ludlow 10	Tenbury 7	140	719
19	Kimbolton....m t & to	Huntingdon.	St. Neots...8	Brington 5	Huntingdon..10	64	1584
23	Kimcote ....pa	Leicester ...	Lutterworth ..3	Mt. Harboro' 9	Leicester ...12	91	505
29	Kimerston..........to	Northumb	Wooler.....5	Coldstream ..7	Belford 11	325	....
18	Kimpton ....pa	Herts	Welwyn 4	Luton.....6	Hitchin 7	27	944
16	Kimpton ....pa	Hants	Ludgershall..3	Andover.....6	Amesbury ..9	67	366
12	Kincombe, Nether and Over......ti	Dorset......	Beaminster ..6	Cerne Abbas.7	Bridport.....8	127	159
0	Kinder............to	Derby.....	C -le-Frith...4	Mottram 8	Hayfield 1	172	129
7	Kinderton‡ ....to	Chester.....	Middlewich .2	Northwich ..5	Tarporley ..10	167	493
39	Kineton§ ....m t	Warwick...	Warwick ..11	Stratford ...10	Southam ...11	83	1102
35	Kinfare ....pa	Stafford.....	Stourbridge ..3	Kidderminst. 3	Hales Owen..8	126	1831
24	Kingerley ....pa	Lincoln.....	Mt. Raisin...5	Glan. Bridge 9	Caistor 8	147	84

KILNSEA. the well-known promontory of Spurnhead, the southernmost point of Holderness; it may be called an island, as it is joined to the mainland by a narrow neck of sand, about a mile and a half in length, which is frequently overflowed by a high tide; it contains two light-houses and a few cottages, and it is also a station for a life-boat.

* KIMBLE, Great. This place is said to derive its name from the British King, Cunobelin, and, from several fortifications and trenches in the vicinity, is supposed to have been the place where the brave sons of that monarch opposed the progress of the Romans. A hill at a short distance hence still bears the name of Belinesbury.

Seat of the Duke of Manchester. † KIMBOLTON, a small market-town, celebrated only for its magnificent castle, the seat of the Duke of Manchester; it is a quadrangular building, of most superb construction, which contains a fine collection of paintings. Queen Catherine resided in this town for a considerable time after her divorce from Henry VIII.

Market, Friday.—Fairs, Friday in Easter week, for pedlery and sheep; and December 11, for cattle and hogs.

Cheshire barons. ‡ KINDERTON, a township in the parish of Middlewich, and hundred of Northwich, generally believed to be the Condate of the Romans. It gave title to one of the ancient barons who composed the Parliament of Earl Lupus. This was the family of Venables, now represented by Lord Vernon, of Kinderton, the only lineal successor of the eight Cheshire barons that has descended to the present times.

King John occasionally held his court here. § KINETON, a small market-town and parish, in the hundred of Kington. A castle existed here at an early period, which was situated westward of the town, where King John occasionally held his court; and a neighbouring spring is still named King John's-well. Kineton is pleasantly situated on the banks of a stream which falls into the Avon; and it comprises two streets, through one of which passes the turnpike-road from Warwick to Banbury. Lord Willoughby de Broke, who is the proprietor of the manor, has a noble seat at Compton Verney, about two miles and a half from the town.

Market, Tuesday, St. Paul (January 25) for seed and corn; St. Luke, (October 18) for cattle and cheese.

Map	Names of Places.	County.	Number of Miles from			Dist. Lond.	Popu-lation.
31	Kingham ....pa	Oxford	Chip. Norton 4	Burford 8	Deddington 14	79	504
21	Kinghamford ......hun	Kent				....	1669
11	Kingsbridge* .....m t	Devon	Dartmouth ..9	Modbury 8	Plym. Earls.16	208	1586
41	Kingsbridge......hun	Wilts				....	966
25	Kingsbury..........pa	Middlesex ..	Stanmore ...5	Hampstead ..4	Brentford....8	8	360
34	Kingsbury ....hun	Somerset ...				....	19962
39	Kingsbury..........pa	Warwick...	Coleshill ...5	Tamworth ..6	Birmingham 12	108	1314
34	Kingsbury, Episcopi pa	Somerset ...	Langport 3	Bridgewater 13	Taunton....13	128	1695
17	King's Caple ....pa	Hereford ...	Ross.......5	Hereford 8	Monmouth..13	129	271
16	Kingsclere ......hun	Hants				....	18070
16	Kingsclere† ....m t	Hants	Basingstoke.10	Whitchurch 8	Odham 17	54	3151
28	King's Cliffe‡.....pa	Northamp ..	Duddington ..4	Rockingham 11	Peterboro'..12	85	1173
15	Kingscote ....pa	Gloucester..	Tetbury 9	Berkley 6	Wotton 5	109	266
34	Kingsdon..........pa	Somerset ...	Somerton ..2	Wincanton .13	Ilchester ...3	122	610
21	Kingsdown vil	Kent	Deal 3	Dover 6	Canterbury .16	71	....
21	Kingsdown ......pa	Kent......	Sittingbourn .4	Maidstone ..11	16	39	75
21	Kingsdown ......pa	Kent	Wrotham ..3	Dartford.....7	Gravesend ..8	24	438
5	Kingsey ....pa	Bucks	Thame.....3	Aylesbury ..7	Wendover ..8	46	204
42	Kingsford........ham	Worcester..	Kidderminst. 2	Stourbridge..5	Bewdley 5	128	....
17	Kingsham ....pa	Hereford ...	Presteigne ..3	Leominster .10	Kington 7	148	107
30	Kingshaugh......ham	Nottingham.	Tuxford 3	Chesterfield..8	Ollerton 10	140	....
15	Kingsholme......ham	Gloucester..	Gloucester ..1	Newent 3	Tewksbury. 10	109	....
17	Kingsland§.......pa	Hereford ...	Leominster ..4	Presteign...10	Ludlow 12	141	1074
25	Kingsland ‖ .....ham	Middlesex ..	Hackney 1	Islington 1	Tottenham ..4	2	....
7	Kingsley ....to	Chester....	Frodsham ..4	Northwich ..6	Tarvin 7	180	934
16	Kingsley ....pa	Hants	Alton 4	Farnham 6	Haslemere ..9	47	373
35	Kingsley ....pa	Stafford	Cheadle....2	Leek 7	Ashborn....10	148	1416
7	King's Marsh....ex pa	Chester	Gt. Neston .11	Frodsham ..10	Eastham 8	184	46
9	Kingsmoor ......ex pa	Cumberland	Carlisle 2	Wigton 10	Longtown ...7	304	162
21	King's North.......pa	Kent	Ashford 3	Tenterden ..9	Hythe......11	58	372
42	King's Norton ......pa	Worcester..	Birmingham .5	Bromsgrove..9	Stourbridge 11	116	3977
17	King's Pyon ......pa	Hereford...	Weobly 3	Hereford ...10	Leominster ..7	147	376
16	King's Sombourn ..hun	Hants				....	7962
28	King's Sutton ....hun	Northamp ..				....	11897
11	Kingsteinton ....pa	Devon	Newt.Bushel 2	Chudleigh ..5	Totness 10	186	1288
28	Kingsthorpe........pa	Northamp ..	Northampton 2	Welford....11	Mt.Harboro'13	68	1344

* KINGSBRIDGE, a small market-town, pleasantly situated on an islet of the English Channel, called Salcombe river; it derives its name, according to Risdon, from the bridge by which it is connected with Dodbrooke. David Tolley, a celebrated scholar of the time of Henry VIII., was a native of this town. — *Birthplace of Tolley.*

Market, Saturday.—*Fair*, July 20, for horned cattle, cloth, and shoes.

† KINGSCLERE. *Market*, Tuesday.—*Fair*, April 2, and October 15, for sheep.

‡ KING'S CLIFFE, a parish in the hundred of Willybrook, formerly a market-town, which derives its name either from King John having had a hunting-seat here, or merely from its belonging to the crown. The inhabitants of this parish being tenants in ancient demesne, are exempted from the payment of tolls throughout England. The Rev. William Law, a celebrated polemical and non-juring divine, was a native of King's Cliffe, where he was born, in 1686, and lived in retirement, having refused preferments on account of the required oaths. — *Singular privilege.*

Market, Tuesday, disused.—*Fair*, October 29, for cheese, homespun linen, and turners' ware.

§ KINGSLAND. This parish was part of the great inheritance of the Mortimers; in the reign of Edward I., Margaret, widow of Lord Mortimer, procured a grant for a market and fair; the former has long been disused. It is said that Kingsland formerly had a castle, in which King Merwald was buried.

Fair, October 10, for horses, horned cattle, hops, cheese, and butter.

‖ KINGSLAND, a hamlet in the parish of Hackney, Tower division of the hundred of Ossulton, now forming a portion of the north-eastern suburb of the metropolis. It consists principally of irregular ranges of buildings, extending from Shoreditch-church to Stoke Newington, along the high road from London to Royston and Ware.

Map	Names of Places.	County.	Number of Miles from			Dist. Lond.	Popu-lation
6	Kingston ....pa	Cambridge .	Caxton......3	Royston ...10	Cambridge ..8	46	279
11	Kingston ....pa	Devon......	Modbury 3	Plym Earls ..8	Kingsbridge .8	211	504
17	Kingston ....pa	Hereford....	Hereford ...7	Hay 15	Monmouth..17	142	406
21	Kingston ....pa	Kent	Canterbury ..5	Dover 12	Ashford 11	58	301
34	Kingston ....pa	Somerset ...	Ilminster ...2	Crewkerne ..4	Chard 4	135	892
16	Kingston ....pa	Hants	Newport ...6	Brading 9	Newtown ...8	95	68
35	Kingston ....pa	Stafford....	Uttoxeter ...4	Abb.Bromley 3	Stafford 11	132	368
38	Kingston ....pa	Sussex	Lit.Hampton 4	Worthing ...4	Arundel 6	57	61
42	Kingston ....pa	Worcester..	Worcester . 9	Alcester....7	Droitwich..8	106	153
4	Kingston Baypuze ..pa	Berks	Abingdon ..7	Farringdon ..8	Oxford.....10	63	306
31	Kingston Blount ....to	Oxford.....	Tetsworth...4	Thame.....5	Watlington..5	41	....
41	Kingston Deverill...pa	Wilts......	Mere.......4	Warminster .6	Hindon 6	102	380
46	Kingston upon Hull .. seaport & bo to	E. R. York.	Beverley....9	Hedon......6	Gt. Driffield 22	174	32958
38	Kingston by Lewes..pa	Sussex	Lewes......2	Brighton.....6	Newhaven...6	52	160
4	Kingston Lisle ti & cha	Berks	Wantage....5	Farringdon ..5	Shrivenham .5	65	357
12	Kingston Russell..ex ....pa ham	Dorset......	Dorchester ..2	Cerne Abbas.9	Bere Reges .12	118	76
38	Kingston by Sea ....pa	Sussex	Shoreham....2	Brighton 5	Steyning.....6	57	60
34	Kingston Seymour ..pa	Somerset ..	Axbridge....9	Wrington ...5	Bristol......14	132	368
30	Kingston upon Stour pa	Notts	Nottingham 10	Loughboro' ..7	Derby 14	116	175
37	Kingston upon Thames ....m t	Surrey	Brentford....6	Epsom 7	Staines 10	10	7257
12	KingstonWinterbornpa	Dorset......	Blandford ...7	Bere Regis..3	Wareham ...10	110	56
18	Kings Walden .....pa	Hereford....	Hitchin 4	Luton 5	Welwyn.....8	32	1004
11	Kings Weare......pa	Devon......	Brixham ...3	Dartmouth ..1	Totness.....10	204	275

* KINGSTON-UPON-THAMES. Kingston is situated on the eastern bank of the Thames, over which there was a bridge leading to Hampton, in Middlesex, mentioned in records of the reign of Henry III., and consequently supposed to have been originally founded at an earlier period than any other on the river, except that of London; but the present structure has very recently been erected at the expense of £40,000, advanced as a loan, by Government. It seems to have been the site of a Roman station, coins, urns, and other antique remains having been discovered here. Under the Anglo-Saxons it was a place of great importance, and a royal residence, several monarchs having been crowned here. A council was held at Kingston, by Egbert, in 838; and some writers mention a castle as existing at this place, in the reign of Henry III., who is said to have captured it in his war with the barons; but it was probably only a temporary fort, as there are no traces of any considerable fortress ever having stood here. Towards the end of the civil war, under Charles I., a skirmish took place at Surbiton-common, near Kingston, in which Lord Francis Villiers, brother of the Duke of Buckingham, was killed on the side of the royalists. The first charter of incorporation was granted by King John, in 1199, and others were subsequently given by his successors, the last being that of James II., in 1685; but the town is governed under a charter of Charles I. The petty sessions are held here, as well as the Lent assizes for the county. Members were returned to parliament, for Kingston, in the reigns of Edward I. and Edward II., after which the practice was discontinued on petition of the corporation. The church is a spacious structure, the work of different periods, the oldest part having been apparently erected in the time of Richard II.; it has a square tower between the nave and chancel; and the aisles are modern, having been rebuilt in 1721. An alms-house for six poor men and six women, with a chapel, was founded in 1670, and endowed with landed property, by William Cleave, alderman of London. There is a free grammar-school, for thirty boys, which was founded by Queen Elizabeth, in 1561. In the market-place stands the town-hall, first erected by Elizabeth, but partly rebuilt by James I., when the windows were ornamented with stained glass. In this hall the Lent assizes for the county were formerly held; but a plain brick edifice has been erected within a few years, to which the courts of assize are transferred. The market is held under a charter granted by James I., and renewed by his successor, which, among other

Margin notes: Discovery of Roman coins, &c. / Corporation granted by King John. / County assizes held here.

Map.	Names of Places.	County.	Number of Miles from			Dist. Lond.	Popu-lation.
35	Kingswinford* ....pa	Stafford....	Stourbridge..4	Dudley 4	Wolverhamp.7	130	15156
5	Kingswood ......ham	Bucks......	Aylesbury ..9	Bicester 8	Thame 8	48	....
15	Kingswood† vil	Gloucester..	Bristol.....3	Bath.....9	Sodbury....9	115	....
34	Kingswood .....ham	Somerset....	Wiveliscomb.7	Watchet....4	Minehead...11	153	....
37	Kingswood ....lib	Surrey......	Gatton 2	Reigate 3	Dorking....7	18	....
39	Kingswood ....to	Warwick	Henley 5	Solihull 5	Warwick ..10	102	....
41	Kingswood....vil & pa	Wilts	Wotton un E.1	Wickwar....3	Tetbury ...10	109	1447
16	Kings Worthy.....pa	Hants	Winchester..2	Alresford....7	Basingstoke.16	61	345
43	Kingthorpe ....to	N. R. York.	Pickering ...2	New Malton.8	Scarborough.16	228	....
15	Kington ....ti	Gloucester..	Thornbury...1	Chepstow ..11	Bristol......12	123	4044
17	Kington‡ ...m t & pa	Hereford....	Leominster .14	Weobly 8	Hay.......14	155	3111
12	Kington Magna ...pa	Dorset......	Shaftesbury..7	Wincanton ..7	Sherborne..11	108	539
41	Kington, St. Michael } .... pa & to	Wilts	Chippenham 3	Malmsbury..8	Bath 14	96	1091
41	Kington, West ....pa	Wilts	9	Bath 9	Malmsbury .12	102	298
9	Kingwater ....to	Cumberland.	Carlisle 16	Brampton ..8	Longtown ..18	317	365
34	King Weston ....pa	Somerset....	Somerton...4	Ilchester 6	Wells 10	122	122
33	Kinlet ....pa	Salop......	Bridgenorth..8	Bewdley....8	Clesbury Mtr.5	157	532
17	Kinnaston ....ham	Hereford....	Ledbury.....5	Hereford....11	Ross 10	126	....
33	Kinnerley ....pa	Salop......	Oswestry ...7	Shrewsbury.12	Welchpool ..10	166	1158
17	Kinnersley ....pa	Hereford....	Weobly.....5	Kineton 7	Hay 11	152	351
33	Kinnersley ....pa	Salop	Wellington ..4	Newport 5	Shrewsbury 14	144	295
53	Kinnerton ....to	Flint	Wrexham ...8	Chester....8	Mold. 10	180	....
7	Kinnerton, Lower ..to	Chester....	9	9	Flint 10	180	104
9	Kinneyside ....to	Cumberland.	Egremont ..4	Whitehaven .4	Workington.10	294	....
30	Kinolton ....pa	Notts	Nottingham .9	Bingham....7	Newark ...18	116	389
42	Kinsham ....ti	Worcester..	Tewksbury .4	Upton.......6	Pershore....6	102	....
12	Kinson, or Kinstanton ti	Dorset......	Pool 6	Wimborne ..6	Ringwood...7	99	....
4	Kintbury ....pa	Berks.....	Hungerford ..3	Newbury....6	Reading. ...23	62	1781
17	Kinton ....to	Hereford....	Ludlow 9	Presteign...9	Leominster ..14	152	....
35	Kinvaston ....lib	Stafford....	Stafford....16	Wolverhamp.2	Walsall.....9	123	23
39	Kinwaldsey ......ham	Warwick....	Coleshill....6	Kenilworth .9	Birmingham 12	105	19
39	Kinwardton ......pa	Warwick ..	Alcester 2	Stratford on..8	Henley in Ar. 7	103	40

provisions, ordains that no other market shall be kept within seven miles of the town.

Market, Saturday.—*Fairs*, Thursday, Friday, and Saturday in Whitsun-week, for horses and toys; August 2, for toys; August 3 and 4, for fruit and pedlery; and November 13, for horses, cattle, and toys.

Side note: KINGSTON-UPON-THAMES.

* KINGSWINFORD. A parish in the north division of the hundred of Seisdon, celebrated for its extensive glass and earthenware manufactories. The canals to Dudley, Stourbridge, Wolverhampton, and Stafford, affording facility of communication with the principal rivers of the kingdom, it has become a place of considerable trading importance and opulence.

Side note: Glass and earthenware manufactures.

† KINGSWOOD. An irregularly built village, called also Kingswood-hill, partly within the parish of St. George, Bristol, and partly within that of Bitton, in the upper division of the hundred of Langley and Swineshead, and anciently a part of the royal forest, or chase of Kingswood. Here are numerous coal-mines, many of which are of great depth; and from this neighbourhood the city of Bristol was formerly entirely supplied with fuel. It was at this place that John Wesley, the founder of Methodism, in an early period of his religious career, began preaching to the colliers; and he is said to have effected a considerable reformation of conduct among the dissolute population of Kingswood. There is still subsisting here a seminary, called the Wesleyan School, instituted by Mr. Wesley, in 1748, for the support and classical education of 100 boys, the sons of Methodist ministers. The establishment is under the direction of a governor and six assistant-teachers; and it is chiefly supported by annual contributions.

Side note: Numerous coal mines.

‡ KINGTON, or Kyneton, a market-town, parish, and township, situated on the Black Brook, under Bradnor Mountain; the town in general is well built, and the inhabitants are principally employed in the manufacture of narrow cloth, which is carried on here to a considerable extent. The church is a very irregular structure, having a detached tower,

Side note: Manufacture of cloth.

Map	Names of Places.	County	Number of Miles from			Dist. Lond.	Popu-lation
43	Kiplin..............to	N. R. York.	Catterick ...3	N. Allerton. .7	Darlington ..13	228	103
45	Kippax ......pa & to	W. R. York.	Ferrybridge .6	Leeds 8	Tadcaster ..10	183	1901
39	Kirby Monks ....pa	Warwick ..	Rugby......7	Lutterworth .6	Coventry ...10	92	1637
14	Kirby in le Soken..pa	Essex	Manningtree 10	Harwich ...11	Colchester..15	65	972
38	Kirdford...........pa	Sussex	Petworth....5	Horsham ...11	Godalming..13	46	1653
9	Kirk Andrews upon Eden ....pa	Cumberland	Carlisle 3	Longtown ...7	Wigton.....11	304	107
9	Kirk Andrews upon Esk* ....pa & to	Cumberland	Longtown ...3	Longholm...7	Carlisle.....12	313	2053
9	Kirk Bride ....pa	Cumberland	Wigton....6	Annan......8	12	313	383
46	Kirk Burn.....pa & to	E. R. York .	Gt. Driffield .4	Beverley ..11	Poklington..15	195	489
22	Kirkby .....to & cha	Lancaster...	Prescot.....6	Ormskirk...6	Liverpool...7	203	1190
24	Kirkby............pa	Lincoln.....	Mt. Raisen ..5	Brigg.......10	Lincoln ...15	148	214
45	Kirkby ....to	W. R. York	Wetherby .. 5	Knaresboro'.8	Leeds 10	198	....
30	Kirkby in Ashfield..pa	Notts	Mansfield....5	Nottingham.8	Alfreton....6	137	2032
24	Kirkby upon Bane ..pa	Lincoln.....	Horncastle ..6	Tattershall ..3	Lincoln....19	101	596
27	Kirkby Bedon......vil	Norfolk....	Norwich 4	Bungay.....12	Yarmouth ..16	113	245
23	Kirkby Beler ....pa	Leicester ...	Melton Mow. 3	Leicester ..12	Lougborough13	109	250
27	Kirkby Cam.......pa	Norfolk....	Beccles.....5	Bungay.....4	Yarmouth ..14	110	385
43	Kirkby in Cleveland ....pa & to	N. R. York.	Stokesley...5	Guisborough .9	Helmsley...16	235	469
43	Kirkby, Cold .....pa	N. R. York.	16	Thirsk.....8	6	219	185
24	Kirkby, East ......pa	Lincoln....	Spilsby 5	Horncastle...7	Tattershall..10	130	396
43	Kirkby Fleetham ...pa	N. R. York.	Catterick...4	N. Allerton..7	Bedale 7	230	625
23	Kirkby Frith ......lib	Leicester ...	Leicester ..4	Loughboro' .10	Ashby Zouch14	102	32
24	Kirkby Green......pa	Lincoln.....	Sleaford 7	Tattershall ..9	Lincoln.....12	122	74
16	Kirkby Grinddlythe ....pa & to	E. R. York .	New Malton .5	Gt. Driffield.11	York 27	207	414
45	Kirkby Hall ....to	W. R. York	Aldborough..5	Knaresboro'. 8	12	203	50
43	Kirkby Hill....pa & to	N. R. York.	Boroughbrid. 2	Ripon 5	Thirsk.....12	204	524
43	Kirkby on the Hill ..to	N. R. York.	Richmond....5	Barnard Cas.10	Darlington..13	234	118
22	Kirkby Irelith ....pa	Lancaster...	Ulverstone ..5	Dalton 3	Broughton. .6	266	3234
13	Kirkby Knowle pa & to	N. R. York.	Thirsk 5	N. Allerton .9	Helmsley. ..12	219	507
24	Kirkby la Thorpe ...pa	Lincoln....	Sleaford 2	Boston.....16	Lincoln....20	115	170
40	KirkbyLonsdale† m t } ....& pa	Westmorld .	Burton 5	Kendal 12	Kirkby Step.24	252	3949
45	Kirkby in Malham Dale.....pa & to	W. R. York	Settle 6	Skipton ...10	York 54	226	1033

KINGTON. Remains of a camp.

surrounded by a spire of singular form. Here are a free grammar-school and a charity-school, the former was erected and endowed by a Lady Watkins. On the summit of Bradnor Mountain are the remains of a square camp.

Market, Wednesday.—*Fairs*, Wednesday before February 2; Wednesday before Easter; Whit Monday; August 2; Wednesday before Old Michaelmas; and September 19, for horses and cattle of all sorts.

Destruction of rebels in 1745.

* KIRK-ANDREWS-UPON-ESK. Near the church is an ancient border fortress, consisting of a large square tower of three stories, with small windows, and formerly defended with an iron door. At Glinger Burn is a good bridge, near the place where several of the rebels lost their lives in crossing the Esk, in 1745, when closely pursued by the Duke of Cumberland. Here are two stone bridges across the river Sark, and at Garristown a cast-iron one crosses the Esk.

Singular cross.

† KIRKBY LONSDALE, a market-town and parish, situated, as its adjunct name implies, in a valley, watered by the river Lon, and on the southern border of the county. Over the river is a stone bridge of three arches, for the repairs of which the grant of pontage was made in the third year of Edward I.; and in the market-place is an ancient cross of unusual structure. The church is a large Gothic structure, with a tower and steeple, which were erected in 1705. Near it is a school-house, founded through the benefactions of various individuals, for the use of a free grammar-school, established by letters patent of the thirty-third of Elizabeth, under the management of twenty-four governors. The town consists chiefly of two streets, through the principal one passes the high road from Settle, in Yorkshire, to Kendal; and it is intersected by the other at right angles. Most of the houses are good buildings, and they are all covered with slate, which gives them a uniform appearance. Courts

Map.	Names of Places.	County.	Number of Miles from			Dist. Lond.	Popu-lation.
23	Kirkby Mallory.....pa	Leicester ...	Hinckley . . .5	Mt.Bosworth 4	Leicester 9	104	2261
45	KirkbyMalzeard* m t }..........pa & to }	W. R. York	Ripon 6	Masham.....5	York 30	218	4707
43	Kirkby Misperton.pa }.............& to }	N. R. York.	Pickering . . .4	New Malton .6	24	220	864
43	Kirkby Moorside† m t }.............& pa }	N. R. York.	 7	12	29	224	2324
23	KirkbyMuxloe to & cha	Leicester ...	Leicester 5	AshbyZouch14	Hinckley....10	103	275
45	Kirkby Overblows pa }..........& to }	W. R. York.	Wetherby ...6	Harrowgate..5	York 20	200	1528
43	Kirkby Ravensworth }.........pa & to }	N. R. York.	Richmond ...6	Barnard Cast.9	Darlington..14	235	1727
45	Kirkby, South..pa & to	W. R. York.	Pontefract...8	Doncaster...10	York 32	172	1478
40	KirkbyStephen‡ m t &pa	Westmorlnd	Brough 5	Appleby....13	Kendal....24	266	2798
40	Kirkby Thore..pa & to	Westmorlnd	Appleby ...5	Penrith ...10	27	275	1231
46	Kirkby Underdale ..pa	E. R. York.	Pocklington .7	NewMalton 10	York 15	214	350
24	Kirkby Underwood .pa	Lincoln.....	Bourn 5	Folkingham. .4	Lincoln . . .31	102	162
7	Kirkby, West..pa & to	Chester....	Gt. Neston ..8	Liverpool....9	Chester 19	201	1289
46	Kirkby Wharfe.pa & to	W. R. York	Tadcaster ..2	Cawood 6	York 10	186	492
44	Kirkby - upon - Wisk }..........pa & to }	N. R. York.	Thirsk 5	N. Allerton..7	Ripon......12	219	872
22	Kirkdale ....to	Lancaster ..	Liverpool...2	Ormskirk...11	Prescot......7	204	2591
44	Kirkdale§ ....pa	N. R. York.	Helmsley . . .5	Kir. Moorside 2	York 28	223	1107

leet and baron are held under the lord of the manor; and there is also a court for the recovery of small debts. The principal manufactures here are those of carpets and blankets; and on the stream that passes through the town are mills for grinding bark and grain. The river affords an abundant supply of salmon-trout and other fresh-water fish; and the market is well stocked with provisions.

Market, Thursday.—*Fairs*, Holy Thursday, for horned cattle; St. Thomas, December 21, for woollen cloth.

KIRKBY LONSDALE.

* KIRKBY MALZEARD. *Market*, Wednesday.—*Fairs*, Whit Monday, and October 2.

† KIRKBY MOORSIDE, a market-town, situated on the river Dove, and nearly encompassed on all sides by steep hills. On the Dove and other streams near the town are corn-mills: limestone and freestone are dug in the vicinity, and the malting trade is carried on here, the surrounding country being very productive of grain. This place is remarkable as having been the last retreat of George Villiers the younger, Duke of Buckingham, the unprincipalled minister and profligate favourite of Charles II. Having lost his interest at court, and by his extravagance involved himself in pecuniary difficulties, he retired to this town, in the neighbourhood of which he had some landed property, and here he died, April 16, 1688.

Extensive trade in malt.

Market, Wednesday.—*Fairs*, Whit Wednesday for horned cattle and horses; and September 18, for sheep, linen, and woolen cloth.

‡ KIRKBY STEPHEN. *Market*, Monday.—*Fairs*, Easter Monday; Whit Tuesday; and October 29; for black cattle, sheep, and flax.

§ KIRKDALE, a parish and village, romantically situated in a fruitful vale, surrounded by hanging woods, and watered by a small brook. This parish is famous on account of a cave in one of the calcareous hills which bound the vale of Pickering on the north, and the waters from which fall into the Derwent. In the summer of 1821, quarriers working here discovered by accident the opening of this cavern, which had been closed by rubbish overgrown with bushes; and on entering which, to the distance of about 200 feet, it was found to be studded with stalactites, hanging from the roof, and on the floor covered with diluvial loam, thickly interspersed throughout its substance with organic remains, or bones of various animals. These were examined by Professor Buckland, of Oxford, by M. Cuvier, and other naturalists, who discovered the bones to be chiefly those of hyenas, mixed, however, with bones of the elephant, rhinoceros,

Remarkable cavern.

Fossil remains.

Map.	Names of Places.	County.	Number of Miles from			Dist. Lond.	Popu-lation.
22	Kirkham*..m t pa & to	Lancaster ..	Preston 9	Poulton 8	Lancaster ..22	226	11630
46	Kirkham......ex p lib	E. R. York.	New Malton.6	Pocklington 13	York 13	212	31
29	Kirkhaugh..........pa	Northumb ..	Hexham....19	Alston 4	Haltwhistle .7	275	309
29	KirkHeaton ex p & cha	Northumb ..	11	Morpeth ...15	Newcastle..18	291	182
29	Kirk Hill.......ham	Northumb ..	Morpeth 9	Alnwick ...20	22	295	....
9	Kirkland ....to	Cumberland	Cockermouth 7	Wigton 9	Carlisle 20	307	....
9	Kirkland ......pa & to	Cumberland	Penrith 9	Appleby ...8	23	278	765
22	Kirkland..........to	Lancaster ..	Garstang ...2	Kirkham 8	Lancaster ..13	230	458
40	Kirkland ....to	Westmorlnd	Kendal......0	Kir.Lonsdale12	Ambleside..14	261	1250
10	Kirk Langley .....pa	Derby	Derby 5	Wirksworth10	Ashbourn ..8	131	553
44	Kirk Leatham†.pa & to	N. R. York .	Guisborough 5	Yarm 15	York 54	248	1074
44	Kirk Leavington pa & to	N. R. York .	Yarm.......2	Stokesley....7	41	233	517
29	Kirkley.............to	Northumb ..	Newcastle..11	Morpeth 8	Alnwick ...27	284	165
36	Kirkley ....pa	Suffolk ..	Lowestoff ..2	Beccles 8	Southwold..12	112	374
30	Kirklington ....pa	Notts	Southwell ...4	Mansfield....9	Nottingham 13	133	243
44	Kirklington....pa & to	N. R. York.	Bedale......6	Ripon 6	York 27	214	486
9	Kirk Linton..pa & to	Cumberland	Longtown ...4	Carlisle 8	Wigton...19	309	1892
29	Kirknewton....pa & to	Northumb ..	Wooler......5	Berwick....19	Alnwick ...24	325	1674
9	KirkOswald‡m t pa & to	Cumberland	Penrith 8	Carlisle 15	Appleby....16	292	1033

KIRKDALE.   hippopotamus, horse, ox, deer, rat, hare, tiger, wolf, and a few other animals. Several of the species differ from any at present existing; and it has been concluded that this cave was an antediluvian den of wild beasts, an opinion which has been corroborated by the discovery of collections of bones in similar situations in other parts of England, and also in France and Germany.

Handsome town.

* KIRKHAM, or Kirkham-in-the-Field, a market-town, parish, and township, situated between the Ribble and another small river. The town is handsome, well built, and is rapidly advancing in improvement, but contains nothing remarkable. Its principal manufactures are sail-cloth, cordage, and course linens, and latterly cotton has been introduced. In 1670, Henry Colburne, of the Drapers' Company, founded a free-school which has three masters. Here is also a charity-school for girls, and a large well-built workhouse. The Lancaster canal passes within three miles of the town.

Market, Tuesday.—*Fairs*, June 24, for horses and horned cattle; and October 18, for toys and small ware.

Munificent bequests.

† KIRK LEATHAM. Here is an hospital which was endowed in 1676 by Sir William Turner, lord mayor of London, for twenty poor persons and twenty children; it is a handsome building, forming three sides of a square, in the centre of which is a small chapel of great beauty, with a window of painted glass, representing the offering of the magi at the nativity of Christ; the hospital contains a valuable library. Sir W. Turner also left by will £5000. for founding a grammar-school, which was erected in 1709, but the benevolent purpose for which it was intended has been abandoned for some years.

Ancient church.

‡ KIRK OSWALD, an ancient market-town, situated on a pleasant and fertile spot, near the confluence of the river Eden and Raven Beck, which derives its name from the celebrated king and martyr of Northumberland. The houses are irregularly built, on the declivity of a gentle eminence, and the principal employment of the inhabitants arises from the operations of husbandry. The church is an ancient, irregular structure, and contains some elegant monuments; the belfry stands on a hill at some distance from the church. Here is a small endowed school and a dissenting meeting-house. At a short distance from the town are the ruins of an ancient castle, which appears to have occupied an extensive area, of a square form, bounded on three sides by a fosse, and skirted on the other by the brook, which supplied it with water; it is said to have been once a very magnificent residence.

Market, Thursday.—*Fairs*, Thursday before Whit Sunday; and August 5, for horned cattle.

	Names of Places.	County.	Number of Miles from			Dist. Lond.	Popu- lation.
46	Kirk Sandal ....pa	W. R. York	Doncaster ...5	Thorne.. ...6	York 34	167	200
46	Kirkstall* ....ham	W. R. York	Leeds......3	Bradford ...9	28	192	....
24	Kirkstead ....pa	Lincoln.....	Horncastle ..7	Tattershall ..2	Lincoln ...20	130	179
45	Kirkthorpe ......ham	W. R. York.	Wakefield ..2	Pontefract..10	York 29	180	....
20	Kirkton ....pa	Notts	Ollerton ...2	Tuxford ...5	Nottingham 22	139	247
29	Kirk Whelpington pa }............& to }	Northumb..	Morpeth....15	Newcastle..21	Alnwick ..22	294	789
24	Kirmand in theMire .pa	Lincoln.....	Mt. Raisen ..6	Louth ...12	Lincoln ...21	154	74
24	Kirmington ....pa	Lincoln.....	Caistor 8	Barton.. ...8	32	164	310
6	Kirtling.............pa	Cambridge..	Newmarket .4	Linton 12	Cambridge..16	61	735
31	Kirtlington .....pa	Oxford......	Woodstock . 5	Bicester .. .7	Oxford....8	62	687
24	Kirton† ......m t & pa	Lincoln.....	Brigg........7	Gainsborough9	Lincoln ...18	151	2147
36	Kirton ....pa	Suffolk.....	Ipswich ...9	Woodbridge .7	Harwich 8	79	624
28	Kislingbury ....pa	Northamp ..	Northampton 4	Towcester ..8	Daventry ...9	68	683
34	Kittesford..........pa	Somerset..	Wellington ..4	Milverton ...4	Taunton....11	152	171
24	Knaith ....pa	Lincoln.....	Gainsborough4	Kirton ...11	Lincoln.. ...14	147	63
34	Knapp ....ti	Somerset..	Taunton 6	Ilminster.. ...8	Bridgewater .8	136	....
23	Knaptoft ....pa	Leicester ..	Lutterworth 7	Hinckley... ..4	Leicester ...14	96	53
23	Knaptoft in Walton }.........ham }	Leicester. ..	6	6	10	95	....
27	Knapton ....pa	Norfolk	N. Walsham.3	Cromer......8	Norwich ...19	128	327
45	Knapton.........to	W. R. York.	York........3	Wetherby ..11	Boroughbridge 14	200	....
46	Knapton......to & cha	E. R. York .	New Malton.6	Gt. Driffield 16	York 24	223	120
6	Knapwell ....pa	Cambridge..	Caxton......4	Royston 13	Cambridge ..9	50	128
45	Knaresborough‡ ..bo }......m t pa & to }	W. R. York	Leeds 18	Ripon 12	York 19	197	5296

* KIRKSTALL. This place is celebrated for the ruins of Kirkstall-abbey, which was founded by Henry de Lacy, in the reign of King Stephen, 1147, for monks of the Cistercian order. A part of the cloisters, the dormitory, the refectory, and the chapter-house, are all that remain of this monastery, which was beautifully situated in a fertile vale, on the banks of the Aire, and surrounded by pleasant hills and woods.

[margin: Ruins of Kirkstall abbey.]

† KIRTON, or Kirktown. Market, Saturday.—Fairs, July 18, and December 11, for all sorts of cattle and merchandise goods.

‡ KNARESBOROUGH, a borough, market-town, parish, and town-ship, situated on the side of a hill, on the north-east bank of the river Nidd, commanding extremely beautiful prospects. The town is large and handsome, with two bridges over the Nidd ; and the houses, many of which have been constructed with the stones of the ruined castle, are well built ; the market-place is very spacious. The manufacture of linens, which has been long established, is very considerable, and some branches of the cotton trade have been lately introduced. The church appears to have been erected at different periods, but presents nothing remarkable ; it contains several elegant monuments. The Rev. Robert Chaloner en-dowed a free-school here, in 1616. Situated on a craggy rock, are the remains of an ancient castle, said to have been built by Serlo de Burgh, soon after the Conquest ; it was a strong place of defence till the time of the civil wars, when it was dismantled by order of Parliament. A part of the keep, with a few dilapidated arches and semicircular buttresses, are all that now remain of this once formidable fortress. Near the centre of these ruins is the court-house, and also a prison for the liberty of the forest of Knaresborough ; a chamber is still shown, in which the unfortunate Richard II. was confined after his deposition. Near the lower bridge are some entire dwellings, excavated out of the cliffs, which have been inhabited from time immemorial. One of these was produced by the industry of a poor weaver and his son, who employed, during six-teen years, all the time they could spare, from their necessary avocations, to accomplish it. At a short distance from this monument of persever-ance is St. Robert's-chapel, elegantly cut out of the solid rock, above which is a hermitage. St. Robert, the reputed founder of this curious chapel, was an anchorite of the thirteenth century, and son of a mayor of York ; he, by the austerity of his life, attracted the admiration of the

[margin: Beautiful prospects.]

[margin: Richard II. confined here.]

KNARES-
BOROUGH.

Scene of the
murder by
Eugene
Aram.

populace, among whom he is said to have performed many miracies. About a mile further down the river, is St. Robert's-cave, another excavation in the rock, which is supposed to have been the same holy man's usual residence. This gloomy cave is awfully memorable, on account of a horrid murder committed there, in 1745, by Eugene Aram, a schoolmaster of extraordinary abilities and learning, which, by a train of singular circumstances, was discovered, after a lapse of nearly thirteen years, and the murderer brought to justice. In the year 1758, a man, whilst digging for lime-stone, near this place, found the bones of a human body Suspecting these to be the remains of some one who had been murdered, he gave information of his discovery in the town of Knaresborough, where the people, thrown into great excitement by the intelligence, endeavoured to recollect if any one had of late years been missed from that neighbourhood. It was remembered by a particular individual, that one Daniel Clarke, a shoemaker, had disappeared about thirteen years before, and had never again been heard of. On further inquiry, it was ascertained that he had disappeared under circumstances which occasioned a suspicion of his having acted fraudulently. He had borrowed a considerable quantity of plate, under pretence of being commissioned to collect that article for exportation. Being then just married, he had also borrowed some articles of household furniture and wearing apparel, for the purpose, as he pretended, of giving an entertainment to his friends. After his disappearance, two persons named Houseman and Aram were suspected of having aided him in the fraud. Their houses were searched, and some of the miscellaneous articles found, but no plate, which it was then supposed that Clarke must have made off with; and thus the matter ended. It was now recollected that the wife of Aram, who was subsequently deserted by him, had said to some one that she knew what would peril the life of her husband and some other persons. An inquest being held upon the skeleton, all these circumstances were brought forward as evidence. To this inquest the coroner summoned Richard Houseman, one of the individuals suspected at the time of having assisted Clarke in his fraud. This man entered the room in a state of great agitation, and with strong marks of fear in his countenance and voice. Taking up one

of the bones, he used the remarkable expression, "This is no more Dan Clarke's bone than it is mine; which convinced the jury that he knew something more about the matter. He was ultimately prevailed on to acknowledge that he was privy to the murder of Clarke, and that his bones were buried in St. Robert's Cave, not far from the place where those now before the jury had been found. On a search being made, the bones were found exactly in the place and posture which he described. He stated the actual murderer to be his former friend, Eugene Aram, who now acted as usher in the school of Lynn, in Norfolk. A warrant was

immediately sent off for the apprehension of Aram, who was found peacefully engaged in his ordinary business. The profession of this man, his mature age, and the reputation which he bore for great learning, conspired to render his apprehension as a murderer a matter of the greatest surprise to the inhabitants of the place where he lived. He first denied that he had ever been at Knaresborough or knew Daniel Clarke, but, on the introduction of a person who was acquainted with him at that town, he saw fit to acknowledge his former residence in it. Eugene Aram was a native of the West Riding, and connected by birth with some of the families of gentry in that county. The circumstances of his parents are not stated, but he appears to have entered life in the character of a poor scholar. Having adopted the business of teaching, he devoted himself to the acquisition of knowledge with an ardour equalling that of the most distinguished scholars. After acting as an usher in various situations, he had settled, in 1734, at Knaresborough, where, eleven years after, he committed the crime for which he was now apprehended. By an early and

Map.	Names of Places.	County.	Number of Miles from			Dist. Lond.	Popu- lation.
29	Knaresdale ....pa	Northumb ..	Hexham....19	Haltwhistle .6	Alston 6	277	566
43	Knayton............to	N. R. York .	Thirsk.. 4	N. Allerton. .6	York 27	218	....

imprudent marriage, he had added to the embarrassment of his circumstances; yet his pursuit of knowledge continued unabated. When we learn that the man who associated with such low persons as Clarke and Houseman was deeply skilled in the ancient and modern languages, including the Hebrew, Arabic, and Celtic, and was alike conversant in the belles lettres, in antiquities, and in several branches of modern science, our wonder amounts almost to disbelief; yet there can be no doubt of the fact. He had even, before his apprehension, advanced a great way in a comparative polyglot lexicon, upon a new, and, for that age, profound plan, in which it seems not unlikely, that, if it had been carried into effect, he might have anticipated some of the honours of the German philologists. He had also composed several tracts upon British antiquities. At the trial of Aram, which took place before the York Assizes, on the 3d of August 1759, Richard Houseman was admitted as king's evidence, and gave a minute narration of the murder, slightly distorted, it was supposed, in order to lighten his own share of blame. According to the witness, Clarke had received his wife's fortune, amounting to £160., on the night before he was murdered. He called at Aram's with this sum in his pocket, and also carrying the plate which he had obtained among his friends. He and Houseman, at the request of Aram, walked out in the direction of St. Robert's Cave, where the party had no sooner arrived than Aram knocked down Clarke and murdered him. Houseman, according to his own account, then retired; but it afterwards appeared that he had assisted in burying the body in the cave. The clothes of the murdered man were brought to Aram's house, and burnt, but not until betraying the secret to Mrs. Aram. After this and other evidence had been given, Aram delivered a written defence, in which he endeavoured, by the exercise of much ingenuity and a show of curious learning, to make up for the want of living exculpatory evidence. Notwithstanding this elaborate but specious defence, the guilt of Aram was too clear to admit of doubt, and he accordingly received sentence of death. He afterwards confessed the crime to the clergyman appointed to attend him, and ascribed it to the passion of jealousy. On the morning of his execution he was found almost dead in bed, in consequence of a wound which he had inflicted upon his arm with a razor; a paper, in which he attempted a justification of suicide, being found upon the table by his side. His body, after execution, was exposed in chains at the scene of his guilt. In Caulfield's Portraits there is a genuine likeness of this singular man—an intellectual but melancholy countenance, forming a touching commentary on his history. On the opposite bank of the river to the castle, is the famous dropping, or petrifying well, which remarkable spring rises in the declivity of a hill, spreads itself over the surface of a spongy rock, which projects over its base about fifteen feet, whence it trickles down in about thirty apertures, with a sort of a musical tinkling; it is saturated with a sparry matter, which incrusts in a short time every thing it falls upon. Near this place was born, in 1488, the celebrated Mother Shipton. Here also was born, John Metcalf, a most extraordinary person, who had the misfortune to lose his sight when only four years old, notwithstanding which he became a musician, a guide over the forest, a common carrier, a builder of bridges and houses, a contractor for making roads, and a skilful player at whist; he died in 1810, at the advanced age of ninety-three.

Market, Wednesday —*Fairs*, Wednesday and Thursday after January 13, for sheep; Wednesday after March 12; next day sheep; May 6 and 7, sheep; ditto after August 12; Tuesday and Wednesday after October 10; and Wednesday after November 22, statute; Wednesday and Thursday after December 10; and every Wednesday fortnight, cattle market.

Side notes:
KNARESBOROUGH.

Trial of Aram.

His execution.

Birthplace of Mother Shipton.

d/n p	Names of Places.	County.	Number of Miles from			Dist. Lond.	Popu- lation.
18	Knebworth........pa	Herts......	Hertford 4	Ware 4	Stevenage ...7	25	259
16	Knedlington ....to	E. R. York.	Howden ...1	Selby 10	York 19	179	123
30	Kneesal ....pa	Notts...	Ollerton 4	Newark ...10	Nottingham 20	134	613
6	Kneesworth .....ham	Cambridge..	Royston 3	Caxton ...10	Cambridge..11	40	191
54	Knelston...........pa	Glamorgan..	Swansea...10	Penrice.....3	Lloughor 7	216	125
36	Knettishall ....pa	Suffolk	East Harling.6	Bottesdale ..7	Thetford 8	86	67
30	Kneveton ....pa	Notts	Newark ...8	Bingham 4	Nottingham 12	128	119
35	Knightley ....to	Stafford	Eccleshall ..3	Newport....7	Stafford 7	140	....
58	Knighton*........m t	Radnor ...	Bish. Castle.13	Ludlow.....16	Hereford ...26	165	259
23	Knighton ..ham & cha	Leicester ...	Leicester....2	Mt.Harboro'14	Lutterworth 13	97	402
16	Knighton ....ham	Hants	Newport ...5	Ryde......5	Portsmouth.10	82	....
35	Knighton ....to	Stafford	Drayton ...6	Eccleshall ..10	Stafford 17	152	156
12	Knighton upon Teame { ....pa }	Worcester..	Tenbury 4	Bewdley ...10	Worcester . 19	130	553
12	Knighton, West ....pa	Dorset......	Dorchester ..5	Weymouth ..8	Wareham ..15	122	308
25	Knightsbridge†....ham	Middlesex ...	Hammersmit.3	Vauxhall....2	Fulham 3	1	...
23	Knight Thorpe ...ham	Leicester ...	Leicester .. 12	Loughboro'..1	Ashby......12	110	79
12	Knightwick ....pa	Worcester..	Bromyard ...6	Malvern ...7	Worcester...8	119	169
17	Knill ....pa	Hereford	Kington 3	Presteign ..4	New Radnor.6	158	94
10	Knipe.............ham	Westmorlnd	Orton 10	Penrith.....8	Kendal ...19	280	....
3	Knipton..........pa	Leicester ...	MeltonMow.10	Grantham ...7	Oakham ..15	111	322
13	Knitsley ....to	Durham ...	Durham ...10	Wolsingham 7	Newcastle..14	263	....
10	Kniveton ....pa	Derby......	Derby 14	Ashbourn...3	Wirksworth .6	140	342
10	Knock ....ham	Westmorlnd	Appleby 5	Penrith ...13	Aldston ...14	275	....
33	Knockin..........pa	Salop......	Oswestry ...6	Ellesmere ..11	Shrewsbury.13	167	311
36	Knodishall ....pa	Suffolk	Saxmundham 3	Aldborough..6	Dunwich 7	93	315
21	Knolton ....pa	Kent......	Wingham ...4	Deal 6	Dover......8	67	30
11	Knook ....pa	Wilts	Warminster .5	Heytesbury . 1	Salisbury ...15	90	282
23	Knossington .....pa	Leicester ...	MeltonMowb.8	Oakham ..4	Leicester ...15	99	240
3	Knotting ....pa	Bedford	Higham Fer. 5	Kimbolton ..8	Bedford....10	60	165
15	Knottingley ..to & cha	W. R. York	Ferrybridge..1	Pontefract ...2	York 24	176	3666
39	Knowle.... ham & cha	Warwick...	Henley in Ar. 8	Birmingham .8	Warwick ..10	100	1120
35	Knowle End........to	Stafford	Newcastle ..4	Sandbach....9	Stafford....20	153	282
22	Knowsley‡..........to	Lancaster...	Prescot......3	Liverpool ...7	Ormskirk....8	200	1162
11	Knowstone........pa	Devon......	Bampton ...10	South Molton 8	Exeter 23	171	521

Picturesque town.

* KNIGHTON, or Tref-y-clawdd. A market-town situated upon an agreeable hill, sloping towards the margin of the river Teme. It consists of two principal avenues, intersecting each other at right angles; and the gentle acclivity of the streets gives a picturesque appearance, affords a grateful view of the enclosing valley, and is attended with cleanliness. The living is a perpetual curacy in the diocese of St. David's and province of Canterbury, of the certified value of £10. per annum; patrons and impropriators, the Warden and Trustees of the hospital of Clun, in Shropshire, which was founded and endowed in the reign of James I., by an earl of Northampton. The petty sessions for the hundred are held here once a month. A small free-school, in this town, is endowed, by a Mr. Barnsley, with £1. per annum; and here are six alms-houses for the

Offa's-dyke.

accommodation of the poor. The famous boundary, called Offa's-dyke, enters the parish on the north, and running due south for two miles, may be traced through the parishes of Norton, Whitton, Discoed, and Old Radnor, in this county, after which it passes into Hereford.

Market, Thursday.—*Fairs*, May 17, June 21, August 18, October 1, Wednesday before November 12, and Thursday before December 25.

† KNIGHTSBRIDGE, a hamlet, partly in the parishes of Chelsea and St. Margaret, Westminster, and partly in that of Kensington, besides a small part which extends into the parish of St. George, Hanover-square, in the hundred of Ossulton. This village extends from Hyde Park-corner to Kensington Gore, and consists of a street of irregular buildings, forming the grand ingress to the metropolis from the great western road. On

Barracks for the horse-guards.

the north side of the street are extensive barracks for the life-guards, communicating with Hyde Park; and on the opposite side, near Hyde Park-corner, are barracks for the foot-guards.

‡ KNOWSLEY. Knowsley-park is the seat of the Earl of Derby; the mansion stands on an elevation, and has evidently been erected at different periods; the most ancient part is of stone, and has two round towers; it

Map.	Names of Places.	County.	Number of Miles from			Dist. Lond.	Popu- lation.
41	Knoyle, East*......pa	Wilts	Hindon 2	Shaftesbury..5	Salisbury...17	96	1028
41	Knoyle, West ......pa	Wilts	Mere 3	Hindon.....3	18	97	206
7	Knutsford†...m t & pa	Chester....	Manchester 15	Macclesfield 12	Chester 25	176	2823
7	Knutsford,Over pa & to	Chester.	Knutsford ...1	11	26	175	217
12	Kommeridge........pa	Dorset......	Corfe Castle .4	Wareham ...7	Dorchester..21	117	124
13	Kyloe........pa & cha	Durham.. ..	Belford.....5	Berwick onT11	Alnwick...19	327	927
24	Kyme, North ....to	Lincoln	Sleaford ...6	Tattershall ..7	Lincoln ...18	121	322
24	Kyme, South ..pa & to	Lincoln	7	7	20	122	....
13	Kyo.................to	Durham	Durham ...10	Gateshead ..10	Chester le St. 7	268	412
42	Kyre, Great ....pa	Worcester..	Tenbury ...5	Bromyard ...7	Worcester..17	128	159
42	Kyre, Little ..to & cha	Worcester..	5	8	16	127	....

contains a very large and valuable collection of paintings, principally by the old masters. The surrounding park, which is extensive and beautiful, commands many fine views, and is well wooded.

KNOWSLEY.

* KNOYLE, EAST. This place is remarkable for having given birth to the celebrated architect and mathematician, Sir Christopher Wren, who was born here 20th of October, 1632.

Sir Christopher Wren, born here.

† KNUTSFORD, a market-town, situated in a fertile part of the county, on the great road from London to Liverpool. The town is divided into Over and Nether, or Higher and Lower Knutsford, by a branch of the river Birkin which rising about half a mile south of this place, passes under the turnpike-road, and falls into Tatton-mere. In Nether Knutsford is the market-place, and also a spacious county prison, near which is a handsome and convenient town-hall, or sessions-house, where sessions are held in the months of July and October. Knutsford was formerly included in the parish of Rostherne, but it was made a distinct parish, by act of Parliament, in 1741. The church is a handsome, modern edifice of brick and stone, with a square tower. The principal manufactures carried on here are those of sewing thread, worsted, and tanned leather. Races are held annually in July, near the town, much to the emolument of the inhabitants, as they usually draw together a con- siderable number of persons of rank and fortune. This place is distin- guished by a curious custom or ceremony, practised at the marriage of parties belonging to the town or neighbourhood. The friends and acquaintance of the wedded pair strew the streets before their doors with brown sand, upon which they form various fanciful figures with white sand, and over the whole scatter the flowers which happen to be in season.

The county prison.

Curious ceremony.

Market, Saturday.—*Fairs*, Whit-Tuesday; July 10; and November 8, for cattle and drapery.

RIVERS.

Name.	Rises.	Falls.	Name.	Rises.	Falls.
Keach	Cardigansh .	Tivy.	Kensey	Cornwall ...	Tamar.
Kebby.........	Monmouthsh	Usk.	Keriog	Merionethsh	Dovey.
Kebeck	Yorkshire ..	Nyde.	Keriog.........	Denbighshire	Dee.
Kelyn..........	Merionethsh	Troweryn.	Kery	Cardigansh.	Tivy.
Kemlet	Shropshire .	Severn.	Kevenny.......	Monmouthsh	Usk.
Kemlet	Denbighshire	Tanot.	Kevenny........	Anglesea ...	Sea
Ken	Westmorlnd	Irish Sea.	Kinver	Cardigansh .	Dovey.
Ken	Devonshire .	Ex.			

L.

Map.	Names of Places.	County.	Number of Miles from			Dist. Lond.	Population.
24	Laceby ....pa	Lincoln	Gt. Grimsby .3	Caistor 8	Barton 17	165	616
12	Lacerton ....ham	Dorset......	Blandford ...3	Shaftesbury ..9	Sturminster..8	106	....
7	Lach Dennis........to	Chester....	Northwich ..4	Knutsford ...5	Middlewich .4	173	32
7	Lachford .....to & cha	Chester....	Warrington..2	Altringham ..7	Northwich .10	183	....
43	Lackenby ....ham	N. R. York.	Guisborough 5	Stockton ..14	Whitby 20	250	....
36	Lackford..........pa	Suffolk	Bury........6	Mildenhall ..7	Thetford....12	74	198
14	Lackindon.........pa	Essex	Burnham ...5	Maldon......7	Rochford 7	43	536
34	Lackington, White..pa	Somerset ...	Ilminster ...2	Crewkherne .7	Ilchester ...11	133	254
41	Lacock* ....pa	Wilts	Chippenham 4	Melksham .. 4	Calne 7	94	1650
39	Ladbroke..........pa	Warwick. ..	Southam ...2	Warwick ..11	Kington.... 9	84	268
8	Ladock ....pa	Cornwall	Grampound..4	Truro 7	St. Austell ..9	252	761
16	Lainston ....pa	Hants	Winchester..4	Stockbridge..5	Sutton 5	66	40
43	Laith Kirk ...to & cha	N. R. York.	Barnard Cas. 9	Brough 15	Wolsingham15	255	....
41	Lake ....to	Wilts	Amesbury ...3	Salisbury 6	Wilton......6	81	....
27	Lakenham ....pa	Norfolk.....	Norwich 1	N.Walsham 14	Wymondha. 10	109	3810
36	Lakenheath........pa	Suffolk	Brandon ...5	Mildenhall ..6	Newmarket 17	75	1209
8	Lalent Uny ....pa	Cornwall ...	St. Ives.....3	Penzance....9	Redruth....11	274	1305
25	Laleham† ....pa	Middlesex ..	Staines.....2	Chertsey ...2	Walton 4	18	588
54	Laleston‡ ....pa	Glamorgan..	Bridgend ..6	Neath......10	Merthyr T. .20	187	442
14	Lamarsh ....pa	Essex	Halstead ...7	Sudbury 4	Neyland 7	53	323
24	Lambcroft.... ...ham	Lincoln	Louth 5	Mt. Raisin..13	Wragby....13	151	34
21	Lamberhurst§ ....pa	Kent and Sussex ...	Maidstone ..14	Goudhurst ..4	Tunbridge .. 9	39	1521
37	Lambeth‖ ....pa	Surrey......	Wandsworth 5	Tooting.....5	Streatham ..4	1	87856

Curious monuments. * LACOCK, a parish in the hundred of Chippenham, situated in a fertile vale, on the banks of the river Avon; it formerly had a market, which is now disused. The church is an ancient edifice, and contains many curious and beautiful monuments. Here was formerly a nunnery, parts of which have been entirely removed, and others considerably altered, but the cloisters and some other portions still remain in a perfect state.

Fairs, —July 7, and Decemher 21, for horned cattle, sheep, and horses.

† LALEHAM, a parish in the hundred of Spelthorne, delightfully situated on the banks of the Thames. This place is much resorted to by the lovers of angling, and the surrounding scenery is extremely beautiful and picturesque.

Lalys, the architect. ‡ LALESTON, or Lalyston, a parish in the hundred of Newcastle, containing two hamlets, called Upper and Lower Laleston. This place is supposed to derive its name from Lalys, an eminent architect, brought hither from the Holy Land, in the year 1111, by Grenville, Lord of Neath. He built several abbeys, castles, and churches here, and afterwards became chief architect to Henry I. of England.

Ancient mansion. § LAMBERHURST. Here is Scotney-castle, an ancient castellated mansion, it formerly had a round machiolated tower at each angle, of which the southern alone is now remaining. The modern house is a handsome building, erected from a design of Inigo Jones.

Fairs, April 5, and May 21, for cattle.

‖ LAMBETH. This parish, which is sixteen miles in circumference, is bounded by those of Newington Butts, Camberwell, Streatham, Clapham, Croydon, by the river Thames, and by the parishes of Christchurch, and St. George, Southwark. It is divided into four liberties, and subdivided into the following eight precincts :—the Bishop's, the Prince's, Vauxhall, Kennington, Lambeth-marsh, Lambeth-walk, Stockwell, and

Map.	Names of Places.	County.	Number of Miles from			Dist. Lond.	Popu- lation.
30	Lambley ....pa	Notts	Nottingham..5	Bingham 7	Southwell...7	129	824
29	Lambley on Tyne..pa } ....& to }	Northumb..	Hexham ..20	Alston.....8	Haltwhistle..7	298	252
4	Lambourn* m t pa & to	Berks	Newbury ..12	Wantage ...8	Hungerford .7	68	2386
4	Lambourn, Up.....to	Berks......	14	7	Lambourn ..2	70	387
14	Lambourne .....pa	Essex	Epping.....5	Romford ...6	Chip. Ongar .8	12	778
40	Lambrigg ....to	Westmorlnd	Kendal.....5	Sedberg ...6	Orton 9	266	176
34	Lambrook, East ...pa	Somerset ...	Langport ...6	Ilchester ..7	Ilminster...5	129	....
34	Lambrook, West ....ti	Somerset ...	4	7	6	129	....
57	Lambston..........pa	Pembroke ..	Haverford W.3	Milford.....8	St. Davids ..12	267	286
13	Lambton ....to	Durham	Chester le St. 2	Sunderland ..7	Durham.....7	266	256
18	Lamer..........ham	Herts......	Welwyn ...4	Luton 7	St. Albans ..7	27	....
11	Lamerton† ....pa	Devon	Tavistock ..2	Launceston 10	Oakhampton15	209	1208

Lambeth-dean. Lambeth is mentioned in history as the place at which Hardicanute, the son of Canute the Great, died suddenly, in 1041, whilst celebrating the marriage-feast of a noble Dane, whose name was Osgod Clapa; and here Harold II. is said to have placed the crown on his head with his own hands, after the death of Edward the Confessor. About 1191., Baldwin, Archbishop of Canterbury, having been obliged to abandon a project which he had formed for the foundation of a college for secular canons at Hakyngton, near Canterbury, determined to carry his design into execution elsewhere. He accordingly commenced the erection of a fine chapel at Lambeth, which he intended to make collegiate, and endowed for the support of canons or prebendaries, in honour of his predecessor, Sir Thomas à Becket. But the monks of Christchurch, Canterbury, who had prevented the foundation at Hakyngton from taking place, were equally hostile to this new scheme, and the chapel was but just finished by Archbishop Hubert Walter, the successor of Baldwin, when the monks, by their interest at the court of Rome, procured an order for its demolition. A compromise, however, afterwards took place, in consequence of which, part of the building was suffered to remain as an archiepiscopal residence belonging to the see of Canterbury. The oldest portion of the existing edifice was rebuilt about 1250; Archbishop Chichele erected the tower called the Lollard's-tower, in the middle of the fifteenth century; and subsequent additions have been made by the prelates Warham, Cranmer, Cardinal Pole, Parker, and Juxon; besides the brick building between the great hall and the gateway, which was the work of Archbishops Sancroft and Tillotson. The palace has recently been repaired in a manner corresponding with the original style of its architecture, under the direction of Mr. Edward Blore. The archiepiscopal library, which is extremely rich, especially in MSS., was founded by Archbishop Sancroft, and has been greatly augmented by his successors, particularly by Dr. Charles Manners Sutton. Lambeth was noted in the sixteenth century, on account of a museum of natural curiosities, collected by the family of the Tradescants, who laid the foundation of the Ashmolean Museum at Oxford; here are situated Vauxhall-gardens, opened as a place of public amusement in the beginning of the eighteenth century, and deserving of notice as the most splendid exhibition of the kind in this country.

*LAMBOURN. About three miles from Lambourn is the figure of a white horse, formed on the side of a steep and chalky hill; it is said that Alfred ordered it to be made as a trophy of the signal victory which he obtained over the Danes in the year 871, and it is considered to be the most remarkable antiquity in this county.

Market.—Thursday.—*Fairs,* May 12; October 2; and December 4, for horses, cows, boots, shoes, and young foals.

† LAMERTON, or Lamberton. In the church are the effigies of Nicholas and Andrew Tremayne, twins, who were so like each other as scarcely to be distinguished, even by their parents; they were subject to

Margin notes:
LAMBETH.
Harold II. crowned himself here
Splendid library.
Remarkable antiquity.

6 Q

Map	Names of Places.	County.	Number of Miles from				Dist. Lond.	Popu. lation.
13	Lamesley.....to & cha	Durham	Gateshead ...3	Chester le St. 5	Sunderland .10		261	....
27	Lammas ....pa	Norfolk.....	Aylsham 5	N. Walsham 6	Norwich 11		120	303
9	Lamonby ....to	Cumberland	Penrith......7	Hesket......4	Carlisle....15		290	544
8	Lamorran ....pa	Cornwall ...	Tregony 4	Truro.......4	Grampound..8		257	96
	Lampeter, see Llan Bedr						....	....
9	Lamplugh .. ..pa	Cumberland	Whitehaven.8	Cockermouth 7	Workington .8		298	683
28	Lamport ....pa	Northamp ..	Northampton 9	Mt. Harboro' 8	Rothwell ...6		75	250
34	Lamyat ....pa	Somerset ...	Bruton......2	Shep. Mallet 7	Castle Carey.4		111	204
22	Lancaster* ....co	Lancaster...	....	....	....		....	1336854

LAMERTON.　the same pains and appetites, although at a considerable distance, and
were killed together at Newhaven, in France, in 1564. About three miles

Bren-tor rock.'　north-east of Lamerton is Bren-tor, a vast mass of craggy rock, which
serves as a sea-mark to mariners in the British-channel, though more than
twenty-miles distant. The summit is frequently enveloped in clouds, but
in clear weather commands a very extensive and interesting prospect, and
the ships in Plymouth harbour can be distinctly seen.

　　* LANCASTER, a maritime county, bounded on the north by Cumberland and Westmorland, on the east by Yorkshire, on the south by
Cheshire, and on the west by the Irish Sea. It consists of two portions
of very unequal extent, which are separated by Morecambe-bay and the
estuary of the river Ken. Under the sovereignty of the Normans, this county
was called the Honour of Lancaster; and Henry III. created his youngest

First Earl of Lancaster.　son, Edmund Crouchback, Earl of Lancaster, in 1267, which title continued in the family of that prince till 1353, when his descendant, Henry
Plantagenet was raised to the dukedom. He was succeeded by his son-
in-law, John of Gaunt, the fourth son of Edward III.; through his
interest Lancashire was, in 1376, made a county palatine by royal patent.
John of Gaunt left the dukedom to his son Henry, Earl of Hereford and
Derby, who being chosen king after the deposition of Richard II., the title
of Duke of Lancaster has since been usually borne by the reigning sovereign; and from the property belonging to the duchy arises a considerable
part of the land revenue of the crown. From a survey made in 1610, it
appears that it contained sixteen castles and forts, forty parks, thirteen
forests, and two chases. The principal officer of the duchy is the chancellor, under whose authority various courts of law are held in different
places within the extent of his jurisdiction. In the civil war, under
Charles I., the influence of the Earl of Derby, one of the great landed
proprietors of this county, was strenuously exerted in support of the
royal cause; and that nobleman at length sacrificed his life to the service
of the king; for being taken after the battle of Worcester, he was beheaded
at Bolton-le-Moors, October 15, 1651. Among the most memorable
events of that disastrous period were the gallant defence of Lathom-
house against the Parliamentarians, by the Countess of Derby; and the

Victory gained by Cromwell.　victory gained by Cromwell over the Duke of Hamilton, at Walton-le
Dale, August 17, 1648. This county was distinguished in the sixteenth
and seventeenth centuries by the prevalence of popular superstitions rela-
tive to witchcraft. In 1594, Ferdinand, Earl of Derby, died, probably
from the effect of poison; and his death and previous sufferings, were
attributed by himself and his attendants to magic and sorcery; in 1612,
nineteen poor women were arraigned and tried as notorious witches at the
summer assizes at Lancaster; and in 1633, other persons were accused,
in consequence of which an investigation took place before the king and
his physicians, when the discrepancies in the evidence of the witnesses
occasioned the acquittal of the prisoners. The national delusion on this
subject, however, long survived this period, though it has now happily
disappeared before the progress of knowledge; and the phrase of " Lancashire witches " has of late years been applied by way of compliment to
the females of this county on account of their personal charms. The out-

line of the county of Lancaster is extremely irregular; it is divided from Yorkshire and Westmorland by moors, mountains, and rivers, and on the west side the coast is indented by bays and harbours. There is a great variety of soil and surface, but in general it is not well adapted for cultivation; hence the ancient thinness of its population, shown by the comparatively small number of parishes into which it is divided. The northern detached part, commonly called the hundred of Furness, but belonging to that of Lonsdale, partakes of the romantic character of the neighbouring district of the lakes. It is a wild and rugged region, abounding in iron ore and slate, and covered with groves of underwood, successively cut down and converted into charcoal for the supply of the iron furnaces. This county includes some mountain heights of considerable elevation, among which the most remarkable are Pendle-hill, two miles east of Clitheroe, according to the Trigonometrical Survey of England, 1803 feet above the level of the sea; Rivington-hill, near Bolton, 1545 feet; Wittle-hill, 1614 feet; and Coniston-fell, in Furness, 2577 feet. The more southern part of the county may be regarded as consisting of two unequal portions; the smaller one extending between the borders of Westmorland and the Ribble, and the larger including the country between that river and the Mersey. Lancashire is watered by numerous rivers, of which the following are navigable :—the Mersey, the Ribble, the Lion, or Lune, the Irwell, the Douglas, the Wyre, the Ken, the Leven, the Dudden, and the Crake. The principal lakes are, Winandermere, between this county and Westmorland; Coniston-mere, in the centre of the Fells of Furness; and Easthwaite-water, situated between the two preceding. Lancashire is noted in the annals of gardening as having furnished the first potatoes which were raised in England; and what are called fancy flowers, especially the auricula, are here cultivated more generally than in any other part of the country, except near the metropolis. The climate of Lancashire is distinguished for its humidity; and it appears from a register kept at Liverpool, from 1784 to 1792, that the smallest quantity of rain which fell during any one year was 24⅜ inches, in 1788; and the largest quantity, 54¼ inches, in 1792. At Lancaster, in the year last mentioned, the entire quantity amounted to nearly 66 inches. The mean degree of heat at Lancaster, from 1784 to 1790, was 51¾. The prevailing winds are those from the south, the south-west, and the north-east. Fogs are not of frequent occurrence; there are no stagnant waters of considerable extent; and hence the climate on the whole is not unhealthy. The most important mineral products of this large county are coal, copper, lead, and iron. The great coal-tract commences on the south of Prescot, and crossing the county in a north-easterly direction, passes into Yorkshire; but coal is likewise found in abundance near Manchester, and northwards beyond Lancaster. Copper ore occurs in the rough barren mountains, towards the northern extremity of the High Furness or Fell district, and especially at Coniston, Muckle-gill, and Hartriggs; but it has not been discovered to the south of Lancaster-sands in quantities sufficient to bear working with advantage. Lead ore is chiefly met with in the northern and north-eastern parts of the county, but it is by no means abundant. At Anglezark, near Chorley, is a lead-mine, the ore of which, galena, is intermixed with carbonate of barytes. Iron ore has been already mentioned as the principal product of the district of Furness; and though found in some other parts of the county, it is there only sufficiently plentiful to render the working of it profitable. Lancashire is distinguished as the grand seat of the cotton manufacture, one of the principal sources of the wealth and commercial prosperity of Britain; and in this county have originated various inventions for the improvement of machinery and the consequent abridgment of labour. Fabrics of silk, wool, and linen, as well as cotton, are largely manufactured in this county, and here are carried on hat-making, calico-printing, bleaching, dyeing, machine-

Marginal notes:

COUNTY OF LANCASTER.

Abounding in iron ore.

Potatoes first planted here.

Mineral productions

Great cotton manufactories.

Map.	Names of Places.	County.	Number of Miles from			Dist. Lond.	Popu- lation.
!	Lancaster * .. m t & bo	Lancaster...	Manchester 53	Liverpool ..53	Preston 22	240	12613
15	Lancaut......cha & to	Gloucester .	Chepstow ...2	Blakeney ..12	Monmouth..12	130	....
13	Lanchester.... pa & to	Durham	Durham 7	Chester le St. 7	Wolsingham .8	266	5076
8	Lancing..........pa	Sussex	Worthing...3	Shoreham...2	Steyning 4	55	695

COUNTY OF LANCASTER.

making, iron-founding, and the manufacture of paper, glass, and earthen-ware. Steam-carriages, though not invented in Lancashire, were here brought to perfection, and experiments with them on a large scale were first made on the rail-road between Liverpool and Manchester, where they are now very extensively employed in the conveyance of goods and passengers.

* LANCASTER, a market, borough, seaport, and county town. It is situated on the southern bank of the river Lon or Lune, at a considerable bend of the stream towards the south-west, before it becomes an estuary, or open harbour. A fortress existed at this place, under the government of the Anglo-Saxons, which is said to have been destroyed by the Picts and Scots; and after the Norman Conquest a grant of the lordship of Lancaster was obtained by Roger de Poitou, who erected a castle, and founded the church of St. Mary, the advowson of which he gave to the abbey, of Seez, in Normandy. The great entrance-tower of the castle, which is still standing, has been noticed as a specimen of early Norman architecture, but it may with greater probability be ascribed to the age of Edward III. That prince, in the fiftieth year of his reign, created his son John of Gaunt, Duke of Lancaster; and during the civil wars between the rival houses of York and Lancaster, this town suffered so much on account of the adherence of the inhabitants to the Lancastrian cause, that it was nearly depopulated. On the renewal of the charter to the corporation, by Charles II., with the grant of additional privileges, the town revived, and it has ever since been increasing in extent, population, and trade. The corporation, under the new act, in 1835, consists of a mayor, six aldermen, and eighteen common-councilmen, with other officers. The county assizes are held twice a-year at Lancaster, according to the provisions of a statute of thirty-sixth of Edward III. The duchy court is held at Lancaster-castle and at Preston, generally under the presidency of the vice-chancellor. There is also a court, called the duchy court, held at Westminster, in which are tried all causes relating to the revenue of the Duchy of Lancaster. These courts were originally established by Henry IV., on his accession to the crown, when he separated the duchy, which he held in right of his mother, with the property belonging to it from the crown lands, and afterwards bestowed it on his eldest son. Besides the county assizes and quarter sessions, here are held quarterly courts for the borough, a court of wapentake for the hundred of Lonsdale, for the recovery of sums under forty shillings, on the first Wednesday in every month. Lancaster first returned members to Parliament in the reign of Edward I., but returns have taken place un-interruptedly only since 1547. Besides an ancient free grammar-school, here are a blue-school for girls, and national schools for children of either sex. Among the other charitable institutions are the County Lunatic Asylum, on Lancaster-moor, a handsome stone structure, capable of accommodating 300 patients, with a chapel attached to it, opened in 1816; Gardyner's Charity, for four poor persons; Penny's-hospital, for the reception of twelve poor men; Gilleson's-hospital, for eight unmarried women; a dispensary; a house of recovery; and a lying-in charity. Here also may be noticed the Lancaster Institution for promoting the fine arts, the Mechanics' Library, the Bible, Religious Tract, and Church Missionary Societies. The appearance of the town has been greatly im-proved since the passing of an act of Parliament for that purpose in 1784; several new streets and squares having been erected, which are commo-diously arranged and well paved. The principal public building is the

Attack of the Picts and Scots.

Nearly de-populated in the civil wars.

Charitable institutions.

Map.	Names of Places.	County.	Number of Miles from				Dist. Lond.	Popu- lation.
6	Landbeach ....pa	Cambridge .	Cambridge .. 6	Ely........10	Soham 9		57	422
11	Landcross ....pa	Devon	Bideford 2	Torrington ..4	Barnstaple..10		200	96
8	Landewenack ....pa	Cornwall ..	Helstone ..12	Lizard-point .1	Falmouth ..16		286	406
41	Landford ....pa	Wilts	Salisbury ...10	Romsey 6	Southampt..12		79	226
36	Landguard* .. ....fort	Suffolk	Harwich 2	Ipswich ...12	Woodbridge 12		73	....
7	Landican ....to	Chester.....	Park Gate ..5	Flint 10	Liverpool . ..6		198	61
11	Landkey..........pa	Devon	Barnstaple ..3	Torrington..12	SouthMolton10		190	790
43	Landmoth ....to	N. R. York.	N. Allerton..4	Stokesley ..14	Thirsk 6		221	53
29	Landon ....to	Northumb ..	Wooler......7	Coldstream ..8	Kelso 13		327	....
8	Landrake ....pa	Cornwall...	Saltash......4	Callington ...6	Liskeard ...10		224	872
57	Land Shipping Quay.to	Pembroke ..	HaverfordW. 6	Pembroke ...4	Milford......6		256	....
8	Landulph ....pa	Cornwall ..	Saltash......3	Devonport ..7	Callington ..7		223	570
6	Landwade.........pa	Cambridge..	Newmarket . 4	Soham 4	Ely.........9		65	25
8	Laneast ....pa	Cornwall ...	Launceston ..7	Camelford ...8	Bodmin ...16		221	279
35	Lane End† ....m t	Stafford	Newcastle ..4	Burslem 6	Stone........7		147	1488

castle, now used as a county gaol. This commanding **LANCASTER** eminence affords a prospect of vast extent, comprehending the hills of Cumberland and Westmorland, the plain of South Lancashire, and the whole extent of the vale of the Lune, with the Irish Sea in the distance. The area within the walls of the castle includes a space of 10,525 square yards, comprehending, besides the usual prison accommodations, various apartments appropriated to the classification of the prisoners, the county and crown halls, nisi prius and crown courts, a residence for the governor, &c. The estimated expense of these and other improvements made at different periods, has been stated to be more than £140,000. On the north and south sides of the castle are terraces, which form a fine promenade beneath the walls of this massive structure, which may hence be viewed with advantage in contrast with the neighbouring country. Other public buildings are the town-hall, erected in 1781 ; the custom-house, on St. George's Quay, built in 1764 ; the public baths, in Moor-street ; the assembly-rooms, in Back-lane ; and the theatre, at St. Leonard's-gate. To these may be added the new bridge over the Lune, erected at an expense of £12,000, by Mr. Harrison ; and the grand aqueduct bridge, which conveys the Lancaster-canal over the same river, and which is supposed to be the most magnificent work of the kind in England. Lancaster has long been noted for the manufacture of mahogany furniture and upholstery, much of which **Extensive commerce.** is made for exportation. Sail-cloth, cordage, linens, and candles, are likewise made here to a considerable extent. In the parish are cotton-mills, a factory for silk-spinning, and another for spinning fine worsted yarn ; there are two yards for ship-building, and upon the Holton Water are corn-mills.

Market, Wednesday and Saturday.—*Fairs*, May 1, for cattle, cheese, and pedlery ; July 5 ; August 11, for ditto and wool ; October 10, for ditto and cheese.

* LANDGUARD, or Langer-fort, situated in the parish of Felixtow on a point of land at the south-east extremity of the county and at the mouth of the Orwell, commanding the sea from the entrance of Manning-tree-water. At high water it has the appearance of an island. The fort **Strong fortification.** has been lately enlarged, and has a strong garrison and a platform with guns to defend it ; the entrance is by a drawbridge, and over the gateway is the chapel, which has lately been converted into a barrack-room. Fresh water is conveyed by pipes from Walton, a distance of about three miles.

† LANE END, a populous market-town, where commercial enterprise has, withing a comparatively recent period, drawn together a dense population of skilful and industrious manufacturers. The abundance of coal found in this part of the county and the argillaceous and silicious earth, adapted for making various kinds of earthenware, have principally con- **Centre of the pottery trade.** tributed to render this spot the centre of the pottery trade, and the canals which have been constructed from hence to different commercial marts and seaports, affording cheap and expeditious **means** for the conveyance of

	Names of Places.	County.	Number of Miles from			Dist. Lond.	Popu-lation.
30	Laneham ....pa	Notts	Tuxford 6	East Retford 7	Gainsboro'..10	143	347
9	Lanercost Abbey* ..pa	Cumberland	Carlisle 14	Haltwhistle .9	Bewcastle .. 6	315	1608
30	Langar ....pa	Notts	Nottingham 11	Bingham 4	MeltonMow.13	116	274
45	Langbar............to	W. R. York	Skipton 7	Keighley 7	Otley.......8	210	..
45	Langcliffe ....to	W. R. York	Ingleton 10	Settle 1	Skipton ...17	228	550
10	Langdale ....ham	Westmorlnd	Orton......5	Sedberg...7	Kendal 10	270	...
10	Langdale, Great and Little ...to & cha	Westmorlnd	Ambleside ..5	Hawkeshead 5	Ravenglass .16	283	314
14	Langdon Clay ......pa	Essex	Billericay ...4	Horndon 5	Raleigh......9	25	574
14	Langdon Hills ....pa	Essex	 7	 2	10	26	224
21	Langdon, East......pa	Kent	Dover......4	Deal 5	Sandwich ..10	72	322
21	Langdon, West ....pa	Kent	 3	 6	11	72	86
14	Langenhoe ....pa	Essex	Colchester ..6	Maldon....14	Witham...15	53	146
45	Langfield..........to	W. R. York	Halifax 12	Haslingden. 10	Rochdale...8	206	2514
3	Langford ....pa	Bedford	Biggleswade .2	Baldock ...7	Shefford ...4	44	726
4	Langford ....pa	Berks and Oxford	Lechlade ...4	Farringdon ..6	Bampton 5	74	673
14	Langford...........pa	Essex	Maldon.....2	Witham ...4	Chelmsford .10	38	273
27	Langford ....pa	Norfolk....	Watton 7	Swaffham ...9	Thetford 9	87	36
30	Langford ....pa	Notts	Newark 4	Tuxford ...10	Lincoln ...14	128	125
34	Langford ....ham	Somerset ...	Axbridge ...5	Bristol.....13	Wells 13	131	....
34	Langford Budville .to & cha	Somerset ...	Wellington .3	Wiveliscomb.5	Milverton....3	151	603
41	Langford, Little ....pa	Wilts	Wilton......5	Amesbury ..8	Hindon 10	86	39
41	Langford Steeple....pa	Wilts	 6	 8	10	86	587
27	Langhale ....pa	Norfolk	Bungay.....7	Norwich ...9	Wymondha. 12	113	...
14	Langham ....pa	Essex	Dedham ...2	Colchester ..7	Neyland ...5	58	821
32	Langham ....pa	Rutland	Oakham 4	Uppingham .11	Stamford ...17	100	608
34	Langham ....ham	Somerset ...	Crewkherne .8	Ilminster ...6	Taunton...12	139	..
36	Langham ....pa	Suffolk	Bury St. Ed. 10	Ixworth ...3	Stowmarket 10	81	264
27	Langham, Great ...pa	Norfolk....	Holt......5	Cley.......4	N.Walsingha.6	119	375
27	Langham, Little ....pa	Norfolk.....	 5	 4	9	119	....
22	Langhoe..........cha	Lancaster...	Clitheroe 5	Blackburn ..4	Haslingden ..9	212	....
4	Langley ....ham	Berks	E. Ilsley ...4	Newbury...7	Wallingford 11	56	....
10	Langley ....to	Derby	Derby.....10	Belper 7	Nottingham 10	136	....
13	Langley ....to	Durham	Durham ...6	Chester le St. 6	Wolsingham 10	264	97
14	Langley...........pa	Essex	Saff. Walden 7	B. Stortford.11	Royston ...6	41	384
21	Langley...........pa	Kent	Maidstone ..4	Smarden ...7	Lenham ...7	38	244
27	Langley...........pa	Norfolk....	Acle 7	Beccles......9	Norwich ...11	114	361
31	Langley‡...........ham	Oxford	Burford 5	Chip. Norton 7	Charlbury ...4	73	67

LANE END. goods, have widely extended the benefits of this great source of national prosperity. The canal from Manchester and Liverpool to London, passes within two miles of this town; and through it runs a small stream, on which have been erected several mills where flints are ground for the potteries. Enamelling, ornamental gilding of china, engraving, and other arts subservient to the manufacture of the finer kinds of earthenware, are extensively practised here. There are two convenient market-houses, and the markets are held twice a-week, that on Saturday being the most considerable; the fairs are chiefly for the sale of woollen cloth, hardware, and pedlery.

Remarkable ruins. * LANERCOST ABBEY. This place is remarkable for the ruins of its priory of Augustines, which are situated in a romantic valley, and consist of the remains of the conventual church, a part of the cloisters and some of the walls of the refectory and other buildings, which display many specimens of Gothic architecture. Within this parish is Gilsland Spa, the waters of which are sulphureous chalybeate. It supplies all the usual accommodation to visitors, and the surrounding scenery is beautiful.

Beautiful cascades. † LANGDALE, GREAT and LITTLE. Here is a school, which was erected by the Gunpowder Company of Elterwater, in return for a plot of ground given them for the use of their mill, and other charities providing for the poor of the village. In the neighbourhood are the beautiful cascades of Skelwith and Colwith-forces, and a cluster of very fine mountains, yielding blue slate.

‡ LANGLEY, a hamlet in the parish of Shipton, situated on the borders of Winchwood-forest. Here was formerly a royal palace, built by King John, which was last occupied by Charles I. No traces of this

Map.	Names of Places.	County.	Number of Miles from			Dist. Lond.	Popu. lation.
33	Langley ....ham	Salop	Birmingham .8	Dudley..... 5	Stourbridge..5	117	....
33	Langley ....cha	Salop	M. Wenlock.6	ActonBurnell 1	Shrewsbury..7	154	86
16	Langley ....ham	Hants	Beaulieu ...4	Southampton 9	Lymington .. 12	85	....
16	Langley..........pa	Hants	Lyndhurst ..4	Romsey 6	Southampton 5	79	....
39	Langley ....to	Warwick....	Henley in Ar. 4	Warwick.....6	Strat. onAvon6	96	164
41	Langley ....ti	Wilts.....	Chippenham .2	Marlborough20	Malmesbury .8	95	520
41	Langley Burrell ..pa	Wilts	 2	19	 9	94	438
13	Langley Dale*......to	Durham ...	Staindrop...3	B. Auckland .9	Bernard Cast. 5	246	217
18	Langley, Kings †...pa	Herts	Watford 5	St. Albans...6	Berkhampste.7	19	1423
5	Langley Marsh......pa	Bucks	Colnbrook ..2	Windsor.....4	Uxbridge....5	19	1797
10	Langley Meynell....to	Derby	Derby......5	Ashbourn ...9	Belper.... .9	131	....
23	Langley Priory ex p lib	Leicester ...	Ashby.....7	Derby......12	Loughboro' .10	119	16
34	Langport‡...m t & pa	Somerset ...	Somerton ..5	Ilminster ..10	Taunton....14	129	1245
21	Langport, Old ...man	Kent	Lydd......3	New Romney 2	Appledore ..8	71	....
24	Langrick Ville ......to	Lincoln	Horncastle .1	Wragby ...10	Louth......11	135	202
34	Langridge ....to	Somerset ...	Bath.......4	Sodbury 9	Marshfield ..3	107	109
34	Langridge ....to	Somerset ...	Dulverton ..3	Bampton ...5	SouthMolton12	166	....
9	Langrigg............to	Cumberland	Wigton 7	Allonby 7	Ireby......6	309	269
16	Langrish...........ti	Hants	Petersfield ..4	Droxford ...9	Alton 13	58	....
45	Langsett...........to	W. R. York	Penistone...4	Sheffield...13	Huddersfield12	176	320
16	Langston§..........to	Hants	Portsmouth .3	Cosham 5	Havant.....7	73	....
43	Langthorne ....to	N. R. York	Bedale.....3	Catterick...5	Middleham ..7	226	136
43	Langthorpe ....to	N. R. York	 3	 5	 7	226	196
45	Langthwaite ....to	W. R. York	Doncaster ..4	Thorne.....8	Pontefract ..12	166	28
24	Langtoft ....pa	Lincoln....	Mt. Deeping .3	Bourne......5	Stamford....7	93	606
46	Langtoft ....pa	E. R. York .	Gt. Driffield .7	Bridlington .11	Scarborough 14	200	523
13	Langton............to	Durham	Bernard Cast. 9	B. Auckland.7	Darlington..10	247	107
24	Langton .... pa	Lincoln....	Horncastle ..4	Tattershall ..6	Lincoln 20	136	115
24	Langton‖.........pa	Lincoln....	Spilsby 4	Alford 9	Louth 12	137	230
24	Langton..........pa	Lincoln....	Wragby ...1	Lincoln 12	12	144	206

building are, however, at present visible, although there is an entry in the parish register of a French boy having been buried from the court of Langley, in the reign of James I.

* LANGLEY DALE. Here is an ancient tower, which was formerly used as an outpost and guard to Raby-castle, and also the Gaunles smelt-works, which yield about 400 pigs of lead and 4000 ounces of silver per week.

† LANGLEY, KING'S, or Chiltern. Henry III. built a palace here, in which Edmund V., son of Edward III., was born. In the church was buried the unfortunate Prince, Richard II., after his death at Pontefract; whose body was subsequently removed by Henry V. to Westminster-abbey.

‡ LANGPORT, a town and parish of great antiquity, was formerly a royal burgh, and is seated on the river Parret, near its junction with the Ivel, which is navigable to Bridgewater, and consequently has a good trade, chiefly in timber, stone, coal, iron, salt, and corn. The river abounds with eels. The town consists of two good streets, and is divided into two parts, called Eastover and Westover. The church is a handsome building, with a tower, containing five bells. At a short distance hence is an old building, commonly called the Hanging-chapel, which is now used as a free-school, founded in 1675, by Thomas Gillett.

Market, Saturday.—*Fairs*, Monday before September, for fat cattle; second Wednesday in August; last Monday but one in September, for fat cattle and sucking colts; and last Monday in November for fat cattle, hogs, and sheep.

§ LANGSTON. Langston-harbour is capable of containing the whole navy of England, but the entrance of large ships is rendered very difficult in consequence of a sand-bank. It is, however, very convenient for conveying timber from the Hampshire and Sussex forests to the dock-yard at Portsmouth. Here are three hulks, each having about 200 convicts on board, many of whom are daily sent on shore to work in the dock-yard.

‖ LANGTON. This place is noted for having given birth to three distinguished characters, Stephen Langton, who was created a cardinal and promoted to the archbishopric of Canterbury, by Pope Innocent III.,

LANGLEY.

Smelt-works.

Richard II. buried here.

Extensive trade.

Capacious harbour.

Map.	Names of Places.	County	Number of Miles from			Dist. Lond.	Popu-lation.
46	Langton.............pa	E. R. York	New Malton 3	York 17	Pickering ..12	212	341
23	Langton, East ......to	Leicester ...	Mt. Harboro' 4	Billesdon 6	Leicester ...11	87	281
43	Langton, Great.pa & to	N. R. York .	N. Allerton ..5	Richmond ..9	Darlington..12	230	230
12	Langton Herring....pa	Dorset......	Abbotsbury..3	Weymouth ..6	Dorchester..10	129	205
43	Langton, Little .....to	N. R. York .	N. Allerton..4	Richmond ...9	Darlington..13	229	97
12	Langton, Long......pa	Dorset.	Blandford ..2	Wimborne ..9	Bere Regis ..9	105	187
12	Langton Matravers..pa	Dorset......	Swanage...2	Corfe Castle .3	Wareham ...9	119	676
23	Langton Thorpe.. to { ....& cha }	Leicester ...	Mt. Harboro' 4	Rockingham .9	Billesdon....7	86	230
23	Langton Tur ..to & cha	Leicester ...	5	11	6	87	332
23	Langton, West......to	Leicester ...	4	11	8	86	98
11	Langtree............pa	Devon......	Torrington ..3	Bideford ...8	Holsworthy.12	195	888
22	Langtree............to	Lancaster...	Wigan 4	Chorley 5	Bolton.....11	204	....
9	Langwathby ....to	Cumberland	Penrith....5	Kirk Oswald.5	Appleby....12	291	250
10	Langwith.......pa & to	Derby	Mansfield ..6	Bolsover ...4	Worksop....7	144	165
30	Langwith............to	Notts......	6	5	7	144	437
46	Langwith............to	E. R. York .	York 6	Pocklington .9	Selby.....12	195	44
8	Lanhy Drock ......pa	Cornwall ...	Bodmin.....3	Lostwithiel .3	Liskeard ...9	238	239
8	Lanivet ....pa	Cornwall ...	2	4	10	237	922
8	Lanlivery ....pa	Cornwall ...	Lostwithiel ..1	Bodmin......7	St. Austel ..8	235	1687
8	Lanreth ....pa	Cornwall ...	6	West Looe ..6	Fowey 5	240	651
8	Lansallos ....pa	Cornwall ...	7	6	3	240	884
8	Lanteglos ....pa	Cornwall ...	7	7	2	241	1208
8	Lanteglos ....pa	Cornwall..	Camelford ..2	Padstow ..14	Bodmin ..12	230	1359
29	Lanton............to	Northumb.	Wooler......5	Coldstream ..8	Berwick....16	324	73
54	Lantwit Fayrdre...pa	Glamorgan..	Llantrissant .2	Caerphilly .. 8	Cardiff....12	173	727
54	Lantwit, Lower....pa	Glamorgan..	Neath 1	Swansea ...7	Llandilo V..20	198	1117
54	Lantwit, Major* ...to	Glamorgan..	Cowbridge ..4	Bridgend ...8	Cardiff 16	177	998
11	Lapford............pa	Devon......	Bow......5	Chumleigh...5	Crediton ...9	178	700
35	Lapley.............pa	Stafford	Penkridge ..3	Brewood ...3	Stafford 7	134	1042
11	Lapslode..........cha	Devon......	Chudleigh .. 6	MoretonHam..4	Exeter......9	181	....
39	Lapworth ....pa	Warwick....	Henley in Ar..4	Warwick.....7	Solihull 7	97	656
22	Larbrick ....to	Lancaster...	Poulton 4	Garstang....5	Preston.....12	228	....

LANGTON.

which circumstance produced the rupture between that pontiff and King John, and its consequences. Dr. William Langton, president of Magdalen-college, Oxford, in the time of James I.; and the late Bennett Langton, whose name is associated with that of Dr. Johnson, both by epistolary and literary productions.

Very ancient town.

* LANTWIT MAJOR, an ancient town in the parish of Lantwit Major, situated in the Great Vale of Glamorgan, within one mile and a half of the Bristol Channel. It consists of a number of humble dwellings scattered over a surface disproportionately large, and is surrounded by the ruins of its ancient halls, colleges, &c. Here are two parish churches and a parsonage and glebe. In the year 508 a church and college were erected here by St. Iltatus, at the latter of which, amongst 2000 scholars, Gildus, the historian; Paulinus, Bishop of Leon; Sampson, Archbishop of Dol, in Brittany; Talhaim, the bard; and the famous Talicon, received their education. It is said that there are 400 houses and seven halls here for the accommodation of the students. The ruins of the college, monastery, and halls, may still be seen.

Mots ancient church in Wales.

The church is the oldest in Wales; the monastery was removed to Tewkesbury by Fitzhammon; and Henry VIII. bestowed the revenues upon the see of Gloucester. In the old church are two curious monumental stones, brought thither from the Plas Mawr, where a church also stood; and in the vestry-room is a gigantic figure of Prince Richard Hopkins, in the costume of the reign of Henry VIII. Against the wall of the church-porch a large stone leans, bearing an inscription

Singular inscription.

which is thus translated: " In the name of the Most High God, the cross of our Saviour begins, which the King has erected to the memory of Sampson, the Abbot, and to Jathahel and Artmael, for the sake of their souls. May the cross protect me!" Below the old church is an ancient building, much dilapidated, called The Lady's-chapel. The new church consists of a centre and two lateral aisles, and is adorned with a handsome altarpiece. The old town-hall, still standing, is approached by two flights of steps, and contains one spacious apartment. Over the hall is a bell upon which the clock strikes, which is said to have been presented to

Map	Names of Places.	County.	Number of Miles from				Dist. Lond.	Popu-lation.
21	Larkfield ....to	Kent	Maidstone ...4	TownMalling 1	Rochester ...6		30	....
15	Lark Stoke ......ham	Gloucester & Warwick ..	Campden 4	Evesham 5	Stra. onAvon12		94	22
7	Larkton............to	Chester.....	Whitchurch .9	Malpas......4	Nantwich ..10		172	44
27	Larling ....pa	Norfolk.....	East Harling.2	Thetford 9	Watton 9		89	227
43	Lartington..........to	N. R. York.	Bernard Cast. 3	Brough 15	Wolsingham 14		249	183
7	Larton............to	Chester.....	Liverpool 8	Gt. Neston ..8	Chester 18		202	56
15	Lasborough ....pa	Gloucester..	Tetbury 5	MinchinHam.5	Wootton E...5		104	....
43	Lasenby ....ham	N. R. York.	Guisborough 4	Stockton 9	Stokesley .. 9		249	...
43	Laskill Pasture .....to	N. R. York.	Helmsley 1	Thirsk 12	 9		229	85
16	Lassham ....pa	Hants	Alton 4	Basingstoke..7	Odiham ...7		51	236
15	Lassington ....pa	Gloucester..	Gloucester ..3	Newent 6	Michel Dean .9		108	60
43	Lastingham ....pa	N. R. York.	Pickering .. .8	Kir.Moorside 5	Whitby 18		230	1766
31	Latchford ....ham	Oxford......	Tetsworth ..2	Thame 5	Oxford 11		44	35
5	Lathbury ....pa	Bucks	Newport Pag.1	Olney 5	Sto. Stratford 7		51	172
22	Lathom*..........to	Lancaster...	Ormskirk....3	Wigan 9	Prescot......9		222	3272
5	Latimers ....cha	Bucks	Chenies......2	Chesham ...3	Amersham ..4		23	..
14	Latton ....pa	Essex	Harlow......1	Epping......6	Bish.Stortford7		23	319
41	Latton ....pa	Wilts	Cricklade....2	Cirencester ..6	Fairford 6		86	360
49	Laugharne†. ......m t	Carmarthen	Carmarthen .12	Narbarth .. 14	Tenby......20		246	2020

St. Illtyd, by one of the popes of Rome. Here was a large building belonging to the rectorial tithes, in which were many spacious rooms, they have been occupied by the parish school-master. The jail is demolished, but the name of Gallows-way marks its situation. The number of streets or causeways, the many high roads passing through the extensive remains of ancient architecture, and the remnants of a quay and harbour at Colhugh, near this place, sufficiently confirm the truth of the history which represents this as having once been a place of consequence, and thickly peopled.

LANTWIT MAJOR.

Remains of ancient architecture.

Market, Friday.—*Fair*, June 23.

* LATHOM. Here is Lathom-house, the magnificent seat of Lord Skelmersdale. The ancient structure is celebrated in English history for the heroic resistance manifested by Charlotte de la Tremouille, Countess of Derby, against the parliamentary forces, during three months, when the siege was relieved by the arrival of Prince Rupert. The mansion stood upon a flat boggy ground, and was surrounded by a wall of two yards in thickness; this wall contained nine towers, each mounted with six pieces of ordnance, so placed as to command the approaches in every part. A moat, twenty-four feet broad and six deep, encircled the whole. It is said that the besiegers lost 2000 men in this attack; after which the countess retired to the Isle of Man, and Lathom-house endured another siege till the ruin of the royal cause, when it was yielded up by command of the king, in 1645, and the following year the fortifications were dismantled. The existing mansion was chiefly erected about the middle of the eighteenth century, from designs by Leoni; it is a beautiful and spacious structure, 156 feet by seventy-five, having the offices attached by colonnades, supported by pillars of the Ionic order. The park and grounds are about five miles in circumference, commanding many extensive views, among which are the river Ribble, the sea, and the mountains which divide Yorkshire and Lancashire.

Heroic resistance of the Countess of Derby.

Extensive park.

† LAUGHARNE, or Llacharn, a small seaport-town, situated upon an estuary, into which the rivers Tave and Cowen discharge their waters. It is a very retired place, and derives little advantage from its maritime position. It is governed by a corporation, who possess lands and a share in commons, bestowed on them by Sir Guido de Brian, the younger, in the reign of King John. His mantle, richly embroidered in purple and gold, is still preserved in the parish church. The charity-school here is endowed with £6 per annum, by Mrs. Foster, which sum is intended to defray the expense of instructing twelve children. There is no trade of any value at this port. The petty sessions for the district are held in the

Map.	Names of Places.	County.	Number of Miles from				Dist. Lond.	Popu- lation.
24	Laughterton ....to	Lincoln	Lincoln.....10	Gainsborough 9	E. Retford..12		143	....
23	Laughton ....pa	Leicester ...	Harborough..5	Lutterworth.8	Leicester ...12		87	154
24	Laughton ....pa	Lincoln.....	Gainsborough 5	Epworth 6	Kirton.. 5		154	75
24	Laughton......pa & to	Lincoln	Corby 5	Bourn 6	Falkingham..2		104	441
38	Laughton ....pa	Sussex	Uckfield 6	Lewes 6	Hailsham ...7		50	804
45	Laughton......pa & to	W. R. York	Worksop....9	Rotherham ..6	Tickhill 5		154	1232
8	Launcells...... ....pa	Cornwall ...	Stratton 1	Launceston .16	Camelford ..17		222	848
8	Launceston*bo m t & pa	Cornwall ...	Bodmin 21	Plymouth ..24	Oakhampton18		214	2231
12	Launceston Tarrant. pa	Dorset.....	Blandford ...5	Wimborne...9	Shaftesbury.12		98	72
22	Laund,Old...ex pa & to	Lancaster...	Burnley 3	Colne 4	Clitheroe....6		214	476
23	Launde ......ex pa lib	Leicester ...	Uppingham . 7	Oakham 7	MeltonMow.12		96	60
31	Launton ....pa	Oxford.....	Bicester ...2	Buckingham 10	Aylesbury ..15		53	553
14	Laurence, St. .. ...pa	Essex	Bradwell 3	Burnham 5	Maldon 10		48	229
21	Laurence, St. ....pa	Kent	Ramsgate ...1	Margate.....5	Sandwich ...4		70	1601
22	Laurence, St. ..ham & cha	Lancaster...	Preston......6	Garstang 6	Kirkham 8		223	....
57	Laurence, St. .....pa	Pembroke ..	HaverfordW. 8	St. Davids ..14	Fishguard ...7		264	211
16	Laurence, St. ....pa	Hants......	Newport ...10	Ryde 14	Brading 10		91	102
36	Laurence, St. ....pa	Suffolk	Bungay......3	Beccles.....5	Halesworth . 7		103	565
38	Lavant, East and West† ....pa	Sussex	Chichester...3	Midhurst....9	Arundel 11		59	407

LAUGHARNE.

Origin of its name.

town. Here are several military antiquities ; an ancient barbican and curtain wall stand in a private garden. Close to the sea-side are the ruins of the noble castle of Guido de Brian, built in the reign of Henry III. ; and not far from the latter stands Roche-castle, whose history is lost. The original name of this parish was Tal-Llacharn, *i. e.*, above the Great Lake ; a name which, it is supposed, has been corrupted in its present form from General Laugharne, who besieged and took the castle in the year 1664.

Market, Friday.—*Fairs*, May 6, and September 28.

* LAUNCESTON, or Dunhevid, a borough, market-town, and parish, pleasantly situated on the side of a hill, on the Attery, which falls into the river Tamar, about three miles below the town. It has sent members to Parliament since the twenty-third of Edward I. The town consists of several streets, which are narrow, but many of the houses are well built ; it was formerly surrounded by a wall, some parts of which still remain ; it is governed, under the new act of 1835, by a mayor, four aldermen, and twelve councellors. A branch of the Bude-canal has recently been brought within four miles of the town. The church is a handsome Gothic structure, with a lofty tower, situated near the centre of the town, it is built with square blocks of granite, every one of which is enriched with carved ornaments, executed in a very singular manner. On the east side, placed in a niche, is a fine figure of St. Mary Magdalen, in a recumbent posture. Here are two good charity-schools for forty-eight children of both sexes, and a free-school, founded and endowed by Queen Elizabeth. A priory, belonging to monks of the order of St. Augustin, is said to have been established here by Warle-wast, Bishop of Exeter. Reginald, Earl of Cornwall, built a strong castle which is the most important object in the town ; its mouldering walls occupy a considerable extent of ground, and prove it to have been a very strong and important fortress, the tower of which is still used as a prison.

Handsome Gothic church.

Market, Saturday.—*Fairs*, first Thursday in March, a free market ; third Thursday in April ditto ; Whit-Monday ; July 6 ; November 17 ; December 6, for cattle.

Seat of the Duke of Richmond.

† LAVANT, EAST and WEST. Near this place is Goodwood, the splendid seat of the Duke of Richmond, agreeably situated in a spacious park, and commanding extensive and delightful prospects. The stables and offices westward of the house, form a handsome quadrangular build-ing, inferior to few, if any, in the kingdom ; and the kennel for the hounds exceeds, in magnificence and conveniences of every kind, any structure perhaps ever raised before for a similar purpose. Goodwood races, established by the duke, are annually run in this park, and every year become more important.

Map.	Names of Places.	County.	Number of Miles from			Dist. Lond.	Popu-lation.
5	Lavendon ....pa	Bucks	Olney........2	Bedford 10	Wellingboro 10	57	664
36	Lavenham* ..m t & pa	Suffolk	Bildeston 6	Sudbury 7	Bury........11	62	2107
14	Laver, High† .....pa	Essex	Chip. Ongar..4	Bish.Stortford9	Dunmow ...11	23	495
14	Laver, Little ....pa	Essex	5	9	10	24	112
14	Laver, Magdalen....pa	Essex	5	9	12	21	206
41	Laverstoke ....pa	Wilts	Salisbury....1	Downton 6	Andover....17	81	817
16	Laverstoke ....pa	Hants	Whitchurch .3	Kingsclere ..7	Basingstoke..9	54	117
15	Laverton ....ham	Gloucester..	Campden 6	Evesham 6	Winchcombe 6	93	....
34	Laverton ....pa	Somerset ...	Frome......4	Bath........9	Trowbridge..7	106	196
45	Laverton ....to	W. R. York	Masham 5	PaitleyBridge6	Ripon 7	215	457
24	Lavington...........pa	Lincoln	Corby 4	Falkingham..4	Grantham ...7	109	341
41	Lavington, East‡.m t ....& pa	Wilts......	Devizes......5	Westbury ..10	Salisbury ...18	90	....
41	Lavington, West....pa	Wilts	5	9	19	91	1322
42	Lawern............ham	Worcester..	Worcester .. 1	Droitwich ...6	Pershore ...9	111	....
14	Lawford............pa	Essex	Manningtree .2	Neyland 8	Colchester .. 8	59	794
39	Lawford Church ....pa	Warwick ..	Rugby 4	Brinklow 3	Coventry 8	86	320
39	Lawford, Little§ ....to	Warwick ..	4	4	9	36	28
39	Lawford, Long ......to	Warwick ..	2	5	10	84	478
57	Law-Haden ....pa	Pembroke ..	Narbarth....3	HaverfordW. 8	Tenby 11	258	....
8	Lawhitton..........pa	Cornwall ..	Launceston ..2	Callington ..10	Tavistock....10	214	485
45	Lawkland ....to	W. R. York	Settle 4	Ingleton 7	Kir.Lonsdale15	239	351

Custom of Borough English.

* LAVENHAM, or Lanham, a market-town agreeably situated on a branch of the river Brit, in a valley encompassed by hills on every side, except towards the south. This place consists of several small streets, with a spacious market-place, in the centre of which is a stone cross. Estates in land, within the manor of Lavenham, descend to the youngest son, according to the custom of Borough English. The church is a handsome Gothic edifice, built towards the close of the fifteenth century ; the walls are constructed of freestone, with curious decorations in flint-work, exhibiting the armorial bearings of distinguished persons who were probably benefactors to the church. The porch, of highly ornamental architecture, is likewise embellished with shields of arms. In the interior, the timber-ceiling is admirably carved ; and there are two pews, the carvings on which are of exquisite workmanship, resembling the style of the chapel of Henry VII. There are chapels for Wesleyan Methodists and Independents, and several charitable institutions, including a free-school and almshouses. The market has almost fallen into disuse, but two annual fairs are still held here.

Market, Tuesday.—*Fairs,* Shrove-Tuesday, and October 10. for butter and cheese.

Monument to the memory of Locke.

† LAVER, HIGH, or KING'S. On the south side of the churchyard is a tomb of black marble, to the memory of the celebrated philosopher, John Locke, who spent the latter part of his life, and died at Otes, near this place, 1704.

Considerable trade in malt.

‡ LAVINGTON, EAST. A market-town and parish in the hundred of Swanborough, called also East Lavington, to distinguish it from the neighbouring parish of West, or Bishop's Lavington. This place is situated on the northern border of Salisbury Plain, and it was formerly noted as a great corn-market, whence its adjunct appellation, but the trade in grain now is less considerable than it was, the farmers and dealers chiefly resorting to the markets of Devises and Warminster. The charitable institutions include a free-school for thirty six children, liberally endowed, and two alms-houses. The malting trade is carried on here to some extent ; but the labouring people are chiefly employed in agriculture. Dr. Thomas Tanner, a learned and industrious cultivator of monastic archæology, who died Bishop of St. Asaph, in 1735, was a native of this town.

Market, Monday and Wednesday.

§ LAWFORD, LITTLE. Here was the seat of Sir Theodosius E. A. Boughton, Bart., who was poisoned by a distillation of laurel-leaves, substituted for a bottle of medicine by Captain Donellan, his brother-in-

Map.	Names of Places.	County.	Number of Miles from			Dist. Lond.	Popu- lation.
33	Lawley ....to	Salop..	Wellington ..2	Madeley Mt. .4	Broseley 6	142	....
14	Lawling..........pa	Essex	Burnham...6	Maldon..... 7	Rochford ...8	44	....
57	Lawnenny........pa	Pembroke ..	Pembroke ..5	Tenby 8	Narbarth ...9	260	422
36	Lawshall.........pa	Suffolk	Lavenham ..5	BurySt.Edm. 7	Sudbury....9	63	885
7	Lawton Church ...to	Chester....	Congleton ..5	Burslem 6	Chester ...32	156	..
36	Laxfield..........pa	Suffolk	Framlingham 6	Halesworth..8	Eye........10	93	1158
28	Laxton...........pa	Northamp ..	Kingscliff ..4	Weldon 5	Rockingham .7	90	188
30	Laxton ....pa	Notts......	Tuxford ...3	Ollerton ..4	Newark ...10	135	659
46	Laxton.....to & cha	E. R. York.	Howden ...4	Goole 5	M.Weighton14	185	281
45	Laycock..........to	W. R. York	Keighley ...2	Skipton ...12	Halifax ...12	209	..
14	Layer Breton.....pa	Essex	Colchester .. 6	Coggeshall .8	Witham ...9	47	262
14	Layer de la Haye...pa	Essex	4	8	11	49	637
14	Layer Marney ......pa	Essex	8	6	7	45	275
36	Layham ....pa	Suffolk	Hadleigh ..2	Neyland ..6	Ipswich ...10	62	552
34	Laymoor. ....ti	Somerset ..	Crewkherne .0	Chard 8	Yeovil 9	132	..
17	Laysters..........pa	Hereford ..	Tenbury ...5	Leominster . 6	Ludlow ...10	135	212
43	Laysthorpe ....to	N. R. York.	Helmsley ...4	Kir.Moorside 7	New Malton 12	219	...
18	Layston..........pa	Herts......	Buntingford..1	Puckeridge ..6	Royston 8	32	1093
46	Laytham..........to	E. R. York..	Howden ...8	Mt. Weighton8	Pocklington .7	189	138
22	Layton...........to	Lancaster..	Blackpool ..1	Kirkham ...8	Poulton ...3	233	943
44	Layton, East ......to	N. R. York .	Greta Bridge.6	Richmond ...7	Darlington ..9	236	156
44	Layton, West ....to	N. R. York.	7	7	10	236	94
14	Laytonstone .....ham	Essex	Barking 5	WalthamAb. 9	Epping ...11	6	..
9	Lazonby......pa & to	Cumberland	Kirk Oswald.1	Penrith....7	Carlisle ...15	290	841
7	Lea ....to	Chester....	Chester 6	Tarporley...8	Wrexham ..10	178	56
7	Lea ....to	Chester....	3	Gt.Neston ..9	Liverpool ..15	185	92
7	Lea ....to	Chester....	Nantwich ..4	Sandbach ...9	Newcastle ..12	160	..
15	Lea ....pa	Gloucester & Hereford	Ross........5	Michel Dean .2	Newent 7	115	161
22	Lea ....to	Lancaster..	Preston......4	Kirkham ...3	Garstang ...10	221	687
24	Lea ....pa	Lincoln....	Gainsborough 2	Kirton 10	Lincoln.. ..16	149	197
41	Lea ....pa	Wilts......	Malmesbury .2	WottonBass. 9	Chippenham 10	96	419
15	Lea Bailey.......ham	Gloucester..	Ross........5	Michel Dean 2	Newent 8	115	108
10	Lea Dethwick ...to	Derby......	Matlock....2	Wirksworth 4	Alfreton ...6	144	518
39	Lea Marston.........pa	Warwick ..	Coleshill ...3	Tamworth . 8	Birmingham 10	107	269
7	Leach.............to	Chester....	Chester 3	Hawarden ..4	Wrexham ..10	185	170
35	Leacroft..........lib	Stafford	Cannock ...1	Penkridge ..6	Rudgley 6	123	456
53	Leadbrook, Major ..to	Flint........	Northop ...2	Flint........2	Holywell 5	199	83
53	Leadbrook, Minor ..to	Flint........	2	2	5	199	24
24	Leadenham, Long .. pa	Lincoln....	Sleaford ...9	Newark ...10	Lincoln ...12	121	565
45	Lead Hall vil	W. R. York.	Selby....7	York 9	Sherburn ..6	186	59
17	Leadon...........to	Hereford ..	Bromyard .. 5	Ledbury ...9	Hereford ...15	123	80
15	Leadon, High .....ham	Gloucester..	Gloucester ..5	Newent.... 4	Michel Dean.9	110	98
31	Leafield..........ham	Oxford....	Witney 4	Burford 5	Charlebury .5	70	656
22	Leagram............to	Lancaster..	Clitheroe ...9	Garstang ...10	Blackburn . 11	220	384
24	Leake............pa	Lincoln....	Boston 8	Wainfleet...8	Spilsby ...14	125	1744
30	Leake, East ......pa	Notts....	Nottingham 10	Loughborough6	Derby.....16	115	975
30	Leake, West ......pa	Notts....	10	6	15	115	203
39	Leamington, Hastings ....pa	Warwick ..	Southam....4	Rugby 7	Coventry ..12	84	464
39	Leamington Priors* ..pa	Warwick ..	8	Warwick ...2	10	90	6209
16	Leap...........ti	Hants	Beaulieu ..4	Southampton 9	Lymington..11	84	..
29	Learchild..........to	Northumb ..	Rothbury ..6	Alnwick ...6	Wooler ...15	305	20
29	Learmouth........ham	Northumb ..	Wooler ...11	Coldstream .3	Kelso 8	331	..
24	Leasingham, North and South .....pa	Lincoln.....	Sleaford 2	Lincoln ...16	Newark ...15	117	358

LAWFORD, LITTLE.

law; for which that individual suffered the utmost rigour of the law. This case made a considerable noise at the time, in consequence of a premature opinion conveyed, in a charge to the grand jury, by Judge Buller; but no rational doubt has ever been entertained of the guilt of the condemned.

Fashionable watering-place.

* LEAMINGTON PRIORS, a parish in Kenilworth division of the hundred of Knightlow, situated nearly in the centre of the county, and comprising within its limits the fashionable watering-place called Leamington Spa. Since the year 1797, the mineral waters have been rising in reputation, on account of their efficacy in the treatment of cutaneous diseases, glandular obstructions, bilious and dyspeptic complaints, and other maladies, for which they are used both internally and externally. Various new springs have been discovered within the last twenty or thirty years, and Leamington, from an inconsiderable village, has become a place of crowded resort for the votaries of health or pleasure. The public spring is enclosed in a handsome stone edifice; and a pump-room

Map.	Names of Places.	County.	Number of Miles from			Dist. Lond.	Population.
33	Leasowes*........ham	Salop......	Birmingham .6	Dudley.....6	Hales Owen .2	115	....
37	Leatherhead†......pa	Surrey......	Epsom 4	Dorking 5	Guildford...12	19	1724
45	Leathley ......pa & to	W. R. York	Otley........3	Harrogate ..8	Ripley 10	196	413
22	Leathwaite .....cha	Lancaster...	Ulverston ..5	Broughton ..5	Dalton 6	266	190
33	Leaton ....to	Salop.....	Shrewsbury .5	Wem........9	Oswestry .. 15	159	....
35	Leaton ....ham	Stafford	Stourbridge..7	Bridgenorth..8	Wolverham 10	133	....
46	Leavening ....to	E. R. York .	New Malton .7	Docklington 12	York 17	207	354
43	Leavington Castle ...to	N. R. York.	Yarm.....3	Stokesley....5	N. Allerton.14	234	....
43	LeavingtonKirk pa & to	N. R. York .	3	5	14	234	517
43	Leavisham ....pa	N. R. York .	Pickering...5	Whitby 16	Scarborough 17	227	168
24	Lebthorpe.. ......ham	Lincoln.....	Colsterworth 2	Corby 6	MeltonMow.12	100	....
15	Lechlade‡.........m t	Gloucester..	Highworth ..6	Burford 8	Cirencester .13	77	1244

LEAMINGTON PRIORS.

The baths.

and baths of elegant architecture, ornamented with a spacious Doric colonnade, have been erected at a great expense, for the accommodation of visitors. The baths are handsomely and tastefully fitted up, abundantly supplied with the mineral water, by means of a powerful forcing-engine. Here, as at Cheltenham, the different springs are variously impregnated. The original Spa, which is mentioned by Sir William Dugdale, in his "History of Warwickshire," contains a large proportion of common salt, besides sulphate of soda, muriate of magnesia, and sulphate of lime; and there are also chalybeate and sulphureous springs, the water of the latter being chiefly used externally. The church was originally erected as a chapel of ease to the neighbouring parish of Wootton. There are also another episcopal place of worship, a chapel called Union-chapel, a chapel appropriated to the Roman Catholics, a third to the Independents, and a fourth to the Wesleyan Methodists. Among the charitable institutions established here, are national schools, a general hospital and dispensary, and free baths for the benefit of pauper invalids. One of the principal ornaments of Leamington is the bridge over the river Leam, which connects the New Town with the original village of Leamington, called, by way of distinction, the Old Town.

Public buildings.

Among the public buildings not already mentioned are the assembly-rooms, erected in a style of grandeur and elegance rarely excelled, and comprising a ball-room, a refectory, billiard-rooms, card-rooms, and reading-rooms. There is likewise a new suit of concert and ball-rooms; and in 1814 was erected a handsome theatre. Two public libraries, a spacious picture-gallery, a museum, and Ranelagh-gardens, contribute towards the accommodation and amusement of the visitors of this place. A customary market is held on Wednesday, which is abundantly supplied, especially with provisions.

* LEASOWES, a hamlet in the parish of Hales Owen. The celebrated poet, Shenstone, was born here in 1714, and died in 1763.

† LEATHERHEAD, a parish and small town, situated nearly in the centre of the county, on rising ground, on the eastern bank of the river Mole, which is crossed here by a bridge of fourteen arches. The church is an ancient cruciform edifice, consisting of a nave, chancel, and transept, with lateral aisles and a vestry. There was formerly a weekly market, but it has been discontinued for more than a century. A large fair for horses, swine, pedlery, &c. is held annually in a field on the north side of the town. The trade and manufactures are inconsiderable, but some advantage in the way of commerce arises from the situation of the place, as a thoroughfare on the high road from London to Guildford and Farnham.

Norbury-park.

In the town and neighbourhood are some handsome villas and gentlemen's seats, among which Norbury-park may be noticed, as distinguished for the picturesque beauties of its situation and embellishments.

‡ LECHLADE, a small market-town, situated at the confluence of the little river Leach with the Isis or Thames, and near the point of junction of the counties of Gloucester, Berks, and Oxford. It consists principally

Map	Names of Places.	County.	Number of Miles from			Dist. Lond.	Population.
22	Leck ....to & cha	Lancaster...	Kirkby Lons. 2	Hornby 7	Settle......14	251	326
13	Leckby ....to	N. R. York.	Boroughbridg,6	Thirsk.....7	Ripon......7	208	....
16	Leckford.........pa	Hants	Stockbridge..2	Andover 6	Sutton......6	65	221
4	Leckhampsted.....cha	Berks	East Ilsley...5	Newbury....7	Wantage ..10	63	402
5	Leckhampsted......pa	Bucks	Buckingham .4	Sto.Stratford 5	Brackley ...10	57	499
15	Leckhampton*.....pa	Gloucester..	Cheltenham..2	Gloucester ..9	Painswick ..10	96	929
46	Leckonfield.......pa	E. R. York.	Beverley 3	M.Weighton10	Gt. Driffield 10	183	301
5	Ledburn........ham	Bucks	Leighton Buz. 3	Ivinghoe 5	Aylesbury ...8	39	181
17	Ledbury†....m t & pa	Hereford....	Hereford ...16	Ross 13	Bromyard...14	120	3909
15	Leddington .. ....ham	Gloucester..	Newent....4	9	Tewksbury .14	112	....
7	Ledsham ....to	Chester	Chester 7	Gt. Neston ..5	Liverpool .. 12	189	....
45	Ledsham ......pa & to	W. R. York	Ferry Bridge.4	Sherburn 4	Leeds......11	181	944
45	Ledston ....to	W. R. York	5	4	11	181	236

LECHLADE. of one long and wide street of well-built houses; and here is a bridge over the Thames, called St. John's-bridge, up to which the river is navigable for vessels not exceeding eighty tons burden. The church is a handsome structure, with a tower and spire at the west end. In a meadow near St. John's-bridge, an hospital, dedicated to St. Nicholas, was founded in the reign of Henry III., by Lady Isabella Ferrars, but the establishment falling into decay, the revenues were appropriated to the support of a chantry in the parish church, which, at the Reformation, became the property of the crown. Here is a Sunday-school, as also a place of worship for Baptists. The market is become inconsiderable, but an extensive transit trade is carried on here, cheese, butter, and other articles being brought to the wharfs at this place, to be conveyed by the Thames to London. Coal also is brought hither by the Thames and **Supposed to be a Roman station.** Severn-canal, which here terminates in the river Isis or Thames. Lechlade is supposed by some antiquaries to have been a Roman station; and, in a meadow near the town, were discovered, several years ago, the remains of tessellated pavements, and the foundation of a building which appears to have been an ancient hypocaust or Roman bath. Thomas Coxeter, a bibliographer and antiquarian of some eminence, was born at Lechlade, in 1689; he died in 1747.

Market, Tuesday.—*Fairs*, August 5 and 12, for cattle and toys; and September 9, for cheese and cattle.

Ancient monuments. * LECKHAMPTON, a parish in the hundred of Cheltenham, part of it a rich pasture, and the remainder a mountainous tract, including some of the boldest and most lofty of the Cotswold-hills, one of which, from its craggy and gigantic form, is called the Devil's-chimney. The church contains some ancient monuments, among which are the effigies of a knight, cross-legged, and his lady. The manor-house is an ancient structure, supposed to have been erected in the reign of Henry VII.; it occupies three sides of a square, and though situated at the base of the Leckhampton-hills, commands a fine view over the vale of Gloucester.

Spacious church. † LEDBURY, a market-town, situated in the eastern angle of the county, at the southern extremity of the Malvern-hills, and on the declivity of a small eminence, about a mile westward from the river Leddon or Leden, which gives name to the place. It was anciently a borough, and returned members to Parliament twice in the reign of Edward I., but the elective franchise was not afterwards exercised. The church is a spacious edifice of Norman architecture, with alterations and additions made at different periods. It comprises a nave, aisles, and chancel, with a chapel called St. Catherine's, and a detached tower, terminating in a finely proportioned spire, about sixty feet high. Hugh Foliot, Bishop of Hereford, in 1232, founded here an hospital to the honour of St. Catherine, for a master and several poor brethren and sisters; and its dissolution having taken place in the reign of Henry VIII., it was refounded by Queen Elizabeth, in 1580, for a master, appointed by the dean and chapter of Hereford, seven widowers and three widows, with stipends of

Map.	Names of Places.	County.	Number of Miles from			Dist. Lond.	Popu- lation.
31	Ledwell ....ti	Oxford	NeatEnstone 4	Deddington ..4	Chip. Norton 8	71	....
5	Lee................pa	Bucks	Gt.Missenden 2	Chesham 4	Wendover .. 4	30	186
21	Lee................pa	Kent	Greenwich ..1	Woolwich ..4	Eltham......3	6	1108
16	Lee ....ti	Hants	Romsey 2	Lyndhurst ...8	Southampton 6	75	....
33	Leebotwood........pa	Salop......	Shrewsbury..9	Chur.Stretton4	M; Wenlock 10	157	223
33	Lee-Brockhurst... ..pa	Salop......	 10	Whitchurch 10	Wem.......3	163	150
16	Lee Britain ....ham	Hants	Gosport 4	Fareham 4	Tichfield 4	77	....
33	Lee Bridge.......ham	Salop.....	Shrewsbury 10	Whitchurch 9	Wem........3	156	....
14	Lee, East ....cha	Essex......	Tilbury Fort .2	Gra.Thurrock4	Horndon.....5	27	20
29	Lee, St. John ....pa	Northumb ..	Hexham 2	Corbridge....2	Bellingham .16	282	1952
29	Lee Mailing ....to	Northumb ..	16	Haltwhistle.16	Rothbury .. 22	296	....
16	Lee Mark ....ti	Hants	Fareham 3	Gosport 7	Titchfield....0	76	....
29	Lee Ward ....to	Northumb ...	Morpeth....10	Alnwick....12	Rothbury....3	302	103
14	Lee, West ....cha	Essex......	Tilbury Fort .2	Gra.Thurrock3	Horndon 4	26	..
21	Leeds..............pa	Kent	Maidstone .. 5	Lenham 6	Smarden....10	39	613
45	Leeds*............m t	W. R. York	Manchester 41	York 25	Sheffield....33	186	123393
43	Leek ....pa & to	N. R. York.	Thirsk 6	Nor. Allerton 6	Yarm 14	220	1083

£6. 13s. 4d. per annum each. There are also other alms-houses, a free grammar-school, founded about the middle of the sixteenth century, a charity-school, founded and endowed by Mrs. Elizabeth Hall, a national school for children of both sexes, and a school of industry for girls. Here are places of worship for the independents, the Baptists, and the Wesleyan Methodists. The town consists of two principal streets, intersecting each other nearly at right angles. The principal commerce at present depends on the produce of the neighbouring orchards and hop-grounds; the hops, cider, and perry, from the adjacent district, being all of excellent quality. The trades of malt-making and tanning afford employment for many persons; and near the town are quarries furnishing abundance of limestone, and marble for chimney-pieces and other purposes of decorative architecture. A charter for a market on Saturday was procured for the townsmen, by Betun, Bishop of Hereford, in the reign of King Stephen; but this becoming obsolete, Queen Elizabeth granted a charter for a market on Tuesday, and two annual fairs. The Gloucester and Hereford-canal passes by this town.

Market, Tuesday.—*Fairs*, first Monday after February 1, for horses, cattle, pigs, sheep, &c.; Monday before Easter, and May 12, for horned cattle and cheese; June 22, ditto and wool; first Tuesday in August, and October 2, for horned cattle, hops, cheese, and pigs; Monday before St. Thomas (December 21), for horned cattle, cheese, and fat hogs.

LEDBURY.

Its commerce.

* LEEDS, a large and populous market-town and chartered borough, distinguished as the principal seat of the clothing manufacture in the north of England. The town is situated on the declivity and summit of a hill, rising from the north bank of the river Aire, over which there is a noble stone bridge, leading to the extensive suburb on the opposite border. Its extent from east to west along the river is about a mile and a half, and its breadth from north to south somewhat less than a mile. A castle formerly existed here, which was besieged by King Stephen, in 1139; and in this fortress Richard II., after his deposition, in 1399, was confined for a short time previously to his removal to Pontefract, where he is supposed to have been put to death by order of his successor. There are no vestiges of the castle now remaining, but it is conjectured to have occupied the spot called Mill-hill. Leland describes Leeds as ‘ a pretty market-town, subsisting chiefly by clothing, reasonably well builded, and as large as Bradford, but not so quick as it.” The town received its first charter of incorporation from Charles I., in 1626, when Sir John Savile, afterwards ennobled, was made the first honorary alderman; and in compliment to him, the arms of the town are very appropriately decorated with Lord Savile's supporters, two of the Athenian birds, sacred to Minerva, the goddess of wisdom, and patroness of the arts of spinning and weaving. A second charter was given to the town by Charles II., in 1661, and renewed by James II., in 1684. The, corporation, under the new act of 1835, consists of a mayor, sixteen alder-

Castle besieged by King Stephen.

Incorporated by Charles I.

LEEDS.

The parish thirty miles in circumference.

Numerous places of worship.

Famous for the manufacture of cloth.

The Mixed cloth-hall.

men, and forty-eight common councilmen. The sessions are held quarterly, for the borough, in January, April, July, and October. The general quarter sessions for the West Riding, at Michaelmas, are also held at Leeds. In 1818 a vagrant office was established, as an appendage to the police of the town, for the more effectual suppression of medicity. The parish of Leeds, which is thirty miles in circumference, extending seven miles and a half from north to south, and seven and a quarter from east to west, is divided into ten townships, besides the township of Leeds, which includes the town itself, and the village of Woodhouse, about a mile distant from it. The church is a cruciform edifice, with a central tower; the nave was erected in the reign of Edward III., and the remaining parts of the building about the beginning of the sixteenth century; it has over the altar a painting of the Last Supper, and on the ceiling of the nave, one in fresco of the Ascension, by Parmentier; and there are several fine sepulchral monuments, particularly one in commemoration of two British officers, natives of Leeds, killed in the battle of Talavera, adorned with sculpture, by Flaxman. There are several other churches, or rather chapels, belonging to the establishment. St. John's, erected in 1634, was founded and endowed by John Harrison, a native of the parish. The church of the Holy Trinity is a handsome structure of moorstone, with ornaments, chiefly of the Doric order, and at the west end, a square tower and spire; the building was commenced in 1721, and completed at the expense of £4560. St. Paul's church is a noble fabric, embellished in front with Ionic pilasters and a pediment, surmounted by a domed tower; the cost of its erection was nearly £10,000; and it was consecrated in 1793. The church, dedicated to St. James, is an octagonal stone building. The churches of St. Mark, Woodhouse and St. Mary, Quarry-hill, are edifices of recent erection, by the commissioners. There are places of worship for Presbyterians, Unitarians, Quakers, Independents, Scotch Seceders, Baptists, Wesleyan Methodists, Seceding Methodists, and other sects of dissenters; together with a Roman Catholic chapel. The free grammarschool, founded in the reign of Edward VI., and subsequently endowed by Mr. Harrison, the founder of St. John's-church, and other benefactors. Here are likewise national and Lancasterian-schools, and various almshouses. The buildings of the town in general are of brick; the streets in the higher parts are narrow, but elsewhere they are broad, and the houses uniformly planned and arranged; and many of them display elegance, especially those in Park-place and Park-square, some of which command fine prospects of the neighbouring hills. Leeds has long been famous, not only for the manufacture of woollen cloth in general, but also as a mart for the two varieties of mixed and white broad cloths. The mixed cloths are those which are made with dyed wool, which, in the seventeenth century, were exposed for sale on the battlements of the long and wide bridge over the Aire, and afterwards in the open air in the street, called the Briggate. The inconvenience and damage to the cloth, from exposure to the weather, suggested the necessity of a different arrangement; and in 1758 the Mixed cloth-hall was erected at the general expense of the merchants and manufacturers. This is a quadrangular edifice, surrounding a large open area, from which it receives the light abundantly, by a great number of lofty windows; it is 128 yards in length, and sixty-six in breadth, divided in the interior into six departments, or covered streets, each including two rows of stands, amounting in number to 1800, held as freehold property by various manufacturers, every stand being marked with the name of the proprietor. The markets are held on Tuesdays and Saturdays, and only for an hour and a half each day, at which period alone sales can take place. The market-bell rings at six o'clock in the morning in summer, and at seven in winter, when the markets are speedily filled, the benches covered with cloth, and the proprietors respectively take their stands; the bell ceasing, the buyers enter to bargain for the cloth they may require, and business is thus summarily transacted, often involving an exchange of property to a vast amount. When the time for selling is terminated, the bell again rings, and any merchant staying in the hall after it has ceased, becomes liable to a penalty. Similar in its plan to the preceding, is the White Cloth-hall, which is divided into five streets, each with a double row of stands, amounting in all to 1210. The markets are held here on Tuesdays and Saturdays, but they do not commence till after the conclusion of those at the Mixed Cloth-hall, and are subject nearly to the same regulations. Besides these principal halls, there is also a small hall of more recent erection, under the concert-room, in Albion-street, appropriated to the use of such clothiers as are excluded from the others in consequence of not having served as apprentices to the trade. Though the coarser kinds of cloth long constituted the staple manufacture of the town and its vicinity, it has of late years been somewhat superseded by that of superfine cloth; and more recently large quantities of fancy goods have been made, such as swansdowns, toilinets, and kerseymeres, as well as cloths of a thick, coarse kind, called bear-skins. Here also are manufacturers of shalloons, stuffs, Scotch camlets, blankets, carpets, pelisse-cloths, and shawls, in great variety. Mills have been erected on an extensive scale, for the manufacture of tobacco and snuff; within a mile of the town, are potteries, where large quantities of earthenware are made, and exported thence to Scotland, Ireland, Holland, Germany, Russia, the Baltic, and the Mediterranean; here are establishments for making canvas, sacking, thread, &c.; others for the finer kinds of linen; and in or near Leeds are several cotton-mills, chiefly worked by means of steam-engines. Here are also iron and brass foundries, with establishments for making various kinds of machinery; oil and mustard-mills, paper-mills, silk-mills, and works for the preparation of oil of vitriol, aquafortis, and other chemical articles. Within the parish are several productive coal-mines, and abundant supply of slates and flagstones for paving. Among the public buildings, connected with commerce, besides the cloth-halls, are the Corn-exchange, advantageously situated at the top of the Briggate; and a handsome edifice, erected a few years ago, called the Commercial-buildings, or Exchange News-rooms, near the entrance into the Mixed Cloth-hall; it is a stone structure, with a circular portico in front, adorned with noble massive columns. In York-street are gas-works, for lighting the principal streets, shops, and manufactories; and there is also an oil-gas company, established in 1824. The new court-house and prison, erected in 1813, has been regarded as a beautiful and highly-finished specimen of modern architecture, and has been praised for its internal arrangement. The horse-barracks, constructed on a very extensive scale, are situated near Buslingthorpe; the building, with the parade-grounds, and other appendages, occupy a space of about eleven acres; and the expense of erecting this establishment was defrayed by a grant from government of £28,000. The Philosophical-hall is a handsome stone structure, erected for the use of the Leeds Philosophical and Literary Society. Here is a society for the encouragement of the fine arts, called the Northern Society, the gallery belonging to which adjoins the music-hall. There are several public libraries, called the Leeds, the New Subscription, the Parochial, the Methodist, the Eclectic, and the Mechanics' Libraries. The chief places of public amusement are the theatre, in Hunslet-lane, usually open in the months of May and June; the assembly-rooms over the north side of the White Cloth-hall; and the concert-rooms, in Albion-street. The charitable institutions in this town, exclusive of the schools and alms-houses already mentioned, are the general infirmary, near the Mixed cloth-hall, supported by benefactions and annual subscriptions, opened in 1771; the dispensary, and the house

Marginal notes:
LEEDS.
The White Cloth-hall.
Manufacture of tobacco and snuff.
Coal-mines.
Places of amusement.

6 s

Map.	Names of Places.	County	Number of Miles from				Dist. Lond.	Popu- lation.
39	Leek Wootton......pa	Warwick ..	Warwick....3	Kenilworth .2	Leamington..4		94	433
35	Leeke*.....m t & pa	Stafford	Manchester 32	Stafford 24	Newcastle..12		154	10780
35	Leeke, Frith........to	Stafford	Leeke 5	Congleton ..8	Longnor 9		159	873
43	Leeming.....to & cha	N. R. York .	Bedale 2	Catterick 6	N. Allerton..7		223	562
43	Leeming, Little ...ham	N. R. York .	 2	6	7		223	....
7	Lees ....to	Chester	Middlewich..3	Northwich ..6	Knutsford ...7		170	126
10	Lees................to	Derby	Derby 6	Ashbourn....9	Burton 10		132	....
22	Lees ......ham & cha	Lancaster...	Oldham 2	Rochdale....7	Ashton-un-L. 4		190	....
23	Leesthorpe ......ham	Leicester ...	Melton Mow. 4	Oakham 7	Billesdon 9		103	....
7	Leftwich ....to	Chester	Northwich ..1	Middlewich .5	Tarporley ..10		171	1799
24	Legbourn ....pa	Lincoln	Louth 3	Alford 8	Saltfleet....10		143	499
24	Legsby...........pa	Lincoln....	Mt. Raisin...5	Wragby 5	Louth......12		148	236
23	Leicester†.........co	Leicester ...	....	....	....		....	197003

LEEDS. of recovery, both in Vicar-lane, the lying-in hospital, in St. Peter's-square, and the guardian asylum, in St. James' s-street. Leeds confers the title of Duke on the family of Osborne.

Market, Tuesday and Saturday.—*Fairs*, July 10 and 11, for horses and hardware; October 8, and every Monday fortnight, for cattle, &c.; and November 9, for horned cattle, horses, and hardware.

* LEEKE, or Leek, a market-town and parish, situated on the river Churnet, a tributary stream to the Trent, in the moorlands of Stafford-shire, and on the great road from London to Manchester. The church is an ancient Gothic structure. In the churchyard, at the south-east angle of the chancel, are the remains of a pyramidal stone cross, about ten feet high, supposed to be of Danish origin. A free grammar-school has been founded here, to which is attached a small endowment; and alms-houses for eight widows were founded in 1696, by Mrs. Elizabeth Ash. The principal commerce of the town arises from the silk manufacture, and here are made bandana and other handkerchiefs, ribbons, ferrets, galloons, twists, and thrown silk. Buttons formerly constituted a staple article of manufacture, now on the decline; but the cotton-trade has been extended hither from Lancashire. Blue Hills, in the neighbourhood, abound with mines of coal; and from one of the hills issues a salt spring. In the neighbourhood are remarkable eminences, called Leek Rocks and Hen Clouds. A branch from the Trent and Mersey Navigation extends within about a quarter of a mile of the town. Besides the market and fairs, there are markets for fat cattle, held once a fortnight, on Wednesdays, from the 28th of July to Christmas.

Remains of an ancient cross.

Abounding in coal.

Market, Wednesday.—*Fairs*, February 7; Easter-Wednesday; May 18; Whit-Wednesday; July 3 and 28, and Wednesday after October 10, for cattle of all sorts, and pedlers' ware; Wednesday before Old Candlemas; and November 13, for cattle and pedlers' ware.

* LEICESTER, an inland county, situated nearly in the centre of the kingdom; and bounded on the north by Derbyshire and Nottingham-shire; on the east by the counties of Lincoln and Rutland; on the south by Northamptonshire; and on the west by Warwickshire and Derbyshire. When William, Duke of Normandy, ascended the throne, Leicestershire experienced a complete revolution as to territorial rights and privileges, the Danish or Anglo-Saxon proprietors being universally deprived of their estates, or obliged to become the feudal tenants of the Norman chiefs and barons, among whom the king distributed the lands and lordships of the county, to be held by the tenure of knights' service. These intruders, in order to secure their newly-acquired possessions, erected on their respec-tive estates strong and magnificent castles, to awe the vanquished Saxons, and secure themselves against their attacks or those of neighbouring nobles, with whom they often engaged in hostilities excited by family feuds or rival jealousy. The whole of this county presents nearly a level surface; and the land is chiefly appropriated to the purpose of grazing. The soil may be generally described as a fine mixture of sand and clay, partaking more of the latter than the former, but highly adapted for culti-vation. From Leicester, which is almost in the centre of the county, the

Its changes in feudal times.

Map.	Names of Places.	County.	Number of Miles from			Dist. Lond.	Popu- lation.
23	Leicester*....bo & m t	Leicester ...	Nottingham.26	Derby......29	MeltonMow.15	98	39306
23	Leicester Abbey..ex ....p lord	Leicester ...	Leicester 1	Loughboro' .11	Ashby......17	99	18

land rises towards the east, and also in some degree towards the south, but more especially in the west, towards Charnwood Forest. An extensive vale intervenes, through which passes the river Soar, anciently named the Leire, which is a tributary stream to the Trent. The other rivers are the Wreak, a branch of the Soar, the Swift, the Welland, the Avon, and the Anchor. With the Soar, the Wreak, and other streams, are connected various navigable canals, which have been constructed for the benefit of commerce. The principal mineral products of this county are coal and limestone. In some parts the limestone is blended with rich lead ore. Ironstone is found abundantly on Ashby Wolds, at the depth of about 680 feet; but it does not contain metal enough to pay the expense of smelting. At Swithland, on the east side of Charnwood Forest, are raised large quantities of slate; and freestone and clay for bricks may be found in most parts of the county. The hill of Mountsorrel is composed of a reddish kind of granite, which hardens on exposure to the atmosphere, and forms an admirable article for street pavements. In digging for coal on Ashby Wolds, saline springs were discovered 200 yards below the surface, and baths have since been erected on the spot. Leicestershire is famous as a grazing country, for breeding and feeding cattle and sheep. The Leicestershire sheep are particularly noted. The Leicestershire kine are well known and greatly esteemed in most parts of the kingdom. The principal object of the graziers is to fatten their cattle for the butcher; but in some parts of the county, as Hinckley, Bosworth, along the Trent, on the borders of Derbyshire, and in the vale of Belvoir, the dairy is much attended to. In the neighbourhood of Melton Mowbray is now made the peculiar kind of cheese called Stilton, deservedly styled, for its excellence, the Parmasan of England. Leicestershire has long been noted for useful and beautiful breed of black horses, comprising varieties for the plough and the waggon, or for the race-course and the chase. It is, indeed, one of the first sporting counties in England. To provide food for the horses and stock of the farmer, more than half the land is constantly kept in pasture, and the remaining part is chiefly appropriated to the production of grain and other food for cattle. The manufactures of Leicestershire are almost wholly those of its great staple article, wool, consisting of the combing, spinning, and making it into stockings, either by knitting or weaving. The principal articles of commerce from this county are cheese, worsted hose, hats, lace, and wool; besides great numbers of cattle and sheep, which are sent to London, Birmingham, and other places.

* LEICESTER, a borough and county-town. It is situated in a valley on the banks of the river Soar, anciently called the Leire, from which the town, supposed to have existed at a very remote period, is said to have been denominated by the ancient Britons, Caer Leirion, whence the Saxons formed the appellation, Leir-ceastre, since contracted to Leicester. Various indications of Roman residence have at different times been discovered, several of which are still existing. At the west end of St. Nicholas's church-yard is a curious fragment of Roman architecture, vulgarly styled the Jewry-wall, consisting of a mass of brick-work, stones, and rubbish, with five dilapidated arches, turned with wall tiles firmly cemented; and near it, on a spot called Holy Bones, the bones of oxen have been frequently dug up, whence the ruin is conjectured to have formed part of a Roman temple. Tessellated pavements have repeatedly been discovered here, the most curious of which, found in a cellar near the

LEICESTER.

town prison, in 1675, exhibits figures supposed to refer to the story of Diana and Actæon. Roman coins of various emperors, from Nero to Honorius, and fragments of pottery have been disinterred in vast quantities. But the most remarkable relic of antiquity, which has proved a fertile subject of archaiological discussion, is the military or Roman milestone, discovered in 1771, on the side of the Foss-road, at the distance of about two miles north of the town, and thence removed into it, and fixed on a base or pedestal by order of the corporation; the inscription on the surface was sufficiently legible, not only to identify the nature and design of the stone, but also to decide the name of the station, Ratæ, the distance from

Once a bishop's see.

which it is indicated. About 737, the see of a bishop was transferred from Sidnacester to Leicester; but how long this place continued to be a bishopric is uncertain. The town had anciently a mint, and a series of coins has been collected, which shows that the privilege of coinage was exercised here from the reign of King Athelstan to that of Henry II. The first charter granted to Leicester, was by King John, in 1199, and at the same time the feudal lord of the town, Robert Fitz Parnel, Earl of Leicester, bestowed on the burgesses the power of buying and selling land, and other privileges. Henry VII., in 1504, confirmed, by charter to the burgesses, all the rights and immunities they had previously enjoyed, and empowered the justices of the borough to take cognizance of all capital offences. Queen Elizabeth, in 1584, granted a fresh charter, confirmed by her successor, in 1604. The corporation, under the new act, in 1835, is composed of a mayor, fourteen aldermen, and forty-two common-councilmen. Leicester has sent members to Parliament ever since the reign of Edward I. One of the representatives was formerly chosen by the mayor and his brethren, and the other by the commonalty of the town, or inhabitants in general. This mode of election having excited disturbances, Henry VII. ordained that the mayor and his brethren should choose forty-eight of the wisest and gravest of the commonalty, who should elect all officers of the borough and members of Parliament. This anomalous kind of proceeding continued till the reign of Charles II., from which time, till the passing of the Reform Bill, the right of election was vested in the freemen not receiving alms, and the inhabitants paying scot and lot. Here Cardinal Wolsey, the fallen minister of a

Cardinal Wolsey died here.

tyrannical sovereign, died on the 29th of November, 1530, having been compelled by illness to seek an asylum in the abbey, while travelling as a prisoner to London in the custody of Sir William Kingston, by whom he had been arrested on the charge of high treason. The college of Newark was founded as an hospital by Henry, Earl of Lancaster and Leicester, in 1330, and turned into a college, with an increase of endowment, by his son, in 1355; John of Gaunt augmented the revenue, which, at the dissolution of monasteries, was about £800 a-year. A bed-house, or hospital for a master, a confrater, and twelve men and women, was founded by William Wigston, about the close of the fifteenth century; it escaped destruction at the Reformation, and still subsists; the master having a salary of £160, and the confrater £70; the appointment to these offices being vested in the Chancellor of the duchy of Lancaster. There

Charitable institutions.

was also an hospital dedicated to St. Leonard; and convents existed here belonging to the Austin Friars, Dominicans, the Franciscans, and the friars of the order called De Penitentia. Here are a free grammar-school, a National-school, and charity-school for the parishes of All Saints, St. Margaret, St. Martin, and St. Mary. The other charitable institutions are, an infirmary and a lunatic asylum. The principal streets, which intersect each other at right angles, are paved, and lighted with gas. Several buildings on an extensive scale have, within a few years past, been erected for the prosecution of commerce; and among the public edifices not before noticed, are the exchange, the excise office, the county-gaol, built in 1791, the town-gaol, the new bridewell, and a commodious

Map	Names of Places.	County.	Number of Miles from			Dist. Lond.	Popu-lation.
12	Leigh .... to	Dorset......	Wimborne ..1	Poole 8	Ringwood.. 8	99	532
12	Leigh .... cha	Dorset......	Sherborne....7	Cerne Abbas.7	Yeovil.....8	123	400
11	Leigh, East......ham	Devon	Bideford ...4	Barnstaple...5	Torrington ..6	196	....
14	Leigh ....pa	Essex	Rochford....4	South End ..4	Raleigh....4	40	1251
15	Leigh ....pa	Gloucester..	Tewkesbury .5	Gloucester ..6	Cheltenham 7	103	355
16	Leigh ....ti	Hants	Hambledon ..0	Petersfield..10	Winchester 20	64	....
21	Leigh ....pa	Kent	Tunbridge....3	Seven Oaks. 8	Westerham . 9	29	1011
16	Leigh, East.........ti	Hants	Havant....1	Petersfield..11	Portsmouth 11	65	....
35	Leigh or Lees ....pa	Stafford ...	Uttoxeter ...5	Cheadle 6	Stone........9	140	1038
16	Leigh, Middle .....ti	Hants	Havant.....3	Petersfield..10	Portsmouth 11	64	....
37	Leigh ....pa	Surrey	Reigate.....3	Dorking 5	Crawley 8	24	483
16	Leigh, West........ti	Hants	Havant.....3	Petersfield..11	Portsmouth 10	65	....
41	Leigh ....to	Wilts	Westbury ...1	Warminster .3	Trowbridge..6	100	1420
41	Leigh or The Lea ..cha	Wilts	Cricklade....3	Wotton Bas..7	Malmesbury .9	87	267
42	Leigh ....pa	Worcester..	Worcester ..5	Gt. Malvern .6	Bromyard ..10	116	1933
34	Leigh, Abbot's* ....pa	Somerset ...	Bedminster ..3	Bristol 4	Axbridge ..17	122	402
7	Leigh, High .. to & cha	Chester.....	Knutsford ...5	Altrincham . 5	Warrington . 8	181	983
7	Leigh, Little..to & cha	Chester.....	Northwich ..4	Frodsham ...7	9	174	381
41	Leigh de la Mere ...pa	Wilts	Chippenham 5	Malmesbury .7	Bath......14	98	129
34	Leigh upon Mendip .pa	Somerset ...	Frome 6	Shepton Mal. 6	14	109	640
11	Leigh, North......pa	Devon	Colyton 4	Honiton 4	Sidmouth ..7	153	240
31	Leigh, North. ......pa	Oxford	Witney 4	Charlbury ...4	Woodstock ..5	65	519
11	Leigh, South ......pa	Devon	Colyton 3	Honiton 6	Sidmouth....6	158	320
31	Leigh, South ......pa	Oxford	Witney 3	Ensham 3	Bampton 6	63	339
11	Leigh, West ......pa	Devon.....	Bideford 2	Barnstaple ..7	Torrington...6	202	484
22	Leigh, West†. m t & pa	Lancaster...	Newton.....5	Bolton 7	Warrington 10	197	2780

LEICESTER.

theatre. Many years since a fine public walk was constructed on ground given by the corporation, extending more than a mile from the town, in a south-eastward direction, and affording many delightful views of the surrounding country. The chief manufacture here is that of hosiery, and especially worsted stockings, conducted on so extensive a scale as to furnish employment, according to estimate, to more than 20,000 persons ; and it is stated, that occasionally more than 18,000 dozens of hose, &c. are made weekly in the town and its immediate vicinity. The other manufactures are those of brass and iron work, ropes, twine, sacking, &c., sewing cotton, thrown silk, frames for the stocking-makers, and other machinery. Dr. Richard Farmer, an antiquary and critic, who projected a " History of Leicestershire," and gained great literary reputation by his " Essay on the Learning of Shakspeare," was born at Leicester in 1735 ; he died in 1797.

Its manufactures.

Market, Wednesday and Saturday.—*Fairs*, March 2 ; Saturday before Easter ; and Saturday in Easter week ; May 12, 13, and 14 ; June 1, and July 5, for horses, cows, and sheep ; October 10, largely for horses, cows, and sheep ; December 8, a few horses and cows. New *Fairs*, January 4 ; June 1 ; August 1 ; September 13 ; and November 2.

* LEIGH ABBOT'S. Leigh-court, in this parish, is a splendid seat, not more distinguished for the elegance of its architecture, than for its interior decorations and rich and costly furniture. The picture-gallery contains a collection of works of art unrivalled in the west of England, including the two celebrated landscapes of Claude, from the Altieri-palace, formerly belonging to Mr. Beckford, of Fonthill.

Splendid seat.

† LEIGH, WEST, a parish and market-town, situated in the manufacturing district of Lancashire, and at the junction of the Leeds and Liverpool-canal with a branch from that of the Duke of Bridgewater. It includes the townships of West Leigh and Pennington, the division of which takes place in the centre of the town, so that the market-place stands in the former, and the parish church in the latter of these townships. The church is an ancient stone structure. Here are places of worship for the Independents, the Methodists, and the Swedenborgians, and a Roman Catholic-chapel. In the churchyard is a free grammar-school, founded and endowed by Piers Ranicars, in 1655, and the funds have been since augmented by other benefactors. There is also in the parish an institution called the Bedford Charity-school. Muslins, cambrics, calicoes, and fustians, are the principal articles here manufactured ;

Religious edifices.

Map.	Names of Places.	County.	Number of Miles from			Dist. Lond.	Population.
41	Leigh, Wooley ......ti	Wilts	Trowbridge..3	Bradford 1	Melksham ...6	101	1680
34	Leighland..........cha	Somerset....	Watchet...4	Dunster 6	Wiveliscombe7	160	....
14	Leighs, Great......pa	Essex	Braintree ..6	Witham ...6	Chelmsford ..7	36	756
14	Leighs, Little .. ....pa	Essex	5	7	7	36	189
15	Leighterton...ti & cha	Gloucester..	Tetbury 5	Wooton un E.7	Dursley......8	104	....
7	Leighton ....to	Chester.....	Nantwich ...5	Sandbach....6	Middlewich..7	168	261
7	Leighton ....to	Chester.....	Parkgate ...1	Gt. Neston ..1	Liverpool....9	191	333
19	Leighton .. ..pa	Hunts	Kimbolton ..6	Huntingdon..9	Stilton 10	68	452
56	Leighton....ham & to	Montgomery	Welchpool ..1	Montgomery .9	Newtown ..18	170	213
33	Leighton .. ..pa	Salop	M. Wenlock.4	Wellington ..6	Shrewsbury 11	150	360
3	Leighton Buzzard*..} .... mt & pa}	Bedford	Woburn 5	Dunstable ...8	Aylesbury ..11	41	5149
17	Leintwardine..pa & to	Hereford....	Ludlow 9	Leominster .16	Bish.Castle .15	151	1358
29	Leipscot............to	Northumb...	Morpeth 1	Newcastle..15	Rothbury..15	289	174
23	Leire ....pa	Leicester ...	Lutterworth 4	Hinckley 7	Leicester .. 11	93	485
36	Leiston† ....pa	Suffolk	Saxmundham5	Aldborough..5	Dunwich ...6	95	1070
46	Lelley.............to	E. R. York.	Hull 8	Hedon 2	Patrington .10	179	114
29	Lemington..........to	Northumb ..	Alnwick ...5	Rothbury....6	Morpeth....17	306	85
15	Lemington, Lower ..pa	Gloucester..	Moreton in M.3	Shipston on S.4	Campden 7	87	56
5	Lenborough.......ham	Bucks	Buckingham 2	Winslow.. ..6	Bicester 11	56	75
42	Lench Church ......pa	Worcester..	Evesham 6	Alcester ...7	Pershore 7	102	360

LEIGH, WEST.
Coal-mines.

several new commercial establishments have taken place in and near the town of late years ; and the numerous population of the parish appears to have been greatly augmented. Here are coal-mines, and likewise lime-pits, which furnish a valuable kind of lime-stone, the lime from which has the property of hardening under water.

Market, Saturday.—*Fairs*, April 24 and 25; December 7, and 18, for cattle, swine and horses.

Singular Gothic cross.

* LEIGHTON BUZZARD, a parish and market-town, situated on the south-western border of the county, and on the eastern bank of the river Ouzel. The proper appellation of the town is Leighton Beau Desert, of which the present name is a corruption. In the market-place is a Gothic cross, a pentangular structure, thirty-eight feet in height, and consisting of two stories, that above divided into five niches or recesses, containing so many statues ; the first exhibits a person in an episcopal dress ; the second, the Virgin, with the infant Jesus ; the third, apparently St. John the Evangelist ; the others too much mutilated to be identified. This interesting monument of antiquity was repaired in 1650, a rate having been levied on the inhabitants of the town to defray the expense. The origin of this cross is uncertain ; but as there was at this place a cell to the Cistercian monastery of Woburn, it had probably some connexion with that religious foundation. The church is a handsome cruciform structure, of the Gothic style, with a massive tower, surmounted by an octangular spire, rising from the intersection of the nave and transept. It was formerly a collegiate church. A charity-school was founded and endowed by the Hon. Mrs. Leigh, in 1790 ; and alms-houses, for eight poor women, were founded in 1630, by Matthew Wilkes.

Manufacture of lace, &c.

The manufactures of lace, and straw-plat for hats and bonnets, are carried on here, affording employment to a considerable number of females ; other branches of industry, are lime-burning and brick-making ; and the vicinity of the Grand Junction-canal has given rise to trade of some extent in corn, seeds, timber, iron, and other articles. The market is numerously attended, and amply supplied with cattle, corn, and the manufacture of the town.

Market, Tuesday.—*Fairs*, February 5 ; second Tuesday in April, for horses and cattle; Whit-Tuesday, great horse fair; July 26 and October 24, for cattle; and St. Leonard's-day, November 7.

† LEISTON. This place is remarkable for the ruins of an abbey of Premonstratensian canons, which was founded in 1182 ; great part of the church, several subterraneous chapels, and other offices of the monastery are still standing, and are used as barns and granaries.

Map.	Names of Places.	County.	Number of Miles from			Dist. Lond.	Popu- lation.
42	Lench Rouse .....pa	Worcester..	Evesham 8	Alcester.....6	Pershore.....7	104	280
42	Lench, Sheriff's ...ham	Worcester..	4	9	5	100	79
42	Lench Wick..to & cha	Worcester..	3	9	6	99	....
21	Lenham *.....vil & pa	Kent	Maidstone ..10	Ashford 11	Faversham..11	44	2197
15	Lenhill, Great and } Little ....ham }	Gloucester } and Oxford }	Lechlade 2	Fairford 3	Burford 8	78	....
17	Lenthall, Earl's....cha	Hereford ...	Ludlow 7	Leominster ..8	Presteign .. 10	145	....
17	Lenthall, Starkes ...pa	Hereford ...	6	9	10	146	150
30	Lenton†...........pa	Nottingham..	Nottingham .1	Derby 15	Ashby......20	126	3077
17	Leominster‡ ..m t & pa	Hereford ...	Tenbury....12	Weobly 10	Hereford ...14	137	5249
38	Leominster.........pa	Sussex	Lit.Hampton 2	Arundel 2	Worthing....9	57	715
5	Leonard's, St.. ....cha	Bucks	Wendover .. 3	Tring......3	Berkhampste.6	32	14.

* LENHAM, a parish and village, formerly a market-town near the source of the little river Len, from which it derives its name. It consists principally of two streets, crossing each other, and at their intersection is a square planted with trees, which have an agreeable effect on the appearance of the place. The church is a spacious and handsome structure, consisting of a nave, chancel, and north aisle, with a square tower and a small attached chapel. At the west end of the chancel are sixteen stalls, and on the south side a stone seat or chair ; probably designed for the accommodation of the abbot and monks of St. Augustin, Canterbury, during their occasional visits to Lenham, in which parish was an estate belonging to their monastery. The market having been long disused, an attempt was made, in 1757, to re-establish it under the patronage of the lord of the manor, but without success.

Spacious church.

Fairs, June 6, for cattle and horses, and October 23, for horses, &c.

† LENTON. The church is an ancient structure, containing many curious monuments. Here are the remains of a considerable Cluniac priory. Lenton-priory is a very handsome seat, built in the form of an ancient priory, in the garden of which are several sepulchral memorials, and a curious Saxon font, supposed to have belonged to the ancient priory. In the vicinity are some coal-mines.

Remains of a priory.

Fairs, Wednesday in Whitsun-week, and Martinmas, November 11, for horned cattle, sheep, and hogs.

‡ LEOMINSTER, a market and borough town, situated in a pleasant and fertile valley, amidst meadows, orchards, and hop-grounds, watered by two small streams which pass through the town, and the river Lug, by which it is partly encompassed. In the reign of Edward the Confessor, the manor was held by Queen Eltha, and the town, which seems to have been then a place of importance, was governed by præpositi, or provosts, and other officers. The town was destroyed by fire in the reign of King John, but it was speedily rebuilt. After the death of Edward VI. the men of Leominster distinguished themselves by their promptitude in rising to support the claims of his sister Mary to the crown, in opposition to the ill-concerted conspiracy of Dudley, Duke of Northumberland, in favour of Lady Jane Grey. In recompense for this service, Queen Mary bestowed on the town the first charter of incorporation ; and other charters, with additional privileges and immunities, have been granted by succeeding sovereigns, the last being that given by George I. The corporation, under the new act, in 1833, consists of a mayor, four aldermen and twelve counsellors. The borough has sent members to Parliament ever since the reign of Edward I. The church is an irregular building, the work of different periods, the north side of the nave and the north aisle exhibiting columns, arches, and arcades of Norman architecture, while the south side is manifestly of a later date. The interior was greatly injured by fire more than a century ago, when the ancient monuments, stalls, and wood-work were destroyed. There is now a good organ, and over the altar is a painting representing the Last Supper, from Rubens. A free

Town destroyed by fire.

Map.	Names of Places.	County.	Number of Miles from			Dist. Lond.	Popu- lation.
11	Leonard, St.......pa	Devon	Exeter......1	Topsham 4	Crediton 7	172	467
38	Leonard's, St. ......pa	Sussex	Hastings 2	Bexhill.....4	Battle 6	64	346
46	Leppington...to & cha	E. R. York .	New Malton .8	Pocklington 10	York.......14	205	118
45	Lepton ....to	W. R. York	Huddersfield.4	Penistone....9	Wakefield ...9	186	3320
29	Lesbury ......pa & to	Northumb ..	Alnwick 4	Felton.......9	Belford 16	308	976
8	Lesnewth ....pa	Cornwall ..	Camelford ..5	Launceston 15	Stratton ..13	228	127
27	Lessingham ......pa	Norfolk.....	N. Walsham.7	Norwich ...16	Yarmouth ..20	125	191
21	Lessness ......cha	Kent	Crayford....2	Woolwich ..5	Erith........1	13	....
18	Letchworth ....pa	Herts	Hitchin.....3	Baldock 3	Stevenage ...5	36	76
4	Letcombe Basset ..pa	Berks	Wantage ...3	Lambourn ..5	E. Ilsley....10	63	288
4	Letcombe Regis ..pa	Berks......	2	6	9	62	969
36	Letheringham ......pa	Suffolk	M. Wickham 3	Framlingham 4	Woodbridge .6	84	174
27	Letheringset........pa	Norfolk....	Holt 1	N Walsingh.10	Fakenham ..12	119	278
57	Letterston ....pa	Pembroke ..	Haverford W10	Fishguard ..4	St. Davids ..14	261	493
17	Letton........ pa & to	Hereford ...	Weobly....7	Kineton 8	Hay.......10	150	200
17	Letton ....to	Hereford ...	Knighton ..6	Ludlow ...11	Kineton...11	154	134
27	Letton..............pa	Norfolk....	EastDereham 5	Watton 5	Swaffham ..11	96	133
45	Letwell......to & cha	W. R. York	Worksop ...6	Blythe......5	Tickhill ...4	152	155
8	Levan, St.* ....pa	Cornwall ..	Penzance ...8	St. Burian ...3	Land's End ..4	297	515
35	Levedale ....to	Stafford.....	Penkridge ..2	Stafford.....5	Newport ...12	131	....
21	Leveland...........pa	Kent	Feversham ..4	Lenham 6	Milton 7	47	79
46	Leven.........pa & to	E. R. York	Beverley ...7	Gt. Driffield 10	Hull 14	187	771
40	Levens ....to	Westmorlnd.	Kendal 6	Burton......7	Kir. Lonsdale 9	261	789
22	Levenshulme ......to	Lancaster...	Manchester..4	Stockport ...4	Ashton un L. 6	182	1086
45	Leventhorpe.....ham	W. R. York.	Leeds 5	Swillerton .. 0	Wakefield .. 8	185	....
22	Lever Darcy.. to & cha	Lancaster...	Bolton 2	Manchester .10	Bury........6	196	1119
22	Lever, Great. ......to	Lancaster...	1	9	6	196	637
22	Lever, Little†......to	Lancaster...	3	8	5	195	2231
6	Leverington ....pa	Cambridge .	Wisbeach ...2	March...... 9	Holbeach .. 11	91	1700

LEOMIN- STER. grammar-school was founded and endowed with £20. per annum, by Queen Mary I., and there is likewise a school on the national plan, supported by subscription. An alms-house for four decayed widows, was founded here in 1735, by Mrs. Esther Clarke. The buildings in the outskirts of the town are very indifferent, and many of the streets are narrow and inconvenient; but the High-street is spacious, and contains many modern edifices of a respectable appearance; and the situation of the place, as a thoroughfare on the great road from London to South Wales, has occasioned the erection of several good inns. The town-hall, **Singular structure.** or, as it is commonly called, the butter-cross, is a singular structure of plaster and timber-work, erected in 1633, by John Abel, a noted architect of that period. It stands on twelve oak pillars, with a kind of Ionic capital, and sustained by stone pedestals, the brackets and spandrels above the arches, and the upper parts of the building, are profusely ornamented with carving. A new gaol was erected in 1750; and a market-house in 1803. **Manufac- tures.** The principal manufactures carried on here formerly were those of woollen cloth, hats, and gloves; but the last-mentioned is declining, and the others have almost disappeared; among the existing branches of industry are flax-dressing, rope-making, tanning, malting, and nail-making.

Market, Friday.—*Fairs*, February 13, Tuesday after Midlent Sunday, and May 13, for horned cattle and horses; July 10, for horned cattle, horses, wool, and Welsh butter; September 4, for horned cattle, horses, and butter; and November 8, for horned cattle, hops, and butter.

* LEVAN, ST. Here is the holy well, dedicated to St. Levan, with an oratory; and in this parish is Treryn-castle, a large piece of rocky ground projecting into the sea and enclosed by two formidable ramparts and ditches. On this promontory is the most considerable and curious of **The Logan stone.** the Logan stones; it is poised on the top of an enormous pile of rocks which rises to a fearful height and overhangs the sea; this immense block of granite contains about 1200 cubic feet, and is supposed to weigh nearly ninety tons, yet, from its peculiarity of position, a single person may give it oscillatory motion with perfect ease.

† LEVER, LITTLE. The Bolton-canal passes here over the Irwell, by a lofty aqueduct of three arches. This place gave birth to Thomas

	Names of Places.	County.	Number of Miles from			Dist. Lond.	Popu lation
9	Leversdale...........to	Cumberland.	Carlisle......7	Longtown ...8	Brampton ...4	301	431
4	Leverton............ti	Berks......	Hungerford ..1	Ramsbury ...4	Lambourn ...7	65	...
24	Leverton, North....pa	Lincoln.....	Boston.....7	Wainfleet ...9	Spilsby....14	124	631
10	Leverton, North....pa	Notts.....	East Retford..6	Gainsborough 6	Tuxford ...9	146	305
10	Leverton, South ....pa	Notts......	6	7	8	145	400
18	Levesden ....ham	Herts......	Watford 3	St. Albans...6	HemelHemp. 6	18	...
16	Levington..........pa	Suffolk	Ipswich 6	Harwich 6	Woodbridge .8	78	228
11	Lew, North ....pa	Devon	Hatherleigh..4	Oakhampton.7	Holsworthy.12	202	...
11	Lew Trenchard....pa	Devon	Oakhampton10	Tavistock ...9	Launceston . 9	205	435
8	Lewannick.........pa	Cornwall. ..	Launceston ..5	Camelford ..12	Callington ..11	218	643
31	Lewes.............to	Oxford	Witney 3	Bampton 2	Burford 6	69	...
38	Lewes*......bo & m t	Sussex	Brighton.....8	TunbridgeW24	Hastings....33	50	8592

Lever, an eloquent and popular preacher in the reign of Edward VI., and also to Oliver Heywood, a nonconformist divine, who was born in 1629, and died in 1702. *(marginal note: LEVER, LITTLE.)*

* LEWES, a considerable borough and market-town. It is situated at the eastern extremity of the South Downs, on the banks of a small river, called the Ouse, and about seven miles distant from the sea. This place is supposed to have been a Roman station, from the coins and other antiquities found here, but it cannot be satisfactorily identified with any of those mentioned by ancient writers. Its importance, during the Anglo-Saxon period of our history, appears from the establishment of two *(marginal note: Original importance.)* mints for coinage, in the reign of Athelstan, while there was only one at Chichester. Before the Norman Conquest, the lordship of Lewes was vested in the crown; but William I. gave it, together with the whole rape of Lewes, to his son-in-law, William de Warren, a Norman baron, who either rebuilt from the foundation, or enlarged and strengthened the castle, which had been erected by the Saxons, and made it his principal residence. Lewes continued in the possession of the Earls of Warren till 1347, when, on the death of the last Earl, the property devolved to his nephew, Richard Fitz Alan, Earl of Arundel, whose grandson leaving no issue, his estates were divided between his three sisters, and are still held in coparceny by their descendants. The castle has been long in ruins, but there are still some portions remaining, particularly the gate-house, which appears to have been erected in the reign of Edward III. Near *(marginal note: Great battle fought here)* this town a remarkable battle was fought on the 14th of May, 1264, between the forces of King Henry III. and those of the confederated barons in insurrection against him, under the command of Montfort, Earl of Leicester, who completely defeated the royalists, and subsequently concluded a truce or treaty with the king, called "The Mise of Lewes." Members have been returned to Parliament for this place ever since the 26th of Edward I. The quarter sessions for the eastern part of the county of Sussex have been held at Lewes ever since the reign of Edward III.; in 1504 an act of Parliament was passed for holding the sheriff's or county court at this town and at Chichester, alternately; and here are held the county assizes in the summer circuit. The town anciently contained eleven parishes. Lewes may be considered as the county town, and it is nearly the largest and most populous place in the county, having several good streets and handsome houses, besides public buildings. Among which are the county-hall, a spacious and well-built *(marginal note: Public buildings)* stone structure, erected from the designs of John Johnston, architect, in 1812, at the expense of about £10,000.; and the house of correction for the eastern division of the county, built in 1793, and enlarged in 1817. Here is a theatre for dramatic exhibitions; and races are held near the town every summer, in July or August. The principal manufacture now carried on here is that of paper; and on the banks of the Ouse are extensive iron-works, for casting cannon and other purposes. A monastery of Cluniac monks was founded here by William, Earl of Warren, and his wife, Gundrida, the daughter of William the Conqueror, in 1078,

6 t

Map	Names of Places.	County.	Number of Miles from			Dist. Lond.	Popu- lation.
21	Lewisham* ....pa	Kent......	Greenwich ..2	Eltham.....3	Bromley 5	5	9659
3	Lewknor..........pa	Oxford.....	Tetsworth ...4	Thame.....5	Watlington..3	39	709
12	Lewston......ex p dis	Dorset......	Sherborne ...4	Yeovil.......8	Cerne Abbas.8	120	18
14	Lexden ....pa	Essex......	Colchester ..2	Coggeshall ..9	Witham....12	49	1184
27	Lexham, East ......pa	Norfolk.....	Swaffham ...7	Fakenham ...9	EastDereham 8	100	206
27	Lexham, West .....pa	Norfolk.....	6	10	11	99	103
21	Leyborne...........pa	Kent	Maidstone ..5	Rochester ...8	Wrotham....7	29	299

LEWES.

dedicated to St. Pancras, which was the principal establishment belonging to that monastic order in England; and at the time of its suppression, by Henry VIII., its revenues amounted to £1090. per annum. Here also were hospitals, dedicated to St. James and St. Nicholas, and a convent of Franciscan friars. The famous Thomas Paine, author of the "Rights of Man," in the earlier part of his life was an exciseman at Lewes. Near

Discovery of fossil remains.

this place have been discovered some curious fossil remains, the most remarkable of which are bones of enormous dimensions, belonging to an animal to which naturalists have given the name of Megalosaurus, from its resemblance to the lizard; fragments of the thigh-bones have been found twenty-two inches in circumference. Along with these gigantic relics were also found those of another extinct species of animal, called the Plesiosaurus, and bones of crocodiles, tortoises, cetaceous fishes and birds.

Market, Saturday.—*Fairs*, May 6, for horned cattle; Whit-Tuesday, for horned cattle and horses; July 26, for wool; and October 2, for sheep.

* LEWISHAM, a parish and pleasant village situated on the Ravensbourn, a stream which flows through Deptford into the Thames. The name of this place is supposed to be derived from the Saxon "leswe," a meadow, and "ham," a dwelling. In the village and its vicinity are many handsome houses and detached villas, inhabited by opulent merchants and retired citizens, attracted hither by the salubrity of the air and the beauties of the surrounding country. The church was erected, in 1774, on the site of a former church, and was a few years ago repaired and embellished at a considerable expense. This structure, which was heated by

Church destroyed by fire, in 1830.

means of a large stove and flues, having been opened for divine service on Christmas Day, 1830, it is supposed that the flues becoming overheated, set fire to some of the woodwork of the interior, as at a very early hour on the following morning the building was discovered to be in flames, and notwithstanding every exertion, the conflagration continued till the interior was almost entirely destroyed, leaving only the walls and roof standing. The inhabitants of the parish shortly after raised a handsome subscription to repair the injury thus unfortunately occasioned. Two charity-schools, one of which is a free grammar-school, founded by the Rev. Abraham Colfe, vicar of this parish, in the latter part of the seventeenth century, are under the patronage of the Leathersellers' Company; and there are alms-houses for six poor women, that owe their foundation to the same benevolent individual. Here was formerly a small convent, which was a cell to the Benedictine-abbey of St. Peter at Ghent; and on the suppression of alien priories, by Henry V., it was given to the monastery of Shene, or Richmond.

† LEXDEN, a parish and village, situated on the high road to London. This pleasant village probably occupies the site of the ancient town or fortress of Camalodun, the capital of the Trinobantes, before the invasion of Britain by the Romans. On Lexden-heath are stupendous, irregular earth-works, called Gryme's-dyche, in a peregrination of the liberties of Colchester, in the reign of Charles I.; and at the south-west

King Coel's kitchen.

corner is an excavation, vulgarly called King Coel's kitchen, which Dr. Stukeley supposed to have been an amphitheatre. Numerous traces of British and Roman settlements here have been discovered, whence it

dnnr	Names of Places.	County.	Number of Miles from			Dist. Lond.	Population.
37	Leybourn ....ti	Surrey	Godalming...0	Guildford....4	Farnham ...10	33	1003
43	Leyburn*.........m t	N. R. York.	Richmond ...9	Askrigg 10	Masham 9	235	....
11	Leyhill ....ham	Devon	Honiton. 5	Collumpton..6	Exeter 12	153	....
22	Leyland........pa & to	Lancaster...	Chorley 4	Preston......5	Wigan 11	212	13871
21	Leysdown ....pa	Kent	Queenboro' . 8	Faversham ..7	Milton 9	53	191
14	Leyton †............pa	Essex	Stratford 2	Barking 5	WalthamAb. 9	4	3323
8	Lezant............pa	Cornwall ...	Launceston ..4	Callington ...7	Liskeard....13	220	841
27	Leziate, Lesyate....pa	Norfolk ...	Lynn Regis ..5	Swaffham ..12	Downham ...13	98	159
43	Libberston..........to	N. R. York.	Scarborough .5	Hunmanby ..3	Bridlington .12	215	173
28	Lichborough........pa	Northamp. .	Towcester .. 7	Daventry 6	Northampt. 10	67	412
12	Lichet Matravers. ..pa	Dorset......	Wimborne ..6	Poole........8	Blandford .. 10	106	630
12	Lichet Minster .....pa	Dorset.....	 8	 8	12	108	560
12	Lichfield. ....pa	Hants	Whitchurch .5	Newbury....7	Kingsclere ..6	60	95
16	Lichfield‡........city	Stafford	Birmingham 16	Newc.-un-L 30	Manchester 67	110	6499

LEXDEN.

may be inferred that the Romans, on their conquest of this part of the country, established at this place the station which they called Camalodunum, and which they afterwards removed to Colchester, as a situation better adapted for a military post.

Natural terrace.

* LEYBURN, a market-town, pleasantly situated and surrounded by picturesque and delightful scenery. The town consists chiefly of an oblong square. Here is a beautiful natural terrace, called Leyburn-shawl, which passes along the edge of a ridge of rocks for the distance of two miles. The mineral productions in the vicinity are lead, coal, and lime.

Market, Friday.—*Fairs*, second Friday in February; second Friday in May; second Friday in October; and second Friday in December, for horned cattle and sheep.

Strype, the antiquarian.

† LEYTON, a parish, called also Low Leyton, in the hundred of Becontree, which takes its name from the river Ley, or Lea, passing through it. Camden, Dr. Gale, and other antiquaries, have conjectured that the site of the Roman station, called Durolitum, was near the site of the manor-house; and their opinion derives some confirmation from the discoveries which were made some years since of Roman bricks, or wall tiles, urns, coins, and other antiquities. The church is a brick edifice, consisting of a nave, chancel, north side, and western tower, which last was erected in 1658. John Strype, the antiquary and ecclesiastical historian, held the benefice of Leyton under peculiar circumstances, during the long period of sixty-eight years; for having been elected by the parishioners, in 1669, he was licensed by the Bishop of London, in 1674, to officiate as curate during the vacancy of the vicarage, and he continued to hold the office without institution or induction till his decease, in 1737, at the advanced age of ninety-four. Here are a free-school for twenty poor boys, founded and endowed by Robert Ozier, in 1697; and a school of industry for girls, established in 1794; besides Sunday-schools. Almshouses for eight poor persons were founded here by John Smith, merchant, in 1656, and endowed by various benefactors. The famous Sir Thomas Roe, or Rowe, ambassador to the Great Mogul, in the beginning of the seventeenth century, was a native of Leyton.

Introduction of Christianity

‡ LICHFIELD, an ancient city, forming a county of itself. It stands on the banks of a small stream that falls into the Trent, in the midst of a fine valley, surrounded by gently swelling hills. It is said to have been only a small village, when Oswy, King of Northumberland, having defeated and slain Penda, the Pagan King of the Mercians, about 656, introduced Christianity among his subjects, and built a church and established a bishopric at this place. In 669, Chad, a zealous ecclesiastic, afterwards canonized, was appointed to this see, and under his prelacy Christianity was greatly extended among the people, and Lichfield became a considerable town. Offa, King of Mercia, about 790, obtained a decree from the pope for the division of the province of Canterbury, and erecting

LICHFIELD.

here an archiepiscopal see; but after the death of Offa the government of the English church reverted to its former state. At the time of the Norman Conquest, the town was of so little importance, that, in consequence of an ordinance of Archbishop Lanfranc, for the removal of bishoprics from insignificant places, this see was transferred to Chester; and thence, in 1102, to Coventry; but Roger de Clinton being appointed bishop in 1129, made this place again the seat of prelacy, and his successors ever since have assumed the style of Bishops of Lichfield and Coventry. Bishop Clinton not only rebuilt the cathedral church, but he is also recorded to have erected a magnificent tower, and to have fortified the city, of which works some memorial is preserved in the name of Castle Ditch. Among the few historical events deserving of notice in the annals of Lichfield are the trial of Edward Wightman, before the consistory court of this city, in 1611, on the charge of heresy, as an Arian, or Anabaptist; his conviction and delivery over to the secular power; and his subsequent execution, by being burnt alive in pursuance of the king's writ, dated March 9, 1611. Another event, which has perhaps been the subject of more discussion than it deserved, was the death of Robert, Lord Brooke, a parliamentary officer, during the civil war, who having laid siege to the Close of Lichfield, garrisoned by the Royalists, was killed by a musket-ball, fired from the battlements of the cathedral tower. What rendered this accident remarkable was the report that Lord Brooke, on advancing to the attack, when within half a mile of the city, halted his troops and publicly prayed for a blessing on his undertaking, desiring that God would give him some special token in approbation of his design. The fatal occurrence that followed this act of superstition, and its happening also on the festival of St. Chad, to whom the cathedral was dedicated, inspired the Royalists with the belief that an especial judgment had befallen the rebel chief. The city was anciently under the government of a guild, consisting of a guild-master and four wardens, with twenty-four brethren and sisters. Of this guild, Henry VII., together with the Queen and his son, Prince Arthur, became members. Lichfield was incorporated by Edward VI., in 1549, and his charter was confirmed, with additions, by Queen Mary, who, in 1553, by the authority of Parliament, constituted this city a county of itself. Queen Elizabeth ratified these charters, as also did James I.; and in 1664, Charles II. granted the charter under which the late corporation acted, for though it was surrendered to James II., in 1686, yet it was subsequently restored. The corporation, under the new act of 1835, is composed of a mayor, a bailiff, six aldermen, and eighteen counsellors. Here are held quarter-sessions, a court of piepowder, a court called Maudlin's Court, the great portmote court of the bailiffs and citizens, a court of view of frankpledge, and court-baron, a court of record for the recovery of debts amounting to forty shillings or more, and a court annually held by the bailiffs on Whit-Monday, in the Guild-hall, and adjourned to the open air; this court was anciently called the Court of Array, or View of Men at Arms; and it is attended by the city officers and others, who make processions, bearing garlands of flowers and emblems of their trades, accompanied by morrice-dancers decorated with ribbons, who dance sarabands, &c., and the day concludes with a feast. This custom, the origin of which is uncertain, is said to have existed long before the grant of charters of incorporation, though now under the direction of the bailiffs. Lichfield first sent members to Parliament in the thirty-third of Edward I., and also occasionally in the reigns of Edward II. and Edward III., after which elections were discontinued till 1552, when the franchise was restored by Edward VI., and has been since regularly exercised. The ecclesiastical establishment of the cathedral is said to have consisted of only five priests till the time of Bishop Clinton, who is stated to have first instituted a college of canons or prebendaries at Lichfield. But it is

The city fortified by Bishop Clinton.

Incorporated by Edward VI.

Grand festival.

certain that for several hundred years past, as at present, the ecclesiastical LICHFIELD officers have been a bishop, a dean, a precentor, a chancellor, a treasurer, the four archdeacons of Coventry, Stafford, Salop, and Derby, and twenty-seven prebendaries, besides five priests-vicars, seven lay-clerks, or singing men, eight choristers, and other official attendants. The revenues of the bishopric are valued in K. B. at £559. 17s. 3½d. ; and those of the dean and chapter, at £275. 13s. 4d. The diocese comprehends 557 parishes, of which 250 are impropriate. It contains the entire county of Stafford, except the parishes of Brome and Clent, which are in the diocese of Worcester, the county of Derby, the greater part of Warwickshire, and nearly one-half of the county of Salop. The cathedral church is an elegant structure, chiefly in the decorated Gothic style of architecture. It was originally erected by Bishop Clinton, about the middle of the twelfth century, and dedicated to the Virgin Mary and St. Chad ; Walter de Langton, who became bishop, in 1296, built the chapel of St. Mary, now taken into the choir, raised a splendid monument to St. Chad, and erected the cloisters ; and under Bishop Heyworth, whose prelacy commenced in 1419, the cathedral was brought to perfection. At the Reformation this structure was despoiled of many of its ornaments, and the shrine of the patron saint was removed ; but during the sieges in the time of Charles I., and especially when the Close was taken by the Parliamentary soldiers, the most scandalous injury and waste were committed. The roof was stripped of its lead covering, the monuments and ornamental sculpture were defaced or demolished ; and the beautiful painted windows were broken in pieces. After the restoration of Charles II., Dr. Hacket, being appointed to this see, zealously exerted himself to restore this noble edifice from its dilapidated state, which he in a great measure effected. In 1788 the building was again thoroughly repaired, under the direction of James Wyatt, at the expense of more than £5950., chiefly raised by subscription. The cathedral, which stands on the northern side of the city, on the border of a beautiful piece of water, consists of a nave, choir, lady chapel, and transept, with a tower and spire rising from the intersection, and others at the angles of the west front. The entire length of this noble structure is 411 feet, that of the choir, 110 feet, the lady chapel, fifty-five feet ; the central tower to the top of the spire is 258 feet in height ; and that of each of the western towers, 183 feet. The more prominent parts of the building are richly and often tastefully adorned with sculpture, the west front exhibiting a multitude of figures representing subjects from sacred history, and on the roof is a statue of Charles II., erected by Bishop Hacket. The north portal is also highly ornamented. In the interior the beautiful groined roof of the nave may be mentioned as almost the only part of the building which escaped injury from the indiscriminating violence of the soldiery in the civil war. There are many handsome monuments of modern erection, one of which, displaying two female figures in a recumbent posture, the work of Chantry, has been generally and deservedly admired, both for the classic elegance of the design and the taste and beauty of the execution. Near the cathedral are the bishop's palace, a house for the residence of the dean, and others for the prebendaries, &c. The Close in which these buildings are situated is not reckoned a part of the city, forming a distinct liberty or precinct, within the separate jurisdiction of the dean and canons, who are the sole justices of the peace for this precinct. In the city are one parish and two parochial chapelries. The livings are all peculiars in the patronage of the Dean and Chapter of Lichfield. The free grammar-school of Lichfield, founded by Edward VI., has, at different periods, numbered among its scholars, Elias Ashmole, Addison, Garrick, and Johnson. There are also an English charity-school and several national school. In Bacon-street is an hospital or alms-house, founded by Bishop Heyworth ; there is also an hospital for

Side notes:

Extensive diocese.

The cathedral injured by the Parliamentarians.

Splendid monument.

Map.	Names of Places.	County.	Number of Miles from			Dist. Lond.	Popu- lation.
41	Liddiard Millicent..pa	Wilts.....	Wotton Bas..3	Cricklade....5	Swindon ...5	88	406
11	Liddiard Tregooze ..pa	Wilts......	Swindon...4	Wotton Bas. 3	Cricklade ...6	87	765
32	Liddington. ....pa	Rutland ...	Uppingham . 3	Weldon 7	Kettering...12	87	534
41	Liddington. ....pa	Wilts	Swindon.. ..4	Highworth ..7	Liddington ..8	78	407
11	Lidford* ....pa	Devon	Tavistock ...8	Oakhampton 9	Launceston 10	204	734

LICHFIELD. a master and poor brethren, dedicated to John the Baptist ; and, besides other alms-houses, a charitable institution subsists here for aged widows or unmarried daughters of clergymen, founded and liberally endowed by Andrew Newton. A dispensary and a mendicity society are supported by voluntary contributions. The city is irregularly built, and the streets are narrow, but they are well paved and lighted ; there are many handsome houses, and the inhabitants are abundantly supplied with water ; the general aspect of the place displays convenience and respectability, and in the vicinity are some pleasant gardens and agreeable walks, affording a **Public buildings.** diversity of prospects on every side. The public buildings not previously noticed, include the guild-hall, a neat stone structure, with a pediment displaying the city arms ; and beneath it the gaol appertaining to the county of the city of Lichfield ; a theatre erected in Boar-street, in 1790 ; and the market-house, a light and commodious edifice of stone, occupy-ing the ground where formerly stood the market-cross. The only con-siderable manufactory here is that of carpeting, knit-yarn, &c. ; and the trade is chiefly of a local description, arising from the agricultural and **Birthplace of Dr. Johnson.** other produce of the neighbouring country. Lichfield was the birth-place of Ashmole, the antiquary and founder of the Ashmolean-museum at Oxford, who died in 1692 ; Dr. Thomas Newton, Bishop of Bristol ; and his celebrated contemporary, Dr. Samuel Johnson ; besides other persons of literary eminence.

Market, Tuesday and Friday.—*Fairs*, January 10; Shrove-Tuesday and Ash-Wednesday, for cattle, sheep, bacon, cheese, and iron ; May 12, for sheep and cattle ; and first Tuesday in November, for geese and cheese.

Ancient borough. * LIDFORD, or Lydford, a parish in the hundred of Lifton ; the former including the entire district called the Forest of Dartmoor, and the modern establishment of Princetown. Lidford was a borough in the reign of Edward the Confessor, and in Domesday-book it is stated that forty houses within its walls had been laid in ruins before the Conquest ; probably this destruction happened in 997, when the town was burnt by the Danes. The borough twice returned members to Parliament in the reign of Edward I. The manor of Lidford, belonged to Richard, King of the Romans, and Earl of Cornwall, the brother of Henry III., who, in 1267, obtained a grant for a market to be held on Wednesday, and a fair for three days at the festival of St. Patrick, which have long been obso-lete ; but there is still a fair at Twobridges, on Dartmoor, within the parish, for horses, cattle, and sheep, which takes place on the first Wed-nesday after the 16th of August. Lidford-castle, in which the stannary courts were held, is now in ruins. It contained a prison for offenders against the stannary laws, which, in an act of Parliament, passed in 1512, is described as " one of the most heinous, contageous, and detest-**Dartmoor.** able places in the realm." The extensive district of Dartmoor contains about 130,000 acres. It is a barren mountainous tract, on the surface of which are a number of tors, or craggy heights, some of which are from 1500 to 1800 feet above the level of the sea. Crokern Tor is noted as the place where the stannary parliaments were anciently held, and on this spot, till a comparatively recent period, the commission was opened and the jurors were sworn, after which the court was adjourned to one of the stannary towns. In 1809, a prison was erected on Dartmoor, for the reception of prisoners of war, who had been previously confined in prison-ships at Plymouth. Adjoining was a building for the residence of the

Map.	Names of Places.	County.	Number of Miles from				Dist. Lond.	Population.
36	Lidgate ....pa	Suffolk	Newmarket..8	Haverhill .. 10	Bury St. Ed.12		64	442
3	Lidlington ....pa	Bedford	Ampthill ...3	Woburn 6	Bedford 8		48	814
15	Lidney* ....pa	Gloucester..	Blakeney....4	Coleford 7	Chepstow ...9		127	1534
7	Lidsham.............to	Chester.....	Chester.....7	Gt. Neston ..5	Liverpool...12		189	70
31	Lidston ....to	Oxford	NeatEnstone 1	Chip. Norton 3	Charlbury ...4		72	....
11	Liftont ....hun						....	11685
11	Lifton‡............pa	Devon.....	Launceston ..4	Oakhampton15	Tavistock ..10		210	1535
15	Lightcliffe..ham & cha	W. R. York	Halifax......3	Bradford 6	Huddersfield.7		196	....
3	Lightgrave ....ham	Bedford	Luton......3	Dunstable ..3	Market St. ..5		34	685
39	Lighthorne·.......pa	Warwick...	Kineton 4	Warwick 8	Southam.....7		86	346
28	Lilbourn ....pa	Northamp ..	Daventry ...10	Mt.Harboro' 13	Northampt. 17		83	274
29	Lilbourne, East.....to	Northumb ..	Wooler......5	Belford 8	Alnwick ...11		315	95
29	Lilbourne, West ....to	Northumb ..	 3	 7	13		317	235
23	Lilford.............pa	Northamp ..	Oundle......3	Thrapston ..5	Weldon 7		80	127
34	Lillesdon ....ti	Somerset ..	Taunton 5	Langport 9	Ilminster 8		139	....
33	Lilleshall ....pa	Salop	Newport 3	Wellington ..6	Shiffnall 6		141	3569
18	Lilley ....pa	Herts	Hitchin 5	Luton.. 4	Dunstable ...7		35	451
43	Lilling, 'East and' West .. ..to }	N. R. York.	York.......10	New Malton 10	Easingwold..9		206	22C
5	Lillington Dayrell .pa	Bucks	Buckingham .5	Brackley 8	Stoney Stratf. 7		59	15C
31	Lillingston Lovell...pa	Oxford	 5	 9	 6		58	15Ω
12	Lillington ....pa	Dorset.....	Sherborne ..4	Yeovil 7	Cerne Abbas.9		120	205
39	Lillington ....pa	Warwick ...	Warwick....4	Leamington..2	Kenilworth . 5		92	274
4	Lilly ....ham	Berks......	East Ilsley .. 4	Newbury....9	Wantage 8		59	....

LIDFORD.

governor; and, at the distance of a quarter of a mile, barracks, in which were stationed troops, forming the military guard. In the vicinity were erected inns, bakehouses, slaughter-houses, a brewery, and many other public and private buildings, together with a chapel, forming a vill or town, called Prince-town. This place declined greatly on the conclusion of the late war, and the consequent removal of the prisoners; the buildings in general being unoccupied, and in danger of falling into decay. It was proposed at one time to appropriate the prison to the purposes of a workhouse, on a large scale, under the patronage of government; but since the construction of the Plymouth and Dartmoor-railway, which commences at this place, the granite dug here has become a considerable article of commerce, and the population of the neighbourhood has increased.

Increased population.

* LIDNEY, or Lydney, a parish, and formerly a market-town within the district called the Forest of Dean. The church is a large edifice, with a spire at the west end, and a small chancel on the north side of the principal one. This place appears to have been the Roman Statio Trajectus, on the western bank of the Severn, mentioned by Richard of Cirencester; for here are traces of a large intrenchment, with the foundations of ancient buildings, among which are the ruins of a supposed Roman bath, or hypocaust; and many coins have been discovered of the emperors Galba, Hadrian, and Antoninus. In the middle ages, Lidney was a place of some importance; but the market formerly held here has long since been discontinued, and the town had sunk into insignificance, from which there is a prospect of its recovering in consequence of the recent construction of the Severn and Wye-railway and canal; the former, which was originally called the Lidney and Lidbrook-railway, terminating at Lidney, and the canal, extending from that place to the Severn, with which it communicates by locks and a basin, furnishing ample facility for the conveyance of timber, coal, stone, and iron ore, the products of the Forest of Dean, and giving rise to a considerable commerce in those and other articles.

Once a Roman station.

Severn and Wye-railway and canal.

Market, Wednesday.—Fairs, May 4 and November 8, for horned cattle.

† LIFTON, a hundred situated towards the western side of the county, including Dartmoor, and containing twenty-one parishes and the borough of Oakhampton.

‡ LIFTON.—Fairs for cattle, February 2, Holy Thursday, and October 28.

Map	Names of Places.	County.	Number of Miles from			Dist. Lond.	Popu- lation.
34	Lilstock...........pa	Somerset ...	Bridgewater 11	Watchet....8	N. Stowey...4	152	64
24	Limber, Great.....pa	Lincoln....	Castor 6	Grimsby ...9	Barton 12	163	451
24	Limber, Little ....ham	Lincoln.....	8	11	10	165	242
3	Limbury..........ham	Bedford ...	Luton 2	Dunstable ...5	Hitchin 9	33	....
17	Limebrook.........to	Hereford ...	Presteign....4	Ludlow 12	Leominster .11	149	....
25	Limehouse*.......pa	Middlesex ..	Greenwich ..3	Barking 5	Stratford 2	2	15695
16	Limerston ....ham	Hants	Niton 7	Yarmouth ..8	Newport 6	90	....
27	Limpenhoe ....pa	Norfolk....	Acle........5	Beccles.....9	Yarmouth ..11	118	156
37	Limpsfield ....pa	Surrey......	Godstone 4	Croydon ...10	Westerham..3	20	1043
22	Linacre ....to	Lancaster ..	Liverpool ...4	Ormskirk ...10	Prescot.....10	209	....
29	Linbriggs ....to	Northumb ...	Alnwick....19	Wooler 16	Yedburgh...16	311	64
5	Linchlade ....pa	Bucks.....	LeightonBuz. 2	Woburn 5	Aylesbury ..11	43	390
38	Linchmere† ....pa	Sussex	Haslemere .. 3	Midhurst....7	Petersfield..10	45	301
24	Lincoln‡.......county					....	317244

Origin of its name.

* LIMEHOUSE, a parish, now forming a part of the eastern suburb of London, situated on the north bank of the Thames, in the Tower division of the hundred of Ossulton. According to Stowe, the original name of this place was Limehurst, and it was so called from the number of lime-trees anciently growing here. It was formerly a hamlet belonging to the parish of Stepney, from which it was separated by act of Parliament, in 1730. The church is one of the fifty new churches directed to be built in London, by act of Parliament, in the beginning of the last century; it was commenced in 1712, and completed in 1724, but not consecrated till September 12, 1730. It is a massive structure, principally of Grecian architecture, with a square tower at the west-end, which, as well as the church itself, designed by Nicholas Hawksmoor, has been severely criticised by some writers, and greatly praised by others. A charity-school, for poor boys belonging to this parish and that of Poplar, was founded by Dr. Gloster Ridley, lecturer here in 1737; and there is another school for the gratuitous instruction of children of both sexes, instituted in 1779. The principal manufactures carried on here are such as are connected with maritime commerce, as sail-cloth making, mast, oar, pump and block making, the manufacture of patent chain cables and anchors, and that of ropes and cables on an improved plan, at the establishment of Sir Joseph Huddart and Co. There are also dock-yards for ship-building.

Ludicrous representation of our Saviour's birth.

† LINCHMERE. Here is a considerable part of Shelbred-priory, which, being converted into a farm-house soon after the suppression, escaped the fate of many other monastic establishments; upon a square tablet in one of the rooms is the following ludicrous representation of the nativity of our Saviour, under this inscription : *Ecce virgo concipiet et pariet filium, et vocabitur nomen Jesus.* Uppermost stands a cock in the act of crowing; from his beak is a label, with these words : *Christus natus est.* Next is a duck, from whose bill issues another label, inscribed : *Quando? quando?* which is answered in like manner by a raven : *In hac nocte.* A cow bellows : *Ubi? ubi?* And lastly, a lamb seems to bleat out, " In Bethlehem."

Earliest inhabitants.

‡ LINCOLN, a maritime county, the largest in England, except Yorkshire. It is bounded on the north by the estuary of the Humber, which separates it from Yorkshire ; on the east by the German Ocean ; on the south by Cambridgeshire and Northamptonshire ; and on the west by the counties of Rutland, Leicester, Nottingham, and York. The earliest inhabitants of this part of the country, of whom we have any account, were the Coritani, or Coitanni, a tribe of the ancient Britons, on whose subjugation by the Romans, several military stations were fixed here ; and in the ultimate division of the island, under the Roman government, Lincolnshire was included in the province called Flavia Cæsariensis. Three British, or Roman roads, traversed the county, these were the

Fossway, the Ermin-street, and the Upper Saltway; and within its limits were the Roman stations, called *Lindum* (Lincoln), *Causennis* (Ancaster), *Vernometum*, *Croccolana*, *Ad Abum*, *Margidunum*, and *Ad Pontem*, the sites of which are somewhat uncertain. Lincolnshire is divided into three districts, differing in size, as well as in their natural features and products. The part or district of Lindsey, is by far the most extensive, comprehending the whole of the county north of the Fossdike and the river Witham; and the highest ground is here situated, but the eminences are so inconsiderable, that there is scarcely one which deserves the name of a hill. Towards the north-east is a large tract of heathy land, called the Wolds, extending from Barton-on-the-Humber to Spilsby, consisting principally of sandy loam and flint; and on the western side the substratum is a sandy rock. Throughout this tract are bred large flocks of sheep, of a kind distinguished for their long, thick wool, much used in the manufacture of worsted stuffs and coarse woollens. Here also were formerly kept a great number of rabbits, their skins and fur being valuable articles of commerce; but the rabbit-warrens, in many places, have been destroyed of late years, and the ground broken up for tillage. The north-western part of Lindsey includes the river island of Axholme, formed by branches of the Trent, the Dun, and the Idle, a low fertile tract, in which flax is much cultivated, as also hemp, rape, and turnip-seed. The rivers here are the Trent, which crosses a corner of the county; and the Ancholme, a small stream, noted for producing fine eels, which falls into the Humber. The district of Kesteven contains the western part of the county, from near the centre to the southern extremity. Its soil exhibits considerable diversity; but though some tracts of heath occur, it is on the whole a fruitful country; the heaths, particularly those of Ancaster and Lincoln, having been enclosed and cultivated. A long ridge of high ground forms an abrupt boundary of this district to the west, beginning near Grantham, and continuing with but little interruption to the north of Lincoln. The principal river of Kesteven is the Witham, which rises near Grantham, and flowing north-east to Lincoln, makes a semicircular sweep, and taking its course south-eastward, falls into the German Ocean, below Boston. It is in the former part of its channel a shallow stream, but becomes navigable at Lincoln, where it communicates with the Fossdike. The jack, or pike, is a fish said to be very abundant in this river. The fens, for which Lincolnshire is noted, are partly in the district of Kesteven, but by far the larger portion of them belongs to the district of Holland, so called from its characteristic feature, being hollow or low land, like the province of the Dutch Netherlands bearing a similar appellation. Holland consists of two divisions, upper and lower, both composed of fens and marshes, many of which have been reclaimed, and converted to the purposes of agriculture by the construction of numerous drains and canals, together with raised causeways. The lower, or southern division, is the most watery, and is only protected from the devastating effects of inundations by immense embankments on the sea-coasts and the borders of the rivers. Where the operations of draining have been carried into effect, the air though damp, is not unwholesome, and hence intermittent fevers, rheumatism, and other diseases of marshy countries, have become comparatively unusual. Human industry has here introduced comfort and opulence, by forming excellent pasture-land out of swamps and bogs, and even rendered them capable of producing abundant crops of corn. The fens, too, even where they are left in their native state, are not destitute of objects of utility, and they also present many subjects interesting to the naturalist. The reeds, which grow abundantly in the watery marshes, are annually collected in large quantities, for thatching and other purposes. Among the undrained fens are bred vast flocks of geese, which form a considerable source of commerce, on account of their quills and feathers, and also as an article of

COUNTY OF LINCOLN.

Large flocks of sheep bred here.

The rivers.

The fens.

Map.	Names of Places.	County.	Number of Miles from			Dist. Lond.	Popu lation.
24	Lincoln*..........city	Lincoln.....	Boston....36	Hull 41	Peterboro'..52	133	11892
22	Lindale ....cha	Lancaster...	Lancaster ...3	Hornby. 6	Burton.. 9	242	....
30	Linderby..........pa	Notts	Nottingham .8	Mansfield ...7	Southwell ..12	132	460

COUNTY OF LINCOLN.

Wild fowl in abundance.

Productions of the county.

provision. The principal decoys in England for wild ducks, teal, widgeon, and other water-fowl, are in this district; and hence the London markets are chiefly supplied. Wild geese, grebes, godwits, wimbrels, coots, and a numerous variety of other aquatic birds, breed here abundantly, and obtain a plentiful supply of food from the fishy pools and streams. Stares, or starlings, resort hither during the winter to roost in the reeds, and in such vast multitudes, as to crush the stalks by their weight. Near Spalding is said to be the greatest heronry in England, where the herons build their nests like rooks, in clusters, on the tops of lofty trees. The avoset, or yelper, distinguished by its bill, which curves upwards, is found in considerable numbers in the neighbourhood of the Fossdike; as likewise are those delicacies for the table, knots and dottrels. Among the agricultural products of Lincolnshire in general, are grain of all sorts in the higher grounds; and in the lower, oats, hemp, flax, wood, &c. But its distinguishing character is that of a grazing county, and its pastures are noted for rearing different kinds of stock of the greatest size and weight. Lincolnshire oxen are proverbially remarkable for their immense bulk; the sheep have been already noticed; and the horses bred here have long been held in high repute, both for the saddle and for harness, while those from the southern part of the county are especially valuable as draught horses. The mineral productions of Lincolnshire are of but little importance in commerce, the only articles deserving of notice being a kind of variegated marble, the ore called the sulphuret of iron, and the sub-phosphate of the same metal. This is not considered as a manufacturing county, but, in some towns, canvas and sail-cloth are made in considerable quantities. Lincolnshire is celebrated for the number of its handsome churches erected during the middle ages, several of which are highly ornamented; and it is remarkable that the most splendid of them are found in low, fenny situations, still difficult of access, and doubtless much more so at the periods when they were founded. Some of these churches, however, as those of Boston, Louth, and Spalding, are crowned with lofty towers or spires, and one object of their erection probably was that of furnishing landmarks for travellers.

Once occupied by the ancient Britons.

* LINCOLN, an ancient city, the capital of the county to which it gives name. It occupies the summit and sides of a hill, at the base of which flows the river Witham, in three channels, crossed by several bridges; and from the level nature of the surrounding country, its buildings, and especially the cathedral church, are advantageously seen in several directions at a considerable distance. Here, no doubt, was situated one of the towns, or hill-forts, of the ancient Britons. The vestiges of Roman residences, stated to have been discovered here at different periods, some of which are yet remaining, are evidences of the ancient extent and importance of the colonial settlement. On the north side of the city is an arched passage, called The Newport-gate, from the adjoining suburb of Newport, to which it leads; and the wall, in which this archway is formed, is described by Mr. William Wilkins, in a paper in the "Archæologia," as one of the most interesting specimens of Roman masonry remaining in this county. In the time of Edward the Confessor, the town contained 970 mansions; and it is stated, though on uncertain authority, that it comprised fifty-two parishes. In 1068 William the Conqueror erected, or built the castle; and in the reign of that prince, Lincoln became the seat of a bishop, the see being removed hither from Dorchester, in Oxfordshire. During the contest for the crown

between Stephen and the Empress Matilda, this place became the scene of renewed hostilities; for the castle, having been garrisoned by the partisans of Matilda, the king advanced and laid siege to it, on which the Earl of Gloucester hastened hither with an army to the relief of his friends, and an obstinately contested engagement took place, in which Stephen was defeated and made a prisoner. Henry II., in the fourth year of his reign, subsequently to his coronation at Westminster, was a second time solemnly crowned, together with his queen, according to Hoveden, at Wikeford, without the walls of the city of Lincoln, the ceremony having taken place at the church of St. Mary de Wigford, probably in consequence of the cathedral being at that time under repair. Several parliaments were held at Lincoln in the reigns of Edward I. and his two immediate successors. This city was governed by a portreeve till 1314, when a charter of incorporation was granted by Edward II., under which the chief officer had the title of mayor; and Edward IV., in the fifth year of his reign, constituted the city, with the adjacent villages of Branston, Waddington, Bracebridge, and Canwick, a distinct county, or separate liberty. Charles I., in 1629, granted a new charter, vesting the municipal government in a mayor, twelve aldermen, two sheriffs, twenty-eight common-councilmen, and four chamberlains, with a recorder, a deputy-recorder, a steward of the courts of the borough, a town-clerk, four coroners, and other officers. Under the new act, in 1835, the corporation consists of a mayor, six aldermen, and eighteen counsellors. The assizes for the county at large, are likewise held here, in the county-hall, Castle-yard. Lincoln was one of the places to which writs were directed for the return of members to the parliament, summoned by the authority of the Earl of Leicester, the forty-ninth of Henry III.; and representatives have been regularly sent from this city ever since the reign of Edward I. The diocese of Lincoln, soon after the removal of the see from Dorchester, acquired a vast accession of territorial jurisdiction and wealth; and though Henry II. dismembered it by the foundation of the bishopric of Ely, and Henry VIII., by founding those of Peterborough and Oxford, it is still considered as the largest in England. The revenues also were much reduced in the reigns of Edward VI. and Elizabeth. Remigius, who had been Bishop of Dorchester, and who transferred the see hither, commenced the erection of the cathedral church, the episcopal palace, and houses for the dignitaries and officers of the diocese; and on his death, in 1092, they were completed by the succeeding prelate, Robert Bloet, who increased the number of prebends from twenty-one to forty-two. The ecclesiastical officers at present, besides the bishop, are a dean, a precentor, a chancellor, a sub-dean, six archdeacons, fifty-two prebendaries, four priest-vicars, eight lay-vicars, or singing-men, an organist, seven poor clerks, eight choristers, &c. Fifty-eight bishops have occupied this see since its establishment at Lincoln; and among the numbers were Robert Grosseteste, Cardinal Beaufort, Cardinal Wolsey, Dr. Robert Sanderson, Dr. Thomas Tenison, and Dr. Edmund Gibson. The cathedral first erected having been partly destroyed by fire, in 1124, it was repaired by Alexander, the third bishop, who vaulted the aisles with stone, but the great tower falling some time after, Bishop Hugh, of Burgundy, who succeeded to the see in 1186, found it necessary to undertake the re-erection of a great part of the edifice. He, however, built only the eastern part, from the great transept to the end of the choir, together with the chapter-house; and the nave and transept were erected by Bishops Hugh de Wells and Grosseteste. Henry de Lexington, the next prelate, enlarged the church towards the east, extending the choir; and this is considered as the most beautiful part of the whole structure. Many additions were afterwards made till about the year 1400, when the building seems to have attained its completion; and the subsequent introduction of chapels, oratories, and other ornamental structures, may be regarded as so many superfluous additions. The

LINCOLN.

Henry II. crowned here.

Largest diocese in England.

The cathedral.

LINCOLN.

Robbery
of the
cathedral.

Magnificent
Gothic ar-
chitecture.

The "Great
Tom of
Lincoln."

The Jew s
house.

splendour and value of the decorations of this church may be estimated from the fact, that Henry VIII., in 1540, took away 2621 ounces of gold, and 4285 ounces of silver, besides diamonds, and other precious stones of great value. In the reign of Edward VI. it was stripped of its remaining treasures, and its tombs, statues, shrines, and altars, were destroyed. It suffered again in 1645, when, it is said, the parliamentary soldiers made it a stable for their horses. This edifice consists of a nave, with its aisles; a transept at the west end, formerly crowned with angular towers and wooden spires, the latter of which were taken down in 1808, and two other transepts, one near the centre, and the other towards the eastern end; also a choir and chancel, with their aisles, and a large central tower. The entire length of this edifice is 524 feet; the breadth of the western front, 174 feet; the length of the great transept, 250 feet; the length of the lesser or eastern transept, 170 feet; the breadth of the body of the cathedral, eighty feet; the height of the central tower to the top of one of its angular pinnacles, 300 feet; and that of the two western towers, 180 feet. The most striking part of this edifice is the grand western front, which Lord Burlington has characterized as an unrivalled specimen of the magnificence of Gothic architecture. It was formerly ornamented with statues of the kings of England, from William I. to Edward III., which, with other decorations, suffered from the destructive violence of the fanatics of the sixteenth and seventeenth centuries. Some variety of style is exhibited by different parts of this cathedral, as might be expected from the distant periods at which they were erected, and from the alterations it has undergone since its original foundation; not-withstanding which, it may be justly regarded as one of the most regular, as well as the most extensive structures of its kind in England. On the north side of the upper transept, and connected with it, are the cloisters, of which three sides only remain in their original state. Attached to the cathedral, on the north side, is the chapter-house, in form, a decagon, with an elegantly-vaulted roof, supported by a central pillar. Over the north cloister is the library, containing some ancient manuscripts, and a curious collection of Roman and other antiquities, found in the vicinity of Lincoln. In one of the towers is one of the largest bells in England, called "Great Tom of Lincoln;" it was cast in the reign of James I., and weighed 9894 pounds; its greatest circumference was twenty-two feet and three quarters; it broke while under repair, in 1831. This city is divided into two parts, designated Lincoln above-hill, and Lincoln below-hill, the former constituting the chief residence of the clergy and gentry, and the latter of the merchants and tradespeople. It compre-hends two principal streets, extending longitudinally, and several smaller ones in transverse or parallel directions with the former. Modern im-provements have made considerable alterations in the general aspect of the place, which contains several handsome buildings of recent erection, though the remains of antiquity are still numerous and interesting. Of the castle, erected by William the Conqueror, the principal portions now standing are fragments of the old wall and the gateway; and the area of the ancient fortress is occupied by the county-hall, a modern brick build-ing, and the county-gaol. The castle, which was improved and enlarged by John of Gaunt, probably stood on the site of the Roman citadel. The keep was not, as usual, encompassed by the castle wall, but stood half within and half without the wall, having a communication with the other buildings of the fortress by a covered way. In the north-eastern angle of the area is a small structure, strongly built, called Cobb's-hall, and supposed to have been used as a dungeon; and on the western side is a square tower, in which is an arch, resembling, in its masonry, that of the Newport-gate. Among the ancient edifices here may also be mentioned one called the Jew's-house, said to have been the residence of a wealthy Jewess, who was hanged for coining, in the reign of Edward I.; and

Map	Names of Places.	County.	Number of Miles from			Dist. Lond.	Population.
40	Lindeth ....ham	Westmorlnd	Kendal 8	Ambleside .. 7	Cartmel 10	269	....
38	Lindfield and Lindfield Bardolph* pa	Sussex	Cuckfield....3	E. Grinstead.8	Lewes......11	37	1485
23	Lindley.....ham & cha	Leicester ...	Hinckley 4	Nuneaton .. .3	Atherstone ..4	103	....
45	Lindley........... to	W. R. York.	Huddersfield 3	Halifax......5	Rochdale .. 16	192	2306
45	Lindley ....to	W. R. York.	Otley 4	Ripley 9	Knaresboro' 11	200	125
42	Lindon ....to	Worcester..	Bewdley 5	Cleobury 4	Tenbury 9	129	...
22	Lindreth...........to	Lancaster ..	Lancaster....9	Burton 5	Kendal.....13	248	...
45	Lindrick.....ex pa dis	W. R. York.	Ripon 5	Ripley.......8	Masham 8	211	2
42	Lindridge ....pa	Worcester..	Tenbury 6	Cleobury 5	Bewdley 9	130	180?
14	Lindsell...........pa	Essex	Thaxted 4	Dunmow 4	Braintree....8	42	38?
36	Lindsey ....pa	Suffolk	Hadleigh.. ..4	Lavenham ...6	Sudbury 9	64	256
9	Lineside.. ....to	Cumberland	Longtown ...3	Carlisle 8	Brampton .. 10	312	137
27	Linford ....pa	Norfolk.....	BrandonFerry5	Swaffham ...10	Thetford 9	84	60
5	Linford, Great......pa	Bucks	NewportPag.2	Sto Stratford 5	Fen Stratford6	51	420
5	Linford, Little......pa	Bucks	 2	 5	8	53	55
27	Ling..............pa	Norfolk.....	EastDereham 6	Reepham....4	Foulsham ...6	106	645
34	Ling..............pa	Somerset ...	Bridgewater .6	Taunton 9	Langport 7	136	365
45	Lingarths .. ..to	W. R. York	Huddersfield.5	Oldham 14	Rochdale .. 15	191	758
17	Lingen ....pa	Hereford....	Presteign 4	Leominster .12	Ludlow 13	149	298

there is a curious bridge, of one arch, over the Witham, supposed by Gough to have been standing for more than four centuries. The principal buildings, yet unnoticed, are the guild-hall, in the High-street; the sessions house, and the common gaol, and house of correction for the city, erected in 1809, on the plan recommended by Howard; the county-hospital, built in 1769; the dispensary; the lunatic-asylum; the house belonging to the lying-in charity; the house of industry, &c. Here are likewise assembly-rooms, news-rooms, and a theatre. Lincoln was a commercial mart of great importance in ancient times. It is probable that, previously to the Norman Conquest, the Witham was navigable for ships, as a tideway to this place; and that it was so at a very early period, may be inferred from the circumstance that the Fossdike-canal was cleared by order of Henry I., in 1121, for the purpose of forming a navigable communication between the rivers Trent and Witham, at Lincoln, which William of Malmesbury, writing in the reign of Stephen, states to have been one of the richest and most populous cities in England, and a principal mart for all goods brought by land or water. Though this place is now the seat of no peculiar manufacture, it affords advantages for the prosecution of commerce, and has consequently an extensive trade in corn and wool, of which articles large quantities are sent into Yorkshire, by vessels which return laden with coal and other merchandise for the use of the city and the surrounding country. There are five principal market-places, the butter-market, in the High-street; the meat-market, in a lane called the Butchery; the cattle and sheep-market, near St. Swithin's-church; the corn-market, in an open area, called Corn-hill; and the fish-market, at the High-bridge.

Market, Friday.—*Fairs*, April 24, and three following days, for sheep and pedlery; July 5; last Wednesday in July; and every other Wednesday, for cattle and sheep; October 6, and November 28, for horses, cattle, &c.—*Bankers*, Smith, Ellison, and Co., draw on Smith, Payne, and Co.—*Inns*, Rein Deer, White Hart, and Saracen's Head.

* LINDFIELD. The charitable institutions at this place are a school of industry, established by William Allen, Esq., of London, for the education of children of both sexes, not only by affording them common instruction, but also by teaching them the processes of agriculture, and various manual operations, as spinning and making nets, shoe-making, printing, &c.; and the Lindfield Benevolent Society, the very useful object of which is to give relief to such industrious individuals and families among the poor as do not submit to the degradation of receiving parochial aid. The fair held here in August, for the sale of lambs, is said to be the largest in the county.

Fairs, May 12, for horned cattle and horses; August 5, for cattle and sheep; and October 28, for pedlery.

LINCOLN.

Public buildings.

Extensive trade in corn and wool.

Charitable institutions.

Map.	Names of Places.	County.	Number of Miles from				Dist. Lond.	Popu- lation
37	Lingfield ....pa	Surrey......	Godstone....6	E. Grinstead 4	Reigate 12		26	1814
27	Lingwood ....pa	Norfolk.....	Acle.........3	Norwich ...9	Yarmouth ..13		118	294
16	Linkenholt ....pa	Hants	Gt. Bedwin..8	Hungerford ..9	Andover ...9		66	87
37	Linkfield Street .....ti	Surrey......	Reigate 1	Merstham ...2	Godstone ...5		20	....
8	Linkinhorne ....pa	Cornwall ..	Callington .. 5	Launceston ..8	Liskeard....8		220	1159
33	Linley ....pa	Salop	Bridgenorth..4	Broseley....3	M. Wenlock 5		142	111
29	Linmouth...........to	Northumb ..	Morpeth......8	Blyth.......7	Alnwick ...21		290	23
29	Linop ....to	Northumb ..	Wooler......8	Rothbury ..11	14		312	74
22	Linsdale ....ham & cha	Lancaster...	Ulverston....9	Cartmel.....3	Lancaster .16		256	....
29	Linsheeles..........to	Northumb ..	Alnwick ...21	Jedburgh...20	Bellingham .16		311	105
9	Linside.............to	Cumberland	Longtown ...3	Carlisle.....8	Brampton ..10		312	220
36	Linstead, Great ....pa	Suffolk	Halesworth..5	Harleston....7	Framlingham 9		97	110
36	Linstead, Little ....pa	Suffolk	3	7	11		99	186
21	Linsted ....pa	Kent	Sittingbourn 3	Faversham ..4	Lenham 7		43	295
9	Linstock ....to	Cumberland	Carlisle.....3	Brampton ...7	Longtown ..9		307	228
43	Linthorpe ....to	N. R. York.	Stockton 3	Stokesley...8	Yarm 7		242	229
45	Linthwaite ....to	W. R. York	Huddersfield 4	Oldham....15	Rochdale .. 16		190	2852
6	Linton* ....m t & pa	Cambridge..	Cambridge...9	Newmarket 13	Royston ...14		48	1678
10	Linton.............to	Derby	Burton 5	Ashby 5	Derby.....15		120	267
11	Linton† ....pa	Devon	Ilfracombe..14	Barnstaple..16	SouthMolton17		185	792
17	Linton.............pa	Hereford....	Bromyard ...3	Ledbury....12	Hereford ..16		127	636
17	Linton ....pa	Hereford....	Ross.......5	10	Newent 5		117	500
21	Linton ....pa	Kent	Maidstone ...4	Tunbridge ..10	Cranbrook ..10		38	723
45	Linton.............to	W. R. York	Wetherby ...2	Harewood ...5	Tadcaster...8		196	166
46	Linton, East.....ham	E. R. York .	Howden 4	South Cave ..9	M.Weighton 10		184	....
46	Linton Grange ...ham	E. R. York .	New Malton 8	Gt. Driffield 13	Bridlington .20		209	....
46	Linton, West ....ham	E. R. York .	Howden 3	South Cave 10	M.Weighton10		183	....
43	Linton upon Ouse ...to	N. R. York.	Easingwold..7	Boroughbrid. 8	York 12		208	343
45	Linton in Wharfdale pa	W. R. York	Skipton 9	Settle 12	Ripon 22		220	2113
13	Lintz-Green ....to	Durham	Gateshead ...8	Durham....12	Chester le St. 7		272	650
16	Linwood ....ham	Hants	Ringwood ...3	Fordingbrid. 4	Ellingham ..1		92	....
24	Linwood............pa	Lincoln.....	Mt. Raisin...3	Wragby 6	Lincoln 14		147	169
16	Liphook‡ ....ham	Hants	Haslemere .. 5	Petersfield ..8	Farnham ...12		46	....
29	Lipwood ....to	Northumb ..	Hexham.....8	Haltwhistle .8	Alston 1		282	583
7	Liscard ....to	Chester.....	Gt. Neston .11	Liverpool....2	Chester 20		202	967
5	Liscombe ....ham	Bucks.....	LeightonBuz. 3	Woburn 6	Fen. Stratford5		44	....
8	Liskeard§ ....m t	Cornwall ...	Callington ..8	Lostwithiel 12	Launceston 17		224	4042
46	Lisset ....to & cha	E. R. York .	Bridlington .8	Hornsea 8	Gt.Driffield .9		193	102

* LINTON.—*Market*, Thursday.—*Fairs*, Holy Thursday, and July 30, for horses and lambs.

Beautiful scenery.

† LINTON. Here is a small pier for the benefit of vessels in the coasting-trade; and there are many fish caught in the vicinity. Here are several lodging-houses for the accommodation of visitors, by whom Linton is much frequented, in consequence of the wild beauty of the coast and scenery. The lord of the manor holds an annual court-leet, when a port-reeve, tithing-man, and ale-taster, are appointed.

‡ LIPHOOK. *Fairs*, March 6, and June 11, for horned cattle and horses.

Battle between the Royalist and Parliamentary forces.

§ LISKEARD. This town is singularly placed, partly on rocky eminences, and partly in the valley at their base; in consequence of which the streets are extremely irregular, and the houses so arranged on a kind of terraces, that the basement stories of some houses are on a level with the chimneys of others near them. This borough has returned members to Parliament ever since the reign of Edward I. On the 19th of January, 1643, a battle was fought near the town, between Sir Ralph Hopton and the Parliamentary forces, when the latter were defeated, and Sir Ralph marched into the town. On the 2nd of August, in the following year, the king, on his entrance into Cornwall, halted here, and remained till the 7th of that month. Liskeard is situated in a district abounding with tin-mines, and was anciently the principal place for the coinage or stamping of tin; but it seems to have declined in importance after the establishment of the corporation; for Norden, who wrote in the reign of James I., describes it as a poor town, whose ruins argued its pristine glory to have been great. Its trade has since revived, and it has become a thriving and populous town. The principal commerce carried on arises from the produce of the neighbouring tin, lead, and copper mines; but here are also tanneries, rope-walks, and manufactories of serge and blankets. On a hill, to the north of the town, may be traced the foundations of the

Map.	Names of Places.	County	Number of Miles from			Dist. Lond.	Popu- lation
24	Lissington..........pa	Lincoln.....	Mt. Raisin..4	Wragby 5	Lincoln 13	146	182
14	Liston............pa	Essex	Sudbury ...3	Clare........6	Lavenham ...6	58	88
27	Litcham..........pa	Norfolk....	Swaffham ..8	EastDereham 8	Fakenham ..8	101	771
10	Litchurch ....to	Derby	Derby 1	Nottingham 15	Belper.....8	127	516
22	Litherland ....to	Lancaster ..	Liverpool....5	Ormskirk....9	Prescot......9	209	789
11	Lithewell ....cha	Devon	Chudleigh ..1	NewtonBush.5	Dawlish.... 6	183	....
6	Litlington..........pa	Cambridge..	Royston 5	Baldock ...5	Cambridge 17	42	622
38	Litlington ....pa	Sussex	Seaford......4	Newhaven ..6	Eastbourne..6	59	143
22	Littleborough* . ham & cha	Lancaster...	Rochdale....4	Burnley...14	Halifax....13	201	....
30	Littleborough ......pa	Notts	East Retford 8	Gainsborough8	Tuxford....10	147	82
21	Littlebourne ......pa	Kent	Canterbury ..4	Sandwich...9	Ramsgate .. 13	59	733
14	Littlebury.........pa	Essex	Saff. Walden 2	Gt.Chesterfor3	Linton 7	44	875
41	Littlecot ....cha	Wilts	Hungerford ..4	Ramsbury ...1	Froxfield 3	68	....
5	Littlecote ....ham	Bucks	Winslow.. ..5	LeightonBuz. 6	Aylesbury ...7	46	....
29	Littledale...ham & cha	Lancaster..	Lancaster ...6	Hornby......4	Garstang ...12	240	....
4	Littlefield, Green..ham	Berks	Maidenhead .4	Windsor ...6	Reading....11	28	....
11	Littleham ....pa	Devon	Exmouth ...3	Topsham.....7	Sidmouth ...7	170	3389
11	Littleham ....pa	Devon	Bideford 2	Torrington ..5	Hartland ...12	202	424
31	Littlemoor .... to	Oxford	Oxford......3	Dorchester ..6	Wheatley...5	55	380
6	Littleport.........pa	Cambridge..	Ely 4	Chatteris ...11	Downham ...9	70	2644
23	Littlethorpe .....ham	Leicester ..	Leicester....6	Hinckley... .5	Lutterworth 8	97	....
7	Littleton ....to	Chester.....	Chester......2	Tarporley....9	Frodsham ..10	180	48
15	Littleton..........pa	Gloucester..	Chip.Sodbury5	Marshfield ..2	Chippenham12	105	125
37	Littleton ....ham	Surrey.....	Guildford....2	Godalming ..2	Farnham 9	31	....
25	Littleton ....pa	Middlesex..	Staines......3	Chertsey....3	Sunbury .. 2	17	134
16	Littleton ....pa	Hants.....	Winchester..3	Stockbridge .6	Andover....10	63	120
41	Littleton ....ti	Wilts	Trowbridge..3	Melksham ...3	Devizes......7	96	79
41	Littleton Drew ...pa	Wilts	Chippenham.8	Malmesbury .6	Bath........12	101	175
34	Littleton, High ....pa	Somerset..	Bath.......10	Wells.......12	Bristol......10	116	911
42	Littleton, Middle....to	Worcester..	Evesham ... 5	Campden....6	Alcester 8	97	....
42	Littleton, North ....pa	Worcester..	 6	 7	 7	98	360
41	Littleton Pannel .....ti	Wilts	Mt.Lavington2	Westbury...8	Devizes......5	94	....
15	Littleton upon Severn ..pa	Gloucester..	Thornbury ..3	Chepstow ...7	Berkeley....9	118	179
42	Littleton, South ...pa	Worcester..	Evesham 4	Campden....6	Alcester 8	97	110
4	Littlewick Green..ham	Berks	Maidenhead .4	Henley.....6	Marlow 5	30	....
4	Littleworth ....ti	Berks	Farringdon ..2	Bampton 4	Wantage 9	66	....
15	Littleworth .ex pa ham	Gloucester..	Gloucester ..1	Tewkesbury10	Cheltenham 10	106	615
31	Littleworth........ham	Oxford	Woodstock ..3	Charlbury ..4	Witney......7	66	....
10	Litton.............to	Derby	Tideswell...1	Bakewell ...6	Castleton ...6	159	866
17	Litton.............to	Hereford & Radnor.	Presteign ...4	Kington ...6	New Radnor.5	156	92
34	Litton ....pa	Somerset ..	Wells 7	Bath 13	Bristol 14	119	414
45	Litton.............to	W. R. York	Settle.......11	Askrig 11	Skipton....18	229	102
12	Litton Cheney ......pa	Dorset......	Bridport 7	Dorchester ..9	Abbotsbury..6	128	420
36	Livermere, Great...pa	Suffolk.....	Bury St.Edm.6	Ixworth....4	Thetford ...7	77	336
36	Livermere, Little..pa	Suffolk.....	 6	 5	 8	77	185
22	Liverpool†.........b t	Lancaster...	Manchester .36	Lancaster ..53	Preston 31	205	165175

ancient baronial castle, which, in the time of Leland, was in ruins, and has now fallen into complete decay. The surrounding country displays many cromlechs, stone circles, and other monuments, supposed to be of Druidical origin. | LISKEARD. Druidical remains.

Market, Saturday.—*Fairs*, Shrove-Monday ; Monday before Palm-Sunday ; Holy Thursday ; August 15 ; October 2 ; and Monday after December 6, for horses, oxen, sheep, and cloth.

* LITTLEBOROUGH. *Fairs*, March 1, and October 13.

† LIVERPOOL. This great and important commercial town, formerly an inconsiderable hamlet of the parish of Walton, fourteen miles, six furlongs, from north to south, and two miles, one furlong, from east to west. The west side is bounded by the Mersey ; on the opposite side are the borders of the townships of West Derby and Everton ; the northern side joins the township of Kirkdale ; and its southern side is skirted by Toxteth-park. By the Saxons, this place is understood to have been called Lyferpole ; others name it Letherpoole, Lyverpoole, Lyrpole, Ler-poole, Leerpoole, Livrepol, Lyverpol ; and, about sixty years ago, it was mostly spelt Leverpool ; which is justified by some ancient MSS., and a charter as far back as the year 1524. The etymology is not easily ascertained. Some imagine it to have taken its name from a bird, formerly found in this place, called Liver ; but this very bird seems to have had no other than | Origin of the name.

LIVERPOOL.

a fabulous existence. Others consider it to have been derived from a sea-weed, known by the name of Liver, in the west of England; or from the hepatica, or liverwort, found on the sea-coast. Some, again, suppose it might originate from the family of Lever, which is of ancient date, and whose arms are exemplified in a MS. in the Harleian Collection, at the British Museum, supposed to have been written as early as 1567. Respecting the latter part of the name, however, it is generally agreed, that it was owing to a body of water with which this place was formerly overspread like a pool. St. Patrick is said to have visited Liverpool, in his way to Ireland; in commemoration of which a cross was erected, which, though long since destroyed, still gives name to the place where it stood, near the lower end of Water-street. According to Camden, Roger de Poictiers, who had lands given him, in this part of the county, by William the Conqueror, built a castle here in 1076. This Roger held all the lands between the rivers Ribble and Mersey. The statement of Camden is extremely equivocal; but it is probable that Prince John, son of Henry II., erected a fortress here; for that monarch having granted his son the lordship of Ireland, with its dependencies, and as the newly constituted port of " Lyrpul," was most conveniently situated for shipping stores, &c., for that island, it became necessary to secure the place by a military establishment. Henry II., in 1173, granted it a charter, wherein it is stated, " that the whole estuary of the Mersey shall be for ever a port of the sea, with all liberties to a port of the sea belonging; and that place which the men of Lyrpul call Litherpul, near to Toxteth, from each side of the water, they may come and return with their ships and merchandise freely, and without obstruction." In different subsequent charters, the place is spoken of, by each monarch, as " our borough, or vill," of Liverpool; and mention is made of persons holding burgages under the crown. Since the beginning of the present century, the town, although a borough, may be considered as perfectly free, for the purpose of commerce, to all the world. Leland states, that Liverpool was a paved town when he visited it, much resorted to by Irish merchants, &c., and that its small port duties were then deemed attractions to traders. From the town record of November, 1565, however, we find that the merchandise and commerce of the place were then much reduced. Liverpool then contained only 138 householders and cottagers. Besides, in a petition to Queen Elizabeth, in 1571, the place is styled, " her Majesty's poor decayed toun of Liverpool." At this period there were only twelve barks, or vessels, with seventy-five men, belonging to this port, and the whole estimated at 223 tons burthen. In consequence of the extended increase of the town, it was found necessary, in the reign of William III., to obtain an act of Parliament for making Liverpool a distinct and separate parish from that of Walton on the Hill. From this period the town gradually and rapidly advanced in population, building, commerce, and riches. The corporation consists of sixteen aldermen and forty-eight counsellors, and the returning officers are the mayor and two bailiffs. It is evident that the present prosperity of Liverpool has arisen from a combination of causes; amongst which may be chiefly noticed its natural situation, its free water carriage, with the numerous manufacturing towns and mines of the county, and the enlightened policy of its civil government. Seated on the eastern bank of the estury of the Mersey, it possesses a ready and easy communication with St. George's-channel, and thence to the Atlantic Ocean. Ships, when the wind is fair, at about east-south-east, will sail from the docks to the main Irish sea, in a few hours. The river gradually expands between the town and the sea. From the fort to Seacombe-ferry, opposite, it is about 1300 yards across At spring tides, the water sometimes rises thirty feet; but at dead neap, only thirteen feet. Leland, as already observed, states that this port was well frequented by Irish merchants in his time; and its first importance

Marginal notes:

Visited by St. Patrick.

Charter granted by Henry II.

Favourably situated for commerce.

doubtless arose from the low ratio of its import duties. From the flatness of the shore, and other circumstances, the shipping were formerly subject to great inconveniences ; for, though vessels rode safely in the offing, they were obliged to ride there as in a road, rather than a harbour. In the reign of Elizabeth, a mole was formed to lay up the vessels in the winter ; and a quay was made for the advantageous shipping and un- shipping their cargoes. In 1709, an act of Parliament was obtained for the formation of a wet dock, now called the "Old Dock." From the increase of trade, this was soon found insufficient, and another act was obtained, in 1736, for the enlargement of the old dock, for the formation of another, called Salt-house dock, and for rendering the harbour more secure, by erecting a pier. A third act was obtained, in 1761, to enlarge the powers of both the former. Thus, a third dock, called the St. George's-dock, was formed, and piers to secure the outer harbour ; and two light-houses were built. Two other docks have since been made, called the King's-dock and the Queen's-dock, which are situated at the north-west end of the town, and accommodated with a dry basin and two graving-docks. These docks may be described as consisting of three sorts ; the wet-docks, which usually receive such ships as are on foreign service, and consequently have large and heavy cargoes to discharge ; the dry-docks, appropriated to receive the vessels that are employed coast-ways ; and the graving-docks, which, by flood-gates, are calculated to admit and exclude the water at pleasure, for the purpose of caulking, and performing other repairs to the shipping. The uncertainty of the tides, and flatness of the shore at this port, first suggested the necessity of some artificial accommodation for the merchant vessels ; and as early as 1561, a scheme was planned for constructing a sort of dock, as a shelter from storms, &c. ; but it was not till 1710, that an act was obtained to construct a regular dock. Since that time the docks have increased in number, with the increase and population of the town, occupying a space of more than three miles in circumference ; the whole constructed, formed, and built, upon the bed of the river. St. George's, the Old, and Salthouse-docks, communicate ; so that ships can pass from one to the other, and into the graving-docks, without going into the river ; and the King's and Queen's-docks communicate in the same manner, and with their own graving-docks. There are perfect communications, under ground, between all the wet docks, by large tunnels, for the purpose of one dock cleaning or washing another. Each wet dock has a dock-master, with an annual salary, whose office is to regulate the internal decorum of the dock, by allotting the positions of the ships in their loading and unloading ; to direct the management of the flood-gates, and to attend to the docking and undocking of the ships at the time of the tide. The docks have watch, scavengers, and lamps, distinct from those of the town. Fires are not suffered ; and even candles are not permitted to be lighted on board the ships, except secured in lanterns ; nor tobacco smoked, nor any combustible matters left on the decks, or on the adjoining quays, in the night. By these precautions, an accident from fire has happened only once. Large ships, when loaded, cannot pass the dock gates at neap-tides, for want of sufficient depth of water there ; so that when a ship of that description in the dock, is ready for sea during the spring tides, and the wind unfair, it is conveyed into the river, and there remains at anchor, to take the advantage of a favourable wind. If a large ship arrive from sea, during neap-tides, it continues in the same situation till the next spring-tide rise high enough to float it into the dock. Connected with the docks, are wide and commodious quays, with large warehouses, cal- culated to store up such goods as are not immediately delivered to the retail dealers, &c. The Duke of Bridgewater's dock is devoted to the flats and barges belonging to the canals which communicate with Runcorn, Man- chester, and the manufacturing towns in this part of the country. The

6 x

LIVERPOOL. direction and government of the docks are vested in the corporation, as trustees; whose accounts are annually examined, and settled, by seven commissioners. By a comparison of the number of ships which sailed from and to the respective ports of Liverpool and Bristol, and on an average of five years, 1759 to 1763 inclusive, the shipping of the former far exceeded that of the latter; while the customs of Bristol exceeded those of Liverpool. This seeming paradox is solved by adverting to the nature of the articles, and differences of duty, imported into the two ports. From that period, and especially since 1770, in every point Liverpool has been surpassing Bristol; the precedency of which has been attributed to two causes, the ardent pursuit of the African trade by the one, and the humane dereliction of it in the other; and the superior advantages which Liverpool has long enjoyed, by means of her floating-

Public structures. docks. The public structures of this town, connected with its trade and commerce, are the Exchange-buildings, Town-hall, and Mansion-house, Custom-house, Corn-exchange, Tobacco-warehouse, &c. The Liverpool Exchange is the most spacious in plan, and ornamental in architectural elevation. It cost, in erecting, £80,000., raised from 800 transferrable shares of £100. each. The buildings occupy three sides of a quadrangle, having the north front of the Town-hall for the fourth side, and together include an area of 194 feet by 180. The architecture was designed to harmonise and correspond with the north elevation of the Town-hall, and thus constitute a uniform quadrangle. The new building consists of a rusticated basement, with a piazza extending round the whole, and opening to the area by a series of rustic arches, between strong piers. Above this are two stories, ornamented with Corinthian pilasters, and surmounted with an enriched bold cornice and parapet. In the centre of the north side, resting on the basement, is a grand recessed portico, with eight handsome Corinthian columns. This building accommodates the merchants, brokers, under-writers, and others of the town, who are devoted to mercantile pursuits. In the east wing is a coffee-room, ninety-four feet by fifty-two, supported on large columns. Above this is another spacious room, seventy-two feet by thirty-six, appropriated to the under-writers,

Monument to the memory of Lord Nelson. &c., on the principle of that of Lloyd's, in London. In the centre of the area is a splendid naval monument, to the memory of Lord Nelson, designed and executed by Mr. George Bullock, in artificial stone, at the expense £8000., which sum was raised, by subscription, for the purpose. "In the statue of Lord Nelson," observes Mr. Bullock, in the description of the model which he presented to the committee, appointed to decide on its adoption, " I have endeavoured to express the calm and dignified composure for which he was so pre-eminently distinguished in the hour of danger; his effigy is, therefore, plain and simple, placed in a firm and decided attitude; the union flag and anchor are introduced as the distinguishing marks of his professional rank; at the same time pointing out the means by which his fame and glory were obtained. The pedestal on which the hero stands, is encircled with a double coil of British cable, resting on the plinth, and enriched by the representation of his four principal engagements, viz. St. Vincent, the Nile, Copenhagen, and Trafalgar; four figures of Victory, whose hands are united by crowns of laurel, suspended over each battle, are the supporters of this column, representing an unbroken chain of splendid victories. The Town-hall, formerly called

The Town-hall destroyed by fire. the Exchange, in Exchange-buildings, is a large irregular pile of building, which was erected about the year 1750. The ground-floor was intended for an exchange, and calculated to accommodate the merchants with insurance-offices, &c. Unfortunately the whole of the interior was destroyed by fire, in 1795. The corporation consequently resolved to rebuild it on a more extended and improved plan, and to appropriate the whole to judicial and other offices, for the police of the town, for a mansion for the mayor, a suite of public assembly-rooms, and for all the offices devoted to the business of the corporation. The ground story, on the south side, consists of a handsome entrance-hall, leading to a flight of stairs, a committee-room, and a private room for the mayor; on the east side are a vestibule, rooms for the magistrates and juries, and the town-clerk's offices; on the north side, an entrance-hall, leading to the Town-hall, or general sessions-room, to the rotation-office, &c. The summit of this building is terminated by a dome of modern construction, ornamented with several columns. Round the frieze, and in the pediment of the southern front is a profusion of badly finished sculptured decoration. On the 24th of April, 1807, the first foundation stone of a new Corn-exchange was laid in Brunswick-street. It is a handsome structure of plain Grecian architecture, with a stone front. Like the New Exchange buildings, it was erected by subscription; a fund of £10,000. having been raised, by shares of £100, each. It was opened, for the first time, on the 2nd of August, 1808. The Custom-house, on the east side of the Old Dock, presents nothing remarkable. The Tobaccco-warehouse, on the west side of the King's-dock, and various other commercial warehouses, are devoted to the stowage of imported goods. The most ancient of the churches, in Liverpool, called St. Nicholas, or the Old Church, was a very low structure, having windows with pointed arches, and a small tower, crowned by a spire. Near it was a statue of St. Nicholas, the tutelary deity of the maritime part of the place, to which sea-faring people usually made a peace-offering, previously to their embarking; and another, as a wave-offering, on their return, for their successful issue of the voyage. This church was destroyed by the fall of the tower, on Sunday, the 12th of February, 1810. A few minutes before divine service, and just as the officiating clergyman was entering the church, the key-stone of the tower gave way, and the north-east choir, comprising the north and east walls, with the whole of the spire, came down, and with a tremendous crash, broke through the roof, falling along the centre aisle, till it reached near to the communion rails, and, in its fall, carried with it the whole peal of six bells, the west gallery, the organ, and clergyman's reading desk, totally demolishing them, and such seats as it came in contact with. Not more than fifteen or twenty adult people were in the church at the time, and of these the greater part escaped; but the children of a charity-school, who march in procession somewhat earlier than the time of service, had partly entered. The boys, who were last, entirely escaped; but a number of girls, who were either entering the porch, or proceeding up the aisle, were in a moment overwhelmed beneath the falling pile. The crash of the steeple, and the shrieks of terror which issued from those who had escaped in the church, or were spectators in the churh-yard, immediately brought a large concourse of people on the spot, who did not cease to make unabated efforts to rescue the unfortunate victims from the falling masonry, till all the bodies were extricated, notwithstanding the tottering appearance of the remaining part of the tower, of the roof, and church, which momentarily menaced a second fall. Many instances of hair-breadth deliverances occurred. All the ringers, except one, escaped, who was caught in the ruins, and yet was extricated alive by his brethren. The alarm, it is said, was first given to the ringers, by the fall of a stone upon the fifth bell, which prevented its swing; the men ran out, and a moment did not elapse before the bells, beams, &c. fell to the bottom of the tower, and their escape would have been impossible, had not the belfry been upon the ground-floor. The Rev. —— Roughedge, the rector, owed his safety to the circumstance of his entering the church at an unaccustomed door. The Rev. L. Pughe, the officiating minister, was prevented from entering by the children of the school, who were pressing forward. The teacher, who was killed, had just separated the children to afford him a passage, when a person exclaimed, "For God's sake come back!" He

LIVERPOOL.

St. Peter's-church.

stepped back, and beheld the spire sinking, and the whole fell in. A person, named Martin, was seated in his pew, the surrounding seats were dashed in pieces, and heaped with ruins, but he came out unhurt. Twenty-seven bodies were taken out of the ruins, and twenty-two were either killed or expired afterwards. St. Peter's-church was built in the year 1704. It is a plain structure, having a quadrangular tower, the upper story of which is octangular, terminated by eight pinnacles, with a gilt fane. St. George's-church, which was finished in 1744, partakes of a classical style. The body is formed by a Doric range, bearing an attic entablature, with a parapet ornamented with vases. The windows for affording light, both to the aisles and galleries, are disproportionately large. On the south side, is a wide handsome terrace, raised on six rustic arches; at the extremity of which are two wings, consisting of octangular buildings; one of which is appropriated to the clerk of the market, and the other to a cell for confining delinquents. The steeple consists of five tiers, or portions, ornamented with pilasters of the Doric, Ionic, Corinthian, and Composite orders; and above the tower rises a lofty, tapering, octangular spire. St. Thomas's-church, which was built

St. Thomas's-church.

in 1750, is better proportioned, but has an unusual appearance. "The body consists of a rustic base, having two tiers of windows; the upper calculated for a drawing-room, and the lower for a prison; nor is the large semicircular Venetian window, at the east end, in a happier style. The double Ionic pilasters attached to the sides, as they appear to have nothing to support, add little to its decoration. The tower is lofty, terminating in a well-proportioned spire, nearly half the height from the base; but its immediate and appropriate support consists of four couplets of Corinthian columns, on which, as though ashamed of their station,

St. Paul's-church.

stare four crocket pinnacles, combined with four vases." St. Paul's-church, erected at the public expense, and consecrated in 1769, is a miniature imitation of the cathedral of London. "On the west side, a grand Ionic portico forms a suitable vestibule to the building, which is also of the Ionic order throughout. The base is rustic, the walls plain, terminated by a balustrade, decorated, but not crowdedly so, with plain neat vases. The dome is crowned with a lantern, and its finial, a ball bearing a cross. Though the exterior of this building loses all apperance of grandeur or beauty to the eye that has dwelt on the designs of St. Peter's at Rome, and St. Paul's at London, yet it assumes some importance and elegance when compared with the other modern churches of the town, or the generality of those sacred edifices that have been erected since the reign of Henry VIII. Its interior is more imposing than the exterior, from the disposition and character of the pillars that support the dome. Like most buildings with domes, or of circular arrangement, this is very unfavourable for the communication of sound." St. Ann's-church, built by two proprietors, in 1770, is remarkable for having its galleries supported by slender cast-iron pillars; and for being placed north and south, instead of east and west. St. John's-church, which was raised at the public expense, was finished in 1784. Trinity-church, consecrated in 1792, is remarkably commodious and neat. It is private

Christ's-church.

property. Christ's-church is a large and handsome building, with two rows of galleries. The organ, constructed by Mr. Collins, of this town, is divided into two parts, fourteen feet asunder; the organist is placed in the centre, with his face towards the congregation; the swell is behind him on the floor; and the movements are beneath his feet. This church, built by an individual, at an expense of £15,000. was consecrated in the year 1800. St. Mark's-church, a large edifice, raised by subscription, at an expense of £16,000., was finished in 1803. It will hold nearly 2500 persons. The increased population of the town having rendered another church necessary, the first stone of a new one was laid, by the mayor, on the 21st of June, 1816. Besides these churches, there are St. James's, in

Parliament-street, Toxteth-park; St. Mary's, a small chapel, consecrated **LIVERPOOL** about the year 1800; St. Andrew's, in Renshaw-street, consecrated in 1815; St. Phillip's, in Hardman-street, built in 1815; St. Michael's, in Upper Pitt-street, first stone laid 1816; the church of the " School for the Blind," opened 1818; St. Stephen's-church, Byron-street, built in 1722; and St. Matthew's, in Key-street, in 1707. In addition to the churches of the establishment, here are five Roman Catholic-chapels, a Scotch-church, and Welsh-church, a Quaker's-meeting, a Jews'-synagogue, and many meeting-houses for the different sects of dissenters. Several of these are neat and comfortable structures; but what is called the Octagon, claims the most notice, as it unites great convenience with some portion of dignity. The Blue Coat-hospital made its appearance as a **The Blue** charity-school, supported by annual subscription and donation, for the **Coat-** educating and maintaining forty boys and ten girls, A. D., 1709. The **hospital.** building consists of a large body, having two wings; the whole built of brick, and ornamented with stone. At the public Infirmary, all persons, without exception, are admitted, who come properly recommended by a subscriber; and in cases of sudden accident this is dispensed with. This building is composed of brick, coped with stone. The wings form an asylum for decayed seamen, with their widows and children. This charity commenced in 1749, by a drawback of sixpence per month from the wages of every mariner belonging to, or sailing out of, the port. Here is a poor-house, a large plain building, extremely well adapted to its purpose; a dispensary, at which, since its commencement, in 1778, nearly 11,000 persons, on an average, have been annually cured of almost every disorder incident to human nature; an asylum for the indigent blind; and a ladies'-charity, established in 1796, to afford relief and com-fort to poor married women in child-bed, at their own houses. The **The theatre.** Liverpool theatre, situated in Williamson-square, is a large and com-modious pile of building. It was finished in 1772, and cost about £6000., which was raised by thirty proprietors. The Athenæum, in Church-street, constituting a news and coffee-room, and public library, was commenced in 1798. The expense of the building, erected by a sub-scription of £4400., with its establishment and current support, is de-frayed by between 400 and 500 subscribers; 300 of whom paid, on entrance, ten guineas for each share; afterwards the shares were raised to twenty guineas; and, subsequently, they were further augmented to thirty guineas each. The subscribers, also, pay two guineas annually, each. The Union news-room, a similar establishment, instituted on the 1st of January, 1801, cost between £4000. and £5000. It has a stone front in Duke-street. The Lyceum, in Bold-street, consisting also of a coffee-room, library, &c., is a large handsome pile, erected at an expense of about £11,000., which was raised by a subscription of 800 proprietors, who pay annually one guinea each, towards its support, &c. The Com-mercial news-room, in Lord-street; and the Minerva news-room, in Upper Dawson-street, are minor institutions, of a similar nature. The **The Music-** Music-hall, in Bold-street, is a large handsome pile of building, provided **hall.** with every accommodation for concerts, &c. The assembly-room is a part of the Liverpool Arms-hotel, in Castle-street. Liverpool also con-tains a circular room for a panorama; a museum, a freemasons'-hall, a botanic garden, &c. The botanic garden, at the S. E. end of the town, consists of about five acres of ground. It is supported by between 300 and 400 proprietors; who, besides an original advance, pay an annual subscription of two guineas. The streets in the oldest part of the town are too narrow to be either handsome or healthy; and, with respect to many of the modern buildings, greater regard has been paid to conveni-ence than to beauty. There are, however, several handsome streets, and fine houses. Notwithstanding the general prosperity of the town, the cor-poration, by failures and want of money, were, in the year 1793, obliged

LIVERPOOL.

to apply to Parliament for relief. Their income, for the year 1792, was £25,000. 17s. 11d.; their whole property was valued at £1,044,776.; and their debts amounted to £367,816. 12s., leaving a surplus of £676,959. 8s., besides some contingent concerns, estimated at upwards of £60,000. more. Parliament allowed the corporation to issue negotiable notes, for a limited time, which was of great service to the trade of the town. Liverpool was but ill supplied with water, and at a great expense. That useful article used to be carried about the town in carts, and sold for a half-penney a bucket. This deficiency has been completely remedied.

The Bootle-springs.

The Bootle-springs, near 2000 of which concentrate, as it were, at one point, rise upon the estate of Lord Derby, and are situated upon a hill in the village of Bootle, three miles north of Liverpool, and have been brought into the town by great perseverance and expense, and uncommon exertions; so that the inhabitants, at present, daily experience the comforts of abundance of fresh water, without having recourse to the slovenly and expensive mode of water-carts. The immense reservoir constructed at the entrance of Liverpool, receives a sufficient quantity of water to counteract, at any future period, so dreadful a calamity as visited the town some years ago. To supply the shipping, and guard against disappointment to the inhabitants, as in case of accidents to the long train of pipes, this reservoir is capable of containing nearly 4000 tons of water. The borough of Liverpool returns two members to Parliament, who are elected by the votes of the free burgesses, about 2500 in number, and £10.

Incorporated by King John.

householders, about 17427. The town was incorporated by King John; constituted a borough, 23rd of Edward I.; and, in 1729, it was determined, that the right of election was vested in the mayor, bailiffs, and freemen, not receiving alms. All the freemen enjoy this singular privilege, that they are also free of the city of Bristol, and of Waterford and Wexford, in Ireland. The Parliament had a very strong garrison here, in 1644, under the command of Colonel Moore. Prince Rupert, assisted by the Earl of Derby, approached the town, after taking Bolton. It was defended on the east and north by a strong mud wall, with a vallum and foss thirty-six feet wide, and nine deep. On the top of these were placed numerous bags of Irish wool. The south-east side was naturally defended by a wide marsh, inundated from the river; the streets leading to this were shut up, and those towards the land were defended by gates, with pieces of cannon planted in each avenue. It had a strong castle on the south, surrounded with a ditch, thirty-six feet wide, and thirty deep; upon the ramparts of which were cannon, and the entrance defended by a fort of eight guns. A covered way led thence to the river, by which the ditch was filled occasionally with water; and by which, at ebb tide, provisions and stores were brought in. The prince, having gained the heights, encamped on the hill; and having, in vain, summoned the place to surrender, he commenced the siege, which, with continual repulses, and great slaughter, continued one month. From the treachery of the commandant, as has been alledged by some, or the works on the north side being deserted by the troops, as mentioned by others, a breach was then made, and the prince's army entered the town, putting to the sword all they met. The troops from the castle then beat a parley, submitted to become prisoners of war, and the whole town surrendered; but it was soon after retaken by the Parliament army, and Colonel Birch was appointed governor of the castle. After this, the works were dismantled. A fort has been erected on the banks of the river at the north-west end of the town, but this is too trifling and weak to afford much protection.

The public cemeteries.

As appertaining to the religious institutions of Liverpool, some account may here be introduced of the public cemeteries, which are arranged and constructed more on the plan of those of Paris than of any others in this country. The Necropolis, or Low-hill general cemetery, was the first established, by persons of various religious persuasions, under the manage-nent of a joint stock company, at the expense of about £8000. ; and the affairs of the proprietors are stated to be in a prosperous condition. It consists of an oblong quadrangular area, surrounded by a strong wall of brick, thirteen feet high, and containing a superficial space of 24,000 square yards. The house for the registrar, and the chapel, were erected from the design of Mr. John Foster, junior ; and the entrance-front, which is of stone, is ornamented with Doric columns and pilasters, support-ing an entablature, surmounted by a pediment on each side of the gate-way. A border, extending ten feet from the wall, all round the interior, is appropriated for an arcade, or colonnade, roofed with slate, and railed in with ornamental iron-work ; and this border will be used for tombs, with monumental inscriptions, tablets, or sculptural decorations. The centre of the ground is laid out in regular order for the construction of vaults and graves ; such part as is not immediately required for those purposes being planted with ornamental trees and shrubs, under the direction of Mr. John Shepherd, curator of the botanic garden. Another of these repositories of the remains of mortality, called St. James's-cemetery, has been more recently constructed, on ground situated at the ends of Rodney-street and Duke-street. The site was formerly a stone quarry, and that circumstance has afforded a facility for the erection of a number of spacious vaults, excavated in the solid rock. There is a school for the indigent blind, the church or chapel attached to which has been previously noticed. In this interesting institution the pupils are instructed in spinning, making of baskets, twine, cord, fishing-lines, hearth-rugs, mats, stairs-carpeting, floor-cloth, list and worsted shoes, and other articles, the manufacture of which is adapted to the state of their faculties ; they are also taught music, when they display a taste for the art, in which several of them have made such proficiency as to become qualified for the situa-tion of organist. The value of the articles manufactured in this establish-ment, has sometimes amounted to nearly £2000. a-year. There are a considerable number of alms-houses for the necessitous and aged poor ; and besides clubs, or benefit societies, for the labouring classes, there is one for commercial travellers ; and likewise an institution for the relief of decayed actors. The streets in general are well paved, and the town is brilliantly lighted with gas, under the direction of two joint-stock com-panies, one for the production of gas from coal, incorporated by act of Parliament, in 1818 ; and the other for producing gas from oil, in 1823. The public buildings are numerous and important, especially those which are connected with trade and commerce, some of them being formed on a scale of greater magnificence than even those of the metropolis. Among the public works connected with commerce, one of the most considerable is the Liverpool and Manchester railway, which is carried under the town by two tunnels, extending from Edgehill to near the Queen's-dock, about 2200 yards. On the surface of the ground, above the mouths of the tunnels, are two lofty chimneys, shaped like columns, with handsome capitals ; they are more than 100 feet high, and are constructed of brick. In the area below are two stationary steam-engines, to draw up the loaded waggons from the bottom of the inclined plane at Wapping ; and at a short distance from the tunnel is a handsome Moorish archway, built from a design of Mr. Foster, and connecting the two engine-houses on the opposite sides of the area. The principal shaft of this tunnel was com-menced in October, 1826, and it was completed and opened, for the inspection of the public, June 30, 1829. On the 15th of September, 1830, the works on the whole line having been entirely executed, the railway was opened ; on which occasion the Duke of Wellington, and many other persons of rank and eminence, accompanied the directors of the under-taking in steam carriages, prepared for the passage from Liverpool to Manchester, when, owing to an unfortunate accident at Parkfield, seven-teen miles from Liverpool, Mr. Huskisson, then M. P. for that borough,

Marginal notes: LIVERPOOL. — School for the indigent blind. — The Liverpool and Manchester rail-way. — Death of Mr. Huskisson.

having alighted from one of the carriages, was alarmed by the approach of another, and falling down, suffered so much injury from the wheels passing over him, that he died on the following night. The borough-gaol, in Great Howard-street, was formerly a depôt for prisoners of war, but is now appropriated to the confinement of criminals and debtors; it is an extensive, strong, and commodious edifice, the internal arrangements of which are on the plan recommended by Howard. There is a Bridewell in South Chapel-street; and at Kirkdale is the house of correction. The parish workhouse is a spacious building, on Brownlow-hill, erected in 1771, at the expense of £8000.; and it is under the management of the church-wardens and overseers, assisted by a select vestry. At the extremity of the Rock Perch, and close to the bar, or entrance of the river Mersey, a new beacon, or light-house, has been erected, the first stone having been laid in July, 1827. On the north shore is a battery for the protection of the town and harbour; and another has more recently been erected on the opposite shore, at Black Rock, from the situation of which, and the nature of the navigation of the river, security against hostile attacks may be anticipated. At the entrance into the town, from the London road, has been erected an equestrian statue of King George III. The mechanics' institute and lecture-room, in Slater-street, and the public libraries for the use of male and female apprentices, the former founded in 1822, and the latter in 1824. Musical festivals are held every four years, the profits of which are devoted to beneficent purposes; and that which took place in October, 1827, produced a sum of more than £9000., leaving a surplus, after the deduction of expenses, of nearly £6000. The first newspaper, ever issued in Liverpool, was on the 28th of May, 1756, by Robert Williamson, price three-halfpence; and in 1766 the first directory of Liverpool was published, which sold for sixpence. In 1757, the post passed for the first time, through Ormskirk, from Liverpool to Preston; and in 1760, the first stage coach was established from hence to London, which started once a week, and performed the journey in four days. In 1567, a cock-pit was erected; and in 1576, horse races were first instituted here and held on Ascension-day, in every year, upon the shore; the prize being a silver bell, which was tied to the forehead of the winning horse, and hence the phrase, to "bear away the bell," applied to successful emulation. From 1774 to 1786, they took place at Crosby-marsh, near the town, but were afterwards discontinued, till August, 1826, when the corporation gave a silver cup, which prize was contested at a place about six miles from the town. In 1829, the races, for the first time, were held at Aintree, about five miles from Liverpool, on the Ormskirk road, and continued during four days. A grand stand has since been erected, enclosed by iron railings, which will contain about 1500 persons, and the whole building will accommodate about 3000. On the principal floor of this structure, is a saloon, or long room, being ninety feet in length, and twenty-two in breadth, lighted by nineteen windows; besides which there are spacious and convenient lobbies, entrance and refreshment rooms. The principal manufactures of Liverpool are refined sugar, soap, starch, glass, watches, &c.; there are, likewise, salt-works, copperas-works, iron-foundries, brass-foundries, tar and turpentine distilleries, oil-mills, saw-mills, tobacco-manufactories, vinegar-works, and many considerable breweries. Vast numbers of persons are employed in ship and boat building, making ropes, sails, blocks, pumps, &c., and equipping, or repairing, vessels for service. Here are also nail-makers, wire-workers, millwrights, engineers, and steam-engine makers, mill-stone manufacturers, and French burr importers. Near the town are several wind-mills for grinding corn, and other purposes. The merchants of Liverpool have extended their commerce to almost every part of the known world, but the principal trade is with America and the West Indies. Before the abolition of the slave-trade it formed the grand source

Map.	Names of Places.	County.	Number of Miles from			Dist. Lond.	Popu- lation.
45	Liversedge....to & cha	W. R. York	Huddersfield.7	Halifax......6	Wakefield ..10	188	5265
45	Liverton ....to	W. R. York	Guisborough .6	Whitby 13	Stoc. on Tees20	249	281
22	Livesey...........to	Lancaster...	Blackburn ..2	Chorley ...:.7	Preston......9	209	1787
54	Llafernoc..... .....pa	Glamorgan..	Cardiff......6	Cowbridge..13	Llantrissant 15	166	94

of commercial enterprise here, and it has been stated that nearly two-thirds of the population were interested in the traffic of human beings; but their wealth and industry are now devoted to purposes more adapted to the promotion of national prosperity. Many vessels are employed in the trade with Norway, Hamburgh, the Baltic, the Netherlands, France, and the Mediterranean, whence are imported a variety of foreign goods. Intercourse is also carried on with the principal ports of England, Scotland, Wales, and Ireland; and, by means of inland navigation, Liverpool communicates with every important town in the kingdom. Steam packet-boats sail regularly to Whitehaven, Carlisle, Lancaster, Ellesmere, Manchester, Beaumaris, Bangor, Bagillt, Rhuddlan, Glasgow, Greenock, the Isle of Man, Belfast, Cork, Dublin, Dundalk, Londonderry, Newry, and Waterford; and foreign packets, to Boston, New York, Philadelphia, Bahia, Pernambuco, Maranham, Buenos Ayres, Rio de Janeiro, Valparaiso, Vera Cruz, Genoa, Leghorn, Lisbon, and Oporto. There are, in different parts of the town, nine markets; these are St. James's-market, near St. George's-place; St. Thomas's-market, Cleveland-square; St. John's-market, Great Charlotte-street; the market in Derby-square; Islington-market; the markets in Scotland-place, and in Pownall-square; the pig-market, near Gibraltar-street; and the cattle-market, in Lime-street. The market for corn is held Tuesdays and Saturdays; and markets for provisions, &c., may be said to take place daily. There are two annual fairs, and ten days before the commencement of each, a figure of a hand is hung up in front of the town-hall, where it is suffered to remain till ten days after the conclusion of each fair, denoting protection during the whole period, in which all persons going from, or coming to the town, on business connected with the fair, are exempt from arrest for debt by a borough process. Liverpool is rather deficient in promenades or public walks, the most agreeable of which is that called the Parade, on the bank of the river, westward of St. George's-dock, whence there is a noble prospect of the Mersey, with the forest of masts on its surface, and the opposite shore of Cheshire, in the distance. In the vicinity of the town are many delightful situations, among which are the villages of Everton, Kirkdale, and Bootle, towards the north and north-east; and on the east, Wavertree, Toxteth-park, and Allerton. During the season, Liverpool is a place of frequent resort for sea-bathing. In October, 1827, a line of telegraph was completed from Liverpool to Holyhead, by means of which, communications may be made from one extremity to the other, a distance of 128 miles in five minutes, and a plan has been proposed for a similar communication with Manchester. Liverpool gives the title of Earl to the family of Jenkinson. Amongst the distinguished natives of Liverpool, may be particularly mentioned a sculptor, of the name of Deare; Jeremiah Horn, a celebrated astronomer; George Stubbs, a distinguished painter of animals; William Roscoe, author of the "Life of Lorenzo di Medici;" Dr. William Enfield; Dr. John Bostock; and the poetess, Mrs. Hemans.

Marginal notes: LIVERPOOL. / Great foreign commerce. / Singular protection from arrest. / Birthplace of distinguished persons.

Market, Wednesday and Saturday.—Fairs, 25th of July, and November 11.—Bankers, James Aspinall, Temple-court, draws on Sir James Esdaile and Co., London; Branch Bank of England, Hanover-street, Samuel Turner agent, Joseph Langton, sub-agent; Fletcher, Roscoe and Co., High-street, Exchange, draw on Jones, Loyd and Co., London; Heywood, Arthur, Sons and Co., 5, Brunswick-street, draw on Joseph Denison and Co., London; Samuel Hope and Co., Water-street, draw on Sir Richary Glyn and Co., London; Thomas, Richard, and Christopher Bullin, Leyland, King-street, draw on Masterman and Co., London; Moss, Rogers, and Moss, 186, Dale-street, draw on Barclay and Co., London.—Inns and Posting Houses, Adelphi-hotel and posting house, Ranelagh-place; Albion-hotel, Ranelagh-street; Bull-inn, Dale-street; London-tavern, Water-street; Saracen's-head, Dale-street; Coach-an, Angel, Dale-street, &c.

Map	Names of Places.	County.	Number of Miles from			Dist. Lond.	Popu- lation.
57	Llamphey* ....pa	Pembroke ..	Pembroke ...4	Tenby.....8	Narbarth...10	265	197
54	Llamphy ....ham	Glamorgan..	Cowbridge ..1	Llantrissant .7	Bridgend....7	173	177
56	Llan ....to	Montgomery	Welshpool ..3	Oswestry...13	Shrewsbury 19	172	....
55	Llan Aber..........pa	Merioneth ..	Barmouth ...2	Harlech.....8	Dolgelly....13	225	1488
51	Llan-Afan..........pa	Cardigan ...	Aberystwith10	Tregaron...8	Devil'sBridge 7	205	384
48	Llan-Afan-Fawr....pa	Brecon	Buallt 8	Rhayader ..10	Llandovery .18	181	936
48	Llan-Afan Fechan ..pa	Brecon	6	12	16	179	189
47	Llanallgof.........pa	Anglesea ...	Llanerch-y-m6	Amlwch 7	Beaumaris.10	261	417
48	Llan-Aml-Llech† ...{ ....ham & pa	Brecon	Brecon......4	Crickhowel 10	MerthyrTyd.15	163	149
58	Llan-Anno‡.......pa	Radnor....	Rhayader ..11	NewRadnor 12	Newtown ..11	177	343
50	Llan-Armon........pa	Carnarvon ..	Pwllheli 4	Cricceath ...5	Carnarvon . 18	239	613
52	Llan-Armon........pa	Denbigh	Ruthin......5	Wrexham ..12	Chester....18	188	1475
52	Llan-Armon Dyffryn Ceiriog.........pa	Denbigh....	Oswestry .. 10	Llangollen...8	Bala 16	181	307
52	Llan-Armon-Mynydd Mawr.........pa	Denbigh....	Llanfyllin ...8	10	16	181	164
51	Llan-Arth§.........pa	Cardigan ...	Lampeter ..14	Cardigan ...18	Aberystwith20	225	449

Lamphey-court.

* LLAMPHEY, a small village, crossed by the high road between Tenby and Pembroke. The church is adorned with a fine tower, and close by stands an ancient cross. Here are the ruins of the stately mansion of Lamphey-court, one of the seven palaces of the bishops of St. David's, and where the unfortunate Earl of Essex passed his early years. It is entered by an arched gateway, with a niche over it. We come next to a square tower, evidently a porter's-lodge. A paved path then leads by a flight of steps to a room, called the red chamber, the floor of which is of hard stucco. A little way to the right is the chapel; the east window still exhibiting most elegant tracery. A little further, in a projection to the right, occur some of the great rooms, ascended by a staircase from without, finished, on the north side, with an open parapet, and under them the kitchen, pointed at top, and ribbed. Separated by several ruined apartments, vaulted beneath, to the west, ascend by a ladder into a larger and grander room than the former, the door and window casings of free-stone, and at one end a door opening to a retiring chamber. To the east of the chapel which looks into it, is a large paddock, once occupied by the gardens and orchards, in which is still a small fish-pond. It had a warren and park. The north wall of the great barn or granary, attributed to Bishop Vaughan, still exists. The beacon for alarm, in case of an invasion, is placed upon an ancient tumulus near Llanfey.

St. Iltut's hermitage.

† LLAN-AML-LLECH. Upon an eminence, between the village of Llan-aml-llech and Llangasty-tal-y-llyn, is the monument called St. Iltut's hermitage. It was a cistfaen, or stone chest, resembling that which stood at Cerrig-y-Druidion, in Denbighshire, and the saint is said to have used it as his penitential couch. Here are some antique characters, believed to be the workmanship of the recluse. A pillar-stone formerly stood close to the cistfaen. The name Llan-aml-llech, may be translated "the church on many flat stones."

Picturesque ruin.

‡ LLAN-ANNO, a parish in the hundred of Knighton, upon the Ithon river, and adjoining the wild district called Knucklass Forest. Area of parish, about 5000 acres, much of which is high and unenclosed. Here is a mineral spring. The picturesque ruin, called Ty-yn-y-Bwlch, or the house in the defile, occupies the summit of a precipitous rock, in a narrow pass, on the banks of the Ithon, in this parish.

§ LLAN-ARTH. The church stands on the summit of a hill, overhanging the Llethy river. Henry VII. encamped at Wern Newydd, in this parish, the second night of his march through this county. Noyadd-Llan-Arth is the handsome seat of the Brooke family.

Fairs, March 12; June 17; September 22; October 27; and the first Wednesday after December 12.

ador.	Names of Places.	County.	Number of Miles from			Dist. Lond.	Popu- lation.
26	Llanarth ....pa	Monmouth..	Ragland 4	Abergavenny 6	Pontypool ..10	140	340
19	Llan-Arthne* ......pa	Carmarthen.	Carmarthen..8	Llandilo-V...7	Llampeter ..20	208	1839
53	Llan-Asaph ....pa	Flint	Holywell 6	St. Asaph... 8	Denbigh... 11	214	2373
47	Llan-Babo†.........pa	Anglesea ...	Llanerch-y-M4	Amlwch 6	Holyhead .. 11	271	174
51	Llanbadarn Fawr‡..pa	Cardigan ...	Aberystwith 1	Tregaron ...17	Machynlleth18	212	9824
58	Llanbadarn Fawr .. pa	Radnor	Pen-y-Bont . 3	Rhayader....7	Buallt..... 10	174	491

* LLAN-ARTHNE, a village and parish, the latter containing four hamlets, in the hundred of Is-Cenue, situated upon the river Tywi, in a picturesque, and most agreeable valley. The collieries and lime-works in this district employ the inhabitants; and increase of population may also be attributed to the enclosure of an extensive common here. Here is Myddleton-hall; and within the demesne there is a chalybeate spring, held in much esteem; adjacent to it are hot and cold baths, and other accommodations for the convenience and gratification of visitors, completed at a considerable expense and in excellent taste. The Spa is one mile from the village, and the latter adjoins the Milford mail-coach road. The pretty castellated building in the park was erected to the memory of Lord Nelson. The ancient church of Cappel Ddewi, on the banks of the Tywi, is now in ruins.

Chalybeate spring.

Fair, first Monday after July 12.

† LLAN-BABO. The church is said to have been built by Prince Pabo, commonly called Pabo Pôst Prydain, for his support of the Britons against the Picts and Scots, in the year 460. His tomb still survives, and bears his effigy encircled by an inscription.

‡ LLANBADARN FAWR retains some traces of its ancient consequence, but is an extremely remote spot, and has lost its market, which has been transferred to Aberystwith. The parish extends eighteen miles in length, and averages four miles in breadth, and the waste lands occupy 800 acres. It includes ten townships, three parcels, besides the manor, called Y-faenor, which belongs to the Duke of Leeds. The tenures of the crown are free soccage, and courts leet and baron are held in them. The Sunday-schools, in this parish, educate upwards of 500 children. A Roman road, usually called Sarn Helen, passes through the farm Llyn Rhingyll, in this place. Sometime in the sixth century, a church and bishopric were erected here by St. Paternus, a foreigner, who was drawn hither, from foreign countries, by the fame and sanctity of St. Dubricius and St. David. The see continued for years, but was united to that of St. David's, upon the barbarous murder of the Bishop of Llanbadarn, by the inhabitants. The suffragan bishop of this very ancient see was one of the seven who had conference with Augustin the monk, when he attempted to establish his own supremacy over the British Church. The church appears to have been given to St. Peter's, of Gloucester, A. D. 1111, and afterwards appropriated to the Abbey of Vale Royal, in Cheshire. The Danes destroyed the original sanctuary, in the year 987; and it was spoiled a second time by Llewellyn ap Sytsylt, in 1038. The present church is a spacious building, in the early pointed style, consisting of a nave and chancel, and adorned with a massive tower, resting on lofty arches. Lewis Morris, the Welsh antiquary, is interred here. Between this town (once a Roman city) and the sea-coast, is a small ancient fortification, consisting of a separate area, surrounded by a wall, with a tower at one of the angles. A range of wild hills, backed by the stupendous Plinlimmon, forms the opposite boundary of this valley; and at its termination, in the sea-coast, the town of Aberystwith appears on the brink of the sea, with its ruined castle, on a gentle rise, to the left, the Rhydiol flowing on the right. This approach is certainly very striking, and raises expectations which the interior of Aberystwith is not calculated to gratify.

A Roman road.

Once a Roman city

Map.	Names of Places.	County.	Number of Miles from				Dist. Lond.	Popu- lation.
58	Llanbadarn Fynydd .pa	Radnor	Newtown ...8	Rhayader...10	Buallt......19		168	518
51	Llanbadarn Od- wynne........pa	Cardigan ...	Tregaron 4	Lampeter...11	Aberystwith15		226	558
51	Llanbadarn - Tref - Eglwys......pa	Cardigan ...	14	12	16		223	982
58	Llanbadarn - y - Car- reg...........pa	Radnor	Buallt.. ...5	Hay.... ..,.9	New Radnor10		165	98
51	Llanbadarn-y-Creid- dyn-Isaf.. ....ham	Cardigan ...	Aberystwith 1	Tregaron ...17	Machynleth.18		212	891
51	Llanbadarn-y-Creid- dyn ....ham	Cardigan ...	1	17	18		212	743
26	Llanbadock ....pa	Monmouth..	Usk 2	Pontypool ...4	Abergavenn.12		144	389
47	Llanbadrig ....pa	Anglesea..	Amlwch ...5	Llanerch-y-M8	Holyhead ..20		275	1364
50	Llanbadrig ....pa	Carnarvon ..	Pwllheli 4	Nevin 5	Carnarvon ..25		247	459
50	Llan-Bebleg........pa	Carnarvon ..	Carnarvon ..1	Newborough.5	Bangor.....9		244	7642
54	Llanbeddery ......ham	Glamorgan..	Cowbridge ..1	Bridgend 9	Cardiff 13		173	....
48	Llanbedr ... .pa	Brecon	Crickhowel . 3	Hay........14	Abergavenny.7		159	359
55	Llan-Bedr..........pa	Merioneth ..	Barmouth ...7	Harlech 3	Dolgelly....12		228	403
26	Llanbedr ..ham & cha	Monmouth ..	Caerleon ...4	Usk 10	Chepstow ..12		148	56
58	Llanbedr ....pa	Radnor	Hay 7	Buallt 7	NewRadnor 12		163	356
52	Llanbedr - Dyffryn - Clwyd ....pa	Denbigh ...	Ruthin......1	Denbigh 9	Chester.....18		206	527
57	Llanbedr-Felfrey ...pa	Pembroke ...	Narbarth ...4	Tenby 7	Carmarthen.18		251	985
47	Llanbedr-Goch .....pa	Anglesea ...	Beaumaris .. 7	Llanerch-y-M8	Bangor......8		259	437
51	Llanbedr* ....m t	Cardigan ...	Llandovery .18	Newc. in E. 21	Tregaron ...10		211	1317

Picturesque situation.

St. David's college.

Roman remains.

* LLANBEDR, or Lampeter-pont-Stephen, a market and contributory borough, partly situated in the beautiful vale of Teifi, on a level tract, encompassed by hills, and watered by the river Teifi. The College of Llanbedr stands upon the summit of the only eminence in the level country, and presents a remarkably picturesque appearance. The town has improved considerably since the erection of the college. Here is a market-house and shambles, a parish church, two meeting-houses, and a house of correction, besides an excellent inn, and other places, affording comfortable accommodation. The bridge, about half a mile from the town, is said to have been originally erected by King Stephen; and an adjoining field bears the name of the King's-meadow, and a little subterranean passage, now filled up, was called the King's-cellar. There is a lead-mine at a short distance, at a place called Llanfair Clydog, containing a large per centage of silver. There is little trade here, except what may be termed domestic. Quarter sessions are held here regularly. The college of St. David is about a quarter of a mile from the town; it was founded by Bishop Burgess, incorporated by royal charter, and opened for the reception of students on the 1st of March, 1827, the first stone having been laid with due ceremony, on the 12th of August, 1822. The government and instruction of the pupils are intrusted to a principal and four professors, namely, of Hebrew, natural philosophy, mathematics, and Welsh. There are accommodations for about 100 scholars. The students enjoy the same advantage, that is, the direct admission into holy orders, as those of Cowbridge and St. Bees. There is an unendowed grammar-school in the town, and a national school consisting of 100 poor children. This was anciently a place of greater extent, and more densely peopled. The people of St. Peter are frequently mentioned in the Welsh chronicles, and to the west of the town, leaden coffins have been dug up, in a place supposed to be the cemetery of St. Thomas's-church, no part of which building now remains. A priory is also thought to have stood where the priory-house and garden are now situated; and two large mounts, enclosed by fosses, remain near to the town. A Roman road may be traced across the common, and there was a Roman camp near Olwen, where some part of a Roman military mil has been found.

Market, Saturday.—*Fairs*, January 11; March 6; May 11; Wednesday in Whitsun-week July 10; first Saturday in August; first Saturday in September, O. S.; September 26; October 19; and first Saturday in November, O. S.

Map	Names of Places.	County	Number of Miles from			Dist. Lond.	Popu- lation
50	Llanbedr-y-Cennin* ..pa	Carnarvon ..	Llanrwst 6	Conway.....4	Bangor.. ...10	223	516
50	Llanberis†.........pa	Carnarvon ..	Carnarvon ..10	Bangor......8	Llanrwst ...10	227	725
49	Llanbeudy.........pa	Carmarthen	Narbeth ...6	Carmarthen.15	Newc. in E. 15	248	1820
47	Llanbeulan ....pa	Anglesea ...	Llanerch-y-M7	Aberffraw ...5	Holyhead ..10	251	375
58	Llanbister ....pa	Radnor ...	Presteign ..14	NewRadnor 10	Rhayader ..12	165	1508
54	Llanbleiddian ......pa	Glamorgan..	Cowbridge...1	Bridgend....7	Cardiff....14	173	670
56	Llan-Brynn-Mair‡ ..pa	Montgomery	Machynlleth10	Newtown.. 16	Llanydloes .13	191	2040
52	Llan-Cadwaladyr ..pa	Denbigh	Oswestry ...8	Llangollen ..8	Llanfyllin....8	179	205
54	Llan-Carfan........pa	Glamorgan..	Cowbridge ..4	Llantrissant 11	Cardiff 12	172	734
17	Llancilloe.........pa	Hereford....	Hereford ...15	Crickhowell 8	Abergavenny 8	150	76
54	Llan-Ciwg ....pa	Glamorgan..	Neath 8	Swansea....10	Llandilo V. 12	206	1558
54	Llandaff§ ....city	Glamorgan..	Cardiff.....3	Llantrissant .8	Caerphilly ...6	165	1299

* LLANBEDR-Y-CENNIN. *Fair*, October 3.

† LLANBERIS, or Llanperis, a village, situated at the entrance of the grand defile called the Pass of Llanberis, and at the base of the Snowdonian mountains. The village consists of a few cottages, a poor-school, and a tolerable church. A new village, however, is springing up near to the lakes, and here are two inns affording comfortable lodgings, and much frequented by tourists, anglers, and artists, the scenery, in this gloomy valley, being considered the most sublime in the principality. The copper-mines here are beginning to be worked with spirit; and new slate-quarries, conducted upon very improved principles, afford occupation to the inhabitants of this and of the adjoining parishes. The slate and ore are raised close to the margin of the lake, flats are provided to transport them to the extremity, whence they are conveyed by a railroad to Moel-y-Don, on the banks of the Menai Strait. An admirable line of road is carried along the margin of the lower lake, from the New-inn to the town of Carnarvon. In the year 1831, this line of road was continued through the Pass of Llanberis, and opened into the post-road, from Beddgelert to Capel-Curig. The Glider Fawr Mountain, forming the eastern side of the Pass, rises to a height of 3300 feet, and Snowdon, which hangs over the west, is elevated 3571 feet above sea level. The surface of the lakes lies 310 feet above the sea. Llyn Cwm Dwythwch, in the west of the parish, discharges its surplus waters into the Upper Lake of Llanberis, by means of the river called Afon Hwch, which, in its course, falls over a ledge of rocks about sixty feet in height, forming the noble cataract called Rhaiadar-y-Ceynant Mawr. The ancient round castle of Dolbadern, one of the Welsh fortresses, built to guard the mountain passes, stands on the summit of a rocky eminence, protruding from the side of the mountain, and separating the Upper from the Lower Lake. Its position is remarkable, and it constitutes a strong feature in the sublime scenery of this vicinity. Owen Goich, brother of Llewellyn, last Prince of Wales, was confined in this castle for upwards of twenty years.

Sublime scenery.

Ancient castle.

Fair, September 18.

‡ LLAN-BRYNN-MAIR. The feeding of sheep and black cattle, upon the grassy hills here, constitutes the principal source of agricultural revenue in this parish. Here is the pool called Llyn Gwyddion, which is subject to remarkable disturbances from the action of the wind; and the cataract of Frwydafawr consists of a great volume of water, falling over a ledge of rock, down a precipice of 150 feet in depth.

Fairs, Friday before the first fair in Welsh Pool; May 31; September 16; and November 23.

§ LLANDAFF. This ancient city derives its name from the situation of the church, on the banks of the river Taf. It is, in fact, a miserable village of mean cottages, with the exception of a few thinly-scattered gentlemen's houses; and its only traders are a few small shopkeepers. The great object of attraction is the Cathedral. The architecture of the ancient building is partly Saxon; with an occasional mixture of Norman;

The cathedral

Map.	Names of Places.	County.	Number of Miles from			Dist. Lond.	Popu- lation.
55	Llandanwg ....pa	Merioneth ..	Harlech 3	Barmouth....7	Dolgelley...14	229	658
49	Llan-Dauddwr......pa	Carmarthen.	Llangharne ..3	Carmarthen..4	Tenby......12	242	421
49	Llan-Daug ....pa	Carmarthen.	6	11	9	242	19
26	Llandavenny......ham	Monmouth ..	Caerleon ...6	Chepstow...9	Usk........10	145	60

LLANDAFF.

but the prevailing style is that which is usually denominated Gothic. The western front is remarkably handsome, and ornamented with fine lancet windows of various sizes. Immediately over the principal entrance, in this end, and underneath the arch, on a tablet projecting in the centre, is the figure of a bishop with one hand moderately raised, and the other holding the pastoral staff; supposed to have been intended to represent one of the earlier bishops of the see. Above, over the upper range of windows, and near the summit of the building, is another carved figure in a sitting posture, holding a book in one hand. The whole is surmounted by an ancient cross. On the north side is a rich Saxon door way; and on the south is another, less ornamented. At the western end were formerly two magnificent square towers; of which, that at the north-west angle, built by Jaspar, Duke of Bedford, in 1485, alone remains. It is in good preservation, except the pinnacles, which were damaged by a storm, in 1703. Two sides of this tower rest on the walls of the church, but the other sides are raised on two light arches, which spring from a single pillar. On entering the building, some elegant Gothic arches occur on the right and left, which separated the nave from two side aisles. The length of the body of the church is 300 feet, and the breadth eighty. At the east end is a chapel, dedicated to the Virgin Mary; and on the south side stands the chapter-house, a square apartment, having, in the centre, a pillar, from which several Gothic arches diverge in different directions, supporting the roof. The ancient structure having fallen into decay, a new edifice was raised, about the year 1751, within the old walls. "This," observes a modern writer, "may, perhaps, claim the merit of being commodious, for the purposes of public worship; but nothing can be more incongruous than its architecture, placed where it is. The style is Grecian; and it is impossible, on the first view, to avoid the impression of its being a heathen temple built, as if in scorn, in the midst of the venerable remains of a Christian church. This incongruity is carried into the interior of the building, where the altar is placed, beneath a Grecian portico." Llandaff has been the burial place of several persons of distinction, and some of the sepulchral monuments remain, though in a dilapidated state. Near the upper end of the north aisle is the sculptured figure of a female, shrouded in a loose robe, the face and the part of the body which is displayed, exhibiting a striking representation of a delicate frame, emaciated by sickness. Beyond are two alabaster monuments, to some of the Matthews family. At the eastern extremity of the south aisle, is an alabaster monument, with the sculptured figure of a lady, in a long robe, reaching to her feet. Behind are the figures of two monks, holding an escutcheon, on which, probably, were once emblazoned the arms of the person whom it commemorates; supposed to have been the lady of John, Lord Audley, in the reign of Henry IV. Near the cathedral are some remains of the ancient, castellated mansion of the bishop, consisting of a large gateway, and part of the external wall. The destruction of this building, and of the principal portion of the church, is attributed to Owen Glyndwr. The present chapter of Llandaff consists of the bishop, who has the decanal stall, an archdeacon, treasurer, chancellor, precentor, and nine prebendaries. The see comprehends the principal part of Glamorganshire, and the whole of Monmouthshire, except seven parishes. Its revenues, valued in the king's books at £154. 14s. 1d., are computed to be worth, annually, £1600. The foundation of this see has been assigned to the year 180, but upon insufficient evidence.

Tower built by the Duke of Bedford.

Singular architecture.

Remains of an ancient mansion.

Map.	Names of Places.	County.	Number of Miles from			Dist. Lond.	Population.
49	Llanddarog........pa	Carmarthen.	Carmarthen..7	Llandilo Va. 10	Kidwelly ...9	221	1037
49	Llanddausaint ......pa	Carmarthen.	Langadock...5	11	Landovery .. 8	189	407
51	Llanddeiniol.......pa	Cardigan ...	Aberystwith 7	Tregaron...12	Cardigan ...31	218	2610
47	Llanddeiniol-Fab ...pa	Anglesea ...	Bangor......6	Carnarvon ...7	Llangefni...5	257	372
48	Llanddetty........pa	Brecon....	Brecon......9	Crickhowell .8	Mer. Tydvil 10	161	564
48	Llanddew*.........pa	Brecon....	 1	14	19	167	339
54	Llanddewi.........pa	Glamorgan..	Loughor 8	Swansea....12	Llanelly....15	215	178
51	Llanddewi-Aberath†pa	Cardigan ...	Lampeter...13	Aberystwith 16	Cardigan. ..22	224	976
48	Llanddewi - Aber - } Gwesin........pa }	Brecon....	Buallt.....15	Llandovery .13	Rhayader. .15	188	146
51	Llanddewi-Brefi‡ ..pa	Cardigan ..	Lampeter....7	Tregaron....4	Aberystwith20	218	2461
58	Llanddewi-Fach....pa	Radnor ...	Hay 6	Buallt......8	Brecon.....14	162	136
57	Llanddewi-Felfry .. pa	Pembroke ..	Narbarth ...4	Tenby 7	Carmarthen.18	251	786
55	Llanddewi-is-y-Craig } ....pa }	Merioneth ..	Barmouth ...4	Harlech 6	Dolgelly .. .12	224	442
48	Llanddewircwm ....pa	Brecon....	Buallt......2	Brecon.....14	Hay ...... .14	171	230
58	Llanddewi - ystrad - } Ennau.......pa }	Radnor	Rhayader...11	Buallt......15	NewRadnor 11	172	596
47	Llanddogfael.....den	Anglesea ...	Amlwch 7	Holyhead .. 12	Llanerch-y-M8	275	....
47	Llan-Ddona§. ......pa	Anglesea ...	Beaumaris ..4	Bangor.....7	12	255	442

* LLANDDEW, or Llanddewi. This village stands in a retired position, on the eastern bank of the river Honddu, and possesses a spacious church, supposed to have been founded in the earliest ages of Christianity in Britain. Here, also, was one of the palaces of the Bishop of St. David's; and here the dean, and other dignitaries of the diocese, occasionally resided. The bishop holds a court-leet here annually, and formerly held also a court-baron. In the time of the Commonwealth, the manor was sold to David Morgan, but was recovered by the see at the restoration. It is in the diocese of St. David's. The author of the county history conceives that this parish was originally part of the parish of St. David's. Giraldus Cambrensis resided here; and the state and condition of the clerical residences, at this place, in the time of Leland, are mentioned in the "Itinerary." Llanddewi signifies the Church of St. David. *(margin: Spacious church.)*

† LLANDDEWI-ABERARTH, a village, situated upon Cardigan Bay, at the mouth of the river Arth, and intersected by the coast-road, from Aberystwith to Cardigan. The village of Aberaeron is included in the return of the population of this parish. Here is a small harbour, the entrance of which is obstructed by a bar, dry at low water. In a direct line with the parish church is the Sarn Ddewi, or St. David's Causeway, running out into the sea for a distance of about a quarter of a mile. *(margin: St. David's causeway.)*

Fairs, July 5, and December 11.

‡ LLANDDEWI-BREFI, a small hamlet and a parish, situated upon the east bank of the river Teifi, or Tyvi, near to Pont Llanico, and in a very retired part of the county. The church is adorned with a lofty and massive tower, resting upon four Gothic arches, and presents a truly venerable appearance. There are some curious, and very ancient, monuments, in the church-yard. In the year 519 a synod was convened here, at which St. David preached against, and overthrew the Pelagian heresy. St. Dubricius assisted at this synod, and immediately after resigned his see of Caer-lleon to St. David, and retired to Bardsey Island, where he dedicated the remainder of his life to devotion. In the year 1073 a battle was fought at this place, between Gronw and Llewellyn, the sons of Cadwgan-ap-Bleddyn, and Rhys-ap-Owen and Rhyddarch-ap-Caradog, in which the princes of Powys were victorious, and Rhuddarch was slain. In 1187 a college was founded, on the spot where the synod was held, by Bishop Beck, in honour of St. David, and recommended to the patronage of King Edward the Confessor; it consisted of a precentor and twelve prebendaries. *(margin: Battle fought in 1073.)*

Fairs, May 7; July 24; October 9; and November 13.

§ LLAN-DDONA. Here is a precipitous hill, called Arthur's Round-table on the summit of which stands the Dinas Sylwy, or exploratory-

	Names of Places.	County.	Number of Miles from			Dist. Lond.	Popu- lation.
47	Llanddwyn* ....pa	Anglesea ...	Carnarvon ...9	Newborough.3	Llangefni ...12	258	319
47	Llanddyfnan........pa	Anglesea ...	Beaumaris ...7	Llanerch-y-M7	 4	258	678
55	Llandecwyn ....pa	Merioneth ..	Maentwrog ..3	Harlech 5	Carnarvon ..19	217	462
48	Llandefaelog-Fach..pa	Brecon	Brecon 4	Buallt.....11	Hay........15	171	359
48	Llandefaelog Fawr..pa	Brecon	 7	11	10	166	735
48	Llandefael g - Tre'r - } Craig.... ......pa }	Brecon	 4	16	11	167	47
50	Llandegai† ....pa	Carnarvon ..	Bangor......1	Carnarvon ..10	Conway....13	250	2600
47	Llandegfan.... •....pa	Anglesea ...	Beaumaris .. 3	Bangor......4	Llaner.-y-M 12	254	738
52	Llandegla‡........ ...pa	Denbigh	Ruthin.....7	Llangollen ...8	Hawarden..11	192	378

LLAN- DDONA.

fort, besides two raths, conjectured to be of Danish origin, and meant to protect the shipping in Red Wharf-bay.

Abounds with fish.

* LLANDDWYN, or Llanddwyowen, situated upon a promontory, stretching into the sea, on the west side of Carnarvon-harbour. Fish of various sorts are taken here; amongst them, lobsters and crabs, in great plenty. The Arundo Arenaria guards the coast from the advances of the ocean; and mats and ropes, for the Carnarvon market, are made from the sea-reed-grass, which abounds here and in the parish of Newborough. The ruins of the ancient church stand upon the extremity of the promontory, which constitutes the parish. Richard Kyffen, rector of this parish, and afterwards Dean of Bangor, being a warm partisan of the house of Lancaster, concerted measures here, in conjunction with Sir Rhys-ap-Thomas, for the introduction of the Earl of Richmond, then in Brittany, with whom they communicated by means of a number of fishing-wherries. In the time of Owen Glendwr, this was considered a wealthy shrine; in the reign of Henry VIII. its revenues constituted the richest prebend in Bangor-cathedral. Near the sea-side was the oratory of St. Dwynwen, the daughter of Brychan Urth, a pious personage, who flourished in the fifth century. Here, also, was the Ffynnon-fair, or St. Mary's-well, visited by contrite persons, upon whom the monks of the well levied large contributions for expounding to them their future destinies.

St. Mary's- well.

† LLANDEGAI, a village on the banks of the river Ogwen. The parish extends about fifteen miles in length, averages about two miles in breadth, and includes the most mountainous and irreclaimable parts of North Wales, being overhung also by Carnedd Davydd and Carnedd Llewellyn. Although the surface is mountainous and barren, an inexhaustible source of wealth lies beneath, in the excellent material, for roofing, generally called Bangor-slates. The Llandegai quarries occupy about 1500 men, and, consequently, sustain a population amounting to about four times that number. The quarry, now a terrific excavation, has been worked for upwards of forty years; and the scientific means adopted in the detaching and splitting of the blocks, as well as the rapidity and economy used in conveying the slates to Port Penrhyn, where they are shipped, tend to augment this great gulf to a capaciousness, that must excite the astonishment of every visitor. The hydraulic press, sawing-mills, and rail-roads, are amongst the improved means of working and transporting slates adopted at these quarries. The noble Saxon castle, erected in this parish by Mr. Pennant, after a design by Mr. Hopper, is not merely unique, but, perhaps, the most majestic private residence in Great Britain. It is built of marble, brought from the island of Anglesea, and the singular antique style adopted in the design is adhered to throughout with admirable exactness.

Extensive slate quarries.

‡ LLANDEGLA, a village and parish, situated at the source of the river Alen. The fairs here are celebrated for the quality and numbers of their black cattle. About 200 yards from the church, in a quillet called

Map	Names of Places.	County.	Number of Miles from			Dist. Lond.	Popu- lation.
58	Llandegla*.........pa	Radnor	Rhayader ..12	New Radnor.7	Pen-y-bont ..2	169	355
26	Llandegweth ......pa	Monmouth .	Caerleon 4	Usk.. 5	Pontypool ...5	147	146
50	Llandegwning......pa	Carnarvon ..	Pwllheli.....6	Bardsey Isle 10	Nevin......10	249	148
57	Llandeilo†.........pa	Pembroke ..	Narbarth 8	Haverford W13	Cardigan ...12	263	87
19	Llandeilo - Aber - Cywyn ......pa	Carmarthen.	Carmarthen..8	Llangharne ..3	Kidwelly.. ..10	242	90
48	Llandeilo-Arfan ....pa	Brecon	Brecon.. ...11	Llandovery ..8	Buallt......18	182	585
19	Llandeilo-Fawr‡...m t	Carmarthen.	Carmarthen.16	14	Swansea....20	202	5189
58	Llandeilo Graban ...pa	Radnor	Buallt.. 6	Hay........8	Brecon... ...12	164	272
54	Llandeilo-Tal-y-Bont ... .pa	Glamorgan ..	Swansea....10	Pont ar Dulas 3	Llanelly.....7	216	1253
50	Llandeiniolen§ .....pa	Carnarvon ..	Carnarvon ...4	Bangor......6	Holyhead . 25	248	2610

LLANDEGLA
Gwern Degla, is a well under the tutelage of St. Tecla, virgin and martyr, said to be serviceable in the unhappy complaint called the falling-sickness. *Fairs*, March 10; May 6; June 23; August 14; and October 26.

Sulphureous spring.
* LLANDEGLA, or Llandegley, a parish situated upon the Cameron river, in the district called the Forest of Radnor, and including the townships of Swydd, Craig, and Trellan. A spring of sulphureous vitriolic water rises in a field near the road to Radnor, and is much esteemed for its useful properties. In this parish is the curious, bold, rocky prominence, called Llandegles Rocks, resembling the Torrs in Cornwall.

† LLANDEILO. Here is a well, the water of which was supposed to cure coughs, when drunk out of the skull of St. Teilo, the tutelar saint. The skull was kept for that purpose in an adjoining cottage.

Ancient church.
‡ LLANDEILO-FAWR, or Llandilo-Vawr. This town does not possess any particular attractions, but the surrounding country abounds with objects of beauty and interest. Here is a spacious but very ancient church. Quarter sessions are held here in the month of July in each year. Sheriff's courts for the county held monthly. The Bishop of St. David's is lord of the manor. There is a good general country trade at this place, and much tanning carried on here. There are several small brooks within the parish, upon which corn-mills are erected, and woollen manufactories established. Several schools for the benefit of poor children exist here. Of the several chalybeate springs in this parish, that called Ffynnon Craig Ceffyl, possesses valuable medicinal properties. The well of Llan-defaen was deemed beneficial in paralysis. The well in Castell Cenen is merely a curiosity, and the copious spring at Cwrt Brynn-y-Beirdd, is the head of the river Llychwyr. Near to the last well, or spring, is a spacious cavern in the limestone rock, containing many beautiful petrifactions. About four miles from the town are the remains of Cenancastle, supposed to have been built by Gorwnw, prince or lord of Is Cenen, and one of the knights of Arthur's Round Table. One mile from this is an ancient bardish palace, called Cwrt-Brynn-y-Beird, now converted into a snug farm-house; and three miles from the town are the ruins of Capel-yr-ywen, formerly a chapel of ease to the parish church. The famous Hirlas, or drinking horn, presented by Henry VII., when Earl of Richmond, to Dafydd ap Iquan, who entertained the earl and his followers, on the route from Milford Haven to Bosworth-field, is preserved in the mansion of Golden-grove. Cromwell also visited this fine seat upon his approach to Pembroke-castle. Near this is shown a spot called Taylor's-walk, from its having been frequented daily by Dr. Jeremy Taylor, during the period of his adversity. On an eminence in the vale stands Drysburgh-castle, the siege of which proved fatal to Lord Stafford and his party, who were buried beneath its ruins.

Remains of Cenancastle.

Market, Saturday.—*Fairs*, February 20; Palm-Monday; May 5 and 12; June 21; August 23; November 12; and Monday before Christmas-Day. Also, on November 22 at Fairfach.

§ LLANDEINIOLEN. Here are two mineral springs, one of which is considered efficacious in removing scorbutic complaints, the other is a

6 z

Map.	Names of Places.	County.	Number of Miles from				Dist. Lond.	Popu- lation.
26	Llandenny........pa	Monmouth..	Usk 4	Monmouth...9	Abergavenny11		138	371
55	Llanderfel..........pa	Merioneth ..	Corwen 7	Bala........6	Denbigh....19		201	1010
26	Llandevand.ham & cha	Monmouth..	Caerleon 4	Newport....6	Chepstow...10		144	....
17	Llandinabo ....pa	Hereford ...	Ross 7	Hereford 8	Monmouth..12		128	53
56	Llandinam ....pa	Montgomery	Llanydloes ..6	Newtown ...7	Rhayader...14		182	1015
49	Llandingad.......pa	Carmarthen.	Llandovery ..1	Langadock ..6	Llampeter ..15		191	2465
54	Llandoch..........pa	Glamorgan..	Cardiff 4	Cowbridge..10	Llantrissant 11		164	119
54	Llandoch..........pa	Glamorgan..	14	2	8		174	118
52	Llandoged.........pa	Denbigh....	Llanwrst ...2	Conway....8	Bangor.....17		219	257
26	Llandogo ....pa	Monmouth .	Monmouth ..7	Chepstow ...8	Usk........11		136	672
49	Llandovery*.......m t	Carmarthen.	Carmarthen.29	Trecastle 9	Llandilo V. 14		191	1766
52	Llandrillo-yn-Rhos .pa	Denbigh....	Conway 5	Abergele ...8	St. Asaph ..14		233	1133
55	Llandrillo†.......pa	Merioneth ..	Corwen.....5	Bala........8	Llangollen..14		199	806
58	Llandrindod‡.......pa	Radnor	Buallt.......6	Pen-y-Bont..7	Rhayader...10		172	182

LLANDEINI-OLEN.

strong chalybeate. The latter is generally called Ffynnon-y-Cegin Arthur, or the Well of Arther's-kitchen, from which the river Cegin flows. The festival-day here is the 23d of November. Near Penllynn are the ruins of a Llys, or palace, of one of the princes of Wales; this, along with the manor of Dinorweg, was granted by Edward I. to Sir Gruffydd Llwydd,

Roman en-campment.

on his bearing the glad tidings of the birth of Edward II., in Carnarvon-castle, to his majesty. Pen Dinas was a Roman encampment; it is 600 feet high, and is enclosed with a double ditch and rampart.

* LLANDOVERY, or Llan-ym-Ddyfri, a town agreeably and beau-tifully situated in a valley, encircled by hills, clothed with wood, and intersected and watered by several streams. Its name appears to be derived from the circumstance of the confluence of so many streams in the immediate vicinity. The town consists of nine streets, the High, or principal one, being a broad and handsome avenue, enclosed by respect-able houses. This place appears to have originated in a Roman-station,

Its castle overthrown by Crom-well.

at a place now called Llanfair-ar-y-Brynn. Its castle was besieged in 1116, by Gryffyd ap Rhys, and was taken by the Welsh and Normans in 1216, but it was reserved for the army of Cromwell to overthrow its walls. The keep of the castle is still standing, and presents a singularly picturesque appearance, placed upon the summit of an insulated rock, the only elevated object in a plain of much extent. The trade of this place is confined to the supply of the surrounding country, which is both rich, respectable, and thickly inhabited, but the fairs are well supplied and well attended. The Roman station, which gave rise to this settlement, was a quarter of a mile from the present town, and at that place four Roman roads inter-sected. The Rev. Rhys Pritchard was a native of this place.

Market, Saturday.—*Fairs*, Wednesday after January 17; Wednesday after Easter week; Whit-Tuesday; July 31; Wednesday after October 10; and November 26.

† LLANDRILLO. *Fairs*, February 25; May 3; June 29; August 28; and November 14.

Mineral springs.

‡ LLANDRINDOD, or Llan-y-Drindod (the church of the Holy Trinity). This town owes its origin, and what importance it possesses, to the mineral springs discovered here. The wells of this place rise from three springs, within a few yards of each other, and totally different in their quality and characters, being chalybeate, sulphureous, and cathartic. They were known to the inhabitants of the vicinity as early as the year 1696, and began to be visited by persons from various distances, in 1726. Lodging-houses were erected and accommodations provided for the recep-tion of visitors in the year 1749, at which period its utility may be sup-posed to have been fully established. The waters are denominated, first, the Rock Water; which issues from a slate rock, and is strongly impreg-nated with iron, earth, salts, and sulphur. This water is beneficial in chronic complaints, proceeding from weakness in the fibres; also in scor-butic eruptions, nervous debilities, palsies, agues, and kindred diseases. Secondly, the Saline Spring; this is found serviceable in scorbutic erup-

Map	Names of Places.	County.	Number of Miles from			Dist. Lond.	Popu- lation.
56	Llandrinio..........pa	Montgomery	Welshpool ..9	Shrewsbury.13	Oswestry 9	166	863
47	Llandrygan ....pa	Anglesea ...	Llangefni....6	Llanerch-y-M5	Holyhead .. 10	268	449
50	Llandudno * ....pa	Carnarvon ..	Conway.....6	Abergele ...11	St. Asaph ..17	236	662
50	Llandudwen......pa	Carnarvon .	Pwllheli.....5	Nevin.....10	Bardsey Isle 10	248	85
52	Llandulas †........pa	Denbigh..	Abergele ... 3	Conway.. ..10	Llanwrst ...14	218	194
48	Llandulas..........pa	Brecon	Buallt......14	Rhayader...21	Brecon 15	186	159
54	Llandwf ....pa	Glamorgan..	Cowbridge ..3	Bridgend 6	Llantrissant..9	176	130
50	Llandwrog‡.......pa	Carnarvon ..	Carnarvon .. 5	Nevin......14	Pwllheli....17	249	1923

tions, and in the several species of the gravel. Thirdly, the Sulphur, or Blackwater, is adapted both for bathing and for internal use. It is taken with beneficial effects in ulcerous, leprous, scorbutic, rhumatic, and gouty complaints ; and, applied externally, affords relief in chronic cases.

Fairs, (on Howey Common) Saturday before February 11 ; May 11 ; and November 11.

LLAN-DRINDOD.

* LLANDUDNO, a hamlet and parish situated upon the Irish Sea, and including the remarkable promontory of Gogarth, or The Great Orme's Head. Here are extensive copper-mines, in which many persons in this and the adjoining parishes find constant employment. The Promontory of Gogarth, so well known to all navigators of the Irish Sea, presents a grand precipitous front to the sea. The action of the waves has excavated the base of these bold cliffs into caverns of vast depths and heights, in one of which occurred the melancholy wreck of the Hornby Castle, West Indiaman. In the most inaccessible parts of the craggs, gulls, cormorants, herons, razor-bills, ravens, and rock-pigeons, have taken up their abode ; and the species of the peregine falcon, so much valued a few ages back in the fashionable and sporting world, is still an inhabitant of the rocks of Llandudno. Rock samphire is gathered upon the rocks of this promontory, and by modes as perilous as those described by Shakspeare on the cliffs of Dover. On an eminence here, called Dinas, is a circular space, enclosed by a wall of prodigious thickness, and within which are several round caves, supposed to have been the rude abodes of the Aborigines of this country, and resembling the habitations of the Troglodytes of Ethiopia. Near to this is the Maen Sigl, or Self-rocking Stone ; also called Cryd Tudno, i. e., St. Tudno's-cradle, a huge mass, enclosed by a fosse, and approached by a narrow pathway.

Remarkable promontory.

The rocking stone.

† LLANDULAS, a village situated upon the little river Dulas, and washed also by the Irish Sea, on the northern boundary. The great post-road from Chester to Holyhead passes through the parish. In one of the little glens in this parish, Richard II. was attacked by a band of ruffians, employed by the Earl of Northumberland, for the purpose of delivering him into the hands of Bolingbroke, who was then lodged at Flint.

‡ LLANDWROG. In this parish is the interesting remnant of antiquity, called Dinas, in the township of Dinas Dinlle, situated upon the water's edge, and almost in the centre of the bold sweep of coast forming the bay of Carnarvon. The Dinas is raised upon a hill of sand and pebbles, is of a circular form, and 140 paces in diameter. The height of the rampart, on the north and east sides, is twenty yards ; on the south, fifteen yards ; while the western side is elevated only ten yards above the sea, which washes its base. The surrounding fosse is fifteen yards in breadth. The principal entrance was on the east, and was funnel-shaped, and a smaller entrance appears towards the northern side. The area of the Dinas occupies twenty acres of land. A Roman road was constructed from Dinas Dinlle to Segontium, interrupted, at one place, by a river, to which obstruction the name of Rhyd-y-Pedestre is given at the present day.

Interesting remnant of antiquity

Map	Names of Places.	County.	Number of Miles from			Dist. Lond.	Popu- lation.
49	Llandybie* ....pa	Carmarthen.	LlandiloFawr6	Bettws 4	Carmarthen 15	207	2248
49	Llandyvailog ......pa	Carmarthen.	Carmarthen..6	Kidwelly....4	Llangharne ..8	235	1271
49	Llandyfeisant† .....pa	Carmarthen.	LlandiloFawrl	Pont-ar-Dul.13	Llangadog ..8	201	230
54	Llandyfodwg‡ .... ..pa	Glamorgan..	Bridgend ...6	Mer.Tydvyl 15	Neath......15	180	32f
51	Llandyfriog ....pa	Cardigan ...	Newc.in Em. 1	Cardigan ...10	Carmarthen.14	230	854
47	Llandyfrydog§......pa	Anglesea ...	Llanerch-y-M2	Amlwch 5	Llangefni....7	267	853
51	Llandygwydd .....pa	Cardigan ..	Cardigan.. ..4	Newcastle ..6	Carmarthen.20	235	1131
57	Llandylwyf ....pa	Pembroke ..	St. Davids ..8	Fishguard ...9	HaverfordW. 9	266	210
52	Llandyrnog.... ...pa	Denbigh	Denbigh 4	Ruthin......4	Holywell ...10	209	708
51	Llandysil‖.........pa	Cardigan ...	Lampeter ..12	Cardigan ...14	Newcastle...6	223	2724
47	Llandysilio¶ ....pa	Anglesea ...	Bangor.. 2	Beaumaris ...4	Carnarvon.. .9	253	479

* LLANDYBIE, or Llandebie. Fairs, first Wednesday in Easter-week ; and first Wednesday in July.

Intermitting spring.

† LLANDYFEISANT. Here is one of those natural curiosities called an intermitting spring, the water in which ebbs and flows ; the explanation of this is easy, even to those but little acquainted with natural philosophy. The rivulet issuing from this spring is called The Bewitched Brook. The church is supposed to rest upon the fragments of a Roman building, and a vessel of Roman silver coins was dug up in the churchyard, about thirty years ago.

‡ LLANDYFODWG. This is part of the duchy of Lancaster, and the inhabitants are, in consequence, exempt from tolls, in all markets and fairs throughout the kingdom, the vicinities of the universities of Oxford and Cambridge excepted. Iron and coal abound here, and several chalybeate springs arise in their immediate neighbourhood.

§ LLANDYFRYDOG. Agriculture engages one part of the population of this parish, while others find employment in the great copper-mines of Parys Mountain, in the adjoining parish. In this parish are two wells, called Ffynnon Seiriol and Ffynnon Kybi, where those holy men are said to have held religious conferences ; the wells are midway between Holyhead and Priestholme-island, the retreats of the saints. Upon Clorach farm, also, is a pillar-stone, called the Tyfrydog Thief, said to be a thief, who was in the act of stealing the church bible, and who was actually turned into this pillar of stone for his sacrilegious crime. The bunch, on one side of the stone, is said to be the transmuted bible. The parish church was founded as early as the year 450.

Legend of the Tyfrydog Thief.

‖ LLANDYSIL. The river Teifi forms the southern boundary of the parish, and its banks here present scenes of the most agreeable description. The high road between Lampeter and Cardigan, runs through the parish, keeping parallel nearly with the sinuosities of the Teifi. The village is humble, but cheerfully situated. There were formerly six chapels of ease in this extensive parish, the ruins of some may still be seen. Besides several carneddau, here is the Tommen Rhyd Owen ; and Howel's-castle, the history of which is lost, is also within the limits of Llandysil parish.

Market, Thursday.—Fairs, February 11 ; on Palm-Thursday ; and on September 19.

Celebrated suspension-bridge.

¶ LLANDYSILIO, a parish upon the western bank of the Menai Strait, where it is crossed by the celebrated suspension-bridge, and where there was formerly an established ferry. The fairs are held on the water-side, and continue to be designated the fairs of Bangor-ferry. The chapel, erected in the year 630, stands on a little rocky peninsula, which, at high water, is completely insulated. The island, as it may properly be considered, is called Benglas, affords pasturage for half a score of sheep, and is approached, at ebb-tide, by a sarn, or causeway, connecting it with the Anglesea shore.

Fairs, August 26 ; September 26 ; October 24 ; and November 14.

Map.	Names of Places.	County.	Number of Miles from				Dist. Lond.	Popu-lation.
56	Llandysilio ....pr	Montgomery	Welshpool..10	Ellesmere ..17	Montgomery 17		167	633
52	Llandysilio*.......pa	Denbigh	Llangollen ..2	Corwen.....8	Wrexham ..12		186	842
51	Llandysilio-Gogo ...pa	Cardigan ...	Lampeter ..18	Aberystwith 9	Tregaron ..12		229	1468
49	Llandysilio-yn-Nyfed } ....pa }	Carmarthen.	Narbarth ...3	Llangharne .17	Carmarthen.20		253	1045
56	Llandyssul.........pa	Montgomery	Montgomery .3	Newtown ...6	Bishops Cas. 12		161	914
54	Llanedeyrn........pa	Glamorgan	Cardiff 4	Caerphilly ..4	Llantrissant 10		164	315
47	Llanedwent†......pa	Anglesea ...	Carnarvon ..5	Bangor 6	Beaumaris ..8		254	294
49	Llanedy...........pa	Carmarthen.	Llanelly ...8	Pont-ar-Dul. 3	Llandilo V. 10		211	1001
55	Llanegryn.........pa	Merioneth ..	Dolgelly ...7	Towyn.....12	Machynleth.16		209	764
49	Llanegwad........pa	Carmarthen.	LlandiloFawr7	Carmarthen..9	Llampeter ..18		208	2214
47	Llaneigrad.........pa	Anglesea ...	Amlwch ...7	Llanerch-y-M6	Beaumaris ..10		261	740
50	Llanelhaiarn......pa	Carnarvon .	Pwllheli ...9	Carnarvon.. 11	Cricceath...15		245	676
47	Llanelian‡........pa	Anglesea ...	Amlwch ...2	Llanerch-y-M7	Llangeffni ..14		274	1438
52	Llanelian ....pa	Denbigh	Abergele ...5	Conway 8	Llanrwst ...10		230	604
52	Llanelidan........pa	Denbigh	Ruthen......6	Denbigh....12	Bala.......14		211	749
48	Llanelieu........pa	Brecon	Hay 5	Brecon.....12	Crickhowel 14		161	115
26	Llanellen.........pa	Monmouth .	Abergavenny.2	Pontypool ...8	Monmouth.14		143	323
55	Llanelltyd ....pa	Merioneth ..	Dolgelly.....1	Barmouth...8	Harlech.. ..13		203	416
48	Llanelly ....pa	Brecon	Abergavenny.5	Crickhowel ..5	Pontypool ...8		152	4041
49	Llanelly§..........m t	Carmarthen.	Carmarthen.15	Swansea....13	Kidwelly 9		217	7646

* LLANDYSILIO, or Llantysilio. The parish occupies the most picturesque part of the beautiful vale of Llangollen, and is adorned by a chapel, situated in a wooded and sequestered little glen, near to which is Llandysilio-hall. In this parish are considerable slate quarries, besides lime-works, on an extensive scale. The Ellesmere navigation commences near the hall, where a wear is thrown across the Dee, and the slates are conveyed thence to public markets. Here are the admired ruins of the Cistercian-abbey of Llan Ggwest. *[margin: Picturesque scenery.]*

† LLANEDWEN, a village situated upon the Straits of Menai, and having here an established ferry, at a place called Moel-y-Don, remarkable in the history of Wales for a defeat, sustained by the forces of Edward I., from the ancient Britons. The learned Henry Rowlands, author of the "Mona Antiqua Restaurata," was born here, and lies interred within the church of his native parish, beneath a black marble slab, inscribed with a few lines, in the Latin language, full of elegance and feeling. *[margin: Birthplace of Henry Rowlands.]*

‡ LLANELIAN. Porth Elian, in this parish, affords refuge to pilot-boats, and is capable of still greater benefit to mariners, by scientific improvement. Here are a light-house and signal-staff. There is a subscription-school here for poor children. In the fine old church were several portraits of holy persons, now totally effaced; and some stained glass adorned the eastern window. The famous Caswallon Law Hir, or the long armed, endowed this place with many privileges and extensive lands, of which about £20. per annum, is now traceable, appropriated generally to the repairs of the church. There is, in the cloister, an oaken semicircular box, six feet in length, by three in breadth, and about four feet in height or depth. It is secured to the wall, and perforated in the front by an aperture, three feet in length, or height, by one in breadth. During the celebration of the wake, many persons enter the chest through this aperture, and turn themselves round in it three times, which ceremony is said to ensure a continuance of life, accompanied by various blessings, for the space of one year, at least, from that period. The building, containing this chest, was the cloister, or cell, of St. Elian, and appears to have possessed a bell. - In the choir of the church stands another chest, called St. Elian's-cuff, rounded on the top, and studded with large nails. The chest is only opened on St. Thomas's-day, in each year. In digging a grave, in the church-yard, in the year 1793, a deep trench, filled with human bones, was found, extending across the cemetery, for a length of about twenty yards. *[margin: Curious ceremony.]*

§ LLANELLY, a thriving market and borough town, situated upon a creek, in the river Burry, which latter is the estuary of the river Loughor.

Iter	Names of Places.	County.	Number of Miles from			Dist. Lond.	Popu- lation.
58	Llanelwedd.......pa	Radnor	Buallt 1	Rhayader...11	NewRadnor 14	173	196
55	Llanenddwyn.....pa	Merioneth'..	Barmouth ..5	Harlech 5	Dolgelly....12	214	798
50	Llanengan* ......pa	Carnarvon ..	Pwllheli ...5	Nevin.....10	Bardsey Isle 12	248	1010
47	Llanenghenel.......pa	Anglesea ...	Holyhead...6	Llanerch-y-M7	Aberffraw ..10	272	....
56	Llanerchfrochwell...to	Montgomery	Welshpool...3	Llanfyllin ...7	Llanfair 7	179	....
47	Llanerch-y-Medd† .m t	Anglesea...	Amlwch ...6	Holyhead .. 13	Beaumaris ..14	265	375
56	Llanerfyl..........pa	Montgomery	Llanfair 5	Llanfyllin ..13	Dinasmowd. 13	189	989
54	Llanfabon...........pa	Glamorgan..	Caerphilly ..5	Llantrissant..8	Mer. Tydvyl .8	165	741
55	Llanfachreth ....pa	Merioneth ..	Dolgelly ...4	Bala......12	Harlech....12	204	948
47	Llanfachreth ....pa	Anglesea ...	Holyhead...7	Llanerch-y-M9	Llangefni ...11	271	424
47	Llanfaelog...........pa	Anglesea ...	9	Aberffraw ..4	10	270	615
50	Llanfaelrhys........pa	Carnarvon ..	Pwllheli ...13	Nevin......16	Bardsey Isle. 4	256	258
47	Llanfaes............pa	Agglesea....	Beaumaris ...1	Bangor.....5	Llangefni ...10	252	271
47	Llanfaethlu ....pa	Anglesea ...	Holyhead...9	Llanerch-y-M8	14	274	433
50	Llanfaglan ....pa	Carnarvon ..	Carnarvon ..3	Newborough 9	Pwllheli ...16	252	156
52	Llanfair - Dyffryn - Clwyd........pa	Denbeigh ...	Ruthin 2	Llangollen..14	Corwen 12	203	1326
56	Llanfair - ynnghaer - Einion‡......m t	Montgomery	Llanfyllin....9	Welshpool...8	Newtown ...10	184	2714

LLANELLY. The town has lately undergone very considerable improvements; and its trade and population greatly augmented. The church is an ancient, venerable-looking structure. The market-house is particularly convenient. The town is governed by a portreeve, and an unlimited number of burgesses, who possess very valuable estates, the revenues of which are judiciously and honourably expended upon the improvement of the town and harbour. The parish includes the hamlets of Berwick, the Borough, Glynn, Hengoed, and Westoac, or Westowe. The prosperity of this place is attributable to the presence of bituminous coal of an excellent quality, of non-flaming, or stone coal, culm, and fire-clay, which has caused an influx of capital, and induced men of spirit and intelligence to Its manu- establish themselves here. Works on an extensive scale are now esta-
factures. blished, for the manufacturing of copper, brass, iron, lead, fire-bricks, &c. A vast number of hands find employment in the copper smelting-houses. Such extensive manufactures demanded an outlet, free and unobstructed; and to procure this, great expense has been incurred in improving the port and constructing docks. There are three excellent docks, now completed, furnished with loading stages. The graving-dock of the Railway-company, is admirably constructed, and, from one end of it, a break-water extends, enabling vessels to lie in smooth water at all times. Each dock has a scouring reservoir attached to it, and there is besides, one reservoir, of great capacity, for scouring the harbour and the channel. A steam-tug is in attendance to tow vessels in and out, as occasion demands.

Markets, Thursday and Saturday.—*Fairs*, Ascension-day; and September 30.

* LLANENGAN, or Einionfrenin, a parish, situated upon a promontory, stretching into the Irish Sea, the eastern side of which is washed by the strait, called St. Tudwal's-road, and the left by the open harbour
Safe of Hell's-mouth. St. Tudwal's-road is one of the safest asylums for
harbour. shipping on the Welsh coast, and has a good anchorage ground, consisting of a stiff clay. About one mile from the coast lie two small islands, called also St. Tudwal's; they afford a good sheep-walk, and rabbits breed there in tolerable quantities. Vast numbers of puffins frequent their coasts.

Extensive † LLANERCH-Y-MEDD, or L annerch-y-Medd. This town possesses
manufac- a manufacture of snuff, acknowledged to be the only formidable rival of
ture of the famous composition, called Lundy Foot, which has yet been dis-
snuff. covered. The petty sessions for the hundred are held here.

Market, Wednesday.—*Fairs*, February 5; April 25 ; May 6; and Thursday after Trinity-Sunday.

‡ LLANFAIR-YNNGHAER-EINION, a neat, but small market-town, situated upon a hill near the banks of the Fyrnwy (Vierniew) river.

Map.	Names of Places.	County.	Number of Miles from			Dist. Lond.	Popu- lation.
49	Llanfair-Ar-y-Brynn pa	Carmarthen.	Llandovery ..1	Llangadog ...6	Llampeter ..15	191	1485
51	Llanfair-Clydogan ..pa	Cardigan ...	Lampeter....3	Llandovery .16	Tregaron....8	214	385
50	Llanfair Fechan* ...pa	Carnarvon ..	Conway.....7	Bangor.....9	Llanrwst...11	245	653
47	Llanfair-in-Matha-farn-Eithaf.....pa	Anglesea ...	Beaumaris ..8	Llanerch-y-M5	Llangefni ...8	259	739
50	Llanfair-is-Gaer ....pa	Carnarvon ..	Carnarvon ...3	Bangor......7	Newborough.7	252	379
55	Llanfair Juxta Har-leigh ....pa	Merioneth ..	Harlech 1	Barmouth ...9	Dolgelly....14	230	429
57	Llanfair Nantygof...pa	Pembroke ..	Fishguard ..4	HaverfordW. 9	Newport....7	257	243
57	Llanfair Nantygwyn pa	Pembroke ..	Cardigan 6	Killgerran...6	Narbarth ...13	245	267
51	Llanfair Orllwyn....pa	Cardigan ...	Newcastle ..4	Llampeter ..14	Carmarthen.14	226	394
47	Llanfair-Pwll-Gwyn-gyll...........pa	Anglesea ...	Beaumaris ..6	Bangor......3	Llangefni....7	254	497
52	Llanfairtalhairn† ...pa	Denbigh ...	Abergele ...4	Denbigh.....7	Conway......12	217	1355
51	Llanfair-Trelygon ..pa	Cardigan ...	Newcastle...5	Llampeter ..13	Carmarthen.15	225	124
47	Llanfair-yn-Neubwll ....pa	Anglesea ...	Holyhead ..5	Lla.-y-Medd 10	Llangefni ..12	271	319
47	Llanfair-yn-Nghor-nwy........pa	Anglesea ...	Amlwch....9	10	16	275	310
47	Llanfair-yn-y-Cwmwd....pa	Anglesea ...	Carnarvon ..4	Bangor......6	Newborough.8	253	....
49	Llanfallteg.........pa	Carmarthen.	Narbarth....5	Llangharne .13	Carmarthen.17	249	378
58	Llanfareth.........pa	Radnor	Buallt......2	NewRadnor 13	Hay........15	172	183
55	Llanfawr...........pa	Merioneth ..	Bala.......1	Llangollen...20	Ruthin......19	193	1749
56	Llanfechan ....pa	Montgomery	Llanfyllyn ..3	Oswestry ...10	Welshpool..10	186	706
56	Llanfechain ....to	Montgomery	Machynlleth .4	Dinasmowddy9	Llanfair...23	203	379
47	Llanfechel‡.........pa	Anglesea ...	Amlwch 6	Llanerch-y-M7	Llangefni ...13	272	976
54	Llanfedw ....ham	Glamorgan..	Cardiff.....6	Caerphilly ..6	Newport....7	155	346
52	Llanferis...........pa	Denbigh ...	Mold........5	Ruthin......9	Wrexham ..13	200	705
57	Llanfernach........pa	Pembroke..	Newcastle ..9	Narbarth 9	Cardigan....9	236	874
48	Llanfeugan ....pa	Brecon	Brecon 5	Crickhowell 12	Hay........18	169	696
47	Llanffinan.........pa	Anglesea ...	Llangeffni...2	Beaumaris ..7	Bangor.....7	257	163
47	Llanfflewyn........pa	Anglesea ...	Holyhead ..14	Amlwch....9	Llanerch-y-M8	275	133
52	Llanfihangel.......pa	Denbigh ...	Cerrig 2	Ruthin ...12	Denbigh...13	204	452
56	Llanfihangel.......pa	Montgomery	Llanfylin ..4	Lanfair.....9	Dinasmowd. 17	193	906
49	Llanfihangel Aber-bythych§ .....pa	Carmarthen.	Llandilo V. .4	Pont-ar-Dul.12	Carmarthen.13	205	953

Here is an ancient church, besides chapels for Methodists and Independents; and a market-house, or town-hall. The petty sessions for the hundred are held here, as well as courts-leet, the latter opened twice in each year, under the lord of the manor. *(LLANFAIR-YNNGHAER-EINION.)*

Market, Saturday.—*Fairs*, February 19; March 29; May 19; July 26; October 3; November 1; and December 19.

* LLANFAIR-FECHAN, a parish situated upon the sea-coast. The improved and admirable new line of road, at the base of Penmaen Mawr, and along the sea-side, passes through the parish. Adjoining this parish are the Lavan Sands, covering a surface of ninety-six square miles, supposed to have been inundated by the sea, in the sixth century, and never since recovered. *(Great inundation of the sea.)*

† LLANFAIRTALHAIRN. Talhairn was a bard and saint, of the congregation of Catwg, and flourished at the close of the fifth, and opening of the sixth, century; he composed the prayer adopted at the sessions of the bards of Glamorgan. He was domestic chaplain to Emrys-Wledig, but, upon the untimely death of that prince, he turned hermit, and dwelt where the church, dedicated to him, now stands. Hedd Molwynog, a descendant of Roderic the Great, King of all Wales, had a mansion in this parish, at a place now called Yr Hen Llys.

‡ LLANFECHEL. The population are partly occupied in the Parys copper-mines, which are in the adjoining parish. A mineral spring here is said to have cured lameness in many persons. The church is supposed to have been built as early as the year 630. *(Ancient church.)*

Market, Friday.—*Fairs*, February 25; August 5; September 21; and November 5 and 26.

§ LLANFIHANGEL-ABERBYTHYCH. Here is Golden-grove, formerly the seat of the Earls of Carberry, but now of Lord Cawdor.

map	Names of Places.	County.	Number of Miles from			Dist. Lond.	Popu- lation.
19	Llanfihangel - Abercywyn*... ....pa	Carmarthen.	Llangharne ..2	St. Clare 2	Carmarthen..8	241	454
18	Llanfihangel Aber- gwessin ...pa	Brecon	Buallt......15	Rhayader .. 18	Llandovery .15	188	345
19	Llanfihangel - Ar - Ararth.......pa	Carmarthen.	Carmarthen.15	Llampeter ..11	Newcastle..11	222	2090
50	Llanfihangel-Bachel- leth...........pa	Carnarvon ..	Pwllheli.....5	Nevin.......5	Bardsey 12	248	332
18	Llanfihangel - Bryn Pab-Jenan .....pa	Brecon	Buallt......13	Rhayader....5	Llandovery .26	186	952
19	Llanfihangel - Cil - Fargen... ....pa	Carmarthen.	Llandilo V...5	Carmarthen.11	Llampeter ..16	206	71
18	Llanfihangel - Cwm - Du...........pa	Brecon	Abergavenny13	Hay........12	Brecon 10	160	1103
51	Llanfihangel-Fach ..pa	Radnor.....	Rhayader....6	Buallt.......8	Pen-y-Bont..6	178	97
18	Llanfihangel Fechan pa	Brecon	Brecon 5	10	Hay........16	172	204
51	Llanfihangel-Genau'r Glynn ....pa	Cardigan ...	Aberystwith 5	Machynlleth11	Towyn 12	216	3576
50	Llanfihangel-in-Rey pa	Carnarvon ..	Carnarvon ...4	Bangor......7	Llanrwst ...16	244	866
51	Llanfihangel Llethyr Troed†........pa	Cardigan ...	Tregaron 7	Aberystwith .8	Llampeter ..14	219	1213
18	Llanfihangel - Nant - Bran..........pa	Brecon	Brecon 10	Buallt......15	Llandovery .10	177	603
58	Llanfihangel - Nant Melin ....pa	Radnor	New Radnor.4	Presteign ...11	Kington....10	162	419
57	Llanfihangel - Pen - bedw........pa	Pembroke ..	Newcastle...4	Killgarran ...3	Cardigan 4	234	339
19	Llanfihangel - Rhosy- corn..........pa	Carmarthen.	Llandilo V. 10	Llampeter ..10	Carmarthen.15	205	657
58	Llanfihangel - Rhydi- thon..........pa	Radnor	Rhavader...12	Knighton ...12	New Radnor.9	168	350
18	Llanfihangel - Tal - y- Llynn‡.........pa	Brecon	Brecon 5	Hay........12	Crickhowell 12	165	135
17	Llanfihangel - Tre'r - Bardd ....pa	Anglesea ..	Llanerch-y-M3	Almwch.....8	Beaumaris . 12	263	360
17	Llanfihangel - Tyn - sylwy........pa	Anglesea ..	Beaumaris ...4	Lla.-y-Medd 14	Llangefni ...10	255	62
19	Llanfihangel - Uwch- Gwili ....den	Carmarthen.	Carmarthen..7	Newcastle..14	Lampeter...15	228	....
54	Llanfihangel-y-Bont- Faen.........pa	Glamorgan..	Cowbridge...2	Bridgend 7	Cardiff 15	175	48
51	Llanfihangel-y-Creid- dyn...........pa	Cardigan ...	Aberystwith .7	Rhayader...22	Tregaron ...10	205	1971
17	Llanfihangel-yn-Nhy- wyn..........pa	Anglesea ...	Holyhead....6	Llangefni ...10	Llanerch-y-M9	269	225
50	Llanfihangel-y-Pen- nant ....pa	Carnarvon ..	Tremadoc ...5	Carnarvon ..12	Maentwrog ..8	232	563
55	Llanfihangel-y-Pen- nant.........pa	Merioneth ..	Dolgelly 8	Towyn 12	Dinasmowd. 13	216	394

LLANFI- HANGEL- ABER- BYTHYCH.

Cromwell visited this place, with the intent of seizing the noble proprietor, Lord Carberry, but his object being previously known, the earl withdrew to a cottage in the mountains; and the protector, after dining with the countess, pursued his route to Pembroke. The eloquent and learned Jeremy Taylor found shelter in Golden-grove, during the usurpation, and dedicated some of his writings to its noble, loyal, and hospitable proprietor. In this parish are the remains of an ancient British post.

* LLANFIHANGEL-ABERCYWYN. *Fairs*, May 12, and October 10.

Chalybeate spring.

† LLANFIHANGEL-LLETHYR-TROED. Here is a chalybeate spring of some reputation. Evan Evans, the Welsh bard, is interred in the cemetery of the parish church. Many carneddau are scattered about here, apparently sepulchral tumuli.

Fair, October 7.

Beautiful lake.

‡ LLANFIHANGEL-TAL-Y-LLYNN, a village, beautifully situated at the head of the Lake Lynnsafaddan, through which the river Llyffni flows. Tal-y-Llynn signifies the Head of the Lake. This pretty sheet of water extends two miles in length, and averages one in breadth. It abounds with pike, perch, and mud-eels, of an enormous size. The trout appear to avoid the lake, but are taken in quantities in the Llyffni river.

Map.	Names of Places.	County.	Number of Miles from			Dist. Lond.	Popu- lation.
47	Llanfihangel Yscei-fiog....pa	Anglesea ...	Bangor....7	Llangeffni....3	Newborough.7	258	663
51	Llanfihangel-Ystrad.pa	Cardigan ...	Lampeter....6	Tregaron...10	Aberystwith14	217	1183
55	Llanfihangel-y-Trae-than....pa	Merioneth ..	Harlech.....3	Tremadoc....4	Maentwrog..7	229	1026
48	Llanfilo....pa	Brecon....	Brecon.....6	Hay........11	Buallt......13	167	326
26	Llanfoist....pa	Monmouth..	Abergavenny 2	Crickhowel ..7	Pontypool ...9	148	588
55	Llanfrothen....pa	Merioneth ..	Tan-y-Bwlch 5	Harlech.....9	Llanrwst...10	220	657
48	Llanfrynach....pa	Brecon....	Brecon.....3	Crickhowel.13	Hay.......16	165	370
47	Llanfugail....pa	Anglesea ...	Holyhead....7	Llanerch-y-M7	Llangeffni..11	270	152
47	Llanfwrog....pa	Anglesea ...	7	9	13	272	266
52	Llanfwrog....pa	Denbigh....	Ruthin......1	Bala........18	Denbigh.....8	196	343
56	Llanfyllin*.......m t	Montgomery	Oswestry...12	Llanfair...10	Dinasmowd.20	179	1836
49	Llanfynydd†....pa	Carmarthen.	Llandilo V...7	Llampeter ..12	Carmarthen.11	209	1436
56	Llangadfan‡.......pa	Montgomery	Llanfair....7	Llanfyllin...10	Dinasmowd.10	190	1067
49	Langadog Fawr§...m t	Carmarthen.	Llandilo V...8	Llandovery ..6	Llampeter ..17	195	2476
47	Llangaffo....pa	Anglesea ...	Carnarvon ..5	Llangeffni ..6	Newborough 3	254	137
49	Llangain....pa	Carmarthen.	Carmarthen..4	Kidwelly....7	Llangharne ..7	222	423
48	Llangammarch ||....pa	Brecon....	Buallt.....9	Llandovery .13	Rhayader...13	182	1091
49	Llangan....pa	Carmarthen.	Narbarth...7	Llangharne.12	Carmarthen.15	233	733

* LLANFYLLIN. The appearance of this town is neat and agreeable. The church is unadorned, the town-hall modern, and convenient. This is a place of ancient foundation. It was incorporated by a charter of Llewellyn ap Gryffyd, in the time of Edward I. The petty sessions for the hundred are held here. Here is a blue-coat school for twenty-four boys, a second, for twelve girls, who wear blue gowns. Mrs. Vaughan's bequest sustains twenty-four children; and there is a national school here likewise. There are some fine seats in the vicinity.

Market, Thursday.—*Fairs*, Wednesday next before Easter; May 24; June 28; and October 5.

Very ancient town.

† LLANFYNYDD. *Fairs*, July 5; September 28; and November 19.

‡ LLANGADFAN, a village and parish, situated upon the Banwy, and watered by other tributaries to the Fyrnwy river, a little south-west of the posting-station, called Cann-office. There is a great extent of turbary here, used only as fuel; and copper-ore is known to exist in one or two parts of the parish. In the church-yard is the Ffynnon-Gadvan, or Cadvan's-well. This saint was the son of Æneas-Cledwyr, of Armorica, and was interred at Towyn, in Merionethshire. There is a tumulus 210 feet in circumference, at Cann-office; and the ruins of a monastery are still visible in the township of Kyffin. William Jones, a poet of some reputation, was born in this parish, in the year 1729.

St. Cadvan's-well.

§ LLANGADOG-FAWR, a town and parish, lying between the Bran and Swadde rivers, and bounded on the west by the river, Tywi, deriving great picturesque superiority from the scenery in the vales of these beautiful and fertilizing rivers. The parish church is mounted upon an eminence, and the stone bridge over the Tywi is substantial and handsome. Thomas Beck once contemplated the establishment of a collegiate church at this place. Bledri, the son of Cedifov the Great, lord of Gwydigada and Elfed, died in 1119, and was interred here. The ancient castle has long since been demolished.

Picturesque scenery.

Market, Thursday.—*Fairs*, March 12; last Thursday in May; July 9; first Thursday after September 11; second Thursday after October 10; and second Thursday after December 11.

|| LLANGAMMARCH, a village and parish upon the post-road between Buallt and Llandovery. The rivers Dulas, Cammarch, and Camddur fall into the Irvon in this parish, and the parish church is conspicuously placed upon the summit of a rock, projecting between the Irvon and Cammarch rivers. Several ancient mansions in this parish lie deserted. It is supposed there was a chapel of ease at a place in this parish, now called Llwyn-y-Fynwent. At Caerau is a mound eighty feet in diameter,

Map.	Names of Places.	County.	Number of Miles from				Dist. Lond.	Popu- lation.
54	Llanganna*........pa	Glamorgan..	Cowbridge ..4	Llantrissant..6	Bridgend 7		176	261
48	Llanganten .....pa	Brecon	Buallt 3	Rhayader...12	Brecknock..16		176	179
55	Llangar......pa	Merioneth ..	Corwen ...1	Bala.......11	Ruthin....12		195	229
17	Llangarren.......pa	Hereford ...	Ross......5	Monmouth .. 6	Hereford ..14		126	1125
48	Llangasty-Talyllynn pa	Brecon	Brecon 6	Hay.......12	Crickhowell 12		168	175
49	Llangathan†......pa	Carmarthen.	Llandilo V...3	Carmarthen.13	Llampeter ..16		204	1182
26	Llangattock Llyn- goed ....pa	Monmouth..	Abergavenny 6	Monmouth..12	Usk 15		141	202
26	Llangattock.......pa	Monmouth..	4	13	8		142	160
26	Llangattock Vibon Avell ......pa	Monmouth..	11	5	13		134	449
48	Llangattwg, or Llan- gattock‡........pa	Brecon	Crickhowell .1	Abergavenny.9	Brecon ...16		158	....
49	Llangedwyn.......pa	Carmarthen.	Narbarth...8	Newcastle..14	Carmarthen.20		238	250
52	Llangedwyn.......pa	Denbigh	Llanfyllin...6	Oswestry ...7	Welshpool..12		187	323
54	Llangefelach ....pa	Glamorgan..	Swansea....4	Neath 6	Llougher 6		204	7753
47	Llangeffni § ......m t	Anglesea ..	Beaumaris ..12	Bangor.....11	Llanerch-y-M8		259	1753
47	Llangeinwen ....pa	Anglesea ...	Carnarvon ...3	Newborough 1	Llangeffni ...9		252	776
54	Llangeinwr........pa	Glamorgan..	Bridgend ...6	Neath......10	Llantrissant 10		181	292
51	Llangeitho..........pa	Cardigan ...	Llampeter ...9	Tregaron 6	Aberystwith12		210	377
49	Llangeler..........pa	Carmarthen.	Newcastle...4	Llampeter ..18	Carmarthen.14		229	1713

LLANGAM-MARCH.   supposed to have been a Roman *Arx speculatoria.* James Howel, a writer of great versatility of talent, and Theophilus Evans, a pious and learned person were natives of this parish.

Interesting relic.   * LLANGANNA, a parish on the eastern side of the Ewenny river, and intersected by the mail-coach road from Cowbridge to Carmarthen. At the west end of the church stands a cross, the arms enclosed in a circle, of rude workmanship, and supposed to have been erected as early as the fourth century. In front of the church is a beautiful tapering and slender shaft, issuing from the top of a flattened pyramid, and approached by steps on the four sides. The head is sculptured with scriptural subjects, well executed in a durable free-stone. The style of the workmanship is of the thirteenth century, and few of these interesting relics are now to be seen.

Medicinal spring.   † LLANGATHAN, a hamlet and parish, on the north bank of the Towy river, and intersected by the post-road between Carmarthen and Llandeilofawr. The celebrated Grongar-hill, and the castle of Drys-Llwyn are in this parish, and here is also a medicinal spring, used in cases of sore eyes, as well as in rheumatic complaints.

Fair, April 16.

‡ LLANGATTWG, or Llangattock, a village situated upon the southern bank of the Usk river, and united to the town of Crickhowel by a stone bridge across the river. The Brecon-canal also passes through this extensive parish. It is in the centre of a mining district, abounding with iron-stone and lime-stone. The Beaufort iron-works are on the borders of the parish, adjoining the county of Monmouth. In the year 728, a desperate engagement took place upon Mount Carno, in this parish, between Roderic Molwynog, Prince of North Wales, and Ethelbald, King of Mercia. The scene of battle is marked by two carneddau, in one of which a cistfaen was discovered in the year 1806.

Petty sessions held here.   § LLANGEFFNI. This town increases rapidly in population, although it has received a check by the diversion of the great Holyhead and London road, which formerly passed through here, to a distance of one mile and a quarter. The market is supported by purchasers of grain for the miners in the great copper-works of Parys-mountain, and the fairs are attended by buyers of black cattle for the English markets. The petty sessions, for the hundred, are held here. There is a chalybeate spring near the town, held in much esteem, as affording relief to rheumatic persons.

Market, Friday.—*Fairs,* March 14 ; April 17 ; August 17 ; and September 15.

Map.	Names of Places.	County.	Number of Miles from				Dist. Lond.	Popu- lation.
50	Llangelynin........pa	Carnarvon ..	Conway 3	Bangor. 12	Llanrwst ...10		241	279
55	Llangelynin........pa	Merioneth ..	Barmouth....6	Towyn 8	Machynlleth 18		213	1162
48	Llangeneu.........pa	Brecon	Crickhowell .2	Hay........15	Abergavenny.9		155	409
49	Llangennyck.......pa	Carmarthen	Llanelly 4	Pont-ar-Dul. 3	Llougher 5		216	670
54	Llangennydd ....pa	Glamorgan..	Swansea....16	Penrice......6	14		212	411
52	Llangernyw*.......pa	Denbigh	Llanrwst...'..6	Abergeley ...8	Conway 9		224	1036
26	Llangeview........pa	Monmouth..	Usk..........1	Monmouth . 12	Chepstow ..14		141	173
50	Llangian ....pa	Carnarvon ..	Pwllheli 6	Nevin 8	Bardsey Isle 12		249	1211
26	Llangiby..........pa	Monmouth..	Usk.........2	Caerleon 5	Newport....8		144	543
47	Llangoed ....pa	Anglesea ...	Beaumaris ..3	Bangor 6	Llangeffni ..13		254	562
51	Llangoed Mawr†....pa	Cardigan ...	Cardigan 1	Kilgerran ...4	Newcastle .. 9		239	1014
52	Llangollen ‡ ....m t	Denbigh	Chester....23	Wrexham ..12	Corwen 10		184	4498
57	Llangolman........pa	Pembroke ..	Narbarth....8	Haverford W13	Cardigan ...12		243	511
48	Llangors ....pa	Brecon	Brecon......7	Hay........12	Crickhowell 12		168	405
26	Llangoven.........pa	Monmouth..	Ragland 4	Monmouth...7	Usk.........7		136	150

* LLANGERNYW, or Llangerniew. *Fairs*, March 29; May 16; June 16; September 29; and November 29.

† LLANGOED-MAWR, a village upon the eastern bank of the Tyvi river, in a cultivated, well-wooded, and agreeable country. A cromlech may yet be seen here, the leaning stone of which measures nine yards in circumference, and one of its edges now rests upon the ground. The Lech-y-Gowres, or Stone of the Giantess, was demolished, and the great blocks which composed it converted into gate-posts. In another place stand nineteen vast blocks of hewn stone, resembling, in arrangement, a Druidic circle. There was a strong military post, or fortress, on the Aberystwith road, which is yet tolerably perfect; it is now called Bank-y-Warin.

Druidical circle.

‡ LLANGOLLEN, a village, beautifully situated in the vale of Llan-gollen, upon the banks of the river Dee, the great Parliamentary road, from London to Holyhead, passing directly through it. The church is spacious, and in good preservation. The glebe-house is one of the most agreeable residences in the county; and there are two inns here. The influx of tourists, during the summer, to this romantic vale, contributes greatly to the support of the villagers. Manufactures of flannel and cotton, upon an extensive scale, occupy many hands. The Ellesmere-canal, which is conveyed across the Dee, from one side of the vale to the other, by an aqueduct 1007 feet in length, affords commercial facilities of great advantage to this parish. The canal is fed by the river Dee, and extends along the vale from the aqueduct to the Oernant slate-quarries. Amongst the curiosities of this interesting and beautiful vicinity, the bridge over the Dee seems to find a place, although possessing no remark-able features. It is an irregular, unarchitectural piece of workmanship, consisting of five pointed arches, separated by clumsy buttresses, which so obstruct the passage of the waters, in extraordinary floods, that it is very singular the bridge has stood so long. The castle of Dinas Bran, called also Crow-castle, is a remarkable and curious ruin. It stands upon the vertex of a hill resembling an upright cone, the sides of which are so steep as to be with difficulty ascended, even by pedestrians. Considerable remains of the castle are yet visible, which indicate it to have been of Welsh orign. It if not ascertained by whom this ancient fortress was erected, but the lord of Dinas Bran was Gryffydd ap Madawc Maelor, a man of notorious reputation for injustice and oppression, who basely for-sook his countrymen and went over to the Earl of Chester, the general of Henry III. and Edward I. His memory was despised by King Edward, who cut off two of Gryffydd's sons secretly, and bestowed the possessions of the eldest upon John, Earl of Warren. The most picturesque object in this vicinity is the Abbey of Valle Crucis. Near to the village is Plas Newydd, the seat of Miss Ponsonby, and where also dwelt her faithful companion, the late Lady Eleanor Butler. The beauty of the scenery,

Extensive manufac-ture of flannel and cotton.

The Abbey of Valle Crucis.

Map.	Names of Places.	County.	Number of Miles from			Dist. Lond.	Popu- lation.
55	Llangower ....pa	Merioneth ..	Bala.......3	Dinasmowd. 13	Llanfyllin ..20	197	412
51	Llangranwg*......pa	Cardigan ...	Cardigan ...10	Newcastle..11	Aberystwith30	225	921
47	Llangristiolus ......pa	Anglesea ...	Llangeffni ...1	Bangor......9	Llanerch-y-M8	260	873
26	Llangston ....pa	Monmouth..	Newport 5	Caerleon 3	Chepstow .. 13	141	137
26	Llangua ....pa	Monmouth..	Abergavennyl1	Monmouth..14	Hereford ...13	145	81
56	Llangurig.......pa	Montgomery	Llanidloes ...5	Aberystwith 25	Rhayader ..13	182	1847
47	Llangwenllwyfo ...pa	Anglesea ...	Amlwch 4	Llanerch-y-M6	Llangeffni...14	272	543
52	Llangwm..........pa	Denbigh	Corwen 8	Bala.........6	Ruthin 14	202	1011
26	Llangwm..........pa	Monmouth..	Usk.........4	Chepstow ...8	Monmouth..10	139	370
57	Llangwm.........pa	Pembroke...	HaverfordW. 5	Milford.....3	Pembroke ...6	271	697
50	Llangwnodyl†......pa	Carnarvon ..	Pwllheli....12	Nevin......12	Bardsey Isle .5	248	293
47	Llangwyfan ......pa	Anglesea ...	Holyhead....10	Aberffraw ...2	Llangeffni ..11	270	218
52	Llangwyfan ......pa	Denbigh	Denbigh.....3	St. Asaph ...5	Holywell 9	217	264
47	Llangwyllog .. ....pa	Anglesea ...	Llanerch-y-M3	Llangeffni ...5	Holyhead .. 12	264	267
50	Llangwystennin ...pa	Carnarvon ..	Conway.....3	Abergele 8	St. Asaph ..15	233	643
50	Llangybi..........pa	Carnarvon ..	Pwllheli.....7	Criccieth....5	Carnarvon ..16	239	717
51	Llangybi.. ....pa	Cardigan ...	Lampeter....4	Tregaron 7	Llandovery .15	204	275
49	Llangyndeyrn‡......pa	Carmarthen.	Carmarthen..7	Llandilo V. 14	Kidwelly....6	216	2412
51	Llangynfelin......pa	Cardigan ...	Aberystwith 6	Towyn....'.9	Machynlleth12	217	688
52	Llangynhafal§ ....pa	Denbigh	Ruthin 4	Mold........5	Denbigh 8	207	503
49	Llangynin........pa	Carmarthen.	Carmarthen.11	Narbarth....11	Llangharne ..8	229	434
51	Llangynllo.........pa	Cardigan ...	Newcastle ..4	Cardigan ...12	Llampeter ..16	227	644
53	Llangynllo........pa	Radnor	Knighton....5	Presteign....9	New Radnor. 7	170	498
49	Llangynnog‖.......pa	Carmarthen.	Carmarthen..7	Llangharne ..3	Kidwelly....8	225	....

LLAN-
GOLLEN.

and the interest belonging to a story where friendship of the highest and most romantic cast forms the most prominent feature, cannot fail to attract the inquisitive to this spot.

Market, Saturday.—*Fairs*, last Friday in January; March 17; May 31; August 21; and November 22.—*Inns*, Hand-hotel and Saracen's-head.

Eistethua rock.

* LLANGRANWG, a village situated upon the shores of Cardigan-bay. On the top of a hill, near the harbour, is a rock, called Eistethua, where bardic meetings are believed to have been held; and on another hill is a tumulus called Moel-badell. The steps of a rood loft may still be seen within the old church.

Fair, May 27.

† LLANGWNODYL, or Llangwnoddle, a parish situated upon the sea-coast. The fisheries on the coast are auxiliary to agriculture, in occupying and maintaining the inhabitants of this remote parish. Upon one of the columns, in the old parish church, is an inscription bearing the date 750, and upon another pillar are these words, *Hæc ædes ædificata est*, A. D. M.

Abounding in iron ore, &c.

‡ LLANGYNDEYRN, a village situated upon the river Gwendrath Vach. Iron ore, coal, and limestone abound here. It is the great lime depôt for the surrounding county; and a good trade exists here in the quarrying and working of marble. Slabs of a rare description, are constantly raised, and chimney-pieces, as well as sepulchral ornaments, manufactured here for Bristol, and other large towns along the Channel.

Fairs, August 5 and 6, and November 1.

The Moel Famma mountain.

§ LLANGYNHAFAL, a parish, situated upon the eastern side of the noble vale of Clwyd. Moel Famma, the most conspicuous of the Clwydian hills bounds this parish on the east. On its summit, which is elevated 1845 feet above sea-level, an obelisk has been erected to commemorate the fiftieth year of the reign of King George III.

‖ LLANGYNNOG, a parish enclosed between the navigable parts of the Tafe and Towy rivers. Here is a charity-school, where eight poor children are received; it is endowed with a house, garden, and an acre and a half of ground for the benefit of the master. It is said that this charitable institution was founded in thankfulness and commemoration of a cure effected on one of the Vaughans, of Derllys, by the waters of a

Map.	Names of Places.	County.	Number of Miles from				Dist. Lond.	Popu- lation.
48	Llangynnog.........pa	Brecon	Buallt 4	Brecon 12	Llandovery .19		177	77
56	Llangynnog*........pa	Montgomery	Llanfyllin....5	Dinasmowd. 16	Llangollen. .16		194	675
48	Llangynydr†........pa	Brecon	Abergavenny13	Crickhowel ..7	Brecon 11		160	1440
49	Llangynyr ....pa	Carmarthen.	Carmarthen..1	Llandilo V. 14	Kidwelly .. 10		218	1040
56	Llangynyw........pa	Montgomery	Llanfair 3	Llanfyllin....8	Welshpool...8		184	675
54	Llanharan‡........pa	Glamorgan..	Cowbridge...6	Llantrissant .6	Bridgend 3		177	313
54	Llanhary ....pa	Glamorgan..	 4	6	6		177	208
26	Llanhenock ....pa	Monmouth..	Caerleon....2	Usk.........6	Pontypool ...8		146	159
26	Llanhileth ....pa	Monmouth .	 8	12	5		154	481
58	Llanhir ....pa	Radnor	Rhayader...7	Pen-y-Bont..7	Buallt.......8		181	675
52	Llanhychan ....pa	Denbigh....	Ruthin.....2	Denbigh.....6	Mold........8		207	135
57	Llanhywel ....pa	Pembroke ..	St. David's..5	Fishguard .. 11	HaverfordW12		268	186
47	Llanidan§..........pa	Anglesea ...	Carnarvon ...4	Newborough 4	Bangor ..…..8		253	966

fountain, called the New-well, which sprang up adjacent to the school-house. Over the entrance door of the school-room is the following inscription: "Here is a charity-school for ever, built at the recommendation of the Archbishop of Canterbury, by the lord, freeholders, and inhabitants of the manor of Penrin, A. D. 1705." The manor of Penrhyn, extends over the whole of this parish, and 1512 acres of the adjoining parish of Llanstephan.

LLAN-GYNNOG.

* LLANGYNNOG, a village on the banks of the Tanat river, and in a valley, enclosed by the Berwin mountains. Above the vale of Llangynnog rises a stupendous rock of coarse slate, containing white, opaque, amorphous quartz, and abounding in lead and calamine. The produce of these hills is transported to Ruabon founderies. The great lead-mine, in the Craig-y-Mwyn, was discovrred, in the year 1692, the vein there wrought being three yards and a half in thickness; and it afforded, for the space of forty successive years, the enormous revenue of £20,000. per annum to the proprietor.

Great lead-mine.

Fairs, May 6; August 9; and September 3.

† LLANGYNYDR, or Llangynyd. *Fairs*, April 4; October 20; December 7; and Wednesday next before Christmas.

‡ LLANHARAN. Llewellyn Sion, an eminent poet, author or collector of the "Traditional System of Bardism," preserved in the Gorsedd Morganwg, at which he presided, A. D. 1580, was a native of this place, and died, A. D. 1616. The collections are in the possession of the Turberville family. In this parish, also, was born the poet Rhys Llwyd ap Rhys ap Rhiriart, who flourished between the years 1420 and 1460.

Birth-place of Llewellyn Sion.

§ LLANIDAN, a village situated upon the Menai Straits. The church was erected, A. D. 616, and belonged, at one period, to the convent of Beddgelert, the fate of which house it shared, in 1535. Edmund Downham and Peter Ashton, obtained a grant of its possessions from Queen Elizabeth, but made over the same, in 1605, to Richard Prytherch, of Myfyrian, whose daughter married a Llwyd of Llugwy. The estates of this last family were purchased by the Earl of Uxbridge, who bequeathed them to his nephew, Sir William Irby, afterwards Lord Boston. Incorporated with the church wall may be seen the famous Maen Mordhwyd, or stone of the thigh, which Giraldus mentions as possessing a locomotive property. Hugh Lupus resolved to subdue this unnatural quality by chaining it to a stone of greater weight, and casting both into the sea; but tradition asserts, that it returned to its former place, and now, at last, rests tranquil in this wall. The Romans having crossed the Menai, at this place, under the conduct of Suetonius Paulinus, slew an incredible number of the islanders on a spot called Maes Mawr Gad. In the year 67, the Druids having recovered from this shock, resumed their authority, and retained it until the year 76, when the Romans, headed by Agricola, again crossed the Menai, and landing at a place called Pont-yr-Yscraphic (the Bridge of Skiffs), a second time massacred the assembled Druids

Singular tradition.

Map.	Names of Places.	County.	Number of Miles from			Dist. Lond.	Popu- lation.
56	Llanidloes* ....m t	Montgomery	Pwllheli....14	Machynlleth 20	Chester.....69	188	4189
47	Llaniestyn..........pa	Anglesea ..	Beaumaris ...3	Bangor 6	Llangeffni ...9	254	135
50	Llaniestyn..........pa	Carnarvon ...	Pwllheli 8	Nevin 6	Bardsey Isle.12	251	1115
48	Llanigon ....pa	Brecon	Hay.... ...2	Brecon 16	Crickhowell 14	158	655
51	Llanilar .....to & pa	Cardigan ...	Aberystwith .8	Tregaron ...10	Cardigan ...34	211	999
48	Llanilid ....pa	Brecon	Brecon.....9	Llandovery .11	Buallt......19	180	565
54	Llaniliid ....pa	Glamorgan..	Cowbridge...5	Llantrissant .6	Bridgend 5	177	119
54	Llanilltwrn........pa	Glamorgan...	Cardiff.....6	 6	Caerphilly .. 5	166	149
48	Llanilltyd..........pa	Brecon	Brecon 5	Trecastle...5	Llandovery .15	176	....
51	Llanina ....pa	Cardigan ...	Lampeter .. 15	Cardigan ...16	Aberystwith22	226	482
51	Llaniot............to	Cardigan ...	8	Tregaron ...4	20	219	125
54	Llanisan ....pa	Glamorgan..	Cardiff 4	Caerphilly ..3	Llantrissant .8	164	390
26	Llanishen ....pa	Monmouth...	Monmouth...7	Usk........7	Chepstow ...8	136	360

LLANIDAN.

Formerly the residence of the druids.

and their followers, in cold blood. The fields of slaughter are known at the present day by the appellation of Llanailywynon and Bryn Lader. Tre'r Dryw is supposed to have been a dwelling-place of an anti-druid, and some curious remains may be seen there. Bryn Gwyn (the Royal Tribunal), is a circular hollow, 180 feet in diameter, encompassed by a mound of earth and stones. Near this was one of the Gorseddau, or conical heaps of stone, on the summit of which the druid sat while he delivered instruction to the people. The eminent antiquary, Henry Rowlands, was vicar of Llanidan, and is said never to have enjoyed any other literary advantages than what he discovered in his native isle. It is certain that he never travelled further than Shrewsbury from the land of his birth. He died, A. D. 1723, and was interred in the church of Llanedwen.

Extensive manufactory of flannel.

* LLANIDLOES, or Llanydloes, is said to derive its name from the Welsh word *Llan*, a church or village, and *Idloes*, the saint, after whom it was called, hence the appellation, "Llanidloes." The town is cheerfully situated at the confluence of the rivers Severn and Clewedog; over the former are two handsome stone bridges, one of which has been recently erected, at the expense of near £3,000., and upon the streams are several mills and factories, for the carding and spinning of wool. Forty years ago, this was the first town in the county for making flannels; this trade is still carried on to a considerable extent, and the finest and best of this article is made here; the lead mines, in the neighbourhood, contribute, also, to the prosperity of the town. A court-baron is held every third Monday, for the recovery of debts under forty shillings; a court-leet is also held once in the year, at Michaelmas, when a mayor is elected, and a coroner and other officers appointed, in whom is vested the government of the borough; petty sessions are also held on the first Monday in every month, by the magistrates of the county. In the vicinity of this town are several handsome residences, the property of opulent individuals; amongst the most distinguished is Dollys, situated about a mile from the town, on the road leading to Trefaglwys, from which the approach to Llanidloes is highly picturesque; the appearance of the vale, with the Severn beautifully winding, and the hills by which the prospect is bounded, all are in unison to render this spot highly interesting. The lands about the town, and in the vale, are fertile and well cultivated, rich in wood and foliage, while the roads around are well kept up.

Market, Saturday.—*Fairs*, April 5; May 11; June 21; July 17; September 13; and October 2 and 28.—*Inns*, The Queen's-head, and New-inn.

Once a Roman station.

† LLANIO. This was the ancient Loventium of the Romans, and an important station upon the Sarn Helen, or western road, between Carmarthen and Penallt, near Machinllaeth. Several Roman coins, and some culinary utensils, have been dug up here. There are three inscribed stones, incorporated with the walls of two cottages in the vicinity, which may, with some appearance of accuracy, be thus read; on one, " *Caii artis manibus primus* ;" on a second, " *Overioni* ;" and on the third,

Map.	Names of Places.	County.	Number of Miles from			Dist. Lond.	Popu-lation.
49	Llanllawdog........pa	Carmarthen.	Carmarthen..8	Llampeter..16	Llandilo V..12	213	770
57	Llanllawen ....pa	Pembroke ..	Fishguard ...3	Newport 6	HaverfordW11	256	135
50	Llanllechid........pa	Carnarvon ..	Bangor 5	Carnarvon ..10	Conway 14	252	3075
48	Llanlleon-Foel.....pa	Brecon	Buallt 10	Rhayader...12	Llandovery .14	183	226
47	Llanllibio ....pa	Anglesea ...	Holyhead ...8	Llanerch-y-M5	Llangeffni ..10	269	88
26	Llanllowell........pa	Monmouth..	Usk 2	Chepstow..12	Caerleon.....7	144	69
56	Llanllugan ....pa	Montgomery	Llanfair 4	Newtown ...9	Montgomery 12	180	360
49	Llanllwch..........pa	Carmarthen.	Carmarthen..1	St. Clare ...7	Llangharne ..7	219	....
51	Llanllwchaiarn .....pa	Cardigan ...	Aberystwith .4	Tregaron ...14	Devil's Brid. 12	211	390
51	Llanllwchaiarn .....pa	Cardigan ...	Llampeter ..17	Cardigan ...16	Tregaron.. .18	228	1062
56	Llanllwchaiarn .....pa	Montgomery	Newtown ...2	Montgomery .7	Llanfair....10	175	1107
49	Llanllwny.........pa	Carmarthen.	Llampeter ...8	Carmarthen.16	Newcastle..15	219	848
50	Llanllyffni*........pa	Carnarvon .	Carnarvon ...7	Criccaeth...7	Tremadoc ...8	241	1571
54	Llanmadog.........pa	Glamorgan..	Swansea ...14	Lloughor ...10	Llanelly ...16	220	240
54	Llanmaest.........pa	Glamorgan..	Cowbridge .. 4	Cardiff 16	Bridgend 9	177	217
26	Llanmartin ....pa	Monmouth..	Caerleon.....4	Chepstow .. 11	Newport 6	141	227
56	Llanmerewig ....pa	Montgomery	Newtown ...3	Montgomery .5	Llanfair 11	173	201
52	Llannefydd ....pa	Denbigh....	Denbigh 7	St. Asaph...6	Abergeley ...9	217	1173
51	Llannon‡...ham & cha	Cardigan ...	Aberystwith 11	Llampeter ..13	Cardigan ...22	224	....
49	Llannon...........pa	Carmarthen.	Llanelly 6	Kidwelly....9	Lloughor ...9	220	1582
50	Llannor...........pa	Carnarvon ..	Pwllheli.....4	Nevin 2	Carnarvon ..18	247	1137
26	Llanover ....pa	Monmouth..	Abergavenny 4	Pontypool ...7	Usk.........9	145	2359
52	Llanrhaider........pa	Denbigh....	Denbigh....3	Ruthin......3	St. Asaph...9	208	2066
52	Llanrhaidar-y-Moch- nant§.........pa	Denbigh	Llanfyllin...6	Llangollen..12	Bala.......15	182	2344
57	Llanrhiain........pa	Pembroke...	St. David's ..5	Fishguard ..12	HaverfordW15	269	715
54	Llanrhidian‖.......pa	Glamorgan..	Swansea ...10	Lloughor ...7	Llanelly 13	216	1445
57	Llanrhidian ....pa	Pembroke...	St. David's ..9	Fishguard ..8	HaverfordW10	265	158
47	Llanrhwydrys .....pa	Anglesea ...	Amlwch.....8	Llanerch-y-M9	Holyhead ..14	276	188

"*Cohors Secundæ Augustæ fecit quinque passus.*" Masses of brick-work are frequently dug up in the surrounding lands, and one piece, possessing a smooth and polished surface, is used as the floor of an oven in a neighbouring mill. **LLANIO.**

* LLANLLYFFNI. In this parish is the admired scene, called the Nantle Pools, immortalized by the pencil of Wilson. And in the adjoining hills are the small lakes of Llyn Cwm Silin, and Llyn Cwm Dylyn, containing an abundance of trout. Edward I. was so enamoured of the scenery of the Nantle glens, that he built a lodge here, in which he occasionally resided. Craig-y-Dinas, on the Llyffni, is a circular mound 210 feet in diameter, and from it issue two embankments, enclosing a deep fosse. It appears to have been a military station. **Splendid scenery.**

† LLANMAES. Longevity is of frequent occurrence here, and there is an entry in the parish register, of the burial of Ivan Yorath, on the 12th of July, 1621, in the 180th year of his age. He had been in the famous battle of Bosworth field, and resided afterwards at Llantwit Major, where he supported himself by fishing. **Remarkable instance of longevity.**

‡ LLANNON. *Fairs* July 6, and December 10.

§ LLANRHAIADAR-Y-MOCHNANT. The river Tanat takes its rise in this parish, and lofty mountains occupy the whole district. William Morgan, the first translator of the Bible into the Welsh language, was vicar of this parish, and the last rector was the facetious Doctor Robert South. Pistyl Rhaiadar, in this parish, is the noblest cataract in North Wales.

‖ LLANRHIDIAN. At Pen Clawd, in this parish, there are extensive works, established formerly by the Cheadle Copper Company. Lime-stone abounds every where, and some good quarries of freestone are worked here. There is a mineral spring, near the church, deemed effica-cious in scorbutic complaints; and the waters of Holywell, on Cefn Bryn, are supposed to strengthen delicate eyes. There are many subterranean caves in the limestone region of this parish; and, in one place, a stream bursts forth from the rock with such impetuosity, that in the space of two **Mineral spring.**

Map.	Names of Places.	County.	Number of Miles from			Dist. Lond.	Popu-lation.
50	Llanrhychwyn......pa	Carnarvon..	Llanrwst 4	Conway 8	Bangor 10	221	565
52	Llanrhydd.........pa	Denbigh	Ruthin 8	Mold........8	Llangollen..13	206	97
47	Llanrhyddlad......pa	Anglesea ...	Holyhead .. 12	Llanerch-y-M9	Amlwch....10	276	628
51	Llanrhystyd*......pa	Cardigan ...	Aberystwith10	Llampeter ..16	Cardigan ...28	227	1525
17	Llanrothall ....pa	Hereford ...	Monmouth...5	Ross 9	Hereford ...15	129	128
52	Llanrwst†.........m t	Denbigh	Conway 12	Denbigh 20	St. Asaph...20	218	3601
47	Llansadwrn ....pa	Anglesea ...	Beaumaris ..3	Llangeffni ...6	Lla.-y-Medd12	254	371
49	Llandsadwrn‡.....pa	Carmarthen.	Llangadog ..5	Llandovery ..5	Llandilo V. .10	196	1221
49	Llansadwrnen§....pa	Carmarthen.	Llangharne ..2	St. Clare 4	Tenby......13	247	212
51	Llansaintffraid ....pa	Cardigan ...	Llampeter ..14	Cardigan ...24	Aberystwith 13	225	1206
48	Llansaintffraid‖ ...pa	Brecon	Brecon 7	Crickhowell .8	Hay........16	165	190

LLAN-RHIDIAN. hundred yards from its source it turns two mill-wheels. On an eminence, commanding a view of the Burry, stand the ruins of Weobley-castle: on Cefn Ifor-hill may be seen an ancient intrenchment, raised, it is supposed, in the year 1110, by Ifor ap Cedifor, a chief of Glamorganshire, during **Arthur's-stone.** his conflicts with the English. Arthur's-stone is a huge mass, about twenty tons weight, raised upon supporters, five feet in height; and beneath it is a well, which ebbs and flows with the tide.

* LLANRHYSTYD. *Fairs*, Thursday before Easter, and Thursday before Christmas.

† LLANRWST, a good market-town, situated upon the north-eastern bank of the Conway river, which is here spanned by a noble bridge of three arches, designed by Inigo Jones, and in one of the most beautiful and fertile valleys of North Wales, preferred even to the vale of Clwyd. The town consists of a square, in the centre of which stand the market-hall and assembly-room, and, from each corner, avenues issue at right **Ancient church.** angles, with perfect regularity. The church, an ancient structure, is inferior in architectural merit to its beautiful little lateral chapel, also built after a design of the famous Inigo. This is the corn-market for the supply of a district of about 200 square miles. The beauty and fertility of the adjacent country, has drawn hither, also, a wealthy resident gentry. Within the church is preserved the stone coffin in which the remains of Llewellyn, last Prince of Wales, were deposited.

Market, Tuesday and Saturday.—*Fairs*, March 8; April 25; June 10; August 10; September 17; October 25; and December 11.

‡ LLANSADWRN. The ancient estate of Albemarles, in this parish, once the property of Sir Rhys ap Thomas, Knight of the Garter, was purchased from Lord Hawarden, by the gallant Admiral Foley, who erected a splendid mansion from the ruins of "Old Sir Ree's-house."

Fair, October 5.

Broadway-house. § LLANSADWRNEN. Broadway-house, in this parish, was once the residence of that upright man, John Powell, Chief Justice of Common Pleas, Keeper of the Great Seal, and one of those who sat on the trial of the seven bishops, who were sent to the tower by the arbitrary mandate of James II.

Fair, October 5.

‖ LLANSAINTFFRAID, a parish situated upon the banks of the river Usk. A house and two quillets of land, called Tal-y-Brynn, were bequeathed by Mr. Watkin, for the relief of the poor of this parish, the profits to be distributed on the 1st of January in each year, reserving the sum of 6s. 8d. to the minister for preaching an appropriate sermon on the occasion. The stone, mentioned by Bishop Gibson, as inscribed with the name Victorinus, still remains on the turnpike-road to Brecon. Thomas Vaughan, noticed in Wood's "Athenæ," was a native of this parish, and also its rector, until removed by the Oliverians. His brother, Henry Vaughan, M. D., author of "*Olor Iscanus*," and other poems, lies interred in the cemetery of the parish.

Map.	Names of Places.	County.	Number of Miles from			Dist. Lond.	Population.
52	Llansaintffraid Glan Conway* ....pa	Denbigh	Conway 3	Abergeley ...2	Llanrwst 9	226	1334
52	Llansaintffraid - Glynn-Ceiriog ..pa	Denbigh	Llangollen ...3	Llanfyllin...14	Corwen......9	187	543
55	Llansaintffraid Glyn-Dyffrwy ..pa	Merioneth ..	Corwen......2	Llangollen ...8	Ruthin 9	192	60
58	Llansaintffraid - in - Elfel ....pa	Radnor	Buallt 5	NewRadnor 10	Hay.........16	169	343
56	Llansaintffraid - in - Mechain .ham &pa	Montgomery	Llanfyllin....6	Oswestry 8	Welshpool ..10	172	1315
50	Llan-Samled.ham & pa	Glamorgan..	Swansea.....4	Neath 5	Llandilo V. 14	203	3187
26	Llansanfread ....pa	Monmouth..	Abergavenny 4	Usk 6	Monmouth...11	140	....
52	Llansannan† ....pa	Denbigh	Denbigh 9	Abergele 9	Conway 12	222	1383
54	Llansannwr ....pa	Glamorgan..	Cowbridge ..2	Llantrissaint.3	Bridgend 9	174	184
49	Llansawyl‡ ....pa	Carmarthen	Llandilo V. ..9	Llampeter .. 9	Llandovery .11	202	1010
26	Llansay§ ....pa	Monmouth..	Usk 5	Monmouth ..9	Chepstow...10	138	152
52	Llansilyn‖ ....pa	Denbigh	Oswestry 5	Llanfyllin....9	Llangollen ..10	176	1951
48	Llanspyddyd¶ .....pa	Brecon	Brecon 3	Llandovery .16	Buallt......17	174	514
57	Llanstadwell ......pa	Pembroke..	Milford 3	Pembroke...4	HaverfordW. 7	275	733
49	Llanstephan** .....pa	Carmarthen	Carmarthen..8	Llangharne ..4	Kidwelly 6	226	1274
58	Llanstephan ....pa	Radnor	Buallt 7	Hay........8	Kington 17	164	268
57	Llanstinan.........pa	Pembroke..	Fishguard ..3	Newport 7	HaverfordW. 9	257	168

* LLANSAINTFFRAID GLAN CONWAY, a village and parish, situated upon the navigable part of the Conway river. Much corn is grown in this parish, and a few vessels belong to this little port. *(marginal note: Abounding in corn.)*

Fairs, February 14; May 1; August 1; and November 1.

† LLANSANNAN, a village and parish on the banks of the river Aled. The former consists of a few cottages, disposed without any regularity, a parish church, meeting-houses for Methodists, Independents, and Baptists; two schools, one on the national system, and a respectable inn.

Fairs, May 18; August 17; October 26; and November 30.

‡ LLANSAWYL, a village agreeably situated in a close valley, watered by a tributary to the Coethy river. Here is Edwin's-ford, the seat of the ancient and respectable family of Williams, whose ancestors represented the county in Parliament, in the reign of Henry VIII. *(marginal note: Edwin's-ford.)*

Market, Friday.—*Fairs*, first Friday after May 12; July 15; October 23; and first Friday after November 12.

§ LLANSAY, a parish in the upper division of the hundred of Ragland; living, a dis. rectory in the archdeaconry and diocese of Llandaff; valued in K. B. £6. 10s. 10d.; annual value P. R. £103. 15s. 5d.; patron (1829) the Duke of Beaufort.

‖ LLANSILYN. *Fairs*, Easter-Tuesday; July 10; and October 2.

¶ LLANSPYDDYD, a hamlet and parish, and on the banks of the river Usk, which is crossed, in this parish, by three bridges. Miles, Earl of Hereford, who was accidentally slain by an arrow, discharged by one of his own knights, while hunting, granted the manor and advowson of Llanspyddyd to the prior and monks of Malvern. There is a stone in the church-yard, which indicates the grave of Brychan Brecheniog, or more probably of Aulach, his father. *(marginal note: Death of Miles, Earl of Hereford.)*

** LLANSTEPHAN, a village agreeably situated in a woody hollow, at the base of a lofty hill, crowned with the ruins of a fine castle, and near to the embouchure of the navigable river Towy. Superstitious reverence has been paid to St. Anthony's-well here, and miraculous cures ascribed to it. There was a chapel in this parish, called Marble-chapel, which fell into the hands of the Dissenters, during the civil wars, and they have continued in possession ever since. This is also an ancient manor. The castle occupies the summit of a bold hill, hanging over the

7 B

Map.	Names of Places.	County.	Number of Miles from			Dist. Lond.	Popu. lation.
26	LlanthewyRytherch..pa	Monmouth..	Abergavenny..4	Usk........9	Monmouth..11	140	348
26	LlanthewySkirrid...pa	Monmouth..	4	11	12	141	92
26	Llanthewy Vach	Monmouth..	Usk........4	Pontypool...5	Newport....6	146	189
26	Llanthoney Abbey*ham	Monmouth..	Abergavenny10	Monmouth..21	Hereford....19	150	....
15	Llanthony....ext p dis	Gloucester..	Gloucester...1	Stroud.....10	Cheltenham 10	106	....
26	Llantilio Crassenny .pa	Monmouth..	Monmouth...8	Abergavenny.8	Usk........10	137	780
26	Llantilio Pertholey..pa	Monmouth..	15	2	13	144	798
47	Llantrissaint ......pa	Anglesea ...	Llanerch-y-M5	Holyhead....9	Llangeffni ..10	269	998
54	Llantrissaint†.m t & pa	Glamorgan..	Bridgend ...11	Cardiff.....11	Mer. Tydvyl16	171	2789
26	Llantrissent ......pa	Monmouth..	Usk........3	Chepstow ..10	Newport....9	145	304
54	Llantryddyd.......pa	Glamorgan..	Cowbridge..3	Cardiff.....13	Bridgend ..11	173	221
57	Llantyd............pa	Pembroke ..	Cardigan....3	Kilgerran...4	HaverfordW19	242	280
55	Llanuwch-y-Llyn‡ ..pa	Merioneth ..	Bala........5	Dolgelley ...14	Dinasmowd.15	199	1516
26	Llanvaches ....pa	Monmouth..	Caerleon...7	Chepstow....7	Black Rock..6	140	271
26	Llanvair Discoed ....pa	Monmouth..	8	6	6	140	232
26	Llanvair Kilgidin ..pa	Monmouth..	Usk 6	Abergavenny 5	Monmouth..11	140	248
33	Llanvair Waterdine..pa	Salop	Knighton...4	Clun 5	BishopsCast.10	166	566
26	Llanvapley ....pa	Monmouth..	Abergavenny 5	Usk........11	Monmouth..11	140	123
26	Llanvetherine ......pa	Monmouth..	5	14	13	142	161
26	Llanvihangel, near Rogeat ....pa	Monmouth..	Chepstow....8	Caerleon 9	Black Rock..5	139	49
26	Llanvihangel, near Usk ....pa	Monmouth..	Usk........7	Monmouth..12	Abergavenny 5	141	251
26	Llanvihangel Crucornney§......pa	Monmouth..	Abergavenny 5	16	Usk........16	145	108
26	Llanvihangel Llantarnam ....pa	Monmouth..	Caerleon 3	Newport 3	Pontypool ...6	147	621

LLAN-STEPHAN.

entrance of the river Tywi ; it was founded by the sons of Uchtre, Prince of Merionethshire, A. D. 1138, but soon after passed into the hands of the Normans and Flemings.

Ancient structure.

* LLANTHONEY ABBEY. Situated in a deep and solitary valley, surrounded by rocks, are the ruins of Lanthoney-abbey, an ancient structure, built by St. David, who, at this place, led the life of a recluse, in the reign of Henry I. After the death of Henry, the monks being grossly insulted and pillaged by the Welsh, fled from this monastery to another of the same name, which had been built for them at a place near Gloucester. Little remains of this venerable abbey, but the ruins of its conventual church.

† LLANTRISSAINT, a town and parish, situated upon an eminence commanding an extensive prospect of the vale of Glamorgan. This is a borough town, and contributes, with Cardiff and others, in returning one member to Parliament. The Marquis of Bute is lord of the manor, and proprietor of the place.

Quarter sessions held here.

The quarter sessions for the hundred are held here. There are several collieries near the town, and the surrounding district abounds with lead and iron ores. Sir Llewellyn Jenkins, secretary of state to James II., was born in this parish.

Market, Friday.—Fairs, February 13 ; May 12 ; August 12, and October 29.

‡ LLANUWCH-Y-LLYN. Fairs, April 25 ; June 20 ; September 22 ; and November 22.

Singular mountain.

§ LLANVIHANGEL CRUCORNEY, or Crickhornel. Here is a gaping mountain, called Skyrrid-Vawr, which has a peculiarly fine effect ; it is isolated, and rises abruptly from the plain ; the base is ornamented with wood, and enriched with luxuriant corn-fields and pastures, which form a gratifying contrast to the dark aspect of its summit, which is covered with heath and ling, but which commands an extensive, grand, and diversified view, embracing a vast expanse of country ; but the most remarkable circumstances attendant on this mountain, is the enormous chasm which divides it into two unequal parts ; the bottom of this chasm is nearly 300 feet in breadth, and is strewed with immense fragments of rock, supposed to have been broken by a tremendous crash. The rugged side of the larger portion rises perpendicularly, like a wall, to a great and dizzy height ; the other portion is also perpendicular, but less elevated.

Map.	Names of Places.	County.	Number of Miles from			Dist. Lond.	Population.
26	Llanvihangel Pont-y-Moyle........pa	Monmouth..	Usk.........5	Abergavenny10	Pontypool....1	147	173
26	Llanvihangel Tor-y-Mynydd.......pa	Monmouth..	6	Monmouth...8	Chepstow ...8	137	234
26	Llanvihangel Ystern, Llewern ....pa	Monmouth..	10	6	Abergavenny10	135	163
26	Llanvrechoa... ....pa	Monmouth..	Caerleon 2	Pontypool ...6	Usk.........7	146	1092
17	Llanvynoe ....to & cha	Hereford....	Hereford....18	Hay.........9	Crickhowell .9	155	298
17	Llanwarne ....pa	Hereford....	Ross.........7	Hereford 9	Monmouth..11	127	366
56	Llanwddyn * ham & pa	Montgomery	Llanfyllin...11	Llanfair....14	Dinasmowd. 11	200	580
26	Llanwenarth ....pa	Monmouth..	Abergavenny 2	Crickhowell .9	Pontypool ...12	148	2201
51	Llanwenog†.......pa	Cardigan ...	Llampeter ...6	Newcastle..13	Cardigan ...20	217	1647
26	Llanwerne ....pa	Monmouth..	Caerleon.....3	Newport 5	Chepstow ...12	142	29
49	Llanwinio‡..ham & pa	Carmarthen.	Carmarthen.13	Narbarth ...15	Newcastle..10	231	1200
50	Llanwnda..........pa	Carnarvon ..	Carnarvon ...2	Tremadoc ..15	Cricceath...15	244	1264
57	Llanwnda§.........pa	Pembroke ..	Fishguard ...3	St. David's..17	HaverfordW15	260	1046
51	Llanwnen‖.........pa	Cardigan ...	Llampeter ...3	Newcastle..16	Cardigan ...23	214	204
56	Llanwnog¶.........pa	Montgomery	Newtown 6	Llanidloes ...9	Llanfair....11	181	1355
49	Llanwrda ....pa	Carmarthen.	Llandovery ...5	Llangadog ...4	Llandilo V. .11	196	560
56	Llanwrin..........pa	Montgomery	Machynlleth .4	Dinnasmowd. 9	Llanidloes ...19	203	802
48	Llanwrthwl........pa	Brecon	Buallt 14	Rhayader ...2	Llanidloes ..14	183	558
48	Llanwrtyd**......pa	Brecon	13	17	Llandovery .12	186	627
56	Llanwyddellan ....pa	Montgomery	Newtown ...7	Llanfair 4	Welshpool .10	186	530
54	Llanwyno ....pa	Glamorgan..	Llantrissaint.3	Mer. Tydvyl .8	Bridgend ...15	179	1094
33	Llanyblodwell .....pa	Salop.......	Oswestry ...6	Llanfyllin ...8	Welshpool ..12	173	915
49	Llanybyddar††....pa	Carmarthen	Llampter 5	Carmarthen.19	Llandilo V. 16	216	1052
57	Llanycefn ....pa	Pembroke ..	Narbarth ...7	HaverfordW12	Cardigan ...13	253	500
57	Llanychaer ....pa	Pembroke ..	Fishguard ...3	Newport 6	HaverfordW10	256	176
51	Llanychaeron ......pa	Cardigan ...	Llampeter ..10	Tregaron ...11	Cardigan ...25	221	690
57	Llanychllwydog‡‡..pa	Pembroke ..	Fishguard ...4	Newport....5	HaverfordW11	255	169

* LLANWDDYN, a hamlet and parish, situated in a remote and elevated region. There is a place here called Wddyn's-bed, and a track across the mountain called Wddyn's-path. This personage, who has bequeathed his name to the parish, is by some said to have been a giant, but by others, with more reason, considered to have been a holy man, and contemporary with Saint Monacella, of Pen Nant Melangell. *(margin: St. Widdyn's-bed.)*

† LLANWENOG. *Fair,* January 14.

‡ LLANWINIO. *Fair,* November 12.

§ LLANWNDA, a village and parish, situated upon the sea-coast. In the year 1797, a detachment of the French army effected a landing at this place. A cromlech may be seen occupying the verge of a rocky eminence above the village, and other Druidical remains lie scattered through the parish. *(margin: Druidical remains.)*

‖ LLANWNEN. *Fair,* December 13.

¶ LLANWNOG, a parish on a tributary to the Severn river. Several Roman antiquities have been found here, amongst them a brick inscribed, "*Septimæ Victrici Legioni,*" which was presented by Mrs. Tilsley, of Dinam, to Mr. Pennant. In the wall of a farm house at the same place, is a stone with the letters G. I. G. engraven upon it; and at Park, in this parish, now the property of University-college, Oxford, Queen Elizabeth kept a stud of horses. *(margin: Ancient inscription.)*

** LLANWRTYD. Here are two mineral springs of acknowledged efficacy, in relieving gravel, gout, and scurvy. They resemble the Harrowgate waters.

†† LLANYBYDDAR. *Fairs,* July 17, and November 1 and 21.

‡‡ LLANYCHLLWYDOG. The church is said to have been founded by Clydawg, a petty prince of this district, who was murdered in his own territories, while pursuing the chase. Two upright stones, in the churchyard, indicate his grave.

Map.	Names of Places.	County.	Number of Miles from			Dist. Lond.	Popu-lation.
55	Llanycil* ....pa	Merioneth ..	Bala 2	Dolgelly ...16	Llanrwst 19	196	2359
49	Llanycrwys ....pa	Carmarthen.	Llampeter...4	Llandovery .13	Llandilo V. 16	207	374
47	Llanyddansaint ....pa	Anglesea ...	Llanerch-y-M5	Holyhead....8	Llangeffni ..11	270	768
51	Llangwyrddon .....pa	Cardigan ...	Aberystwith. 8	Llampeter ..18	Cardigan ...30	211	661
55	Llanymawddwy ....pa	Merioneth ..	Dinasmowd..4	Bala 12	Dolgelly 8	206	772
52	Llanymyneich† ....pa	Denbigh....	Oswestry 6	Welshpool..11	Shrewsbury 16	169	880
33	Llanymyneich ......pa	Salop....	Oswestry 5	12	16	169	887
48	Llanynys ....pa	Brecon	Buallt......3	Rhayader...15	Llandovery .19	176	195
52	Llanynys ....pa	Denbigh....	Denbigh ...6	Ruthin 3	Mold.......10	208	784
49	Llanypumpsaint ....pa	Carmarthen.	Carmarthen..7	Newcastle..11	Llandilo V..15	216	548
50	Llanystyndwy‡.....pa	Carnarvon ..	Pwllheli 8	Cricceath....5	Nevin 9	239	1115
48	Llanywern ....pa	Brecon	Brecon 4	Crickhowell 15	Llandovery .20	172	138
47	Llecheynfarwy......pa	Anglesea ..	Holyhead....10	Llanerch-y-M4	Llangeffni ...7	266	442
51	Llechrhyd ....pa	Cardigan ..	Cardigan ...3	Newcastle...6	Kilgarran....3	236	392
54	Llechwedd ....pa	Glamorgan..	Cardiff 2	Cowbridge..11	Llantrissaint .9	162	103
48	Llechweddor ....ham	Brecon	Buallt......12	Rhayader...15	Llandovery .13	185	328
47	Llechylched ....pa	Anglesea ..	Holyhead....9	Llangeffni ..8	Llanerch-y-M7	267	405
54	Lloughor§ ....pa	Glamorgan..	Swansea.....7	Carmarthen.17	Kidwelly .. 13	212	283

* LLANYCIL. *Fairs,* June 9; September 11, and October 2.

† LLANYMYNEICH, a village in the parish of the same name, the latter being partly in the hundred of Chirk, partly in Deuddwr hundred, in the county of Montgomery, and partly in the hundred of Oswestry, and county of Salop. It is watered by the rivers Tanat, Morda; and Fyrnwy; and the Montgomeryshire-canal passes through it. Limestone is found here in abundance, and zinc and lead ores also are raised. The navigable Fyrnwy, and the canal, afford an easy and expeditious transport of these productions, as well as the Llangynnog slates, which are passed through here. The Romans excavated an insulated hill in this parish, in search of copper; and several skeletons, Roman coins, and mining implements, have been found in the ogo, or cave, hollowed out by them. Offa's-dyke bisects the parish, and crosses the mineral mountain. Two other dykes also cross it, and a rampart of loose stones, with a deep fosse on one side, supposed to be of Roman workmanship, constructed for the better protection of the mineral region from the intrusion of the Britons. Here stood a vast cromlech, beneath which it was believed a giantess, wearing a golden necklace, was interred, but the prospect of plundering the remains, induced some foolish and mischievous persons to overturn the covering-stone.

Fairs, June 9, and September 23.

‡ LLANYSTYNDWY, a village and parish, situated upon the sea-coast, and intersected by the post-road from Tremadoc to Pwllheli.

Fair, April 17.—*Festival.* June 24.

§ LLOUGHOR, or Castell Llychwr, a town in the parish of the same name, and hundred of Swansea, situated upon the Loughor river, which separates the counties of Glamorgan and Carmarthen, and over which there is a regular ferry at this place, and a ford at low water. It is but an inconsiderable place, as to extent and population, yet is a contributary borough with Cardiff, in returning one member to Parliament. The population of the parish appears to have decreased, owing, it is supposed, to the discontinuance of the works at some of the collieries. The ruins of the castle occupy the summit of a mount, which appears to have been encompassed by ditches. The Romans probably cast up the mount, but by whom the castle was founded does not appear. In the year 1115, it was demolished by Gryffydd ap Rhys, Prince of South Wales; and Henry II. granted it to Hugh de Spenser, who most likely built the castle, the ruins of which are now extant. There is a house in the borough, usually called the Sanctuary, supposed to have belonged to the manor of Millwood, or St. John's, near Swansea, anciently possessed by the knights of St. John of Jerusalem.

Fairs, first Monday in June; St. Ann's-day, and October 10.

Marginal notes:

Abounding in lime-stone.

Destruction of a crom-lech.

Ruins of the castle.

Map	Names of Places.	County.	Number of Miles from			Dist. Lond.	Popu- lation.
33	Llwyntidman ....to	Salop	Llanymynech 2	Oswestry ...6	Shrewsbury 15	168	....
58	Llowes ....pa	Radnor ...	Hay.........3	Buallt......12	Kington 13	159	372
26	Lloyndee ....ham	Monmouth..	Abergavenny 0	Crickhowell .6	Pontypool ..10	141	....
47	Llugwy ....pa	Anglesea ..	Llanerch-y-M5	Amlwch....6	Llangeffni ...7	265	577
48	Llysdinam ....ham	Brecon	Buallt......6	Rhayader....9	Llandovery .24	179	213
50	Llysfaen.....ham & pa	Carnarvon ..	Abergele 3	Conway....8	Llanrwst ...14	228	585
54	Llysfaen.....ham & pa	Glamorgan..	Cardiff 5	Caerphilly...3	Llantrissaint .9	166	552
48	Llyswen ....pa	Brecon	Hay........5	Crickhowell 11	Brecon 14	161	202
54	Llyswerni ....pa	Glamorgan..	Cowbridge ..2	Bridgend 6	Llantrissaint.8	175	178
57	Llysyfran ....pa	Pembroke...	Haverford W 8	Narbarth .. 11	Fishguard ...8	254	202
48	Llywell ....pa	Brecon	Brecon 11	Llandovery ..9	Trecastle....1	182	1699
34	Load ....ham & ch	Somerset..	Somerton ...5	Ilchester ...4	S. Patherton.3	124	....
13	Loan End...........to	Durham ...	Berwick on T 4	Coldstream .9	Belford ...16	338	147
31	Lob ....ham	Oxford....	Tetsworth ..2	Thame......4	Watlington..6	43	....
24	Lobthorpe.......ham	Lincoln....	Colsterworth 3	Corby......4	Stamford ...11	100	....
41	Lockeridge ....to	Wilts.....	Marlborough.2	Calne......10	Devizes ...13	77	....
16	Lockerley ....pa	Hants....	Romsey 6	Salisbury ..10	Stockbridge..8	74	554
10	Lockhay.........cha	Derby.....	Derby.......4	Nottingham 11	Belper 8	126	....
34	Locking ....pa	Somerset..	Axbridge ...6	Wrington...8	Bridgewater 17	134	212
4	Lockinge, East .....pa	Berks	Wantage 4	E. Ilsley....6	Abingdon...9	58	373
4	Lockinge, West ..pa	Berks.....	2	8	9	58	....
23	Lockington ....pa	Leicester ..	Loughborough7	Derby 11	Ashby.....11	116	633
46	Lockington ...pa & to	E. R. York.	Beverley....6	Gt. Driffield .8	M.Weighton10	186	475
34	Lockston ....pa	Somerset ...	Axbridge....4	Wrington...8	Bridgewater 15	134	181
44	Lockton...........to	N. R. York.	Pickering....5	Scarborough 16	Whitby ...17	227	312
45	Lockwood..........to	W. R. York	Huddersfield.2	Rochdale ..17	Oldham 16	190	3134
11	Loddeswell ....pa	Devon....	Kingsbridge..4	Modbury 5	Dartmouth ..12	205	826
23	Loddington.........pa	Leicester ..	Uppingham ..8	Leicester ...14	MeltonMow.12	94	164
28	Loddington ....pa	Northampt .	Kettering....4	Rothwell ..2	Wellingbor' 10	77	218
27	Loddon* ....m t	Norfolk....	Beccles......7	Bungay....7	Norwich ...11	112	1175
12	Loders ....pa	Dorset.....	Bridport.....2	Beaminster ..7	Dorchester .14	133	1002
12	Loders Matravers .ham	Dorset	4	8	13	132	....
44	Lodge ....ham	W. R. York	Settle......1	Kettlewell .13	Clapham 7	236	....
38	Lodsworth ....cha	Sussex	Petworth...4	Midhurst ...4	Haselmere ..7	49	564
14	Lofthouse ....pa	N. R. York.	Guisborough .8	Whitby ...13	Stockton ...22	251	1038
45	Lofthouse†.........to	W. R. York	Wakefield ..4	Leeds 7	Pontefract..11	180	....
46	Loftsome ....to	E. R. York.	Howden ...4	Selby 9	Goole 9	181	....
17	Logaston ....to	Hereford....	Weobley...5	Kineton ...5	Hay.......11	152	....
6	Lolworth..........pa	Cambridge..	Cambridge...6	Caxton 7	FennyStanton4	57	122
48	Londesbrough.....pa	E. R. York.	Mt.Weighton 3	Pocklington .5	Gt. Driffield 15	191	250
25	London‡ ....city	Middlesex & Surrey	Edinburgh.396	Dublin 330	Paris......251	....	123656

* LODDON, a small market-town, situated on the banks of a small stream, which rises near Howe, in Clavering, and falls into the Yare at Hardley-cross. The church is a handsome stone structure, with a fine tower, and contains several ancient monuments; it was erected at the sole expense of Sir James Hobart, Lord Chief Justice of the Court of Common Pleas, in the reign of Henry VII. *(Handsome church.)*

Market, Friday.—*Fairs*, Easter-Monday, for petty chapmen, and Monday after November 21, for horses and hogs.

† LOFTHOUSE, a parish in the east division of the liberty of Langbaurgh. The vicinity abounds with stone and alum rocks, which are worked to a considerable extent. *(Great alum works.)*

Market, (customary) Thursday.

‡ LONDON AND WESTMINSTER. Our account of these great and ancient cities must be comparatively brief; yet the sketch that we shall be enabled to present, will be found to exhibit some lively views of our combined metropolis. London is technically considered as a distinct county; having been designated, under 3 Geo. I., c. 5, "The City and County of the City of London." This, and the contiguous city of Westminster, have distinct privileges and jurisdictions; but in every other respect they are justly considered as forming one grand metropolitan town. Calculating the first degree of longitude from the Royal Observatory, at Greenwich, in Kent, St. Paul's-cathedral, in the centre of London, the seat of the British empire is situated in 5° 37" west longitude, and 51° 31" north latitude. There is no doubt that the present site of London was occupied, as a British town, before the arrival of the

LONDON.

Discovery
of Roman
remains.

Ravaged by
the plague
in 664.

Dreadful
massacre of
the Jews.

20,000 per-
sons died
from starva-
tion.

Romans, who made it a permanent station, surrounded it with a fortified wall, governed it by Roman laws, advanced it from a prefecture to the rank of a colony, and rendered it the seat of the vicarius Britanniarum, and of the commissioners of the treasury, under the emperors. Many remains of the Romans, as tesselated pavements, &c., have been at various times found beneath the surface. When the Romans found it necessary, in the early part of the fifth century, to withdraw their troops from the distant provinces, London again became a British town. In the year 457, the Britons fled hither on their defeat by the Saxons, under Hengist, who afterwards made himself master of London. On his death, in 498, it was retaken by Ambrosius, and retained by the Britons during a considerable part of the sixth century. It was afterwards subjected to the newly established Saxon kingdom of Essex; and, on the conversion of the east Saxons to Christianity, it was nominated as the bishop's see; Melitus being appointed the first bishop, in 604, and a cathedral church was erected in 610, on the present site of St. Paul's. In the year 664, the city was ravaged by the plague; and in 764, 798, and 801, it suffered severely by fires. A wittenagemot, or parliament, was held here in 833, to consult on proper means to repel the Danes. London was, about that period, repeatedly pillaged. In 925, King Athelstan had a palace here; and, from the descent of William the Conqueror, London may be considered as the metropolis of the kingdom. William granted a charter to the citizens, which is still preserved. In 1077, the greatest part of the city was destroyed by fire. In 1078, the king founded the fortress now called the White-tower, for the purpose of keeping the citizens in awe. William Rufus repaired and strengthened the tower. Henry I. granted the city an extensive charter of privileges, among which was the perpetual sheriffwick of Middlesex. On the coronation of Richard I. a dreadful massacre of the Jews, who were settled here, was made by the populace. Richard granted the city a new charter, confirming all its liberties; and four years afterwards, on the payment of £1500., he granted another, providing for the removal of all wears that had been erected on the Thames. On this charter the corporation found their claim to the conservatorship of that river. King John granted the city several charters. By one he empowered the "Barons of the city of London" to choose a mayor annually, or to continue the same person from year to year, at their own pleasure. In the civil feuds, the citizens took part with the barons; and when the monarch was compelled to sign Magna Charta, it was expressly stipulated, that "the city of London should have all its ancient privileges and free customs, as well by land as by water." In the year 1258, a famine occurred, and 20,000 persons died of hunger in London only. King Edward III. granted to the city two charters; by one, all the ancient privileges were confirmed, and additional ones bestowed; by the other, Southwark was granted to the citizens in perpetuity. In 1348, the terrible pestilence, which spread itself through every country on the globe, reached England. Its ravages in London were so great, that various pieces of ground without the walls were assigned for burial-places. In the waste land, now forming the precint of the Charter-house, upwards of 50,000 bodies were deposited. The public entrance of Edward the Black Prince into London, in 1356, after his victory at Poictiers, was celebrated with an unparalleled degree of splendor. In 1380, occurred the desperate insurrection, headed by Wat Tyler. The return of King Henry V. after his victory at Agincourt, in 1415, was celebrated here with great magnificence. The year 1450 was memorable for the insurrection of Jack Cade. They entered the city in triumph, bore down all opposition, and beheaded the lord treasurer, Lord Say, and several other persons of consequence. In 1485, an epidemical disorder, called "the sweating sickness," raged with great violence in London. Two mayors and six aldermen died of this complaint in one week. In 1563, the plague again made dreadful ravages, to which 20,000 persons fell victims in the city. In 1569, the first public lottery was exhibited in London. The prizes were of plate, and the profits were appropriated to the repair of the seaports. In the preparations against the Spanish armada, London took a distinguished share. The preparations for the coronation of King James were interrupted by a dreadful plague, which ravaged the city with greater violence than any similar visitation since the reign of Edward III. The commencement of the reign of Charles I. was marked by the return of the plague, which destroyed, in the metropolis, 35,000 persons. The year 1665 became memorable by the dreadful ravages of the great plague, as it is styled, which commenced in December, 1664, and had not entirely ceased till January, 1666. The digging of graves was soon discontinued, and large pits were excavated, in which the dead were deposited. At length, all regard to ceremony became impossible ; and the rich and the poor, the young and the old, were all promiscuously thrown together into one common receptacle. Whole families, and even whole streets of families, were swept away together. The cessation of public business was so complete, that grass grew within the area of the Royal Exchange, and in the principal streets of the city. The entire number returned in the bills of mortality, as having died of the plague within the year, was 68,950. The aggregate is estimated at 100,000. The great fire of London broke out in the morning of Sunday, September 2, 1666. Impelled by strong winds, the city being principally built of wood, it raged with irresistible fury nearly four days and nights. Within the walls it consumed almost five-sixths of the city ; and without the walls, it cleared a space nearly as extensive as the one-sixth part left unburned within. Public buildings, churches, and dwelling-houses, were involved in one common fate. It is stated, on one of the inscriptions upon the monument, which was raised to perpetuate the memory of this calamity, " that the ruins of the city were 436 acres, viz. 373 acres within the walls, and sixty-three in the liberties of the city ; that of the twenty-six wards it utterly destroyed fifteen, and left eight others shattered and half burnt ; and that it consumed 400 streets, 13,200 dwelling-houses, eighty-nine churches, besides chapels ; four of the city gates, Guildhall, many public structures, hospitals, schools, libraries, and a vast number of stately edifices." The value of the property destroyed in this dreadful conflagration has been estimated at £10,000,000. The city was principally rebuilt in little more than four years, in a style of superior regularity. In the year 1689, an act was passed, by which all proceedings of former reigns against the city charters were reversed, and all the rights and privileges of the citizens were fully re-established. In 1692, during King William's absence in Holland, the queen borrowed £200,000. of the city, for the exigencies of government. The year 1703 was remarkable for a dreadful storm of wind, on the night of the 26th of November. The damage sustained by the city alone was estimated at two millions sterling. An act of parliament was passed, in 1711, for erecting fifty new churches in and about London ; the expense of which was defrayed by a small duty on coals, brought into the port of London, for about eight years. In the winter of 1739-40, occurred one of the most intense frosts ever known in this country. It commenced on Christmas-day, and continued till the 17th of February. Above London-bridge the Thames was completely frozen, and numerous booths were erected on it for selling liquors, &c. to the multitudes, who daily flocked thither. In 1814, a similar frost occurred, and a fair was held on the Thames. In 1780, an insurrection, composed chiefly of the rabble, during a week, bore the most alarming appearance. Newgate, the King's-bench, and the Fleet-prisons were burnt, and the prisoners set at liberty. The popish chapels, and a number of private houses of Roman Catholics, were set on fire, and thirty-six fires were

LONDON.

seen blazing at one time in various parts of the metropolis. By military interference, many of the rioters were killed; 135 were brought to trial, fifty-nine convicted, and upwards of twenty were executed. During the years 1792, 1793, and 1794, London was greatly agitated by the political contention of clubs, debating societies, and political associations. In 1798, a numerous meeting of the bankers, merchants, and traders of London, was held in the Royal-exchange, for the purpose of raising a subscription for the public service. This subscription amounted to more *Grand review in Hyde-park.* than two millions of money. Threats of invasion from France gave rise to several armed associations; and on the 4th of June, 1799, all these volunteers were assembled in Hyde-park, and reviewed by his majesty, George III. On the ratification of preliminaries of peace, in October 1801, the metropolis was brilliantly illuminated. The war breaking out again, the cities of London and Westminster raised a volunteer force of 27,077 men. A patriotic fund was established in London in July, 1803, which, before the end of August, amounted to £152,000. The successive deaths of Nelson, Pitt, and Fox, produced respectively a great sensation in the metropolis, in the years 1805 and 1806. They were celebrated with the highest funeral honours. Covent Garden-theatre was consumed by fire in September, 1808; another fire, in January, 1809, destroyed part of the King's-palace, at St. James's; and a third fire, in February, consumed the whole of Drury Lane-theatre. On the 18th of June, 1814, subsequently to the downfall of Buonaparte, the right honourable William Domville, then lord mayor of London, had the honour to entertain, at the city table in Guildhall, the Prince Regent, Alexander, Emperor of Russia, the King of Prussia, and a distinguished train of royal and noble per- *Splendid procession.* sonages. The Prince Regent commanded a public procession in the city, on this occasion; and during the visit, he raised its chief magistrate to the rank of a baronet. On the 9th of July, of the same year, the Marquis Wellington was received by the lord mayor and corporation, with almost equal magnificence. Thus have we hastily sketched some of the more prominent chronological events connected with the history of this great metropolis. It is considered that the site of London is better adapted for mercantile transactions, than for the display of architectural magnificence. It consists of a gentle slope on the north bank of the Thames, and of an almost uniform flat surface on the southern side of that river.

For the convenience of general reference we shall adopt an alphabetical arrangement, and commence with its

BENEVOLENT INSTITUTIONS.

Bartholomew's Hospital is erected upon the site of a house which belonged to the order of Grey Friars. The building is very extensive, and consists of a variety of irregular parts. Its handsomest front looks into Newgate-street, and is decorated with Doric pillars. The hall, which is a large room, was built at the expense of Sir John Frederic, one *Library founded by Whittington.* of the aldermen of London, who expended upon it £500. The library was founded in the year 1429, by the celebrated Whittington, and has a valuable and extensive collection of books. The room in which they are contained, measures 129 feet in length, and thirty-one in breadth. The court-room, a spacious apartment, designed for the meetings of the governors, contains some valuable paintings, among which the portrait of Edward, by Holbein, merits peculiar attention. Henry VIII., upon the dissolution, founded this hospital upon the ruins of the convent of the Grey Friars, and endowed it with considerable lands. It was further benefitted by the exertions of Ridley, Bishop of London, in the reign of Edward VI., at which period the poor, whom it was designed to relieve, were divided into classes. A mathematical school, with an endowment of £1000. per annum, payable for ten years out of the exchequer, was annexed by Charles II. to this hospital; it was designed for the education of forty boys, of which number ten are annually apprenticed to the sea-service, and their places supplied by a similar number from the foundation.

Bethlem Hospital, Lambeth, for lunatics; " is a huge but comely " edifice, and munificently endowed; it formerly stood in Moorfields, but now ornaments St. George's; it is an immense structure, with an elegant frontage of 300 feet, and cost £100,000. The celebrated reclining statues of raging and melancholy madness, that were formerly exposed to the effects of our "moody climate," after a restoration from Bacon's skilful chisel, are now sheltered in the hall of the hospital.

British Lying-in Hospital (The) was instituted in 1749. The committee have preserved an account of those who have died here. In the first ten years of the institution, one woman died in forty-two; in the fifth ten years, one in 288; in the sixth ten years, only one in 216.

Christ's Hospital, Newgate-street, was founded by Edward VI., for supporting and educating the fatherless children of poor freemen of the city; of whom 1000, of both sexes, are generally maintained in the house, or out at nurse, and are also clothed and educated. Forty boys are qualified for the sea. These wear appropriate badges, and their classes are examined by the elder brethren of the Trinity-house; ten of them are yearly appointed to ship masters, and ten others received into their places. The other boys are apprenticed to different trades, at the charge of the hospital; or, if properly qualified, are sent to Oxford or Cambridge. One scholar is sent every year, except on the return of every seventh year, when two are sent.

City of London Lying-in Hospital, City-road, was instituted in 1750. This hospital, in 1809, had subsisted fifty-nine years; and had relieved, in that time, 24,902 poor married women, of whom 25,196 children had been born. Out of the whole number, 292 women have been delivered of twins, and two women had three children at the birth.

Deaf and Dumb Asylum, in the Kent-road, is an admirable institution, and singular success has attended its efforts—greater than could, without the evidence of the senses, be believed. These two last named charities have acquired a kindred popularity; the objects of each are admitted by ballot, and the numbers who vote demonstrate the extensiveness of their patronage; extraordinary interest is made by the friends of the candidates to secure their election.

Female Orphan Asylum, Lambeth, has been instrumental in rescuing thousands of females from ignorance and its consequent depravity, who have been deprived of their natural protectors; the old asylum has been pulled down, and a new erection has arisen on the spot; it forms three sides of a square, but its dimensions appear contracted, and not of that commanding character expected from the celebrity of this charity.

Foundling Hospital (The) is a noble institution, in Guildford-street, for the reception of deserted children, and flourishes under the patronage of the great and the affluent. Many of those handsome streets and squares, which have arisen within these few years around this once insulated edifice, have greatly enriched the funds of the charity, the ground on which they stand being the property of the hospital. The chapels of this, and the preceding charity, are much frequented, and as the congregations are expected, on their entrance,

" To bribe the chinking plate,"

these voluntary contributions must be very productive; the psalmody, at the Foundling, is a great attraction; it is admirably performed by the children, assisted by professional singers.

Haberdashers' Hospital (The) was erected at Hoxton, in 1692, by the company of Haberdashers, in pursuance of the will of Robert Aske, Esq., who left, for building and endowing it, £30,000. It supports twenty poor haberdashers, and supports and educates twenty boys.

7 c

Marine Society (*The*) is an establishment peculiarly British; its design is the training of boys to the sea service; the society have a fine vessel stationed off Deptford, for the purpose of exercising and instructing the boys in rigging and managing a ship.

Middlesex Hospital (*The*), for sick and lame, and lying-in married women, was instituted in 1745. It is under the direction of a patron, a president, twelve vice-presidents, two treasurers, and a committee of the governors, or those who subscribe three guineas annually, or thirty guineas at one payment. The lying-in ward of this hospital has no communication with those in the sick and lame. The patients are visited by three physicians, an accoucheur, and three surgeons, besides the physician and surgeon of the cancer ward; which last was established, in 1792, in pursuance of the will of the elder Samuel Whitbread, Esq., M. P.

Queen's Lying-in Hospital was founded in 1752, for receiving poor pregnant women, as well married as unmarried, in separate wards, and also of attending them at their own habitations, within a limited circuit, was established at Bayswater, but has been removed to Lisson-green, Paddington. The government is vested in a president, four vice-presidents, a treasurer, and a committee of eighteen governors. An annual subscription of three guineas constitutes a governor, entitled to recommend one in-patient, two to be delivered at their own habitations, and six for advice; and a subscription of thirty-one guineas, at one payment, entitles to the recommendation of one in-patient, six at their habitations, and twelve for advice, yearly. Upwards of 45,000 women are estimated to have received the benefit of this hospital. Her majesty is patroness; and it is under the care of a consulting physician, a physician in ordinary, a surgeon and man-midwife, an apothecary, secretary, matron, nurses, &c.

Small Pox Hospital (*The*) was instituted by voluntary subscription in the year 1746; but the present building, at Battle Bridge, St. Pancras, was not open for the reception of patients till Michaelmas, 1767. Dr. Woodville, physician to the hospital, first introduced vaccination, January 21, 1799, and adopted it generally during the following year. During the year 1808, the patients relieved in the casual small-pox, amounted to 132; those for inoculation to 1266; those of vaccination to 1252; and the total number of the lattter, since 1799, amounted to 23,197; of casual patients, since the first establishment, 21,868; and of variolated patients, 47,471; making a total of 92,536. In this building is also a house of recovery for typhus and scarlet fever, supported by voluntary subscriptions.

St. Luke's is a commodious edifice for the reception of insane persons, erected at the expense of £40,000. by the governors of the last-mentioned institution, on a large spot of ground, which they were enabled to purchase by the increase of their funds. This building is 492 feet long, and proportionably broad, its front is grand but simple. Its interior is divided into three floors, exclusive of the ground floor; the centre of which is occupied by a hall, apartments for several of the resident officers, and the staircase. A spacious gallery occupies either side of each story; the western being allotted to the female, the eastern to the male patients. The apartments of the lunatics occupy the south side of the gallery, the greater part of the northern side of which is opened, by wide, lofty, and well-grated iron windows, to the air. Two different apartments are prepared in each gallery for the patients to take their meals in, according to the degree of their disorder. To each is allotted a small square bed-room, containing a good mattress, with comfortable bed-covering. The whole house is kept most perfectly clean, and well ventilated; and in the rear of it are two gardens for the recreation of the patients of each sex.

St. Thomas's, in the Borough, is an extensive range of buildings, consisting of four spacious quadrangular courts, that have the appearance of

a palace. In the middle of the second is a statue of brass of Edward VI.
There are hot and cold baths, and an excellent circular theatre, where
courses of lectures are delivered to great numbers of students, who come
from all parts of the country to learn the London practice. The hospital
is for the poor who are sick, or who have been maimed by accident, and
is of great utility, relieving, on an average of ten years, 9,000 persons, at
an expense of £10,000. annually.

Westminster New Lying-in Hospital, on the Surrey side of Westminster-bridge, was instituted by subscription, in 1765. A subscription
of thirty guineas constitutes a governor for life, entitled to recommend
yearly, three in-patients, three at their own habitations, and any number
for advice. Besides the Lying-in hospitals, there are two or three institutions for the purpose of delivering poor married women at their own
habitations. One of these dates its rise in 1757, and is under the direction of a president, six vice-presidents, a treasurer, secretary, and governors. An annual subscription of one guinea, or more, or a benefaction of
ten guineas, or upwards, constitutes a governor. During the first fifty
years of this society, the deliveries amounted to 178,983. There is
another institution of the same nature, called "The Benevolent Institution for the sole purpose of delivering poor married women at their own
habitations," established forty years ago.

BRIDGES.

Blackfriars' Bridge was finished in 1769, and is remarkable for the
lightness of its structure; it has eight piers, and nine elliptical arches.
The centre arch is 100 feet wide; those on each side ninety-three, the
third eighty-nine feet, and the fourth seventy. The length is 1100 feet,
and the breadth, forty-two feet.

London Bridge.—The first stone was laid on the 27th of April, 1825.
The construction of the piers proceeded with great rapidity; and the first
arch was keyed in on the 4th of August, 1827. The arches of this bridge
being very flat elliptics, it was necessary that the centres (upon which the
stones and other materials of an arch are supported during the progress
of the work) should be particularly strong. Each centre of this bridge
consisted of nearly eight hundred tons of timber and iron. The bridge
was finally completed on the 31st of July, 1831, having occupied about
seven years and a half in its construction. It was opened by the king on
the 1st of August. London-bridge consists of five semi-elliptic arches.
The least of these is larger than any other stone arch, of this form, ever
erected. The centre arch is 152 feet span, with a rise above high water
mark of twenty-nine feet six inches; the two arches next the centre are
140 feet in span; the abutments are each 130 feet in span. The roadway
is fifty-three feet wide between the parapets, the footways occupying nine
feet each; the rise in the road is only one in 132. The length of the
bridge, from the extremities of the abutments, is 928 feet; within the
abutments, 782 feet. The whole of the bridge is built of granite, and
the total quantity of stone employed amounts to about 120,000 tons.
The new bridge is, like the old one, free of toll. The expense has been
paid, partly by the corporation and partly by the government; the corporation are allowed to levy a tax (which is to last for twenty-six years) of
10*d.* per chaldron on all coals entering the port of London.

Southwark Bridge was proposed by Mr. John Wyatt, with the view
of forming a communication between Bankside, Southwark, and the
bottom of Queen-street, Cheapside. Rennie made the design. It consists of three arches only, of cast iron, from the foundry of Messrs.
Joshua Walker and Co., of Rotherham, in Yorkshire, on massy stone
piers and abutments. The centre arch is 240 feet span, and the two side
arches, 210 feet each.

Vauxhall Bridge is of iron, and is light and elegant; it was cast at

Butterley iron works, Derbyshire, and was erected by Mr. Walker, for £150,000. It has nine cast iron arches, seventy-eight feet in span, and twenty-nine in height; the length of the bridge is 860 feet. The first stone was laid by Prince Charles, eldest son of the late Duke of Brunswick, in 1813; it was completed in 1816.

Waterloo Bridge.—Wednesday, June 18, 1817, the anniversary of the glorious victory of Waterloo, was the day fixed for the ceremony of its opening. The town was all in motion. Crowds were seen at an early hour advancing in all directions. The aquatic excursion embarked near Fife-house. The day was most auspicious, and gave full effect to the splendor of the scene. The banks of the river, from Whitehall to Somerset-house, were crowded to excess, and the houses seemed roofed with people; platforms and scaffolds were erected in every station, commanding a view of the river and the bridge; the latter, which was taken possession of by the horse guards, at ten o'clock, resembled a camp, and had a very picturesque effect. Three rows of benches were erected along the eastern footpath of the bridge, for the accommodation of the spectators, including the subscribers, each of whom had a ticket. Flags were flying in all directions. The river between Westminster and Waterloo-bridges was literally covered with boats, filled with genteel and well-dressed company. Divisions of foot-guards, in their full dress, were stationed in the vicinity of Whitehall, and a captain's guard was stationed in the area of Fife-house, to receive the Prince Regent. The military part of the spectacle was uncommonly interesting, as many of the troops who contributed to the victory of Waterloo were present, with their medals, and sprigs of laurel in their hats. On the wreaths of laurel, in gold, were the words, " Waterloo, 18th of June, 1815." Tuesday night a large cannon, taken at the great battle, was placed on some flag-stones on the bridge; and several pieces of artillery were ranged along the west side of the bridge, to fire a grand salute of 202 guns, the number taken at the battle of Waterloo. The cannon commenced firing precisely at three o'clock, announcing the embarkation of the Prince Regent, the Duke of York, the Duke of Wellington, and the great officers of state, in the royal barges, near Fife-house. The barges belonging to the admiralty, ordnance, navy, the treasurer of the navy, &c., distinguished by their proper flags, previously started from the stairs of the house of the board of control, and passing Whitehall, they awaited the arrival of the Prince Regent. The whole then proceeded towards Waterloo-bridge; the six barges first, the two royal barges next, then the other barges bringing up the rear, having previously taken on board their respective companies. On each side a line was formed, consisting of boats belonging to the Eridanus and Euphrates frigates, manned by their respective crews, under the immediate command of captain William King, of the former ship. The boats belonging to the Thames police, under the superintendence of Captain Richbell, chief magistrate of that office, also attended, and assisted in keeping off the boats of every description, with which the Thames was covered. Bands of music were placed in various stations, in boats, on the bridge, &c., playing martial airs. The procession moved slowly along, the cannon still firing, and the royal barges passed through the centre arch of the bridge amidst the acclamations of the people on shore and in the boats, which were countless. The barges having arrived at the Surrey side of the bridge, the royal party landed, ascended the bridge stairs, where they were received by the committee, paid the toll, and walked over the bridge on the eastern side, the Prince Regent at the head of the procession, attended by the Duke of York, the Duke of Wellington, and all the great officers of state. After having passed the bridge, the procession took water again on the Middlesex side, and proceeded in the royal barge to Whitehall. The Lord Mayor was present in the city state barge. Lord Liverpool gave a superb dinner to several persons of distinction after the ceremonies of the day. The bridge was open to the public at seven o'clock in the evening, and an immense number of persons passed over it. A fair of three days' continuance was held on the Surrey side of the bridge. The whole of the outside courses of Waterloo-bridge is Cornish granite, except the balustrades, which are of Aberdeen granite. The stones were cut to their form before they were brought to the spot. There are 320 piles driven into the bed of the river under each pier, the length of each pile, from nineteen to twenty-two feet, and the diameter, about thirteen inches; there is one pile to every yard square. The four toll-lodges are neat Doric structures. They have a contrivance—an extremely inconvenient one—at each lodge, for the purpose of checking and preventing the keeper's dishonesty to the trust. A kind of iron turn-stiles, which admits of only one person passing at a time, touches some machinery, which communicates with a clock, locked up in an oak box, in each toll-house, the index of which is thereby moved, so that on looking at it, the number of those who have passed is seen. The situation of this bridge is remarkably fine for its view of the river. The bridge, which was only six years in building, is exactly on a level with the Strand, and fifty feet above the surface of the river. The first stone of the bridge was laid on the 11th of October, 1811.

Westminster Bride.—London, for a long period, knew the convenience of only one bridge; but in 1739, Monsieur Labelye began that elegant structure, Westminster-bridge, which was completed in eleven years; the entire expense was £389,000., £40,000. of which was sunk beneath the water; parliament defrayed the cost. Its dimensions are, length, 1223 feet, width forty-four feet, width of the centre arch, seventy-six feet.

CATHEDRALS, CHURCHES, AND CHAPELS.

The edifices consecrated to religious worship are so numerous, that it must suffice for us to notice two only of the most prominent, viz. St. Paul's and Westminster-abbey; the whole number of churches, scattered over the metropolis, exceeds 140, besides many private episcopal chapels, and chapels of ease. There are also about 250 chapels appropriated to the service of the various classes of Protestant dissenters and Methodists, including several meeting-houses for the Society of Friends. There are forty foreign churches and chapels, six Jews' synagogues, and fifteen Roman Catholic chapels; one of the latter, lately erected in Moorfields, is very elegant; the interior is finely decorated, and the painting at the altar has a very impressive effect.

St. Paul's Cathedral is confessedly, with the exception of St. Peter's, at Rome, the noblest existing work of man. The ancient gothic cathedral, destroyed by the great fire, in 1666, stood upon the site of the present church, the ground plot of which contains two acres, sixteen perches, seventy feet, enclosed by an elegant and ponderous balustrade of iron. The stupendous structure that covers this extended area stretches its "giant limbs" from west to east, 500 feet, and from north to south, 285 feet, and its altitude, to the summit of the cross, is 404 feet. The first stone was laid on the 21st of June, 1675, and the last in the year 1710, so that the whole was completed in thirty-five years. Sir C. Wren was the architect, and he lived to see it finished. Shortly afterwards, the queen, and members of both houses of parliament, attended divine service in it. The west front, towards Ludgate-street, has a noble aspect; at the north-west and south-west corners two beautiful turrets are erected, the south containing the clock, and the north the belfry. In front of the great north entrance is a semi-circular portico. The southern door is nearly similar. The east end is semicircular, and ornamented with fine sculpture. The sublime dome rises from the intersecting lines of the great cross, in most beautiful proportion and awful grandeur. On the summit of it is a handsome lantern, adorned with Corinthian columns,

LONDON.

Bridges.

Cathedrals, &c.

and surrounded at its base by a balcony; on the lantern rests a gilded ball and cross, of immense size and weight, which was put up a few years since in lieu of the old one (now exhibited in the Colloseum). The new ball is considered the finest piece of gilt copper work in the kingdom, and has a very grand effect; it is six feet in diameter, and will contain twelve persons; the copper of the whole weighs four tons, twelve cwt., and measures twenty-seven feet from the bottom of the gilding to the top. The ball is in two parts only, and rests upon ornamented gilded brackets; the ironwork necessary for its support in the interior, weighs above three tons, making the entire weight near eight tons. The whole of this ponderous ornament was begun, executed, and placed in its present situation, in the short space of fourteen weeks. Within the south-west pier a circular staircase leads to the whispering gallery, from whence the view is strikingly impressive. The whispering gallery is itself a great curiosity, as the slightest breathed whisper is distinctly heard across the dome, the diameter of which, at this part, is 100 feet. The bell is greatly admired; its tone is readily distinguished from that of all the other bells in the metropolis; it is tolled only on the death of one of the royal family, the lord mayor, the bishop of London, or the dean of the cathedral. Monumental decorations give additional interest to the interior, commemorative of scholars, philosophers, philanthropists, and warriors; in a vault, under the centre of the dome, are deposited all that could die of the illustrious Admiral Lord Nelson. Here strangers, when visiting the *cryptæ*, are shown a sarcophagus of black and white marble, resting on a pedestal, with " HORATIO VISC. NELSON," inscribed thereon. Our space will not allow us to enter into a detailed description of the beauties of this noble building.

Westminster Abbey.—On the site of the present building stood a temple of Apollo, which was thrown down by an earthquke, in the time of Antoninus Pius. From its ruins, Sebert, King of the West Saxons, raised a Christian church, which was ruined by the Danes. It was repaired by Edward the Confessor, who chose it for his burial place. Henry III. took down this fabric, and erected a new church, which occupied fifty years in building. It suffered much by fire in 1274, but was repaired by Edward I., Edward II., and the abbots. In 1700, this church being much decayed, the parliament granted money for repairing it; and the bounty has been frequently repeated. The form of the abbey is that of a long cross. Its greatest length is 489 feet; the breadth of the west front is sixty-six feet; the length of the cross aisle is 189 feet; and the height of the roof is ninety-two feet. At the west end are two towers. The nave and cross aisle are supported by fifty slender pillars of Sussex marble, exclusive of pilasters. In the upper and lower ranges there are ninety-four windows; all which, with the arches, roofs, and doors, are in the Gothic taste. The inside of this church is much better executed than the outside, and the perspective is good, particularly that of the grand aisle. The choir, from which there is an ascent by several steps to a fine altar-piece, is paved with black and white marble; having twenty-eight stalls on the north, the same number on the south, and eight at the west end. The altar is made of a beautiful piece of marble, the gift of Queen Anne, enclosed by a curious balustrade, and upon a pavement of porphyry, jasper, Lydian, and serpentine stones, laid in the mosaic style. On each side of this altar a door opens into St. Edward's-chapel, round which are ten other chapels, ranging from the north to the south cross aisles, and dedicated to their respective saints. In St. Edward's-chapel are still to be seen the remains of the shrine, which, though now in obscurity, and robbed of all its riches and lustre, was once esteemed the glory of England, so far as art and riches could make it. Here are the tombs of King Edward I., and several other kings and queens of England; and here, also, is the famous chair in which the kings of Scotland were crowned at Scone. The chapel of Henry II. is divided from St. Edward's by an iron screen, on each side of which are statues as large as life. St. Andrew's-chapel, next to the north cross, and the others which surround the choir, are crowded with monuments of noble personages. At the corner of St. Benedict's-chapel, an iron gate opens into the south cross aisle; which, from the number of monuments erected therein to celebrate English poets, has obtained the name of Poet's-corner. Here is a most magnificent monument, at the south end, to the memory of John, Duke of Argyle; another to Camden, the antiquary; doctor Isaac Barrow, the divine; and Thomas Parr, who died at the age of 152 years. On the east of the abbey stands the chapel of Henry VII., founded in 1502, and at that time styled the "wonder of the world." It is now one of the most expensive remains of ancient English taste. The original object of this chapel was a royal dormitory; and none have been interred therein, but such as have traced their descent from ancient kings. The tomb of King Henry VII. is magnificent, enclosed by a screen of cast brass, admirably designed and executed. Within the rails are the figures of that king, and his royal consort, in their robes of state, on a tomb of black marble. At the head of this tomb lie the remains of Edward VI. In different parts of this chapel are the monuments of Louis Stewart, Duke of Richmond; George Villiers, Duke of Buckingham; John Sheffield, Duke of Buckingham; Charles Montague, Marquis of Halifax, Edward V., and his brother Richard; the vault of James I. and his queen Anne, and daughter Mary; a lofty monument of Queen Elizabeth, and another of Mary, Queen of Scots; the monuments for Margaret Douglas, daughter of Margaret, Queen of Scots; Margaret, Countess of Richmond, mother of Henry VII.; the vault of King Charles II., and William III.; Queen Mary, his consort; Queen Anne, and Prince George. In a fine vault, under the chapel of Henry VII., is the burying place intended for the royal family, erected by George II. Adjoining to the abbey are the cloisters, built in a quadrangular form, with piazzas towards the court, where several of the prebendaries reside.

DOCKS.

Before the construction of the prodigious docks on both banks of the Thames,

> " Commerce brought into the public walk
> The busy merchant, the big warehouse built,
> Raised the strong crane, choked up the public street
> With foreign plenty; and thy stream, O Thames,
> Chose for his grand resort."

But by these enormous excavations both the "choked street" and the "king of floods" have, in a great degree, been freed from these incumbrances.

East India Docks (*The*), at Blackwall, include the Brunswick-dock, and receive all the East India ships. The prodigious traffic to these depôts led to the formation of the fine Commercial-road, which is seventy feet wide, with a *pavé* of twenty feet in the centre; it extends from Whitechapel-church to Blackwall, a distance of nearly three miles.

St. Katherine's Docks, near the Tower, have occasioned the annihilation of nearly the whole of St. Katherine's parish, together with its venerable church. These were opened, October 25, 1828, seventeen months only after the first stone was laid. They cover twenty-four acres, eleven and a half of which are devoted to wet docks, the remainder to warehouses and quays. The canal leading to the river is 190 feet long and forty-five broad, and by a steam engine of 100 horse power, can be filled or emptied, so that vessels of 700 tons can enter at any time of the tide; the docks and basin will accommodate annually, 1400 vessels. The cost, including that of 1200 houses demolished, was little short of £2,000,000., which was raised by shares. From the newly formed quay of these docks, passengers can enter or quit the various steam vessels

LONDON.

Docks.

without the intervention of boats, by which the public avoid both danger and extortion.

London Docks (The) were commenced in 1802, and contain twenty acres. There are extensive warehouses and cellars on the north quay, which, with a large tobacco warehouse, cover fourteen acres. The east cellar extends over three acres, and will contain 22,000 pipes of port wine; the present capital of the company is £2,200,000.

West India Docks (The) are formed in the narrowest part of the Isle of Dogs; one dock for loading, and the other for unloading; the two contain fifty-four acres, and are capable of accommodating all the shipping in the West India trade. The canal to the south is designed to avoid the circuit round the Isle of Dogs.

INNS OF COURT AND COURTS OF LAW.

Inns of Court and Courts of Law.

Admiralty (Court of), held in Doctors' Commons, by the lords of the admiralty, takes cognizance of all maritime affairs, whether civil or criminal. All crimes committed on the high seas, or on great rivers below the first bridge next the sea, are cognizable in this court only. The proceedings are the same as those adopted in civil law. The plaintiff gives security to prosecute, and, if cast, to pay what is adjudged. In criminal cases, as trial of pirates, and crimes committed at sea, the process, by a special commission, is by a judge, jury, and witnesses, a judge of the common law assisting, on which occasion the court is commonly held at the Sessions-house, in the Old Bailey.

Chancery (Court of) is a court of equity, in which cases of the highest import are tried, but from which there is an appeal to the House of Peers. It consists of two courts, in one of which the chancellor, or vice chancellor, proceeds, according to the precedents and statutes of the kingdom, without the aid of jury; and, in the second, according to equity, judging by the spirit rather than by the letter of the law. The lord chancellor holds his appointment during the king's pleasure, and enjoys precedence over every temporal lord. During the vacations, he sits at Lincoln's Inn-hall, in Chancery-lane; and in his absence, the master of the rolls, or sometimes one of the judges, officiates in his place. The master of the rolls has also his own department, and hears causes in the Rolls-chapel, Chancery-lane; but his decisions may be appealed against to the lord chancellor or vice-chancellor.

Chancery (Inns of) were probably so called because they were anciently inhabited by such clerks as chiefly studied the forming of writs, which regularly belonged to the cursitors, who are officers of chancery. The first of these is Thavies-inn, begun in the reign of Edward III., and since purchased by the society of Lincoln's-inn; Clement's-inn; Clifford's-inn, formerly the house of Lord Clifford; Staple-inn, belonging to the merchants of the staple: Lion's-inn, anciently a common inn, with the sign of the lion; Furnival's-inn; Barnard's-inn; and New-inn. These were considered only as preparatory schools for younger students; and many were entered here before they were admitted into the inns of court. They are now chiefly occupied by attorneys and solicitors.

Common Pleas (Court of) is the second court, in point of rank, and has a concomitant jurisdiction with the King's-bench, in civil actions, besides an exclusive one in some particular cases respecting real property, but it has no criminal jurisdiction. No counsel plead in this court, except serjeants at law. The chief justice has a salary of £4500. per annum; and the other three judges have £3000. a year each. A Court of Common Pleas is also holden, by the lord chief justice, at Guildhall, in the city.

Doctors' Commons, or the College of Civilians, is a college established for the study and practice of the civil law, in which courts are kept for the trial of civil and ecclesiastical causes, under the archbishop of Canter-